POP MUSIC, U.S.A.

by
Dr. Simon V. Anderson

with
Dr. Gerard Aloisio and Dr. Warren J. Anderson

Edited by Colleen M. McSwiggin

CLIFTON HILLS PRESS, INC.

ISBN 13: 978-1500778927
ISBN 10: 1500778923

Copyright © 2014
Clifton Hills Press, Inc.
6746 Jennifer Lynn Drive
Cincinnati, Ohio 45248
Phone: 513-484-0112
cliftonhillspress2@fuse.net

POP MUSIC, U.S.A.
TABLE OF CONTENTS

Chapter 1
The Aesthetics of Music

Since the beginning of recorded history, writers have tried to explain the power and beauty of the "aesthetic experience". It is difficult to define and even more difficult to describe, but it is easy to remember. It's that special moment when all the world seems right, when everything seems absolutely OK! Sometimes the experience is so intense that it is accompanied by goose bumps, even tears, and a tingling sensation. The arts, music especially, can often create this aesthetic experience.

TRADITIONAL PHILOSOPHY

Plato believed that music could refine the character and preserve good health, but too much music would cause one to be "melted and softened beyond what is good." Aristotle held that the aim of art was purification, that music was especially good at drawing off unsocial and destructive impulses into harmless excitement. But he cautioned that too much music was a dangerous thing.

St. Augustine confessed that he had "sinned criminally ... being more moved by the singing than by what was sung." He thought music had its place, however, because "by the delights of the ear, the weaker minds may be stimulated to a devotional frame." German philosopher Arthur Schopenhauer declared that music was the most powerful of all the arts, because it could immediately elevate one above the strife of Will.

Henri Bergson, a French philosopher, considered musical works to be "records of intuitions". Sigmund Freud, the father of psychoanalysis, thought that music was a sublimation process through which a composer converted repressions and unfilled wishes into tonal fantasies to express deep desires. Naturalist Charles Darwin theorized that music preceded speech, originally developed to attract and select a mate.

A NEW PHILOSOPHY

All these intellectual opinions are interesting and entertaining. The blunt truth is, however, that music is just an acoustical disturbance in the air. This disturbance affects the tiny bones, fluids, and nerve tissues in human ears, causing chemical and electrical reactions in the brain which make people feel different from how they felt just previous to the sound of that music. No more. No less. But those acoustical disturbances have changed during the course of human history and, in some instances, have changed history.

What the traditional philosophers were trying to explain, of course, was the connection between the music and the emotional results it causes. Three observations. First, musicians create sounds that seem to say what they want to say. Second, listeners seem to understand what the musicians have said. Third, anyone outside this select dialogue might well be completely unaware of what the musicians have said to the listeners.

Indeed, there is often strong disagreement on what message is being sent – between New Age fans and rock fans, jazz buffs and classical audiences, between the same fans in different countries, races, religions, and even between parents and children within any of the above categories.

At times, music has caused riots and destruction – sometimes when things have gotten out of hand at a concert, sometimes when inciting a certain group to violence to protest an inequality. But music has also been used to heal wounds of nations, to bring the plight of the hungry and the oppressed to the attention of the world, and to raise millions of dollars for causes around the globe. By all objective evidence, music does convey something very potent and powerful to people.

OTHER CULTURES

Music, as with all other communication – speech, facial expressions, body language, hand gestures, etc. – derives from the culture of its origin. It may be completely meaningless outside that culture. A raised eyebrow means one thing in the Sahara Desert, and something completely different at a cocktail party in New York. A hand gesture that draws a laugh in one culture might provoke violence in another.

It is the same with music. American ears do not easily receive and interpret the music of gong-kettles in traditional Thai orchestras, or the single-stringed bowed spike fiddles of Ethiopia. The sounds seem strange, representing concepts of life different from Western values and attitudes. Not only are the scales, harmonies, and instruments completely different, but the symbolic meaning of the music is almost incomprehensible to listeners outside the culture. Like a speech in a strange language, the physical sounds are clear, but the meaning is not.

INTERCULTURAL CANTOMETRICS

Alan Lomax, folklorist and scholar, worked for sixty years to explain why this is the case. In an elaborate system of "cantometrics" (the "measurement" or analysis of song), he recorded, catalogued, and analyzed the song styles of all major ethnic groups. The raw information was codified and matched with information drawn from the *Ethnographic Atlas* (Murdock, 1962-1967), which provides standardized ratings for subsistence type, family kinship patterns, settlement types, political organization, etc. Very simply, Lomax found that music always reveals and reinforces the lives of the people who are creating and listening to that music. It's a lot more complex than "happy people create happy music." It has to do with attitudes, desires, goals, sexual traditions, sibling patterns, child rearing, mother-child relationships, authority models, ancestor figures, and many other concerns - all told, some 47 separate items.

For example, in complex societies, the songs deliver a lot of musical and verbal information; in simple societies, much less is conveyed. In societies where the powerful leaders are constantly changing, the songs are rhythmically very busy and complicated. In societies where strong leaders seldom lose their power, the opposite is true. In societies dominated by men, a distinct leader is always in charge of the musical events. In societies where women have some voice in what happens, the musical events are much more communal and informal in character. Lomax's monumental studies, as seen particularly in 1968's *Folk Song Style and Culture*, reveal what music really means, or, perhaps better, what music really *does* in the various societies of the world.

MUSICAL TASTE

All evidence seems to support the conclusion Lomax drew from his research: musical taste — musical preference — comes from a host of deep-seated sociocultural attitudes and values. Those attitudes and values derive from ethnic roots, race, national traditions, neighborhood location, religious affiliation, family ties, occupational subgroups, cultural bonding, etc.

Now the strange fact of the matter is simply this — that of the several components in the above mix, the most important is not race, nationality, or ethnic similarity, but cultural bonding.

Parents and their teenage adolescents have the same genes, but the kids live in their own teen culture, so they often have arguments over haircuts, clothing style, leisure time activities, and music. Yes, music. Music is surely one of the most obvious, colorful, and potent of any cultural differences. Time and again through history, music that delights one crowd of people greatly offends another crowd. It is, indeed, a continuous thread that runs through *Pop Music, U. S. A.*

CONCLUSION

The "aesthetics of music", then, is really a terribly inexact and misleading term, suggesting some kind of absolute standard of beauty and quality. The inescapable fact is that beauty and quality are culturally determined.

What music does, it does powerfully and immediately. It sends subliminal messages in symbolic sounds and sights. Lomax has established quite convincingly that it is not all that mysterious or abstract at all. It is concrete and predictable, revealing and celebrating the attitudes and values of the culture of its origin.

Chapter 2
Utility to Recreation to History:
Folk to Pop to Art

SPORTS

In *Finnegan's Wake* the novelist James Joyce said, "Pastimes are past times." Communications philosopher Marshall McLuhan explained, "The dominant technologies of one age become the games and pastimes of a later age."

The observations of Joyce and McLuhan help explain the appeal of competitive sports. A caveman, for instance, got a meal by hitting a flying object, a bird perhaps, with a stick. The technology of food gathering served him well. Today, baseball players entertain large audiences with the same kind of skill, and the importance assigned to the act is measured in millions of dollars, because everyone is metaphorically (artistically) reliving the urgency of the original behavior.

Leaping over a creek or large stone may once have been necessary to escape from an enemy, and, to avoid injury, it was important to stay in the air as long as possible. Today, basketball players delight huge crowds with magnificent leaping skills, and devoted fans talk about their favorite player's "hang time".

All the "useless" skills of the modern Olympic stars – weight lifting, jumping, diving, running, throwing the javelin, and the others – had a function and "real value" at one time. Today they are sports entertainment.

Technology may even change, but the instinct will continue. When horses did the work on the farms, the county fair always included at least one horse-pulling match to see who had the healthiest and strongest team of horses. Today, those same county fairs have tractor pulls to see whose tractor is the "healthiest and strongest".

THE ARTS

The same can be said for the arts. The useless skills of modern artists — painters, poets, sculptors, dancers, musicians, and such — all had a function and real value at one time. Cavemen put vivid pictures on the walls of their caves to protect themselves from evil spirits. Wandering tribesmen carried sculptured images of their gods for strength and confidence. Ancient storytellers sang rhymed tales of glorious tribal achievements to delight and inspire the village adolescents.

In opera, the tenor who sings highest notes with the most powerful and beautiful voice gets the attractive woman in the opera, and wins the approval of the audience members who partake of the experience in vicarious joy.

Making noises on taut strings and stretched skins served once to attract desirable game, or perhaps to repel enemy animals. Today classical violinists and jazz drummers offer wonderfully crafted solos — works of art which derive from those earlier utilitarian skills.

ART CATEGORIES AND TERMS

In an effort to draw some sense out of the bewildering development of artistic endeavors, Judeo-Christian art critics created categories of *folk art, pop art*, and *fine art*. They also made a distinction, sometimes, between *artists* and *artisans*, that is to say, between real artists and highly skilled craftsmen.

Music scholars have coined two terms to describe music: "vernacular music" (folk and pop music) as contrasted with "music in the cultivated tradition" (classical music). The terms help to avoid the negative tone which attaches to "folk and pop". And the terms are certainly a big improvement over previous times when classical music was called "serious music", to separate it from all that other stuff which was, somehow, "not serious".

But the terms still suggest that "cultivated" music is superior to music "in the vernacular", which by definition and long association means "down there with the common folk". The terms really do not get to the heart of the matter, either. Such marvelous tunes, for example, as Jerome Kern's "All the Things You Are" and Duke Ellington's "Sophisticated Lady" are certainly the artistic equivalent of an art song by Franz Schubert.

The whole process of assigning labels to, and, by implication, greater aesthetic value to, some forms of human effort over other forms has led to rather arbitrary opinions. Not too many years ago opera singers were considered "better" than jazz and pop singers. Ballet dancers were considered "better" than Olympic gymnasts and basketball players. Composers of classical music were considered superior to composers of musical comedy who were considered superior to those charlatans who wrote pop tunes. All of this is highly suspect today.

In *The Anthropology of Music*, a masterful exploration of the entire field of music, Alan Merriam found that "aesthetic value" is a notion peculiar to only certain cultures. Many societies have no such concept as aesthetic value. The natives of Bali, for example, do not even have a word for "art". They do everything as well – skillfully, beautifully, and meaningfully – as possible (Merriam 1964, 259-276).

The flower children of the 1960s challenged the notion that some forms of resourceful activity are a more valuable human experience than others. Since then, great progress has been made in giving all high-quality creative endeavors their just due, by whatever name.

FOLK to POP to ART

History seems to show that all the academic posturing on "art" is just that – academic posturing. The inescapable evidence is that certain human activities, absolutely essential for survival in one age, become the recreational entertainment of a later age, and finally become the high art of a still later age – that is, the behavior moves from folk to pop to art.

There is no such thing as "popular music" among many of the vast millions who live on the planet. In most non-industrial societies there are only two kinds of music: folk music and ritual music. Folk music includes the large body of utilitarian music for planting, harvesting, fishing, hoisting sails, humming babies to sleep, and for all of the other ordinary daily endeavors of life. Ritual music is music for religious and ceremonial occasions. Some of this music got very complex among the Aztecs, Incas, Egyptians, and other ancient societies, with special instruments, costumes, dancing, and a particular musical style.

But popular music simply did not exist through most of the eons of human history, nor does it exist today in many parts of the world. We may have Euro-American rock on the radios in Ethiopia, and I suppose also among the millions

7

people who live on the island of Borneo, and possibly in the mountains of Mongolia. But very few people in those cultures are probably devoted full time to the business of creating music for financial gain.

"Folk music? Folk music? We're all folk, ain't we? I never heard no horse sing." That line, often attributed to Leadbelly, contains a profound observation. It is, in fact, all folk music. In Europe, that folk music got intellectually formalized for its religious utility in the hands of Pope Gregory's scholars, and later by Guido, Leonin, Perotin, and hundreds of their unknown compatriots, into works for the Roman Catholic Church and the various other Christian religions that were offshoots of it.

Later, the formal religious music became forever separated from its folk roots with the teeming lower classes by Guillaume Dufay, Francesco Landini, and their co-workers. It finally emerged as the high art music of Western Civilization in the hands of Josquin des Prez, Gilles Binchois, Orlande de Lassus, and many others who, in addition to writing for the church, turned out secular music for artistic pleasure – madrigals, chansons, and the like. The secular and religious forms expanded over time to become the concertos of J. S. Bach, the operas of Mozart, and the sweeping symphonies of Beethoven. The overarching term for music of this type is "classical".

It was not until the industrial revolution that a third category began to take shape – pop music (commercial). Although Bach, Mozart, and Beethoven were most certainly being paid for their talents, it was only later that true commercialization of musical works began. The first copyright law for published books was established in England in 1710. As new technologies emerged, types of copyrights were created and capitalized on, to the point where, these days, we have multimedia companies who own film, music, performance, and other rights for songs that are seen and heard internationally. Although the background for "how we got here" will be covered, most of what will be discussed in this book will be about popular commercial music for the masses, in all of its wonderfully diverse variations.

These three categories, folk (communal utilitarian), pop (entertainment), and art (classical music of historical significance) occur in economic terms as well as social levels and the progression always seems to go from poverty to middle class to upper class.

POVERTY to MIDDLE CLASS to UPPER CLASS

Why do new music styles always originate in poverty? Fiske, de Certeau, Eco, and other pop culture scholars explain that "change can come from below: the interests of those with power [those above] are best served by maintaining the status quo" (Fiske 1989, 19). Of course. The establishment businessmen and gatekeepers of the arts like the world the way it is. They live above the teeming masses, and want to keep it that way.

Those in poverty, however, have no real clout in the world, and they carry on constant "guerrilla warfare" [de Certeau's term, quoted in Fiske] to sustain their own "opposition within and against the social order dominated by the powerful" (Fiske 1989, 19).

However, once the rebel guerrillas start a fresh war in the form of a new pop music style (with its attendant dress code, dance, and language), the power establishment always moves in to win the war by ingesting the enemy.

Whole books could be written on language, haircuts, clothing styles, music, dances, and social manners that first began in peasant-level and street-level poverty (either real or self-chosen bohemian), then moved into the middle class, and finally became high society behavior.

Case in point – the punk movement in the late 1960s produced its own fashion, directly expressive of its political posture: down with the establishment, down even with the wealthy rock stars. As Anthony Burgess noted, "The punk musicians wear with snarling pride the marks of the downtrodden. Hair is cropped because long hair holds lice. Clothes are not patched, since patching denotes skill and a seedy desire for respectability; their gaping holes are held together with safety pins" (quoted in Szatmary 1987, 188).

A decade later, in the late 1970s, Saks Fifth Avenue and Bonwit Teller carried gold safety pins for $100 each, and noted British designer Zandra Rhodes created a collection of gowns for Bloomingdale's that incorporated stylized rips and glitter-studded safety pins, at prices of $345 to $1,150 per gown. Finally, in June 1980, *Mademoiselle* magazine offered its readers the choice between "punk" or "preppie" in a four-page spread on the "in" styles.

Another case. The favorite event in a fine arts series at any Eastern Ivy League college will probably be a concert by a blues artist, B. B. King, for example.

The college kids will be genuinely moved by the emotional authenticity of his songs about prison life, oppression, love affairs gone bad, alcohol, and poverty.

How ironic it is that he sings to children whose fathers and grandfathers built and still own the very giant corporations that kept B. B. King's folks in poverty and oppression to begin with. And the fine arts series is funded by a foundation which one the grandfathers established to avoid taxes on the astronomical profits of his huge corporation.

Thus, the blues went from (1) functional emotional catharsis and collective commiseration in the poverty-level lives of B. B. King, Leadbelly, Blind Lemon, and others, to (2) pop-entertainment financial gain for Count Basie and Jack Teagarden, to (3a) an event in the fine arts series for upper class college kids, on one hand, and on the other hand, (3b) the esoteric high-art work of Charles Mingus, John Coltrane, and Cecil Taylor. From folk to pop to art.

A final case, a stunning paradox – the magazine called *Rolling Stone* takes its name from Muddy Waters' classic lamentation which inspired the British rock group to become millionaires by screaming out at the world how bad life is. The magazine clings to its anti-establishment image, of course, with strong articles about graft, greed, corruption, and hypocrisy in the music business, yet stays financially solvent with huge ads bought by those very corporations being attacked on the surrounding pages.

ART IS TIME-PLACE-CULTURE SPECIFIC

The surest evidence that the line from folk to pop to art has completed itself is when government organizations and corporate foundations begin to grant money to preserve that art form. When it's folk music, it's free. When it's entertainment, it pays for itself most handsomely. When it's art, it needs government and foundation funding.

Here's a perfect example. The Smithsonian Institution launched a huge project in the 1990s to research and record all the great Duke Ellington compositions as they might be reconstructed in totality from the various pieces of recorded and written evidence. The message was clear. Ellington is history.

From the late 1920s well into the 1950s, Ellington didn't need any government projects to keep his music alive. His music was a shifting musical metaphor for inner-city black culture in the Roaring Twenties, then the Swing Era of the Great Depression, and then America during World War II, by which time he had made most of his major statement.

In the 1990s, however, the metaphor no longer pertains. The music of Duke Ellington has no current cultural relevance. His music doesn't say anything about the ghetto streets of Los Angeles today as it did about the streets of Harlem in the late 1920s. Wealthy college kids don't go down to Central Avenue in Los Angeles today like they used to go to Harlem in the late 1920s for some exotic, slightly dangerous, and very fashionable night life.

Moreover, the haunting artistic strains of "Mood Indigo" and "Harlem Air Shaft" certainly meant nothing at the time to our Native Americans, Greenland Eskimos, or Chinese peasants in the 1920s and 1930s. Music is no more universal than any other language. However, the urge to create and listen to music *is* universal.

All art is time-place-culture specific. Paintings, musical compositions, novels, buildings, poems, and such grow out of a very special perception of the reality of the moment by a very special human mind. Artworks become universal if that very special human mind reaches so deep into the specific time-place-culture as to touch the collective, the universal, human condition at any time, in any location, in any culture.

Even then, however, the artistic connection is frightfully tenuous. European opera fans are likely to miss the marvelous nuances of genuine Korean opera, even if they have studied the time, place, and cultural roots of that Korean opera.

Then, too, things are always a matter of degree. *I Love Lucy* is not all that different from *The Marriage of Figaro* in dealing with the patterns of class differences. Nor is Hank Williams' "I'm So Lonesome I Could Cry" all that different from the second movement of Tchaikovsky's "Pathétique" Symphony in expressing an unbearable sense of separation from the rest of humanity. The difference is not in the authenticity or depth of the feeling, but merely in the style of its delivery.

CONCLUSION

A book on popular music, then, by definition, examines music that is somewhere on its way from folk (utilitarian) to art (historical significance). As it moves through the middle ground of pop (commercial entertainment), it gets so homogenized that it loses some of its original identity, of course. What remains, though, is still sufficient for enormous financial gain in the world of entertainment.

And when it arrives, finally, at the level of historical significance – of "art" – it has lost its cultural currency, but not its cultural authenticity or art value. As art, it reveals strong and abundant evidence of the values, attitudes, and desires of a certain crowd of people, in a specific geographic location, at a given moment in the past.

That's what makes art museums, recorded archives, halls of fame, ancient ruins, and such so important and valuable. We see, hear, and feel – in greater depth and immediacy than possible any other way – the magnitude and beauty of another time, place, and culture that is always remarkably similar to our own at the deepest levels of human experience.

The arts tell us – in symbolic gestures delivered in time, stone, canvas and oil, acoustical sounds, body movements, in the spaces between the printed words, and such – who and what we are. It all happens at such a deep intuitive, psycho-emotional, and non-verbal level that we are often at a loss to even understand it ourselves, much less explain it to anyone else.

Purists don't want to acknowledge it, but pop music is most assuredly among the American art forms. The fact that it is created for financial gain doesn't mean it can't be art. Indeed, it means that pop music must reach, instantly, that deepest level of the pre-conscious aesthetic recognition – with razor-sharp precision. There aren't many second chances on a Broadway opening night.

In Duke Ellington's long career he had a few short dry spells. During one of those times, a well-known music critic said, "Don't worry Duke, future generations will be fond of your music." Ellington smiled and said, "Thank you, but I don't care about future generations, I want the people to like my music now!"

Time now to trace the growth and development of American popular music, that special product created for the unashamed purpose of financial gain – with its creators knowing full well that there will be no financial gain unless they connect with something deep in the collective sensibilities of their market audience.

It's a colorful narrative of talented and ambitious entrepreneurs, and we'll cover the whole story from colonial times to the present day as we travel through the diverse territories of *Pop Music, U.S.A.*

Chapter 3
Colonial Times

The colorful story of America's popular music industry opens in 1620 with the separatist Puritans, who settled in the area of Plymouth, Massachusetts. Called Pilgrims because of their travels to find a land where they could practice their religion freely, the *Mayflower* passengers brought with them Henry Ainsworth's psalter, a collection of 150 psalm and hymn texts (just words, no music) for thirty-nine familiar melodies.

In 1630, non-separatist Puritans landed a few miles to the north, bringing with them a similar collection, the Sternhold and Hopkins psalter. By the end of the century, the groups began to merge into what finally became the Congregational Church.

SACRED MUSIC

Church Music

The first book printed in America was a hymnal, the *Bay Psalm Book* (1640). Like European models, it contained only words, not music, since everyone knew the melodies to which the words had been set. Those melodies are similar to modern country and gospel music: regular phrases, simple chords, repetitive sections, straightforward "on the beat" rhythms, and melodic lines which are a little high for the normal male voice.

By the 1700s, the Eastern Seaboard was alive with industrious settlers carving out their new way of life. Among their favorite tunes were a few that are sung even today: "We Gather Together", a popular Thanksgiving hymn; "Praise God from Whom All Blessings Flow", known as the Doxology but called "Old Hundred" because it was No. 100 in the Anglo-Geneva psalter of 1561; and "Auld Lang Syne", sung today by large crowds of celebrants on New Year's Eve.

In church (called a "meeting house") they sang without instruments because the elders thought that instruments had no place in formal worship. In their private homes, however, they may have sung the same hymns with instrumental accompaniment. And they undoubtedly sang their secular tunes with some kind of instrumental assistance.

Singing in the local churches was a favorite activity, and folks took to it with great enthusiasm. Some of the more eager singers, apparently, would now and then add a few notes to the basic melody, and before long the pastors were complaining that singing had deteriorated into a free-for-all with no discipline or control whatsoever.

Singing Schools

In what has become an American characteristic, entrepreneurs saw a social need, and set out to meet it for a profit. Several enterprising pastors and musicians soon opened schools to teach note reading and correct singing.

As early as 1721, John Tufts, pastor at the Second Church in Newbury, Massachusetts, wrote a music instruction book in which he recommended the "fa-sol-la-mi" system of notation much used in England. Rev. Thomas Walter wrote a similar book, "Fitted to the meanest Capacities", and he complained about the "tortured and twisted" manner of church singing which produced "confused and disorderly Noises."

Andrew Law (1748-1821), William Billings (1746-1800), James Lyon (1735-1794), and many other singing school masters devoted their lives to the improvement of music in the colonies. Writing and publishing their own music and textbooks, they traveled far and wide to conduct two-week singing classes. They were, in a sense, the first public school music teachers. Had their native musical style not been washed aside by later waves of highly trained European musicians, the history of music in America might have been substantially different.

Untrained in traditional methods, these teacher-composers produced a body of music with a kind of straightforward charm, which by European standards sounds a little crude and uninformed. Such techniques as gapped scales, unconventional chord progressions, parallel fifths and octaves, irregular phrases, unprepared suspensions, primitive contrapuntal techniques, and a fondness for melody in the tenor voice brought great criticism from the sophisticates. The singing school masters carried on, though, with considerable success. The composition style and performance traditions can still be heard today in some sections of the South.

Following Tufts, the singing school masters took a simplified approach to reading music. They modified the ancient system of *solfeggio* (singing by syllables rather than letter names), picked up some English variations of that system, and came up with their own American improvement by making each syllable's notation a different shape on the page. Thus the widely used shape note system came to be. The most popular of the second generation of these shape note music books was *The Sacred Harp* by White and King (1844). That book and other, newer, versions featuring the same shape note system are still used today, with Sacred Harp singing communities found in many areas of the United States and beyond.

SECULAR MUSIC

The War for Independence

During the Revolutionary War (1775-1783), musical activities did not disappear from the land. There were long stretches when no fighting occurred at all, and during the winter months, music flourished in the homes, churches, public meeting places, taverns, village commons, and in the army field headquarters.

Four different kinds of musical activity were evident during the War. First, the Revolutionary Army took its signals from the many corps of fifers and drummers who were attached to each regiment. The basic information on what to do – "Reveille" (arise in the morning), "To Arms" (we're being attacked), "Pioneer's March" (camp maintenance duties) – was conveyed by the drum beat-pattern. Superimposed on the beat-pattern was a fife tune, usually a popular folk tune. The drummers and fifers were often mere boys in their teens. Each battalion had three or four of these "musicianers" in the ranks.

Second, contrary to conventional historical accounts, the Americans did have bands during the War for Independence. These little bands of, say, two flutes, an oboe, a bassoon, and perhaps a clarinet or French horn, were separate from the troops, and therefore the names of the bandsmen do not appear in the official military records. The musicians were hired independently by a battalion colonel, and they served at his pleasure only. He used them for military parades, weddings, funerals, and social events where a fife and drum unit would be too crude.

Third was a very common social event, the dancing assembly, a subscription series of dinner dances for the military top brass and local VIP's. A group of "sponsors" would meet, identify a suitable location, and hold a series of perhaps 12-15 weekly or biweekly parties – dinner, cards, dancing, games, "Songs of Liberty", and such. One of the battalion bands would provide the music. It was the historical antecedent of Saturday night at the country club in modern America.

Fourth, there was an active musical theater season during the War. English ballad operas were in vogue then, and performances were held in Boston, New York, and Philadelphia during the winter months each year of the War. The performances, with a few "professionals" and many amateurs, would be much like the community theater groups so common in America today. Unlike sophisticated European opera, ballad opera addressed itself to common people in lower class situations, and the songs were folk and popular songs with immediate appeal.

Broadsides

Broadsides were distributed throughout colonial America as early as the middle 1600s right up through the Revolutionary War and well beyond. A broadside was a single sheet of paper about 12" by 18" in size, on which a poem that could be sung to a familiar song was printed. Written by a local political agitator or journalist, the topic was usually highly critical, satirical, burning with strong emotions, and always witty and inventive.

Broadsides were eagerly anticipated and they quickly sold for a penny each. In addition to political events, all manner of social, topical, and just plain newsworthy items found expression in broadsides. As late as the Civil War, broadsides still served their dual purpose of information and musical entertainment.

CONCLUSION

All in all, musical life in America from the early 1600s through the War for Independence was just what might be expected. The simple folk had no time or inclination for the exalted styles and traditions of Europe.

There were some remarkable exceptions, of course. The Moravians in Pennsylvania formed trombone choirs and singing societies to perform classical music. And in the South, classical music was an integral part of the social life of the wealthy plantation owners. Concerts were occasionally presented by resident church organists, and traveling musicians and singers would often perform in the large room of a plantation mansion.

The music that leads to the subject of this book, however, was mostly functional and utilitarian – perfectly consistent with the life style of that mixed crowd of robust individuals known as "the colonists".

Chapter 4
European-American Traditions

The Revolutionary War was a most unusual conflict in many ways. It was as much an economic conflict as it was a political conflict. The many aspiring businessmen in the colonies saw the British taxation policies in a financial light first, then in a philosophical light. Indeed, only one-third of the colonists wanted to break away from England. Another third wanted to remain a loyal British colony, and the final third didn't care much one way or the other.

The War was also unusual because it was driven by aristocrats – highly sophisticated and immensely wealthy upper-class citizens. For this reason, there were few cases of wanton cruelty, savage killing for pleasure, and the other many barbaric acts so common to most wars. And there were several long months during the winter each year when no fighting was done by either side.

During those winter months, the colonists began to cultivate their own talents and ingenuity. The War cut off most European trade, and the colonists now had to provide for themselves such routine items as books, jewelry, musical instruments, furniture, household utensils, clothing, glass, and tools.

It was the beginning, the real beginning, of that special thing called the American character. Margaret Mead, Jacques Barzun and many others have spoken cogently about it. It's that special kind of brash and breezy confidence with a youthful innocence and arrogance to it. It's a unique optimism in all matters – spiritual, financial, philosophical, and moral. It's a pronounced suspicion of anything truly intellectual or refined.

In popular music, two major traditions began to take shape in American society, the European-American heritage, discussed now, and the African-American heritage, discussed in the next chapter. The European-American heritage appeared in two distinct styles: mainstream Anglo-Saxon music and a specialized Anglo-Celtic music.

ANGLO-SAXON POPULAR MUSIC

This is the music that eventually leads to MOR (middle-of-the-road) popular music – Bing Crosby, Julie Andrews, Barbra Streisand, and Frank Sinatra. Its roots lie in the late 1700s and early 1800s when certain talented musicians began to ply their skills for commercial gain. Prior to that time, most musicians had been farmers or tradesfolk in their primary livelihood. Three major areas are evident.

Standard Fare

As the citizens of the new nation turned their attention from the War back to their normal daily affairs, they sang a plentiful supply of standard popular songs with predictable topics: love, fulfilled and unfulfilled; shipwrecks, storms, and other calamities; the excitement of city (or village) life; the serenity of country life; songs for and against alcohol; songs about fashions, trends, and diversions; novelty songs; and sentimental ballads.

Benjamin Carr (1768-1831), Raynor Taylor (1747-1825), James Hewitt (1770-1827), and several other foreign-born musicians were active and successful composers of popular sheet music, but the first American-born pop music composer seems to have been a blind songwriter, Oliver Shaw (1779-1848). Although known mostly for his religious compositions and classical organ skills, Shaw turned out several marches and songs that were highly respected at the time. One of his tunes, "There's Nothing True but Heav'n", brought in $1,500 in sales – quite a bit of money for a religious pop tune.

The first songster (collection or anthology) came out in 1789, *The American Miscellany*, a selection of popular verses to be sung to familiar melodies. It was about the size of a modern vest pocket appointment calendar, and was designed to be used on a moment's notice on any occasion.

Francis Hopkinson's (1737-1791) "My Days Have Been So Wondrous Free" (1759), the first known secular pop tune by a native American composer, and Alexander Reinagle's (1756-1809) "I Have a Silent Sorrow Here" (1799) seem to have been sung often.

Political and War Songs

Broadsides for and against foreign entanglements for the new nation flourished, and when America entered the War of 1812, a batch of new war tunes appeared. "Yankee Doodle" was brought out again after serving so well for so long during the second half of the 1700s. Its exact origin is still debatable, even after enormous scholarly efforts by Oscar Sonneck, S. Foster Damon, and several others. "Hail Columbia" (words by Joseph Hopkinson, Francis Hopkinson's son, and music by Philip Phile) first came out in 1798, and soon became one of America's favorite patriotic airs.

By the middle of the 1800s, "Hail to the Chief" had become the official ceremonial music for the president of the country, and remains so even today. Even though the battle occurred after the war had officially ended, Andrew Jackson's victory at New Orleans on January 8, 1814, was celebrated in a fiddle tune from Britain, "The Eighth of January". (With a new text by Jimmy Driftwood, the tune, retitled "The Battle of New Orleans", was a giant country music hit for Johnny Horton in 1959.)

The words to America's national anthem were written one night during the War of 1812 by Francis Scott Key. The words fit quite well for a familiar British beer-drinking tune, "To Anacreon in Heaven". The song grew famous over the years, and it was finally adopted as our official national anthem by an act of Congress on March 3, 1931. Every few years there is a major campaign to adopt a new national anthem like "America" ("My Country 'Tis of Thee") or "God Bless America" – both of which are easier to sing than "The Star Spangled Banner" – but neither of which convey the perilousness of the United States' survival at a critical time in history.

Theater Music

The first genuine American stage work came from Francis Hopkinson. In his own words, *The Temple of Minerva* was "an oratorical entertainment", an allegory in praise of American and French political harmony. *Minerva* is best categorized as a political ballad opera, and it represents a class of theater works very popular in early America. The first of the genre, and still the most famous, *The Beggar's Opera* (1728) by John Gay, was done often in the late 1700s throughout the colonies. It returned two hundred years later as *The Three Penny Opera* (1928) by Bertolt Brecht (playwright) and Kurt Weill (composer). This show was revived off-Broadway in 1954. Weill's big hit, "Mack the Knife", was, of course, not part of the original 1728 work.

Dozens of these ballad operas – *Tammy, The Archers, The Padlock* and others – are mentioned in personal diaries and journals and in newspaper accounts of early American show business, indicating how widespread they were. The ballad opera concept (write your own story with your own lyrics set to well-known popular tunes) is alive and well all over America, today. Senior citizens groups, college Greek organizations, and community theater companies often put on at least one such "original" each season.

Burlesque, too, was popular in the early 1800s. This was not dirty jokes and strip-tease dancers, but burlesque in its original form, more of a comedy affair. More on that later. Minstrel shows were also popular entertainment for European-Americans, although their contents were really bastardized versions of African-American traditions.

"Variety entertainments" seem to have been common, also. Novelty acts, trained chickens, feats of magic wonder, strong men, midgets, jugglers, virtuoso musicians, and such were well received throughout America. This kind of entertainment package later developed into vaudeville.

ANGLO-CELTIC FOLK MUSIC

Separate from the musical activities of the urban, middle-class Anglo-Saxons, there existed a great body of lower-class folk music. The oral traditions of this Anglo-Celtic music (Welsh, Irish-Gaelic, and Scotch-Gaelic) go all the way back to the non-literate subcultures of the peasant serfs in the feudal societies of the late Middle Ages.

The Anglo-Celts were a high-strung independent crowd, not given much to the polite niceties of village living, so, in the early 1700s, they began to move out of the (for them) congested cities of Boston, Philadelphia, and New York. They moved into the Appalachian Mountains in what would eventually become the states of West Virginia, Kentucky, Tennessee, the Carolinas, and Georgia.

After many generations of separation from mainstream America, the mountaineers became distinctly different from their Anglo-Saxon compatriots in the big cities of the East Coast. The whole culture – language, values and attitudes, dreams and desires, sense of justice, and music – was frozen in time for nearly one hundred fifty years.

Not until the late 1800s did their music really come to light through the efforts of a Harvard English professor, Francis James Child (1825-1896). In the early 1900s, Child's pioneer studies were used as the basis for five volumes of Appalachian folk songs catalogued by scholar Cecil J. Sharp (1859-1924). Then Bertrand H. Bronson clarified and amplified all the previous research with several scholarly volumes from the 1950s through the 1970s.

We find a surprising number of ballads about violent family entanglements. "The Twa Brothers" (Child 19) tells of a boy who stabs his younger brother to death (Hamm 1983, 49). "Earl Brand" (Child 7) is the story of a young woman who elopes with her lover. When her father and brothers set out to bring her back, her lover ambushes them. He is wounded in the battle, though, and goes home to his mother to die (Hamm 1983, 49).

William, in "Fair Margaret and Sweet William" (Child 74), marries another woman, dreams of Margaret lying in her bed in a pool of blood, and goes to her house to find that she has indeed killed herself. "The Cruel Mother" (Child 20) kills her illegitimate twins with a knife, and is then haunted by visions of them (Hamm 1983, 49).

The details are different, but "somebody done somebody wrong songs" are still popular in Nashville. Indeed, in many other ways – melodic intervals, irregular phrases, that high and lonesome vocal style, gapped scales, simple triadic harmonies, etc. – colonial Anglo-Celtic music lives on, strong and healthy, even today, in the field of country music.

Chapter 5
African-American Traditions

The first slaves landed on American shores in 1619. For nearly 300 years thereafter, very little was known about authentic black musical practices. Fragmentary evidence found in colonial diaries and journals suggests that plantation life was rich in musical occasions.

While the white community moved toward a commercial version of modified British folk music, the black community sang and danced in a wide variety of bicultural patterns. The blacks absorbed the ingredients of European music – melody, harmony, rhythm – but reworked each ingredient into a special artistic expression. The result was a new music, a new language of communication.

It was not European. It was not American. It was not African. It was African-American – growing out of artistic sensibilities that were absolutely unique in world history.

Most imported slaves had come originally from the kingdoms and city-states of the west coast of Africa, and these Ashanti, Benin, Dahomey, Gambia, Oyo, and Senegal societies included a rich body of music and dance in all public and private ceremonies, rites, festivals, and celebrations. All daily activities had musical embellishments – boating, hunting, instruction of the young, planting, cattle raising, fishing, harvesting, storytelling, and even legal proceedings where "the litigants charged or sang their arguments to the accompaniment of drums and occasional singing of the assembled villagers" (Southern 1983, 8).

GENERAL CONDITIONS IN AMERICA

These powerful instincts and traditions sustained the slaves in their new environment, and led to a kaleidoscopic array of musical activities: 'Lection Day ceremonies (patterned after the white Election Day), during which the blacks elected their own governors; Pinkster Day (Pentecost Sunday) which sometimes lasted a full week; religious services, sanctioned and unsanctioned; the now famous

23

ring shouts; all kinds of work songs; dance and play songs; field and street hollers; spirituals and poetic forms which eventually led to the blues; and even forced singing and dancing on the auction block.

Colonial newspapers carried regular advertisements of slaves for sale, and often made reference to the slaves' musical skills. Town records describe events where black musicians performed. Court documents show that run-away slaves were more eagerly searched out if they had musical talent. So valuable were the gifted singers and instrumentalists that their masters put them on display at every opportunity. Sometimes a slave would be called up to the planter's mansion to perform, and sometimes the slave owner would take his guests down to the slave quarters to watch a particular frolic or ring shout. Fiddlers led all in prestige and fame. Solomon Northrup (recently portrayed in the film *12 Years a Slave*), Polydor Gardiner, and many others played for their masters' dances and parties, and were also loaned out to neighboring plantation owners.

Students in the South occasionally took their slaves with them to college. Since there were no slave quarters on campus, the slaves lived in the same rooms as the students, and often went to classes with their young owners. Scholars think some of the slave musicians learned many useful things during those music lessons that were required of proper young Southern men and women.

Five thousand blacks fought in the Revolutionary War. Drummers and fifers Barzillai Lew, Jazeb Jolly, William Nickens, and Negro Tom carried themselves through many a battle with courage and dignity. During the War of 1812, musicians George Brown, Cyrus Tiffany, and Jessie Wall served in the navy with distinction. At first, blacks were not permitted in the military, but General Andrew Jackson gave his permission in 1814. There must have been a good enlistment of black musicians because, right after the war, a large number of African-American brass bands appeared. By 1820, black musicians were well established in America as singers, dancers, instrumentalists, and music teachers.

By the early 1800s, three distinct areas of black music were evident: religious music, theater music, and dance music. Much of what makes America's jazz and popular music so different and distinctive comes from that special black feeling so evident in each of the above areas. In the 1970s this unique and hard-to-describe characteristic was called "soul".

RELIGIOUS MUSIC

Church Music

As black churches appeared, African-American music began to gain the authority of its own voice. When they no longer had to modify their musical declarations as a courtesy to the white members of the congregation, the gifted black musicians could follow their own instincts with confidence and emotional conviction. The result was the real beginning of what eventually led to blues, ragtime, gospel, Dixieland, big band, and all the other styles and periods which make up the world of today's African-American music, and, by extension, rock and roll.

George Leile was the first black to get a license to preach, and he was largely responsible for the formation of the first black congregation, the African Baptist Church of Savannah, Georgia. Other churches soon followed. The most important, by far, was the church formed by Richard Allen in 1816 in Philadelphia, the African Methodist Episcopal Church. Music historian Eileen Southern describes the immediate effect of these churches:

> *The Negro church did more than just provide religious experiences for its congregations. For black folk – who were denied participation in the social, economic, and political life of the white American community – the church was at once a religious temple, a school for children and adults, and a social center, a training ground for potential leaders of the race, and, like the Catholic Church of early Europe, a patron of the arts, particularly music.*
>
> *Significantly, since their beginnings in the eighteenth century, Negro churches have occupied an important place in the lives of black folk; many black leaders have been ministers, and many black musicians have begun their careers in church choirs* (Southern 1971, 84-85).

One of the first things Richard Allen did for his new A.M.E. Church was to publish a hymnal. He collected hymns from various sources, as was the custom of the day, and added a few of his own works. With texts only (many which were not attributed to any composer or writer), the few who could read would guide others through this familiar territory with no trouble whatsoever. Allen altered some of the hymns, adding a two-line refrain to the basic stanzas of the originals, thus establishing a model for future gospel tunes both black and white.

As Southern outlined above, the black churches – then, as is often the case today – nurtured most of the strong leaders in African-American life: preachers, of course, but also educators, politicians, doctors, lawyers, business professionals, singers, dancers, and musicians. Many of the big stars in black music today speak with fondness of their formative years in the church. Their musical style comes from strong childhood memories.

Camp Meetings

African-Americans also revealed their musical gifts in the outdoor camp meetings that arose in the early 1800s. In the sweep of the "Second Great Awakening", thousands of blacks and whites of all religious persuasions gathered periodically in broad fields and valleys to celebrate their communal revivalist passions. These faithful Christians would often spend an entire weekend in this combined religious and social occasion.

Witnesses were stunned by the expressive lamentations of the blacks who identified with Old Testament tales of captivity and with New Testament promises of freedom and salvation. As they sang these poignant songs – some stately and majestic, some brilliantly syncopated – they would shift weight from one foot to the other, producing an audible sound which was then further embellished by hand clapping and thigh slapping. Since they often formed a circle, these activities came to be called *ring shouts*. The repetition of memorable melodic fragments and the punctuation effect of exuberant "Hallelujahs" and "Amens" created an emotional experience of great depth and beauty.

The blacks would often sing far into the night, long after the whites had retired for the evening. And they sang their own permutations of the familiar hymns, freely modifying the melodic and rhythmic components to suit their needs. They invented new texts for old tunes, and new tunes for old texts, and completely new texts and tunes of their own. They also might keep the old text and tune, but break it up in question-and-answer form to give it a more potent emotional thrust.

At sunrise on the last day of the camp meeting, the blacks would tear down the wooden fences that separated the black and white participants, and then perform a kind of ritual conclusion to the festivities, the "grand march". It was, obviously, a rich experience to live through a camp meeting in the 1800s. Generations later, jazz musicians Fletcher Henderson (in the 1920s) and Charlie Mingus (in the 1950s) would put camp meeting titles on some of their compositions. They were obviously acknowledging the strength of those collective memories in their family histories.

Late in the 1800s, several performing groups took this great body of black religious music, reworked it a little for concert presentation, and set out to bring it to the attention of the world. The most famous were the Fisk Jubilee Singers who raised $150,000 for their school in six years of touring. For a short time near the end of the 1800s, "Jubilee song" almost replaced "spiritual" as the generic term of choice, but "spiritual" soon regained its favor.

The difference between a spiritual and a gospel tune is not clear in American historical research. Suffice, at the moment, to suggest that spirituals are more likely to be for several voices in conception and execution, and tend to be offered and received in a concert-like atmosphere. Gospel tunes tend to be geared more toward a solo singer (or a small group of singers), and feel more like the pop tunes of their day. This is oversimplified, however, and the line between a spiritual and a gospel tune is not clearly distinguished in many cases.

FOLK MUSIC

For all the ugly and inhuman things that occurred during a typical week on a plantation in the South, there were times when the slaves were allowed to pursue their own social and recreational desires. Most of Saturday night and all day Sunday, the slaves engaged in a great deal of singing, dancing, and performing on fiddles and banjos. The plantation owners would encourage these traditions, ostensibly because it made the slaves more manageable during the week.

In time, these slave get-togethers would be parodied by white performers in blackface in the minstrel shows that became prevalent in the 19th century. (See Chapter 8.)

AFRICAN-AMERICAN DANCE TRADITIONS

A full treatment of what is essentially the black character of America's popular dance forms would surely fill several volumes. It is sufficient at this time to observe that African body language permeates American pop culture, and the tradition is evident in the earliest jigs, breakdowns, buck-and-wing steps, cakewalks, corn husking jigs, reels, jubas, and all the other forms which the slaves had created or been handed down through history from their ancestors.

All societies dance, of course. Dance is one of the great non-verbal communication systems and a pleasurable release of physical needs. The special appeal of African styles over European styles is hard to explain. But somehow the traditional folk dances of France, Italy, Germany, and Great Britain – polkas, waltzes, schottisches, gavottes, bourrees, and the like – began to recede in favor of the black-derived forms. Only the Latin dance forms (tango, mambo, rhumba, cha-cha, bossa nova, samba, and such) ever held their own with the stimulating physical sensations of the highly syncopated African American styles.

From the late 1800s to the present, black forms dominate the field of social dancing. The historical line is nearly continuous – first the slave styles (mentioned above), then various ragtime dances, then specific dances by the dozens. The list is long: the Charleston, the fox trot, the turkey trot, the Lindy Hop, the grizzly bear, the bunny bug, the shimmy, the Hoochie-Koochie, the Black Bottom, the Sugar Foot Strut, the Jitterbug, the Twist, the Watusi, the Mashed Potato, Walking the Dog, the Frug, the Limbo Rock, the Waddle, and the Shake. And then more - right up through James Brown's moves, disco, break dancing, Michael Jackson's unique style, and finally the hip-hop body moves that accompany rap.

Back then, as today, adolescents love, and their parents fear, any new dance craze. By the early 1900s, dancing had moved across American society. Restaurants created hardwood floor space for diners who wanted to dance between courses of a meal, and soon the "nightclub" was born. Big department stores had afternoon dance teas, and some factories even had dancing during lunch hours. John D. Rockefeller took private dance lessons, and wealthy ladies would sometimes commission a special dance for a particularly important cocktail party. Marathon dance contests and "cross country" dancing enjoyed brief but intense popularity.

Tap dancing, too, has a long and complex history. Although it probably evolved from Irish step dancing, English clog dancing, and African-American juba dancing, it seems to have only gained popularity with the rise of minstrel shows. Some scholars believe that secret messages were communicated by tap dancers – messages about escape trails, times and locations of uprisings, and similar information of importance to the slave community – but the certainty of this is not clear, as it is uncertain how much tap dancing actually occurred on plantations. It is true, though, that some that slave owners would not allow drumming to accompany dancing and singing because they feared that the drumming would send hidden codes to other slaves – either as a warning, an "all clear" that it was safe for fugitive slaves to come into the open, or as signals for the start of an ever-dreaded (by the slave owners and overseers) slave uprising.

CONCLUSION

The evidence is abundant and clear. African waters were deep at work in the American soil, delivering unique nutrients to the transplanted European culture, changing forever the character and development of religious music, theatrical entertainment, and dancing styles.

Chapter 6
The Concert Circuit

By the middle of the 1800s, traveling virtuosos of every ilk and hue began to crisscross the nation with all the hype and fervor of modern rock stars. The posters and newspaper ads may have been slower to move around the country, and there were no instantaneous mass television saturation techniques, but otherwise all the ingredients of the modern stadium concert mentality were in place.

There were conductors, instrumentalists, singers, and groups of many different sizes and mixtures. They delivered a broad variety of folk, pop, and semi-classical music. A few names out of the many dozens at large will serve to convey the spirit and style of the entertainment genre.

CONDUCTORS

Frenchman **Louis A. Jullien** (1812-1860) arrived in the United States in 1853, and he exerted enormous influence on the entertainment scene with his series of spectacular concerts. With a trunk full of special arrangements, he would pull into town, recruit and rehearse an orchestra of anywhere from forty to one hundred local professionals, and then put on a concert of classics, popular airs, and novelty numbers. With his combination of outrageous showmanship and brilliant musicianship, he stirred the nation to a heightened interest in all kinds of music.

"He conducted Beethoven in white kid gloves, and for important works he used a jeweled baton." Sometimes he would seize the concertmaster's violin, or take a piccolo from his velvet coat, to finish out a musical piece with the orchestra. His most famous offering was "The Fireman's Quadrille", near the end of which local firemen came through the hall with hoses to put out real flames on stage (Gleason 1955, 66). He abandoned that part of his program after a theater burned down in Boston.

Patrick Sarsfield Gilmore (1829-1892) came from Ireland, via Canada, and organized the Gilmore Band in 1859. While serving as a bandmaster in the Union

Army in 1863, he wrote "When Johnny Comes Marching Home". Taking his cue from Jullien, Gilmore began to stage big concerts, starting in New Orleans with an inaugural celebration for the federal governor of Louisiana, where he conducted a chorus of five thousand and a band of five hundred. They performed "Hail Columbia", accompanied by the firing of several cannons on the beat of the drums and the ringing of all the church bells in the vicinity.

He then assembled another group for the National Peace Jubilee in Boston in 1869, with an orchestra of one thousand and a chorus of ten thousand. In addition, there were cannons, a powerful pipe organ, and one hundred firemen pounding anvils during the "Anvil Chorus" from Verdi's *Il Trovatore*. Finally, he topped it all at the World's Peace Jubilee, again in Boston, this time in 1872, with an orchestra of two thousand and a chorus of twenty thousand. Johann Strauss came from Europe to conduct his "Blue Danube Waltz", aided by one hundred assistant conductors on giant step ladders. Strauss later described the event to friends as an "unholy row".

Francis Johnson (1792-1844), described by diarist Robert Waln as "a descendent of Africa possessing a most respectable share of musical talents," was one of America's first black musical celebrities. Frank Johnson's Colored Band, made up of many woodwinds and a few brass and percussion, performed up and down the Atlantic seaboard, then played for Queen Victoria at Buckingham Palace. Deleting a few winds and adding strings, Johnson was highly successful as a dance band leader, playing for many high society formal balls. For both concert and dance, Johnson wrote much of the music, and had a high skill in improvising. He was, perhaps, America's first jazz musician, although the term does not come into common language for another fifty years.

INSTRUMENTALISTS

Among the many flamboyant superstars, pianist **Louis Moreau Gottschalk** (1829-1869) stands high. Born into an affluent New Orleans family, Gottschalk had all the privileges of material comfort. His English-Jewish father and Creole mother nurtured his musical gifts. They sent him to Paris to study piano and composition, after which he toured France, Switzerland, and Spain, leaving behind a trail of musical triumphs and adoring females.

In addition to the great master piano works, he played his own special brand of extravagant tone paintings, patriotic airs, and sentimental ballads. He performed brilliantly on the then new Chickering piano. To avoid a sex scandal involving the daughter of a wealthy San Francisco family, Gottschalk moved to South America where he staged massive concerts of his own works. He died at age forty in Rio de Janeiro in 1869.

From Norway, **Ole Bull** (1810-1880) made five successful tours of America in the middle 1800s, playing a dazzling array of his own compositions and special arrangements of standard works. With a nearly level bridge and a flat fingerboard, he could play all four violin strings at the same time. One number was a "Quartette, composed for four instruments, but performed on one, by Ole Bull". His bizarre style attracted an enthusiastic public (Gleason 1955, 63). He was doing exactly what **Niccolo Paganini** (1782-1840) had done a few years earlier in Europe, and he generated the same kind of hero worship.

Thomas Bethune (1849-1908), born blind to Colonel Bethune's household slave, Charity Wiggins, astonished everyone when he played difficult exercises at the piano after hearing them only once. By age nine, the "Negro Boy Pianist" was on a touring circuit where his remarkable memory and prodigious technical skill with Bach, Chopin, and Beethoven became the talk of the nation. Among his repertoire of seven hundred compositions were piano "imitations" of waterfalls, rainstorms, and earthquakes, along with complex feats like playing "Yankee Doodle" with one hand, a brilliant hornpipe in a different key with his other hand, while singing "Tramp! Tramp! Tramp!" in yet another key.

VOCALISTS

Jenny Lind (1820-1887), the "Swedish Nightingale", made her opera debut at age eighteen and went on to world fame before age twenty. Her American manager, the colorful P. T. Barnum, presented her right along with his circus attractions. He guaranteed her $10,000 per show, and she drew huge audiences with various classical and popular works. She sang a wide variety of solos, trios with two flutists, and similar crowd pleasers, then often concluded her show with a ravishing treatment of everyone's favorite of the day, "Home, Sweet Home". Audiences wept with joy.

African-American soprano **Elizabeth Taylor Greenfield** (1809-1876) was called "The Black Swan" by the music critics for her beauty and for her "remarkably sweet tones and wide vocal compass." She made her debut in 1851, and went on tour shortly thereafter, finally appearing in a command performance in England for Queen Victoria (Southern 1971, 112). After her concert career, she opened a voice studio in Philadelphia.

VOCAL ENSEMBLES

The **Hutchinson Family**, one of the most successful collective careers in American music, "thrilled audiences for over fifty years." From Milford, New Hampshire, the eleven sons and two daughters gave their first public concert at a local Baptist Church in 1839. Their concert programs consisted of sentimental ballads, dramatic tunes, religious pieces, and a strong brand of political anti-slavery songs.

The famous Frederick Douglass went with them when they toured England in 1846. As the sons and daughters married, they trained their offspring in the family music traditions, and at one time there were three authentic Hutchinson Family groups touring simultaneously in the United States (Jablonski 1981, 80-81).

An African American family became almost as famous as the Hutchinsons. **Alexander Luca** (b. 1805), his wife, and three sons first performed in 1853, and later toured the nation to great acclaim. They teamed up with the Hutchinsons for some concerts in Ohio in 1859, and were generally well received. The youngest Luca son, Cleveland (b. 1838), was the pianist for the family and eventually was hired by the country of Liberia to teach music there. The middle son, John (b. 1832), went on to a distinguished solo career.

CONCLUSION

While the brilliant shows of the superstar performers brought joy and delight to America's new concert audiences, composers were diligently turning out songs for any and all occasions. With the public's insatiable appetite for music, composers rose to a high level of prestige and financial security. Not all, of course, but a good many of them managed to prosper in the rapid development of America's new music industry.

It is a strange fact but true, that long after the performers are forgotten, the composers of the songs are remembered. Even more strange, of course, is the fact that long after the composers are forgotten, the songs themselves live on, in a kind of independent world of their own, a world of dreams and desires, the world of pop music.

Chapter 7
Tin Pan Alley

At the turn of the century, the term "Tin Pan Alley" began to appear in the popular music industry. Dozens of publishers had settled on 28th Street between Fifth Avenue and Broadway in New York. Journalist Monroe Rosenfeld went to 28th Street to gather material for an article on popular music for the *New York Herald.* Songwriter-turned-publisher Harry von Tilzer was working on a tune, and he had put strips of paper between the piano strings to get a special metallic sound which he liked. Rosenfeld heard this sound, and got the idea for the title of his article, "Tin Pan Alley".

But Eddie Rogers, a British song plugger, denied any American origins of the term, and claimed that "Tin Pan Alley" came from Denmark Street in London where twelve publishers had shops. When a musician or singer would come down the street, a song plugger would pull him into the office to hear a new tune. At that moment, all the other publishers on the street would grab garbage can lids and kettles, and bang them together to kill the plug (Palmer 1976, 103).

However its name first arose, "Tin Pan Alley" came to mean the same to everyone in the music business – aggressive sales techniques for tunes cranked out on call. Pop music had become a commercial product to be moved just like any other commodity in the marketplace.

It wasn't always that way. Back in the middle of the 1800s, several excellent composers provided a wealth of song material without the ruthless drive of the Tin Pan Alley song sharks.

EARLY COMPOSERS

Stephen Foster (1825-1864), the most famous of the composers in the middle of the 1800s, wrote over two hundred songs and instrumental pieces, all in the major mode. Every minstrel show of the day would contain one or more Foster tunes – "Old Folks at Home", "Oh! Susanna", and "My Old Kentucky Home", among the most frequent. Foster's melodies have lovely folk-like contours, and he is often considered America's first genuine pop composer.

Septimus Winner (1827-1902) wrote a great many popular songs under the pseudonym Alice Hawthorne. His big melodic hits were "Listen to the Mocking Bird", "Whispering Hope", "Ten Little Indians", and an adaptation of a German tune titled "Oh Where, Oh Where Has My Little Dog Gone?"

Henry Clay Work (1832-1884) left Connecticut to settle in Chicago. Among his best works are "Marching through Georgia" and "Grandfather's Clock". Work was a printer by vocation, and he was active in anti-slavery politics. His father was imprisoned in 1841 for being involved in the Underground Railroad (Jablonski 1981, 97).

In the last half of the century, two black composers added rich material to America's growing body of pop songs. **James Bland** (1854-1911) was certainly the most influential and successful of the black composers of minstrel music, including "Carry Me Back to Old Virginny", "Oh, Dem Golden Slippers", and "Hand Me Down My Walking Cane". Incidentally, during the 1880s, Bland toured Europe with the all-black Haverly's Minstrels and, as a singer and banjo player without blackface, he was invited to give a command performance for Queen Victoria and the Prince of Wales (who later became Edward VII).

Gussie Davis (1863-1899) wrote some three hundred songs while working as a custodian at the Cincinnati Conservatory of Music. "In the Lighthouse by the Sea", "The Hermit", and "The Fatal Wedding" went well, but his best was "The Baggage Coach Ahead" in which a sobbing child reveals that his mother lies in a coffin in the next railroad car ahead. This song was popularized by Imogene Comer, a noted white "female baritone". Observers said that Gussie Davis "did more than his share to open up the tear ducts of America" (Southern 1971, 270).

TIN PAN ALLEY

Foster, Bland, and the others were not really "Tin Pan Alley" composers. They were pioneers in the field of pop music, but the true beginners in what is now a billion dollar industry came along a few years later. Their stories are colorfully different, but remarkably similar in many ways. They were mostly immigrants from Middle and Eastern Europe, a large number of them Jews, passionately driven by the urge to lift themselves up from their humble ghetto surroundings. They were denied access to most mainstream business and professional opportunities, forcing them to go into the "emerging rogue industries of mass entertainment: vaudeville, movies, and popular music" (Palmer 1976, 102).

The whole drama of Tin Pan Alley is wonderfully characterized in the story of M. Witmark and Sons, one of the giant publishing houses in music. In 1886, Isidore (1869-1941) and Jacob "Jay" Witmark (1872-1950), ages 17 and 11, had a small print shop in their home for Christmas cards and advertising leaflets. Their brother, Julius (1870-1929), age 13, was a boy singer in local minstrel shows. Julius was supposed to be paid for introducing into a minstrel show some songs published by Willis Woodward. Woodward reneged, and the boys got angry. They decided to form their own publishing house. Isidore played piano tolerably well, and wrote songs in his spare time.

When President Grover Cleveland married Frances Folsom at the White House, the boys whipped up the first Witmark publication, "President Cleveland's Wedding March", by Isidore Witmark. It was a runaway best seller, and a sure-fire formula had been established: take a current news item, write a tune about it, and plug it with gusto.

Isidore's next tune, "I'll Never Question Tomorrow", was a so-so composition, but he got a French music hall star to sing it on her American tour. It sold well. Isidore became one of America's premier song pluggers, and M. Witmark and Sons was on its way to becoming one of the leading publishing firms in America. Incidentally, the "M." was for their father, Marcus (1834-1910), who had to sign all legal documents since the boys were still underage. He had no financial interest in the concern (Ewen 1977, 104).

The Witmark story, with multiple variations, but in the same general style, was repeated over and over again as the pop music industry entered the 1900s. Ambitious and inventive kids from ethnic ghetto streets in Chicago, Boston, Philadelphia, and especially New York lifted themselves up to stunning fame and wealth by creating and selling tunes that somehow addressed the American dream. Edward B. Marks, Irving Mills, Joseph Stern, Leo Feist, and scores of others followed in the pattern of the Witmarks.

THE MIGHTY FIVE

Of the hundreds of active composers who got started in Tin Pan Alley, five names come up again and again because they wrote so much music and it was of such memorable high quality. These composers established the art form as we know it today.

Irving Berlin

Israel Baline (1888-1989) was one of the first of the early composers. He dropped out of grade school to work as a "busker" (a strolling street entertainer), singing sentimental ballads in saloons and on street corners. He was especially gifted at writing parodies, that is, clever new lyrics for existing folk and pop tunes. Soon he was sweeping floors and singing those parodies in Pelham's Cafe in Chinatown.

When Pelham's pianist, Nick Michaelson, asked for lyrics for a tune he had written, Israel Baline dashed off several verses within a few minutes. "Marie from Sunny Italy" made thirty-seven cents each for its two creators while the publisher, Joseph W. Stern and Co., made several hundred dollars. That lesson was not lost on the young lyricist, now calling himself "Irving Berlin".

In his late teens, Irving Berlin was making a name for himself in the music business as a staff lyricist for music publisher Ted Snyder. He yearned for growth, however, so he purchased a Calvin Weser piano, and began to plunk out tunes to go with the lyrics that came so freely and quickly to him.

The piano had a special lever to move the hammers so they would strike different strings. He could only play in the key of G-flat, but setting the lever would produce a sound in the key of G or F, or some other key, perhaps. After he worked out a song, he would bring in a trained musician to write it down for him.

Rudimentary as it was, the technique worked so well that by age twenty-two, Irving Berlin had placed songs in four Broadway musicals, including the *Ziegfeld Follies* (Dorough 1992, 148). The same year he wrote "Alexander's Ragtime Band", a tune that brought him instant fame and wealth. Keenly aware of the financial realities of the music business, Irving Berlin immediately established his own publishing firm. By age twenty-four, he was a millionaire many times over.

The folk-like purity and simplicity of Irving Berlin's songs have become part of America's common musical language. "White Christmas", "Always", "A Pretty

Girl Is Like a Melody", "How Deep Is the Ocean", "Easter Parade" (which failed as "Smile and Show Your Dimple"), and that grand anthem of the theater, "There's No Business Like Show Business" – are tunes that will surely never die.

Jerome Kern

Equally talented as Irving Berlin, but not driven by memories of ghetto poverty, was Jerome Kern (1885-1945). Born into a middle class Jewish family in New York City, his father was a successful businessman, and his mother, a gifted pianist, gave him his first music lessons. By his teens, he was well known as a promising songwriter.

His parents sent him to Germany to study harmony and music theory. On his way back to the United States, he stopped in London for nearly a year to work as a rehearsal pianist in the vaudeville and operetta productions so abundant at the time. He quickly earned a reputation as a skillful pianist and tune doctor – one who could "cure" a tune by changing a few notes or chords.

When he finally got back to America, he zoomed to the top of the music business, and remained there the rest of his life. Music critic Alan Dale said, "Who is this Jerome Kern? His tunes stand like the Eiffel Tower above the hurdy-gurdy stuff we here so often in the theater."

Kern's masterpiece is *Show Boat* (1927), with lyricist Oscar Hammerstein II, which contains such golden tunes as "Make Believe", "Can't Help Lovin' Dat Man", and the superb "Ol' Man River". From other shows, he had a string of hits – "All the Things You Are", "The Way You Look Tonight", "The Last Time I Saw Paris", "Smoke Gets in Your Eyes", and "Yesterdays" among them. In total, Jerome Kern wrote more than 700 songs, which were used in over 100 stage works and films. In 1970, he was posthumously inducted into the Songwriters Hall of Fame.

George Gershwin

At age ten, when he heard a boyhood friend play a violin recital, George Gershwin (1898-1937) decided to be a musician. Before long he was passionately plunking out melodies at the piano. His older brother, Ira (1896-1983), was just as passionately writing poems, essays, and newspaper articles. Ira later became George's chief collaborator, and wrote the lyrics to many of George's most famous songs.

George took piano lessons from Charles Hambitzer, who insisted on classical piano studies for the discipline of skilled performance. By age fifteen George Gershwin dropped out of high school to work as a demonstration pianist in the publishing houses of Tin Pan Alley, and by age eighteen some of his original tunes were being sung in New York stage revues.

In 1919, at age twenty-one, Gershwin struck gold with a jazzy tune called "Swanee". When Al Jolson inserted it into *Sinbad,* his show at the time, the tune became an instant giant hit. From then on, Gershwin's career was a non-stop string of major achievements. He wrote hundreds of great songs for dozens of revues and book musicals – "Embraceable You", "Fascinating Rhythm", "Liza", "The Man I Love", "Of Thee I Sing", "Somebody Loves Me", and many, many more.

Even though he was a huge success, Gershwin kept studying harmony and orchestration, and he was ready when Paul Whiteman asked for an extended instrumental work for piano and orchestra, *Rhapsody in Blue.* Written when Gershwin was only 25 years old, *Rhapsody in Blue* is a jazz piano concerto that debuted at Carnegie Hall with Gershwin at the keyboard, with what was essentially the first "Pops" orchestra. (A Pops orchestra plays a mix of classical and popular music that is classical enough to meet the needs of the traditional orchestral crowd, but popular enough to please everyone else. Orchestras today pay their bills with ticket sales from their Pops programs.)

In 1934, Gershwin completed his "American folk opera" written for an all-black cast, *Porgy and Bess*, a masterpiece with lyrics by DuBose Heyward and George's older brother, Ira Gershwin. At the time, *Porgy and Bess* was not well received. Revealing the enormous artistic potential of American popular music, it is now considered one of the great works of the 20th century.

Gershwin died in 1937 of a brain tumor. It was a great loss to American music because he was at the peak of his creative powers and surely would have written several more major works of operatic and symphonic proportions. Even with his untimely death, though, he goes down in history as one of the best American composers in any musical field.

Richard Rodgers

Richard Rodgers (1902-1979) led an upper-class life in New York at No. 3 West 120th Street on the corner of Mt. Morris Park in Manhattan. His father was a wealthy physician, and this was a very comfortable neighborhood, quite a social distance from the Jewish ghettos where Irving Berlin and George Gershwin grew up. In fact, the Rodgers family spent their summers out on Long Island in an equally exclusive neighborhood where father William had a summer office location.

At each home there was a grand piano. Mrs. Rodgers was a gifted pianist, and her husband sang as she played all the tunes from the famous European operettas of the day. She taught her second son, Richard, early and well how to play piano. While still in high school, Richard teamed up with **Lorenz Hart** (1895-1943) to write several songs.

After a few years at Columbia University, Rodgers and Hart moved right out into the professional world. They wrote a wealth of great music together. Seven of their early songs appeared in *The Poor Little Ritz Girl* in 1920. Then came a string of shows that failed, but which produced a few classic pop tunes – "With a Song In My Heart" (1929), "A Ship Without a Sail" (1929), and "Ten Cents a Dance" (1930) come to mind.

Rodgers and Hart soon hit their stride with *On Your Toes* (1937), *Babes in Arms* (1937), *The Boys from Syracuse* (1938), and *Pal Joey* (1940). Among the great tunes by the team were "This Can't Be Love", "Bewitched, Bothered, and Bewildered", "My Funny Valentine", "Little Girl Blue", "The Most Beautiful Girl In the World", "Blue Moon", "Where or When", and the jazz ballet masterpiece "Slaughter On Tenth Avenue" (from *On Your Toes*). In their twenty-five years together, Rodgers and Hart wrote nearly one thousand tunes together.

When Lorenz Hart's health began to fail from alcohol and depression, Richard Rodgers began to search, with Hart's full permission and approval, for another collaborator. Rodgers teamed up with Oscar Hammerstein II (1895-1960) and began the remarkable second half of his illustrious career.

Rodgers and Hammerstein became an industry unto themselves and set a new high level of lyric theater in America with "Oh, What a Beautiful Morning" and "People Will Say We're In Love" from *Oklahoma* (1943), "If I Loved You" and "You'll Never Walk Along" from *Carousel* (1945), "Some Enchanted Evening" from *South Pacific* (1949), "Hello, Young Lovers" from *The King and I* (1951), and "Do-Re-Mi" and "Climb Every Mountain" from *The Sound of Music* (1959). There were a half dozen lesser shows between and among the above masterpieces, also.

After Hammerstein's death in 1959, Richard Rodgers wrote a few more shows with other librettist-lyricists and continued to compose. His most ambitious and successful composition during these later years was a background score for a series of television documentaries, *Victory at Sea*. It is a masterful score that earned Rodgers a special George Foster Peabody Award in 1952.

Cole Porter

Very upscale in style and content were the songs of Cole Porter (1893-1964), born into a wealthy family in Peru, Indiana. As with Irving Berlin, Cole Porter wrote both words and music, and he is remembered more for individual songs than for complete shows. But Porter's lyrics contain more intellectual references to poetry, philosophy, history, painting, and such than do the lyrics of any other Broadway songwriter.

He is best known for the 1934 classic *Anything Goes* with its title tune and "I Get a Kick Out of You" and for the 1938 *Kiss Me, Kate* with "So In Love Am I" and "Wunderbar". Among his big hits from other shows are "What Is This Thing Called Love?", "Night and Day", "Begin the Beguine", "Just One of Those Things", and dozens of others – each of them elegant, refined, charming, debonair and sophisticated.

He was especially fond of off-color innuendos in songs that were sometimes banned in Boston but enjoyed greatly by his high society friends and co-workers – "Let's Do It" and "Love for Sale", for example. Whatever the topic, however, Cole Porter crafted his songs with great skill and attention to internal rhyme patterns and rhythmic flow.

His instinct and gifts were not for the plot-oriented socially conscious works of Irving Berlin, the Gershwins, or Hammerstein-Kern or Rodgers and Hammerstein, but rather for satire-laced witty and urbane entertainment of the highest order.

SONG PLUGGING TECHNIQUES

The "plugging" (marketing) of a tune was as important as composing and publishing it, perhaps more so, because the most beautiful song will remain forever unknown unless it gets brought to the attention of a potential audience.

Many great names in music publishing and some great names in show business started out as song pluggers – Pat Howley, Edward B. Marks, Joseph Stern, Leo Feist, Irving Berlin, Al Jolson, Eddie Cantor, Harry Cohn (later president of

Columbia Pictures), Jack Warner (of the famous movie making brothers) – and hundreds of others.

EARLY PAYOLA

The pluggers would hit fifty to sixty clubs each week to peddle their tunes. They bribed performers with boxes of fine cigars, bottles of expensive perfume, jewelry, large envelopes of money, telephone numbers of attractive young women, and cases of the best whiskey.

Song pluggers would perform their tunes in music shops and five-and-dime stores. They carried "chorus slips" with the words to the chorus (refrain) of their tunes so that the men in the local taverns could join in to sing along with the entertainers on stage.

They would rent a hay wagon, bolt down a piano to the flat bed, and park the rig near the exit gate of a theater, sports arena, or amusement park to catch an audience on their way home. They paid band leaders to play their tunes at dances, and restaurant waiters to hum and sing their tunes. They hired boys to jump up and sing the songs while reels were being changed at the silent picture houses. They induced singers, comedians, and dancers in vaudeville and burlesque shows to use their tunes, and boys to stand on the street corner to sing and peddle sheet music like newspapers. Any possible way to get their "product" (sheet music) into the hands of the public was the order of the day. No questions, no reservations.

Al Jolson and Gene Austin were made "co-authors" (with royalties, therefore) of many songs they knew absolutely nothing about until they saw the sheet music on the streets. Eddie Cantor, Ruth Etting, and many others openly admitted that they received generous payments for introducing songs into their shows. Rudy Vallee boasted that he built a palatial home in Connecticut with song pluggers' "gifts". Al Jolson once received a fine racehorse for plugging a new tune.

Tin Pan Alley was a colorful chapter in the history of American popular music. As the story progresses, it will become evident that things haven't changed all that much since those flamboyant days way back then.

CONCLUSION

There have been hundreds of other composers who worked during and after the Mighty Five – Harold Arlen, Burton Lane, Frederick Loewe, Jule Styne, Arthur Schwartz, Frank Loesser, Jerry Bock, Charles Strouse, Harvey Schmidt, Cy Coleman, John Kander, Marvin Hamlisch, and Andrew Lloyd Webber come to mind immediately.

And lyricists, too – E. Y. Harburg, Dorothy Fields, Alan Jay Lerner, Howard Dietz, Johnny Mercer, Sheldon Harnick, Lee Adams, Tom Jones, Fred Ebb, Tim Rice, and others. And even several of the unusually talented who do both words and music, like Jerry Herman, Bob Merrill, Meredith Willson, Frank Loesser, and Stephen Sondheim.

They have all followed in the mode of the Mighty Five, however, and up to the 1990s there were no major innovations to alter the basic mainstream traditions of the stage musical. Some of the topics covered in the musicals may have changed over the years – for instance, *Hair* (1967) showed illegal drug use and had a nude scene, *Rent* (1994) includes a character who is HIV-positive, and *Bring In 'Da Noise, Bring in 'Da Funk* (1995) covered black history from slavery to the present using tap dancing – but for the most part, the formulas remain the same. That is the subject for a different book, though.

Chapter 8
Early Theater Music

The roots of a great national lyric theater began to spread through the subsoil of the entertainment industry in the late 1800s. It began in earnest right after the Civil War, and soon all America was alive with musico-theatrical activities. Being so open ended as an entertainment experience, "the theater" came in different forms – some story driven, some music driven, some just a series of eye-oriented pleasures, some dance driven, some merely a vehicle for a particular star, some humor driven, and some that were "all of the above".

Theater professionals doing these shows tried to be fairly accurate, but they freely modified their "titles" to bring in the biggest crowd. The theater critics and journalists who reviewed the shows often quarreled in print over a given show's real identity, and scholars came along years later to offer a third opinion.

At least seven distinct kinds of shows had existed through the 1800s, and their general style and manner still can be found in the world of entertainment today.

VAUDEVILLE

For more than fifty years, the dominant form of musical theater in America was vaudeville, and all-embracing stage show derived from English beer hall traditions.

It began with a rotund vocalist with a gift for comedy, **Tony Pastor** (1837-1908). He had spent his youth in minstrel shows and circuses, and at age 24, Pastor began to show his entrepreneurial skills. He opened an "Opera House" in the Bowery in 1865, specializing in what were then called "variety" shows, exactly what the name suggests – jugglers, dancers, dog acts, strong men, singers, comedians, female impersonators, brilliant musicians and such. Variety shows had been getting a little rough and vulgar during the 1840s and 1850s, and Pastor thought that if he cleaned them up, he could get women and children to come. His instincts were good, and he did just that.

He moved to a better section of town, 201 Broadway, and offered groceries, dress patterns, and toys as door prizes. He hired the best variety acts he could find. Before long the shows came to be called "vaudeville", from the French term *vau-de-vires* deriving from a 15th-century tradition of peasants around the Vire River singing and dancing after a day's work. In time, the French term was corrupted to the word "vaudeville" (Ewen 1977, 87).

B. F. Keith (1846-1914) and **E. F. Albee** (1857-1930) left the circus to open their own theater, the Bijou in Boston, in 1885. Instead of the traditional two shows per day, they offered continuous shows from 11:00 a.m. to 11:00 p.m., and soon these shows were a dominant force in the industry. Keith and Albee purchased and built a chain of some four hundred theaters in the East and Midwest, then developed a talent exchange, the Keith-Albee circuit (later called the United Booking Office), which in time handled the bookings for vaudevillians all over America.

The Orpheum Theater in San Francisco and the Majestic Theater in Chicago became the giants through which a Western Vaudeville Association sent an army of talented entertainers. Marcus Loew purchased one hundred fifty smaller theaters from coast to coast, filling in the market for vaudeville in the hinterlands.

The jewel in the Keith-Albee crown of theaters was the Palace Theater located at the intersection of 47th and Broadway in New York. This was the ultimate achievement, the Carnegie Hall of vaudeville. Routine acts at the Palace Theater were "headliners" anywhere else in the nation. Bing Crosby, Bob Hope, Jimmy Durante, Sophie Tucker, Bert Williams, Noble Sissle, Eubie Blake, and the other superstars sang and played the latest popular music of the day – often written specifically for them – at the Palace Theater. When it converted to movies in 1932, the newspapers called it the end of an era. It was.

Soon most of the hundreds of vaudeville theaters in America changed to movie houses, and vaudeville, as a dominant theatrical industry, died a natural death. It lay dormant for a few decades, then came back in an electronic form in the great days of early television, in the 1950s and 1960s, with *The Ed Sullivan Show* and other similar variety shows, which featured dog acts, jugglers, comedians, magicians, singers, strong men, and anything else to capture the interest and delight the senses of a vast audience always hungry for the pleasures of variety entertainment. Today a vague resemblance to vaudeville can still be seen on late-night variety TV shows hosted by the likes of David Letterman, Jimmy Kimmel, Conan O'Brien, and Jimmy Fallon. And vaudeville is still around today on college campuses, in retirement homes, and in summer camps. "Variety" entertainment is always fun.

BURLESQUE

In its original form, a burlesque show was not a striptease affair. That came later. Burlesque (from the Latin *burla*, meaning "joke") was a form of theater specializing in satirical skits and outrageous parodies designed to entertain the audience by revealing the frailties and imperfections of the human condition. Singers and dancers would perform between the skits and other novelty acts.

Longfellow's *Evangeline* and many of the Shakespeare dramas got reworked into musical slapstick. *Hamlet* suffered frequent treatment, as did Friedrich Schiller's *William Tell*. Edward "Ned" Harrigan (1844-1911) and Tony Hart (Anthony J. Cannon, 1855-1891) became the supreme masters of burlesque. Their **Harrigan and Hart** creation, "Mulligan's Guard", satirized all quasi-military groups in situations of crisis. They presented a dozen or so hugely successful "Mulligan's Guard" musicals (burlesques), which established the model that the second generation team of **Joseph Weber** (1867-1942) and **Lew Fields** (Lewis Schanfield 1867-1941) further developed.

Hollywood's "Keystone Cops", the Laurel and Hardy series, and the Abbott and Costello movies continued the great burlesque tradition, as did Sid Caesar, Milton Berle, and Lucille Ball in the days of classic television humor.

By the early 1900s, burlesque moved into its more common association with the female body. May Howard, the first dancer to be called a "burlesque queen", had her own company as early as 1888. Mabel Santley and others often appeared totally nude in "living pictures", and, partially clothed, they danced the "Hootchie-Kootchie" and the "Can-can". Little Egypt (born Fahreda Mazar Spyropoulos, c. 1871-1937) had introduced the "Hootchie-Kootchie" at the Chicago World's Fair in 1893, and it swept the nation.

The piece-by-piece removal of clothing seems to be a later development, and it's not until 1915 that Gaby Deslys did so in *Stop, Look and Listen* to a tune by

Irving Berlin. Soon, Ann Corio, Margie Hart, and Gypsy Rose Lee personalized that "striptease" technique into their own special form of dance routine for Billy Minsky's circuit of theaters.

In fact, there were several burlesque circuits right along with the vaudeville circuits. A booking in the Eastern Circuit of House Managers (burlesque) would guarantee 35 weeks of performances. The same holds true for the Empire Association, sometimes called the Western Wheel (wheel = circuit) for 30-35 weeks. Besides pretty girls, burlesque shows featured a wide assortment of novelty acts, comedy routines, dialect songs (especially Yiddish and "Negro"), jugglers and singers. A popular song presented in a vaudeville or burlesque show on one of the big circuits was heard by thousands of people, many of whom bought the sheet music the next day.

In both its classic forms – satire and striptease – burlesque, too, got replaced by the new film industry. The satire version is still around in "I Love Lucy" reruns, Saturday Night Live skits, Chicago's Second City productions, and in the works of Monty Python, Mel Brooks, and Benny Hill. The striptease version is still around in wet T-shirt contests and the regular strip-joint activities found in the low-rent districts of every major city of the land.

EXTRAVAGANZA

The term "extravaganza" appears here and there in the 1850s and its full meaning becomes evident in 1866 with William Wheatley's production of *The Black Crook*.

> It was a stunning production, lasting five and a half hours, revealing to the startled eye such spellbinding effects as demon ritual, a hurricane in the mountains, a carnival, a "ballet of gems", a march of Amazons, and a splendiferous finale with angels and fairies.
>
> Suggestive dances and partially undraped females added spice to this sumptuously prepared dish. A new quality of sex insinuation was introduced in dance and song, starting the American musical theater on its long journey toward sex exploitation. The girls also did

the cancan, an importation from France that was witnessed in America for the first time (Ewen 1977, 84)

The Black Crook received strong negative reviews from many of America's leading journalists, and was the subject of numerous sermons from outraged preachers. All decent and respectable citizens were offended by this "degrading spectacle", similar, indeed, to "ancient heathen orgies" (Ewen 1977, 84-85). Ticket sales went up, and up, and up, and American show business has mined that field ever since.

Ewen cites the first staging of *The Wizard of Oz* (1902) as a continuation of the extravaganza traditions, with its tornado scene, poppies turning into real girls, and similar stage effects. Spectacular doings reached a zenith in 1905 with the opening of the appropriately named **Hippodrome Theater** at 6th and 43rd in New York. With seating for 5,000 and a stage that must have been the size of a football field, the Hippodrome was the scene of a naval battle (*Battle of Port Arthur*, 1908), an airplane fight (*Sporting Days*, 1908), a tornado and an earthquake (*Under Many Flags*, 1912), and assorted specialty numbers like a giant swimming pool 40 feet deep into which bespangled girls descended never to return, a rush hour Grand Central Station scene (complete with trains), and a colossal presentation of herds of stampeding deer and elephants.

Specific music for these shows was written by music director **Manuel Klein** (1876-1919) from 1905 to 1914 and then later by **Raymond Hubbell** (1879-1954) from 1915 to 1922 (Ewen 1977, 199). Hubbell is remembered fondly for a tune, "Poor Butterfly", which captured all of America in 1916 and became a jazz classic in the 1930s.

The Shuberts built the Winter Garden on Broadway at 51st Street in 1911, and it became the home of many a spectacular musical feast for eye and ear, with special acts by Al Jolson and other giants of the day, and with music written often by Jerome Kern and that early generation of big-time Broadway composers.

The extravaganza is still around, of course, in the form of stadium rock concerts, Las Vegas shows, and half time shows during major professional football games. There is always something compelling about sheer size and volume.

MINSTREL SHOW

Gone now, for good reason, the minstrel show had its roots in the English music hall. The Irish buffoon was a standard item in English entertainment, and in the transfer to America, the character was switched to a stereotyped blackface, with possibly the first professional minstrel show, the Virginia Minstrels, debuting on February 6, 1843, at the Bowery Amphitheater on the East Side of Manhattan. The minstrel show is a terrible chapter in America's history of race relations, but it made a substantial contribution to musical theater traditions and innovations from the 1840s into the early 1900s.

Edwin Pearce Christy (1815-1862), known professionally as E. P. Christy, formed his Christy minstrels in 1843. The troupe is generally credited with the standardization of the minstrel show's three-section structure.

The first section would consist of a Grand Entrance of the whole crowd in ill-fitting, swallow-tail tuxedos, all in blackface except the middle man, Mr. Interlocutor. This entire first part of the minstrel show was a series of vocals solos, virtuoso instrumental performances, several duets, trios, and such, designed to show the audience that the troupe had some genuine high-level talent in its ranks.

But, to keep the spirit light, these musical numbers were interspersed with frequent exchanges between Mr. Interlocutor and his "end men", Mr. Tambo on the right and Mr. Bones on the left. Mr. Tambo (because he played a tambourine) and Mr. Bones (because he played the "bones", a pair of animal rib bones or wooden stick that clicked together) peppered Mr. Interlocutor with verbal gags, double meaning jokes, and one-line zingers. Part One would often conclude with a stirring ensemble number combining voices and instruments.

The second section of the minstrel show, sometimes called the Olio, was a couple of short satire sketches or parody skits on popular social or political topics of the day.

Widely imitated were the jigs and jubas of the black field hands and the cakewalks of the house servants. The plantation stick dance became a standard comedy number for the minstrels in which a white made up as a very old blackamoor tottered on stage in rhythm to do the most amazing steps and leaps over his cane.

"Patting juba" became an accompaniment to a whole series of intricate dance steps. The Negro custom of creating rhythms for dancing without instruments was a big part of many minstrel show routines - striking the hands on the knees, then striking the right shoulder with one hand, the with the other, all the while singing and keeping time with their feet" (Southern 1971, 169).

Part Two would conclude with a major spoof, a black version of *Macbeth*, for example. The entire show would then be wrapped up with Part Three, a General Ruckus or Walk-Around, a spectacular parade of singing, hand clapping, and marching about the stage to celebrate a joyous evening of high-energy entertainment. It was considered a delightful entertainment package at the time, but it feels ugly and cruel in light of today's improved racial awareness and respect.

If there is a "Father of American Minstrelsy", it would be **Thomas Dartmouth Rice** (1808-1860) whose song-and-dance routine, "Jump Jim Crow", enjoyed huge popularity all through the age of minstrelsy. Rice took the shuffling step and verbal mutterings of an old stable hand he had observed one day, and embellished this character concept. Rice gave him an outlandish costume with a wide-brim hat, patched trousers, ill-fitting coat, and a shoe with a sole flapping and a toe sticking out through the top. The new theatrical character, "Jim Crow", became a standard part of the minstrel show for a long time, and the term came to designate racial discrimination in American society.

Jim Crow was a rustic type. His city counterpart, "Zip Coon", was the other side of the coin - a dandy dressed in the latest fashion, a "larned skolar", and an experienced man with the ladies. Two composers, George Washington Dixon and Bob Farrell, claim to have written the original Zip Coon lyrics. The tune goes way back in British history, no doubt. An instrumental version, called "Turkey in the Straw", is stilled played by country fiddlers today.

The black-owned and black-managed Hicks and Sawyer Minstrels, Richard and Pringles Famous Georgia Minstrels, and McGabe and Young Minstrels enjoyed "international vogue", as did the white-owned and managed F. L. Mahara and W. A. Mahara Minstrels along with Callendar's Minstrels. A few minstrel shows were mixed, Lew Dockstader's, for example, even though they did not integrate except for a final number (Southern 1971, 260-261). Some all-girl minstrel shows, either all black or all white, traveled the nation, also, mixing suggestions of a subdued burlesque mentality with the standard minstrel offerings.

The days of minstrelsy were numbered, however, and it was displaced in the big cities by 1915 or so, even though it carried on in rural small towns well into the 1930s. Many of the biggest stars of the 1920s and '30s got their start as minstrel performers. Al Jolson was certainly the most famous of the blackface entertainers. He was adored by millions of Americans both white and black. Missing from Jolson's blackface routines was the insensitivity associated with most minstrel characters. In an unusual way, Jolson's sentimental, likeable black characters actually opened up the industry for real black performers who followed him.

OPERETTA

Often used interchangeably with "comic opera", the term "operetta" came to mean something quite clear and specific in the minds of American theater-goers in the late 1800s — a fantasy world of military brass, noblemen, elegant ladies, beautiful princesses, and bumbling colonial bureaucrats enmeshed in preposterous intrigues in some far off exotic land (Ewen 1977, 202). The model, of course, was the European form so well developed by Gilbert and Sullivan, Johann Strauss II, and Jacques Offenbach.

Americans **John Philip Sousa** (1854-1932) and **Reginald de Koven** (1859-1920) added their operettas to the already abundant repertoire. **Victor Herbert** (1859-1924), **Gustave Kerker** (1857-1923), **Rudolf Friml** (1879-1972), **Sigmund Romberg** (1887-1951), and several other foreign-born but thoroughly Americanized composers flooded the industry with dozens of highly successful operettas, almost interchangeable in their convoluted story lines, romantic lovers, and charming melodies. Romberg was especially prolific, composing 175 numbers for 17 Shubert shows, 15 of which came within a 22-month period (Ewen 1977, 209).

Many of the best of the operettas were turned into movies in the 1930s, so they got a second period of exposure and financial success. **Nelson Eddy** (1901-1967) and **Jeanette MacDonald** (1903-1965) starred in several of them; Romberg's *Maytime*, Herbert's *Naughty Marietta*, and Friml's *Rose-Marie* survive strong and clear on DVD today.

The stage operetta would live on for a few years in the high schools and colleges of America, but by the late 1920s, a new and somehow more satisfying musical had thrust itself center stage. Spunky and irreverent, this new kid on the block would not be denied.

MUSICALS

The "new" musical pushed vaudeville, burlesque, extravaganza, minstrelsy, and operetta into the strange position of gradually looking and "feeling" a little odd, not quite up-to-date "American". It seemed to be more "with it", more consistent with what it was to be a 20th-century American.

Musicals came in several forms, and scholars use different terms for different concepts – "musical comedy", almost a generic term for the entire field, but meaning, usually, that the songs and humor carry the show; "musical play" or "book musical", meaning that the story holds the show together; "American operetta", meaning just that, an American version of the European-conceived form; and "revue", meaning the story is incidental to the individual vignettes presented.

For the sake of clarity, the two least confusing terms have been selected to explain the two basic approaches to a musical – revue and book musical.

Revue

First developed by George Lederer (c. 1862-1938) to give vaudeville a little respect and class, the revue drew on the other current "musical" forms, to be sure, but it paid more attention to artistic details and sophistication. However – and this is what augured well for the future – new compositions were written specifically and exclusively for each revue by established professional composers.

The greatest of all were the revues of **Florenz Ziegfeld** (1868-1932). From 1917 to 1931 (omitting 1926, 1928, and 1929), the *Ziegfeld Follies* stunned the theater world in their imagination and pageantry. Each year seemed to surpass the previous. New stars were created overnight. The best of everything was the rule, and salaries were outrageous.

Others followed suit. Earl Carroll's *Vanities*, George White's *Scandals*, the Greenwich Village *Follies*, Shuberts' *Passing Show,* and the *Music Box Revue* of Sam Harris and Irving Berlin, with music especially composed for each year's edition, lifted American musical comedy to new heights of creativity. All the great composers eventually got involved: Jerome Kern, Irving Berlin, George Gershwin, Sigmund Romberg, Walter Donaldson, Fred Fisher, Gus Edwards, and George M. Cohan among them.

And most of the famous movie stars of the 1930s and 1940s got started in the stage revues of the 1920s. Indeed, they just moved from stage to film when Hollywood began to sign up all the talent in the country. So, for a while, the film revue carried the stage revue tradition quite comfortably into the new age of talking pictures.

But there was something different forcing its way up through the soil, craving air and sunlight. It would forever change the character and identity of America's lyric theater. It would make even the magnificent *Ziegfeld Follies* feel a little shallow and inconsequential. As American as baseball and soon to be as well known and loved all over the world, the "Broadway Show" – called here for scholarly accuracy, the "book musical" – would finally integrate music, words, dance, and story into a substantive artistic whole.

Book Musical

This is what people think of immediately when they say they would like to go to New York to see a Broadway show. This is the art form that pulls together all the diverse energies and inclinations of the previous one hundred years of American show business. It borrows shamelessly from all those earlier (and concurrent) show types – satire, travesty, and slapstick from burlesque; song-and-dance and novelty scenes from vaudeville; clever plot twists among romantic lovers from operetta; lavish sets, scenery, and costumes from revue; one-line zingers and outrageous puns from the minstrel show; strong and original tunes from Tin Pan Alley.

But – and here's the profound difference – the book musical gives its audience something to take home. In addition to stunning sets and imaginative lighting, in addition to electrifying dance routines, and in addition to lovely, haunting, memorable melodies, the book musical gives the audience a modest lesson about the beauty, mystery, and meaning of life. Not just any old life, but American life, as felt subliminally by every member of the audience. No foreign princes and colonial potentates, but genuine American types – businessmen, cowboys, housewives, show girls, New York street folk, ghetto kids, secretaries, politicians, innocent girls from Ohio, factory workers – All-Americans, every one of them. As Leonard Bernstein once said, "The Broadway musical is America's middle-brow opera."

A modest lesson, however, not a serious drama. The history books are full of musical disasters that aspired to give the audience too much to take home. Broadway insiders cautioned each other, again and again, to remember that the tired businessman with his respectable wife (or fashionable mistress) out there in that gaping dark hole called "the house" had just come from cocktails and dinner, had plunged through maddening traffic, had put a couple of big deals on hold, and now wanted an evening of pleasant diversion and entertainment. He did not want to be told that his life lacked depth and significance. Nor did he want some high-brow musical bath. He wanted to tap his toes, smile at the foibles of the characters on stage, and walk out humming a memorable tune.

George M. Cohan

The first man to fully grasp the sum and substance of the book musical was George M. Cohan (1878-1942), sometimes called the Father of the Stage Musical. "Cocksure, egocentric, chauvinistic, energetic, gigantic in scheming and planning, he was a symbol of the new day in America" (Ewen 1977, 210). His first big hit, *Little Johnny Jones* (1904), set the model for things to come. A jockey, Johnny Jones, goes to London to ride in the Derby for King George. He is accused of throwing the race, and is detained in England as his friends sail back to America. Standing on the edge of the pier, he sings, "Give My Regards to Broadway". He is later exonerated, of course, and says, that he wouldn't throw a race. After all, he sings, I am "The Yankee Doodle Boy".

Then followed *George Washington, Jr.* (1906), with its infectious intonation "you're a grand old rag" hurriedly adjusted to "You're a Grand Old Flag" when patriotic groups protested. That was followed by *Forty-Five Minutes from Broadway* (1906), with "Mary's a Grand Old Name" and "So Long Mary". Not among the five hundred songs from forty shows was the most famous of all World War I songs, George M.'s blockbuster, "Over There".

He talked to audiences as if to his barroom friends, pointing a
forefinger at them as he spoke. He was the merchant of corn which
he delivered in song, monologue, and unrehearsed little addresses.

As a creator, as well as a performer, he brought to the musical comedy stage a dynamic American identity. His characters talked in American slang, and they behaved the way Americans do. They sang the kind of simple, sentimental songs to which Americans were partial. Their problems and complications, as well as their dreams and ideals, were those Americans recognized as their own (Ewen 1977, 212).

Al Jolson

"A seminal figure in the history of popular singing and pop song," Al Jolson (1886-1950) sang, danced, and pranced around the stage with such brash exuberance and confidence that he was billed the "world's greatest entertainer" (Shaw 1982, 199). Asa Yoelson from Srednicke, in Russian Lithuania, arrived in 1890 in Washington, D. C., when his father took a position as rabbi in a small synagogue. By age eight, he was out on the streets with his brother, Harry, singing and dancing for pennies. He never once looked back.

In bars, circuses, minstrel shows, burlesque, vaudeville, and finally in big time stage musicals, "Jolie" stole the show every time. He once worked two shows per day in three different vaudeville houses – rushing from one block to another in New York's theater district.

His great gifts were musical delivery and salesmanship. And when the words and melodies seemed insufficient, he broke into whistling and dancing. His best songs were declarations of strong emotion, "I'm Sitting on Top of the World", "Sonny Boy", "My Mammy", and such. His rich, resonant, baritone voice carried the lyrics into the hearts of theater audiences everywhere.

His signature tune, a black-face rendition of "My Mammy", brought listeners to tears. He would fall to one knee, his voice racked with pathos, and belt out the last line, "I'd walk a million miles for one of your smiles, my little Mammy." Vowels and consonants were freely distorted for the sake of dramatic punch. He sold the tune, every time.

After the historic movie, *The Jazz Singer* (1927), he appeared in ten more films and dozens of radio shows. But he was best with live audiences, and a few months before his death, he was still entertaining American military troupes in Korea. "You ain't heard nothin', yet," his favorite remark, really meant, "I ain't through with you, yet!" "He needed applause the way a diabetic needs insulin" (Sieben, quoted in Pleasants 1974, 49).

Jolson combined the best attributes of black and Jewish inflection and emotion with the rhythmic and melodic language of American pop music. The result was stunning. He was the dominant voice of his time.

Ethel Waters

In the 1920s, there were singers in abundance – Norah Bayes, Sophie Tucker, Emma Carus, Bessie Smith, Ma Rainey, Rudy Vallee, Kate Smith, Gene Austin, Jack Norworth, Fanny Brice, Eddie Cantor, George M. Cohan, and hundreds of others. The world of entertainment is often derivative, however, and truly original talent is rare.

Just such an original talent was Ethel Waters (1900-1977). Starting out as a vaudeville blues singer, Ethel Waters quickly moved into pop singing, stage drama, and the movies. Tall and slim, "Sweet Mama Stringbean" then toured with Fletcher Henderson's band and recorded on W. C. Handy's Black Swan label.

In addition to "St. Louis Blues", "Dinah", and "Heat Wave", her special treatment of "Stormy Weather" is best remembered.

> *I was telling the things I couldn't frame in words. I was singing the story of my misery and confusion, of the misunderstandings of my life I couldn't straighten out, the story of the wrongs and outrages done to my people I had loved and trusted. Only those who are being burned know what fire is like. I sang "Stormy Weather" from the depths of my private hell* (Ewen 1977, quoting from *His Eye Is On the Sparrow*).

Ethel Waters was a "transitional figure and a towering one, summing up all that had been accumulated stylistically" from earlier black music, and anticipating the inflections of the swing era (Pleasants 1977, 85).

She absorbed the traits of the best singers, both black and white, who surrounded her, reworked those traits into her own special voice, and then delivered a musical statement that was uniquely hers and ultimately right (Pleasants 1977, 85). She influenced all pop singers who followed.

African-American Musicals

What George M. Cohan did for white musicals, **Eubie Blake** (1887-1983), **Noble Sissle** (1889-1975), **James P. Johnson** (1894-1955), and **Fats Waller** (1904-1943) did for black musicals.

Shuffle Along (book by Flournoy Miller and Aubrey Lyles, lyrics by Sissle, musical score by Blake) opened in 1921, and soon a host of excellent all-black musicals appeared all over New York and environs. Blake did several more fine shows: *The Chocolate Dandies* (1924), *Blackbirds of 1930*, and *Swing It* (1937). Among Blake's best known tunes from those shows are "Loving You the Way I Do", "Memories of You", "Love Will Find a Way", and "I'm Just Wild About Harry".

Jazz keyboard giant James P. Johnson wrote *Plantation Days* (1923) in London, and *Running Wild* (1924) in America. His pupil, and equal, Thomas "Fats" Waller wrote *Keep Shuffling* (1928) and *Hot Chocolates* (1929).

Fats Waller also played organ in many of the burlesque and vaudeville theaters, as did the young William "Count" Basie, during the times when those theaters presented silent films, as they often did. It was a short period for the pipe organs, though, and they disappeared when the "talkies" took over the film industry. Those huge organs – the special creation of the companies Wurlitzer, Page, Morton, and Kimball – are now treasured musico-mechanical marvels being restored throughout America to delight the great-grandchildren of the audiences who first sat transfixed in the glorious sound.

***

Talking films (1927) and the Great Depression (1929) brought an end to most stage musicals, black or white. Only the white book musical survived the competition from the movies, and it soon found its own special voice. More about this topic soon.

Meanwhile, the black musical stage suffered from the "national market mentality" of the Hollywood film moguls who could not quite discern how to keep the black musical stage gifts alive and healthy without alienating certain audiences. When Lena Horne, Fats Waller, and Duke Ellington appeared in 1930s movies, the filming was done so their sequences could be easily deleted when the films were shown in the South.

Chapter 9
Popular Song Types and Forms

By the end of the 1800s, America's popular music industry had taken shape, with the following characteristics still firm today:

1) Music was being written specifically and unashamedly for commercial gain,
2) It was often aimed at a particular ethnic group or socioeconomic class,
3) It was produced, packaged, and marketed with all the inventive energies that go into such business activities,
4) The music arose from, and left its mark on, the immediate social milieu of the day, and
5) Because of the above four characteristics, popular music was scorned by classical musicians and their audiences.

SONG TYPES

The Sentimental Ballad

In pop music, the term "ballad" means, generally, a slow and emotional song. Two kinds are common. First is the love song, with its "boy-girl, moon-June, croon-tune, honeymoon" lyrics. These stock phrases and personal declarations of undying love never wear out. Love songs will be around forever. Why? Because the perpetuation of the species is important business, and it's a completely new and magical experience for each generation.

Second is the song of deep emotion. The musical gestures are much the same as for the love song, but the topic is religion, patriotism, friendship, or, perhaps, the beauty of nature. If the song is set for a choir or large group of singers it will have an added dash of majestic dignity.

The specific character of the sentimental ballad changes from generation to generation, of course, and from style to style. A love song in the 1920s was substantially different from a love song in jazz or musical comedy.

The Narrative Song

Two kinds. The historical narrative holds everyone's interest because a good story is always fun to hear, and the story gains power and depth from its musical setting. The story may be long or short, happy or sad, fully detailed or sparse, with many characters or only a few. Folk singers call this kind of narrative song a "ballad", incidentally, while pop musicians mean a slow sentimental tune when they say "ballad."

The second kind of narrative song is the topical narrative. Quick and clean, like a television commercial perhaps, or a war tune or political tune, it describes a condition or situation in bold, memorable, strokes – the purpose being to make a strong imprint.

The Humorous Song

Again, two kinds. First, some tunes are just plain nonsense tunes, with no specific purpose other than to deliver whimsical and clever lyrics that turn out to surprise and delight the audience.

Second, the dialect song, which has almost disappeared from show business. Once a major source of comedy material, vaudeville routines were loaded with songs that drew their humor from the vocabulary, grammar, and syntax of anyone with other than an Anglo-Saxon speech manner. Imitation Italian, Scandinavian, Jewish, German, Irish, and African-American accents were exaggerated for humorous effect. The dialect song is most rare today, with good reason.

STRUCTURAL DESIGN (FORM) IN POP SONGS

Strophic Design

There are two kinds of strophic design – the single-unit and the verse-refrain construction.

The single-unit package has the same music, over and over again, stanza after stanza, until the complete story has been told, as is the case with "Tom Dooley", "Amazing Grace", and "Blowin' in the Wind". Economy of musical materials is the goal here, and the single-unit strophic design is usually one-part or, occasionally, two-part form, which will be explained shortly.

The verse-refrain strophic design will likewise appear in Spartan simplicity and economy, but in a double package, with the refrain serving as a recurring interlude which throws the verses into bold relief to carry the message. Stephen Foster's "Oh! Susanna" and hundreds of similar camp songs owe their longevity to the psychic pleasures of the crowd joining in on the refrain each time, while the song leader runs through the many verses.

Binary Form

Generally speaking, binary forms will be songs that have only two main parts, regardless of how many times each section is repeated. Two kinds of binary form are found in music. Scholars show the design scheme of these forms, and other musical forms, with a system of letters and numbers, with each letter designating a distinct melody and numbers designating slight variations on a distinct melody.

A-B Design

"America" is a good example of the A-B kind of two-part form: two little sections, one complementing the other:

A   My country, 'tis of thee, sweet land of liberty, of thee I sing.

B   Land where my fathers died, land of the pilgrims' pride.
      From every mountain side, let freedom ring.

A-A' or AB-AC Design

A slightly different kind of binary form is often found. It might be diagrammed as A-A' (A and A-prime) or AB-AC: two sections of music, the second being nearly identical to the first except for a change at the end to tie things up in a satisfying manner. Good examples are Henry Mancini's "Moon River" (as diagramed below), which consists of four basic 8-measure units. In this particular song, the final 8-measure unit has been extended an additional two measures to provide a sense of finality to the whole experience.

AB-AC Design: Moon River

A   Moon River, wider than a mile,
     I'm crossing you in style, some day.
B   Old dream maker, you heart breaker,
     Wherever you're going, I'm going your way.
A   Two drifters, off to see the world.
     There's such a lot of world to see.
C   We're after the same rainbow's end,
     Waitin' 'round the bend,
     My huckleberry friend,
     Moon River and me.

Other excellent examples of A-A' or AB-AC design are Hoagy Carmichael's "Stardust", Jerry Herman's "Hello, Dolly!", Three Dog Night's "Joy to the World", and the jazz standard "Fly Me to the Moon".

Ternary Form

One of the most common forms of all of music, ternary design satisfies a deep human need for the return of familiar melodic material. Of the two kinds of ternary form, the **A-B-A** design is very common in classical music and very rare in popular music, Consuelo Velazquez's 1944 hit, "Besame Mucho," being one of the few pop tunes in A-B-A form. Here's another tune that may be more familiar:

A-B-A Design: "Twinkle, Twinkle, Little Star"

A   Twinkle, twinkle, little star, how I wonder what you are,
B   Up above the world so high, like a diamond in the sky.
A   Twinkle, twinkle, little star, how I wonder what you are.

Often, a psychological need is felt to repeat the first little section of music, to fix it firmly in mind, before the contrasting center section is offered. Thousands of pop tunes come in this **A-A-B-A** design. From the late 1800s to the 1960s it was almost universal. Each unit has 8 measures, 32 measures in all, with the center section changing key and melodic contours as a kind of "bridge" between or "release" from or a "channel" through the opening and closing sections which are nearly identical except for a few notes at the end.

A-A-B-A Design: "Deck the Halls"

A   Deck the halls with boughs of holly,
      Fa-la-la-la-la, la-la-la-la.

A   'Tis the season to be jolly,
      Fa-la-la-la-la, la-la-la-la.

B   Don we now our gay apparel,
      Fa-la-la, la-la-la, la-la-la.

A   Troll the ancient yuletide carol,
      Fa-la-la-la-la, la-la-la-la.

Ternary form was used often, by everybody from Irving Berlin to the Beatles, although the Beatles' "Yesterday" has 7-measure units (instead of 8-measure units) for the first two "A" sections. Ternary form got stretched, occasionally, by Cole Porter and others, and recent works deviate a bit from the pure A-A-B-A scheme, but ternary form still reigns supreme in pop music.

Incidentally, some traditional popular tunes have introductions or lead-ins before the familiar part of the song begins. Many of these lead-in "verses" were important when sung in their original theatrical presentations, as a way to explain a plot point or give details about the emotional state of a character. Since these verses don't always make sense when taken out of context, and because they were very often more spoken on a pitch (usually without a strict tempo) than sung, many traditional pop singers will simply drop the verse to get to the more melodic refrain. And in the days of dancing to instrumental popular tunes, bandleaders dropped the verses to get to the well-known parts of the songs, so the dancers would know what tune they were dancing to.

A fairly recognizable example of a song that usually does not have its verses sung is "Over the Rainbow":

Verse 1 (A)	When all the world is a hopeless jumble And the raindrops tumble all around, Heaven opens a magic door.
Verse 2 (A)	When all the clouds darken up the skyway, There's a rainbow highway to be found, Leading from your window pane To a place beyond the sun, Just a step beyond the rain ...
Refrain (B)	Somewhere over the rainbow way up high, There's a land that I heard of once in a lullaby.
Refrain (B)	Somewhere over the rainbow skies are blue, And the dreams that you dare to dream really do come true.
Bridge (C)	Someday I'll wish upon a star and wake up where the clouds are far behind me. Where troubles melt like lemon drops a way above the chimney tops that's where you'll find me.
Refrain (B)	Somewhere over the rainbow bluebirds fly. Birds fly over the rainbow why, oh why, can't I?
Coda (C')	If happy little bluebirds fly beyond the rainbow Why, oh why, can't I?

An interest in verses has returned, though. Many cocktail pianists and cabaret singers, especially in the better clubs around the country, take pride in knowing and singing the introductions to all the great standard tunes from 1920 through 1950.

Blues Form

The blues is a term used to denote an early historical period in the field of jazz (performed by the likes of Bessie Smith and others); it is also a term used to denote a special kind of authentic and soulful singing-performing. For over one hundred years, the 12-bar blues has carried texts of astonishing depth and diversity. A history of the blues will follow later; for now, a quick sketch of the form will suffice.

As a musical form (that is, a set of chords), the blues is a rigorous structure for the I chord (also known as the tonic), the IV chord (also known as the subdominant), and the V^7 chord (also known as the dominant) in the following scheme (in the key of C):

Measures of music	Chord played
1 through 4	C
5 and 6	F
7 and 8	C
9 and 10	G^7
11 and 12	C

Scholars and theorists use Roman numerals when analyzing classical music. Jazz and pop musicians nearly always use the names of the specific chords. The Roman numerals correspond to the degree of the scale in each key. So, in the above example, if the C is the I chord, going up four tones in the scale brings you to F, so it is, then, the IV chord.

Lots of harmonic deviations can occur within the basic structure. Here is one popular iteration found in many jazz arrangements of blues tunes:

Measure(s) of music	Chord played
1	C
2	F
3	C
4	C^7
5	F
6	F minor
7	C
8	A^7
9	D minor
10	G^7
11 and 12	C

The blues patter, so universally appealing, shows no sign at all of wearing out. Drawn, essentially, from three basic chords (called the primary triads), the blues pattern permits all melodic gestures because the three chords contain every note in the standard diatonic scale.

Hundreds of early rock and roll standards are in blues form. After its eight-measure introduction, "Rock Around the Clock" is pure blues form, as are "Kansas City", "Johnny B. Goode", "See You Later, Alligator", and countless others.

Ragtime Form

Taken from European march construction, ragtime swept the nation in the early 1900s. Seldom with lyrics, ragtime pieces grew out of 16-measure units in a fairly consistent prescription.

Hundreds of titles appeared – "My Ragtime Baby", "Mr. Johnson, Turn Me Loose", "Alexander's Ragtime Band", "Hello, My Baby", and others – which were not true rags, just popular songs generously sprinkled with syncopated rhythms. Genuine rags have a stately charm when played, as they should be played, at a moderate tempo.

Many exceptions occur, however. In Scott Joplin's famous "Maple Leaf Rag", for example, the A-section returns for a single hearing again, after the repeated B-section.

Ragtime form: "Maple Leaf Rag"

* Introduction (optional 4 or 8 measures)
A First Section (repeated)
B Second Section (repeated)
A First Section
C Third Section (repeated)
D Fourth Section (repeated)

Motown Form

The above music forms carried popular music for years, and no one felt a need for change. Not until Motown composer-arrangers Lamont Dozier, Brian Holland, and Eddie Holland began to offer a special binary form, **A-A-B**, did the industry move away from traditional forms. The Motown form steps out from the hundred-year 12-bar blues tradition, which may account for the fresh breeze it brought into rock in the early 1960s. "Stop! In the Name of Love" by the Supremes is a prime example, with its intro "hook" – a catchy phrase or melody that would instantly grab the listener's attention.

A-A-B form: "Stop! In the Name of Love"

Intro	Stop, in the name of love, before you break my heart.
A	Baby, baby, I'm aware of where you go
	Each time you leave my door,
	I watch you walk down the street
	Knowing your other love you'll meet
A	This time before you run to her,
	Leaving me alone and hurt,
	Think it over.
	Think it over.
B	Stop, in the name of love, before you break my heart.
	Stop, in the name of love, before you break my heart.
	Think it over.
	Think it over.

Modified Forms and other Developments

Stephen Sondheim, Burt Bacharach, the Beatles, and others have consciously or unconsciously come up with some slightly different forms, but the very nature of pop music precludes any kind of extended roaming around. Pop music, like political cartoons, must pack a lot of meaning into a few swift strokes.

The Beatles' "Michelle", for example, is a binary form "A" (6 measures), "B" (10 measures) with the "A" section used as an introduction and conclusion. All of this is followed by a 5 measure tag. It's different from, but sufficiently similar to, mainstream pop traditions. The diagram of "Michelle", then, turns out to be AAB-ABB-AC.

Burt Bacharach's "Raindrops Keep Fallin' on My Head" is A-A-B-A, but the numbers of measures in each section are 9-9-10-12. Carole King's "You've Got A Friend" grows out of 16-measure units: AB-AB-CB but the "C" is 10 measures and the final "B" 15 measures.

Two other devices have expanded the psycho-emotional territory a bit: modulation and the fade-out.

First, the modulation up a semitone. Near the end of the 1950s, Nelson Riddle's arrangements for Frank Sinatra would often go up from, say, the key of G to the key of A-flat for the last 8 or 16 measures of a tune. This charming technique kicks new energy into the strict A-A-B-A formal design without running the risk of new melodic material which would overload the pop tune aesthetic. It works well, and can be easily detected in Sinatra's version of "New York, New York".

The modulation up a semitone can be over-used, though and it often is in the field of gospel music when the tune is propelled up a semitone, then another, and another. It's too much of a good thing, and knowledgeable gospel musicians quite understandably grow weary of such spectacular productions. They know that a strong tune need not be driven through the ceiling every time it is performed.

Second, the fade-out. Maybe it was only coincidental, but the fade-out began to appear in popular music in the late 1950s, along with the modulation up a semitone. It has the opposite function. By fading out on a memorable passage, the tune lingers in the mind, leaving a gentle imprint.

As rock and roll tunes replaced the old standards of Irving Berlin, George Gershwin, and Jerome Kern as the main body of America's pop industry, subtle problems emerged as the younger musicians struggled with how to bring their aesthetic experience to a close without being too abrupt and without using the ritards and tags common to the older style. Their solution was ingenious – don't end at all, just fade out. The true ending of the piece then occurs at different times in the minds of different listeners.

But the fade-out can be violated too, just like the semitone upward move. It began modestly at first, but nowadays disc jockeys seldom permit a tune to play out; they come crashing into the fading acoustical time and space with the next tune, full volume. This jolt to the sensibilities precludes any complete musical and aesthetic symmetry and balance, of course, but the disc jockeys fear more than anything else that the listener will move to another station, and they will gladly sacrifice artistic considerations for financial ones. The fade-out as a solution to an aesthetic need has been compromised then, at least during air play. It may still serve to close the musical experience with some style and grace, however, when the listener is in control at home.

CONCLUSION

The American popular tune had assumed nearly all its central identity by the middle of the 1800s. Except for a few technological and marketing techniques, and an occasional timid effort to expand its psycho-emotional territory, pop music is today very much what it was when it first took shape. It has to be. It cannot be anything other and still be "popular".

Absolutely critical to being "popular", is, of course, a song's ability to be grasped and retained immediately, or at most, after only one or two hearings. The 32-measure binary and ternary forms and the 12-bar blues form reigned supreme for most of the history of popular music because they satisfied all criteria.

A song's ability to touch individual hearts and minds is one of the reasons the music is written the way that it is. However, all artistic aspirations aside, popular music is also meant to be a commercial endeavor. It is that aspect of the music business that will be discussed in Chapter 24.

Chapter 10
The Stage Musical

The 1920s stage musicals were a perfect reflection of the Jazz Age. The generic revues satisfied a demand for novelty and humor. The book musicals, a bit more substantial, told an interesting, if not very compelling, story. But almost everyone was happy with the way America's lyric theater was going. Well, almost everyone.

Among the unhappy were **Jerome Kern** (1885-1945) and **Oscar Hammerstein II** (1895-1960), veterans of many successful shows in and around Broadway. Kern, especially, yearned to tackle something more challenging, a real story about real people in real situations, not a story that was "a synthetic product manufactured for specific stars and their specialties, filled with routines which would appeal to the audience but which were not particularly germane to the plot" (Ewen 1977, 353). Hammerstein, too, believed that the public could handle something heavier than what was in vogue, but he cautioned that whatever they might do, it must be entertainment, not education or philosophy.

Kern and Hammerstein had collaborated earlier on *Sunny,* largely written as a vehicle for the stunning Marilyn Miller to follow her successful *Sally.* They worked well together, and shared similar values and attitudes. When Kern mentioned Edna Ferber's novel *Show Boat* as a potential musical, Hammerstein was ecstatic. It was the kind of project he had been seeking for quite some time, and they set out in earnest. The result was a masterpiece – a critical moment in the history of America's lyric theater.

SHOW BOAT

Edna Ferber was reluctant to have her successful novel converted into a musical; she could not envision her story as a "girlie show crammed with conventional musical-comedy attractions" (Ewen 1959, 190). When Kern explained that he had something very different in mind, she consented.

The show opens with Cap'n Andy Hawks' showboat, the *Cotton Blossom*, docked at stage center. Gaylord Ravenal, a handsome ne'er-do-well riverboat gambler, approaches the boat looking for temporary work. He encounters Cap'n Andy's lovely daughter, Magnolia, flirts with her, and sings that even though they have not been properly introduced, they could "Make Believe".

He leaves, and Magnolia asks Joe, one of the black boat workers, if he knows anything about that handsome stranger. Joe says that the riverboat guys are all pretty much the same. Magnolia wonders if her friend Julie might know. Joe then reflects that these wonderful human concerns are interesting, but they pale in comparison to the all-powerful, silent, indifferent, and eternal force of "Ol' Man River". The tune is an absolute masterpiece which brought Edna Ferber to tears when she first heard it.

Magnolia asks Julie about the stranger. Julie is the leading actress on the boat, and she knows a lot more about men than the tender teenager, Magnolia. Julie cautions Magnolia to be careful, and says that Gaylord Ravenal is probably just another no account riverboat drifter. Magnolia says that if he were, she'd just decide not to love him. Julie then offers a bit of advice about men; she says it's not that easy, and sings the somewhat cautionary "Can't Help Lovin' Dat Man".

Next comes a scene that reveals that over the past several months the beautiful olive-skinned Julie has been the object of continued sexual harassment by one of the low-brow boat workers. Her leading man and real-life husband, Steve Baker, finally punches the boat worker, who sulks off mumbling words of revenge.

And revenge it is. Soon, the boat is buzzing that a local sheriff is preparing legal orders to close the showboat. Steve and Julie know, but no one else does, what this is probably all about. So, in full view of everyone in the troupe, Steve takes a pen knife, pricks Julie's finger, and sucks out a little of her blood.

The sheriff arrives with court papers showing that Julie is of mixed ancestry – one of her parents was black. He's going to close the show because miscegenation is illegal. Steve says there is no miscegenation because he, too, has Negro blood in him. Everyone supports his claim, and the sheriff stomps off in disgust. Julie and Steve decide to leave the boat, however, to avoid what are sure to be continued troubles up and down the river.

Over his wife's strenuous objections, Cap'n Andy assigns Magnolia to be the new leading lady. They ponder briefly who might be a good new leading man, when Gaylord reappears. Of course, he gets the job, is very good at it, and within months, he and Magnolia are the most popular make-believe and real lovers up and down the river.

During this early stage of their association, they sing a beautiful operatic duet, "You Are Love". Hammerstein made an art form out of oblique declarations of love. His lovers often reveal their love in an indirect manner – "People Will Say We're In Love" from *Oklahoma*, "If I Loved You" from *Carousel* and "Some Enchanted Evening" from *South Pacific*, for example.

Magnolia and Gaylord marry, and leave the boat to pursue a new life in Chicago. Gaylord's professional gambling career sustains them admirably. They live a life of luxury and pleasure, and are indeed very happy and comfortable. There are three versions of the story from this point on:

1) In the original stage production and in the first movie treatment, a 1929 "part-talkie," they have a daughter named Kim. Then Gaylord's luck turns bad, and he skips out to preserve his masculine ego and to preclude dragging them down into poverty and shame. Magnolia goes back to the boat to be with her parents. After twenty years or so, Gaylord comes back, and all is forgiven.

2) In the 1936 film, same as above, but Magnolia goes it alone, becoming a world famous singer-actress. Daughter Kim is on the edge of a similar career, when they find Gaylord – a custodian in the very theater where Kim is scheduled to make her debut. Before she sings her opening tune, Kim acknowledges her father in the wings. Magnolia rushes into his arms, and all is forgiven.

3) In the 1951 film, Gaylord skips out, but he doesn't know that Magnolia is pregnant. Magnolia has the child, returns to the showboat. Cap'n Andy welcomes her back, and asks her to join the entertainment ensemble. When Kim is just out of diapers, the Cap'n creates an act. The Hawks family trio – grandfather, daughter, and granddaughter – become a riverboat favorite up and down the Mississippi. In a chance

meeting on a gambling boat, Gaylord bumps into Julie. She tells him of the growing fame of the Hawks family trio. Stunned at learning he has a daughter, Gaylord goes back to make amends. All is forgiven, and the show ends.

Analysis

Scholars and critics have never been completely happy with any of the above plot resolutions. Still, everyone agrees it is one of the greatest shows in history. Historians divide the Broadway musical into two big periods: before *Show Boat* and after. It broke new ground in several ways.

First, it deals with genuine people in realistic emotional entanglements. These are not cardboard personalities. The audience gets to actually care for Julie, Magnolia, and Gaylord.

Second, the songs grow out of the dramatic circumstances. There is a reason for a tune to occur, and it's not just to give a star something to sing.

Third, the music is masterful, first-quality all the way. Kern hit his stride, here, and these songs are among the finest works in the history of musical theater.

It was also a feast for eyes and ears, as stupendous as anything producer Flo Ziegfeld had ever presented, but with one major difference – this show had deep and permanent musical and dramatic substance.

THE CLASSIC MUSICAL COMEDY

The model for musical comedy, which crystallized in *Show Boat*, served the industry well for a long time. The elements that were always present are discussed below.

Story

The stories from the 1930s through the 1960s were nearly always about people caught up in love situations that should not work because of class or culture differences. They are eternal variations on the Romeo-Juliet and Cinderella themes that go way back in Judaic-Christian history, perhaps all histories – he's rich, she's poor; he's old, she's young; he's educated, she's not; he's Jewish, she's Protestant or Catholic; she's respectable, he's from the street; or the reverse of all of these situations (she's rich, he's poor, etc.).

The basic conflict, incidentally, is revealed quickly so that everyone knows early in the show who's who and what the problem is. The remainder of the show is simply a matter of watching it all work out, in spite of what seemed to be insurmountable obstacles.

Characterization

The leading characters may be right out of central casting, but the audience will be drawn into a personal relationship with them before the evening is out. These generic types will be particularized early in the show. Audiences really grow fond of the music man, even though he's typical of every traveling salesman in the country. And how many librarians like Marian are there in the Mid-West? Yet, this specific librarian works her way into the collective audience heart in the space of a few scenes.

Libretto

The libretto (little book) compresses the story to set up situations that would be incomplete without a song or a dance sequence. The author of the original story may or may not be involved in doing the libretto, and the librettist may or may not be involved in doing the specific lyrics to the individual songs.

A good libretto will also bring the drama around for a reprise of one of the memorable tunes heard early in the show. And a good libretto will have a crisis at the end of the first act to bring the audience back for the second act. Also, there will be a blockbuster dramatic-musical moment about two-thirds or three-quarters of the way through the show – to lift the audience members who by this time are running low on blood sugar, adrenaline, and attention energies. Finally, it is surprising how many musical comedies take place over a period of a few days or a few weeks. The time line is often nearly continuous.

Subplot

To delay the inevitable, and fairly obvious, conclusion to the primary plot, many shows have a pair of secondary lovers. They are usually friends or relatives of the leading characters, and often provide a comic contrast to the serious love affair in the main plot.

Lyrics

Great song texts (lyrics) have a universal appeal because they can be extracted from the show and still survive. "Tonight" comes out of the dramatic flow of *West Side Story*, but soars on its own even to those who have never heard or seen the show. The same can be said for "You'll Never Walk Alone", sung at many high school graduations with no hint that it came from Rodgers and Hammerstein's *Carousel.*

Song Styles

Every good show has several love songs in solo and duet, also one or more novelty tunes, and surely a couple of ensemble numbers that are often sung and danced at the same time. Some shows will have a long and reflective self-examination, a "soliloquy," by one of the leading characters.

Dialogue

No matter how serious the central story of the show, there will be many moments of high humor. The art form is commonly called "musical comedy" for good reason. Musicals can and do treat heavy topics, too, but they must do so with a few swift strokes, like a political cartoon, and then move on to more pleasurable, less somber events.

PORGY AND BESS

In some ways a splendid example of and in other ways a major exception to the above model is *Porgy and Bess* by brothers **George** (1898-1937) and **Ira Gershwin** (1896-1983). Often called an opera, the show towers high above almost all other shows in the musical genre, but to quibble over categorizing it as an opera or a musical is pointless. It's an overpowering musical and theatrical experience. Gershwin said specifically that he was writing a folk opera.

In 1935, the heart of the Depression, this show spoke to both blacks and whites about the magnitude and beauty of a great love in the face of unspeakable odds. (The following synopsis is drawn largely from David Ewen, 1959, 136-137.)

As the curtain rises, a crap game is taking place in one corner of the court area in front of the African-American tenement, Catfish Row, while in another corner a few people are dancing. Clara is sitting in a third corner, lulling her baby to sleep with one of the most beautiful and popular songs ever composed, "Summertime". When the child just will not go to sleep, Clara's husband, Jake, takes the child and sings a different lullaby, "A Woman Is a Sometime Thing". The baby goes to sleep, and Jake says to his wife, "There, you see, that's how it's done."

As the heat of the crap game rises, a quarrel erupts between Robbins and Crown, and Robbins gets killed. Crown goes into hiding, leaving behind his girlfriend, Bess, who decided to move in with Porgy. Otherwise strong and virile, Porgy is paralyzed below the knees, and has to get around on a small cart drawn by a goat. Bess is a woman of the streets, and Porgy has been attracted to her for quite some time.

The scene shifts to Robbins' room where the mourners are lamenting his death. Neighbors come by to put coins in the saucer on his chest for burial money. The widow, Serena, distraught with grief, gives voice to her tragedy in "My Man's Gone Now", and the religious atmosphere is heightened with Bess' spiritual, "Oh the Train Is at the Station".

In the second act, we find Bess happy in her new life; she has come to love Porgy. Porgy speaks of his new found joy in an exultant refrain, "I Got Plenty of Nuttin'", and the lovers exchange tender sentiments in the duet, "Bess, You Is My Woman Now". At his insistence, Bess leaves Porgy behind as she joins the crowd to go to Kittiwah Island for the lodge picnic.

The picnic gets riotous with singing and dancing. Sportin' Life entertains his friends with a recital of his cynical philosophy, "It Ain't Necessarily So". When the picnic is over and the crowd proceeds back to the boat, Crown – who has been hiding out on the island – stops Bess, breaks down her resistance, and drags her off into the woods.

A few days later, back in Catfish Row, the fishermen are off to sea. While they are gone, Bess returns, delirious and feverish, to be gently nursed by a forgiving and solicitous Porgy. In "I Loves You, Porgy", they repeat their avowal of love.

As a hurricane begins, and the womenfolk huddle in Serena's room to pray for the safe return of their husbands, Crown return and injects a sacrilegious note into the atmosphere by singing "A Red-Headed Woman Makes a Choo-choo Jump Its Track". Just then, from her seat in the window, Clara sees Jake's boat overturn. Taunting Porgy for being a cripple and unable to give help to anyone, Crown runs out into the storm to try to save Jake. But all the fishermen are lost, and when Crown returns for Bess, Porgy kills him.

Porgy is taken off to jail for questioning. Sportin' Life takes Bess to New York where he will pimp for her. She was reluctant, at first, but he broke down her resistance with some "happy dust" (cocaine), singing "There's a Boat That's Leavin' Soon for New York".

Porgy returns from jail since there is no hard evidence to hold him. He's made quite a bit of money shooting craps, and he has a new dress that he bought for Bess. When he learns about Bess and Sportin' Life, he pauses for a moment, and then in a final scene of overwhelming power, beauty, and sadness, he sets out for New York on his goat cart to find his woman, Bess.

Analysis

Strange as it may seem, one of the world's greatest art works, *Porgy and Bess*, got off to a bad start. It confused all the music and drama critics, and ran for only 124 performances. Four revivals starting in 1942 have done extremely well, however, as did a 1959 movie with Sidney Poitier, Dorothy Dandridge, and Sammy Davis, Jr. Manuscripts have been discovered which show that Gershwin's original intent was clearly operatic – continuous music, intense psychological statements made by the orchestra, no spoken dialogue, and such. Over the years, of course, as always, every director has taken great liberty to cut, paste, insert, delete, and otherwise doctor the show to bring it in line with the available time, talent, and budget.

After it caught hold, the show captured the hearts and minds of audiences in every major city in twenty-eight foreign nations, and served as an official instrument of diplomacy for the State Department. In 1976 the Houston Grand Opera staged the work with great success, and in 1983 Radio City Music Hall sold out its 6,000 seats each night for an extended run. On its 50th anniversary, the show entered the repertoire of the Metropolitan Opera. During rehearsals at the

Met, several black opera singers broke down and cried as they struggled with the ambivalence of returning, even professionally, to certain childhood memories.

Porgy and Bess stands as a towering monument in the history of America's musical theater. The deepest human psycho-emotional concerns and convictions suddenly flame up from a particular tale out of a specific sociocultural setting – and they are given singular artistic substance and beauty in some of the very best "popular" music of all time.

THE AGE OF GREAT STANDARDS

Before *Porgy and Bess,* several shows had aspired to step from the flatland of the revue mentality to a little higher intellectual ground, but most of them failed. A good many great tunes came from these shows, however. The tunes are called "standards" by working musicians in the field of American popular music.

"I've Got a Crush on You" came from the Gershwin brothers' *Strike Up the Band* (1930), even though George S. Kaufman's grim antiwar story was so heavy that the show closed on the road.

The haunting "Night and Day" survives from Cole Porter's *Gay Divorce* (1932). "I Get a Kick Out of You", "Blow, Gabriel, Blow", and the title song from *Anything Goes* (1934), also by Cole Porter, are still heard often in nightclubs, as well as Jerome Kern's "Yesterdays" and "Smoke Gets in Your Eyes" from *Roberta* (1934).

"Where or When", "My Funny Valentine", and "The Lady Is a Tramp" came from a Rodgers and Hart show, *Babes in Arms* (1937). *As Thousands Cheer* (1933) by Irving Berlin gave us the perennial standard, "Easter Parade".

Cole Porter provided "Begin the Beguine" and "Just One of Those Things" for *Jubilee* (1935) which ran only 169 performances. Producer Billy Rose moved into the Hippodrome Theater to get enough room for the Rodgers and Hart *Jumbo* (1935), with such fine tunes as "The Most Beautiful Girl in the World", "My Romance", and "Little Girl Blue".

An entire textbook could be written about the nature of the charming and infectious standards which survive from shows that ran only a few months. In most cases, the lyrics deal with universal dilemmas or joys, and the melodies have memorable linear threads which somehow please listeners year after year.

OTHER DEVELOPMENTS

Musical Satire

Aside from the pronounced wealth of great talent and great tunes to be found in 1930s stage musicals, two other developments came to bear. First, there was the rise of satire. The revue-as-satire had its birth in burlesque, of course, and its adolescence in the 1920s *Garrick Gaieties*, but now it came into full maturity. There were no memorable tunes in *Of Thee I Sing*, but it deftly skewered political conventions, beauty pageants, marriage, the Vice Presidency, the Supreme Court, foreign affairs, and motherhood – and it launched a string of impudent satires on everything dear to normal Americans.

Directed by George S. Kaufman from his own book, with words and music by the George and Ira Gershwin, *Of Thee I Sing* received the Pulitzer Prize for drama, a first for a musical. There were extended choral passages, elaborate recitatives, and integrated instrumental sequences which foreshadowed George Gershwin's remarkable musical score for *Porgy*.

Band Wagon (1931) poked a hole in high society's pompous lifestyle, especially the aristocracy in the South. *As Thousands Cheer* (1933) used a newspaper format to blast the foibles of current events. *Pins and Needles* (1937) took a liberal pro-union shot at war-mongers, bigots, reactionaries, Nazis, Fascists, Communists, and the Daughters of the American Revolution, and then, for good measure, delivered a few jabs at the labor movement itself.

Harold Rome's *Pins and Needles* was fun, and ran for 1,108 performances, but Marc Blitzstein's *The Cradle Will Rock* (1938) was too serious, and ran for only 108 performances. Its strong anti-business posture turned away too many music lovers, as did Harold Arlen's *Hooray for What!* (1937) which dealt with poison gas, munitions, diplomatic duplicity, espionage, and warfare.

There is a limit, obviously, to how current and how intense the topics and treatment can be in a "musical comedy".

Ballet

Second, dancing took a turn away from its vaudeville and minstrel roots toward more stylized ballet mannerisms. George Balanchine, the preeminent classical ballet choreographer, broke new ground with *On Your Toes* (1936), with music and lyrics by Rodgers and Hart. The big moment, "Slaughter on Tenth Avenue," became an instant dance classic. Balanchine went on to choreograph *Babes in Arms* (1937), *I Married an Angel* (1938), *The Boys from Syracuse* (1938), *Louisiana Purchase* (1940), and several more.

Dance styles in the stage musical did not change overnight, of course. There was still a great tradition of wondrous bumps and grinds, high kicks, ballroom glides, and crackling tap routines in great abundance. But Balanchine's mark had been made, and later generations of choreographers would have to deal with a new set of aesthetic standards for the body language of the art form called musical comedy.

BROADWAY FROM THE 1960s THROUGH THE PRESENT

A Business Mentality

Beginning with *Camelot* (1960), which was owned from its very inception by CBS Records, most Broadway musicals are now owned by huge media conglomerates. The central vision, purpose, and dream is, therefore, the financial bottom line – not a compelling story told with great music, but rather a vision of marketing strategies guaranteed to return a profit.

Thus comes a parade of shows being marketed beyond belief with TV ads, road tours, T-shirts, posters, CDs, coffee mugs, post cards, umbrellas, and silk jackets – all of which promote *Cats*, *Spamalot*, *Les Misérables*, *Chicago*, *The Phantom of the Opera*, *The Producers*, or *The Lion King*. These shows still have interesting, often wonderful music, powerful dramatic moments, dance routines and the other traditional ingredients of American theater, but the show itself is just one part of a complex marketing strategy that includes souvenir DVD packages, downloadable games, stuffed *Lion King* animals, and anything else that can raise profit margins for investors.

An Operatic Mentality

Opposite forces are also at work in the art form. Stephen Sondheim has created a body of stunning musicals, which pointedly reject the bottom line mentality of corporate thinking. *Pacific Overtures*, *Sweeney Todd*, and *Sunday in the Park with George* are truly operatic in every way, with complex songs with intelligent lyrics.

Topics and Themes in Modern Broadway Musicals

When Oscar Hammerstein died in 1960, it marked the end of an era. Through the 1960s and early 1970s, there were serious efforts to expand the musical in all directions. Everything and anything unusual was tried – nudity in *Hair* and *Oh! Calcutta!*; rock in *Two Gentlemen of Verona* and *Tommy*; religion AND rock in *Jesus Christ Superstar* and *Godspell*; and comic strip characters in *You're a Good Man, Charlie Brown* and *It's a Bird, It's a Plane, It's Superman*.

These shows opened up new and interesting possibilities for the musical, and they revealed the spirit of the turbulent 1960s, with inner-city riots, campus unrest, ghettos on fire, police dogs and water hoses, rampant drug use, a sexual revolution, and civil disobedience everywhere. But Broadway musicals are so frightfully expensive that the investors also played it safe and offered (right in the middle of the turbulent 1960s) some very traditional formula works right along with the experimental fare. *Funny Girl* (1964), *Hello, Dolly!* (1964), *Mame* (1966), and several others came right out of the conventional pattern for success.

Issues of sexuality came to the forefront in a chilling new way in the 1980s when the worldwide AIDS epidemic exploded onto the scene, killing Hollywood superstar Rock Hudson, pianist Liberace, rock group Queen's frontman Freddie Mercury, and countless other performers over the next two decades. The arts have long been a relatively safe place for the gay community to work and prosper. While not a disease exclusive to the gay community, the illness certainly disproportionately affected America's gay community in the '80s and '90s. William Finn's *March of the Falsettos* and *Falsettoland* in 1992 depicted gay men facing life, love, and AIDS with the support of family and friends. *Rent* (1996), which won a Pulitzer Prize for Drama and a Tony for Best Musical, revolutionized what theatre dared to discuss on stage. In *The Full Monty* (2000), gay playwright Terrence McNally had straight characters contend with a budding gay romance in their ranks.

Some of the more recent Broadway musicals have been reworkings of operas, movies, and even comic books. The story of *Madame Butterfly* was given a new time, place, and musical style and became *Miss Saigon*. *La Bohème* was updated as the previously mentioned *Rent*. Even the story of Aida, turned into an opera by Verdi in 1871, was reworked into a modern Broadway musical by Elton John and Tim Rice in 2000.

Walt Disney Productions turned some of their animated films into live stage musicals, and it worked. *Beauty and the Beast*, *The Lion King*, and *The Little Mermaid* were successful beyond anyone's anticipation. An older Disney movie musical, *Newsies*, was also recently turned into a Broadway musical, receiving better reviews than the movie ever did. Not to be outdone, Disney rival Dreamworks turned their blockbuster movie, *Shrek*, into a musical. Even Marvel Comics has gotten into the act with the debut of *Spiderman: Turn off the Dark*. Smaller budget films have made their way into Broadway theaters as well, as evidenced by the productions of *Once* and *Kinky Boots*.

Finally, Mel Brooks turned some of his great films into live stage musicals. *The Producers* was a monumental surprise and an exciting promise for similar efforts. (Only Mel Brooks is respected enough in the entertainment industry to be able to escape public scorn for producing shows with song titles like "Springtime for Hitler.") He followed the success of *The Producers* with a musical production of *Young Frankenstein* and is rumored to be working on a musical adaptation of his comedy classic, *Blazing Saddles*.

Recently the rage in the entertainment industry has been for television superstars to move to the Broadway stage – a complete reversal of the traditional move from Broadway to television. Cash-starved Broadway has discovered that a well-known television or movie star, even one possessing questionable acting abilities and no live theater experience, can still sell lots of tickets. Even Daniel Radcliffe (who portrayed Harry Potter in the film series) and a few recent *American Idol* contestants have been cast on Broadway, certainly due to the star power that their names lend to the shows in which they appear.

Chapter 11
The Film Musical

By the early 1900s, film had been synchronized with sound by Cameraphone, and, in 1923, Phonofilms, Inc. made its debut at the Rivoli Theater with a short program of musical selections by Weber and Fields, Sissle and Blake, and Eddie Cantor. Most movie producers dismissed the new-fangled nonsense. But William Fox and the Warner brothers took interest. Fox rented some Swiss sound equipment, and produced a short feature with his new company, Movietone. Sam, Harry, Albert, and Jack Warner immediately formed the Vitaphone Company, and entered an agreement with Western Electric.

Finally, on October 6, 1927, the Warner brothers presented *The Jazz Singer*, the story of a cantor's son who rejects the synagogue to become a jazz (popular) singer, but substitutes for his dying father at the Day of Atonement services. Only partly in sound, the picture was still a huge success, and Al Jolson has been known ever since as the Father of the Film Musical. The first all-talking (but not singing) movie was *Lights of New York* (1928); the first all talking, all singing, all dancing screen musical was *Broadway Melody* (1928). A new art form had been born (Ewen 1977, 380-381).

It is estimated that eighty-five million people went to the movies at least once a week during the 1930s. With admission prices that were usually twenty-five cents for adults and ten cents for children, many flocked to the movies as an escape from the weariness of the Great Depression.

CATEGORIES

The film musical, sometimes called a screen musical or a Hollywood musical, comes in seven basic categories, with mixtures.

Backstage Musical

The most durable of the film musicals is the musical within a musical, a story about show business – the backstage musical. Dozens of variations can be found, but the story line of the basic show concerns the problems of creating and presenting a show. Such a format means that there are ample opportunities for musical numbers which do not have to be related whatsoever to the central plot of the basic story. And, of course, the final scene of the film is successful opening night of the musical within a musical.

The backstage musical gave the Hollywood studios a good reason to offer short appearances of new and untried talent, as preparation for more demanding roles, later on. Examples are *Close Harmony* (1929), *42nd Street* (1933), *On the Avenue* (1937), *Babes in Arms* (1939), *White Christmas* (1954) and many, many more. The greatest of all was a film musical about the making of a film musical, *Singing in the Rain* (1952), with Gene Kelly and Debbie Reynolds.

Film Revue

With the barest flimsy plot, the big studios would present a string of their talented "property." The singers, dancers, and comedians were under contract to the studios, and the studio moguls had to pay them, work or no work, so every now and then a big revue would appear.

The film revues were celluloid versions of stage revues: *Hollywood Revue of 1929, Paramount on Parade* (1930), Universal's *King of Jazz* (1930), Warner Brothers' *Show of Shows* (1929) and *On with the Show* (the first all-color film musical), right up through Paramount's *Variety Girl* (1947) and MGM's *Hootenanny Hoot* (1963), by which time the studio system was beginning to die out.

Operetta

Film versions of the great operettas by Rudolf Friml (1879-1972), Sigmund Romberg (1887-1951), Victor Herbert (1859-1924), Reginald de Koven (1859-1920), and others brought great joy to Depression audiences. Nelson Eddy and Jeanette MacDonald did eight operettas, beginning *with Naughty Marietta* in 1935. Some operettas were done several times with different stars, and with new tunes interpolated as the producers and directors saw fit.

Like its stage model, the film operetta occurred in a foreign land, with princes, potentates, bureaucrats, and innocent maidens. Many of the great stage operettas were done in the 1930s and then again in the 1950s and 1960s: *Babes in Toyland* (1934 and 1961), *The Merry Widow* (1925 [silent], 1934, and 1952), *Rose Marie* (1936 and 1954), *The Vagabond King* (1930 and 1956), *The Desert Song* (1929, 1943, and 1953), and others.

Campus Musical

The dean is going to discontinue football because the college is in financial trouble, but the quarterback has a nice voice, so the dean's wife suggests to one of the cheerleaders that they put on a musical to raise money for the college, except the chairman of the history department opposes the idea because he thinks any money raised should go to repair the library, so he gives the history class an unusually difficult test which the quarterback fails, making him ineligible for football AND for any extracurricular events, like a campus musical, but the girl who works in the school library is a brilliant history major, and she persuades the professor to put the test scores on a curve, and when she takes off her glasses, the quarterback realizes that she is... Gosh!... beautiful, and she can sing, too, so guess what happens.

Rework that theme forty times with a changing parade of twenty-something and thirty-something movie stars made up to look like teenagers, and the result is pure joy for many years in Hollywood. Some of the best were *Good News* (1930), *Old Man Rhythm* (1935), *Life Begins in College* (1937), *Swing It, Professor!* (1937), *Sweetheart of the Campus* (1941), and, with Mickey Rooney, Judy Garland, and the Tommy Dorsey Band, *Girl Crazy* (1943).

One of the 1952 campus musicals, *She's Working Her Way through College*, involves a burlesque star (Virginia Mayo) who wants to be a serious actress. She enrolls in a drama course in a small college. One of the professors (Ronald Reagan – yes, the man who would later become President of the United States) befriends her, and gets into trouble with his suspicious wife. The burlesque star turns out to be a nice girl, with genuine dramatic talent, of course, so it all works out well in the end.

Horse Opera

Gene Autry, Tex Ritter, Roy Rogers, and several others gave shape and substance to cowboy musicals, "horse operas" as some critics called them. See page 180 for the discussion of Gene Autry's career.

Musical Biography

Most of the famous composers and performers in popular music have had musical film biographies done on their lives – what Hollywood insiders call a "biopic" – Benny Goodman, Florenz Ziegfeld, Sigmund Romberg, Stephen Foster, Jane Froman, Gus Kahn, Eddie Cantor, Helen Morgan, Ruth Etting, Cole Porter, and others. Among the early best were *Till the Clouds Roll By* (1946), depicting the life and times of Jerome Kern, with twenty-five of his great tunes sung by a galaxy of stars, and *The Jolson Story* (1946), with Jolson himself, still in good voice, dubbing in the vocals for actor Larry Parks.

More difficult to do is a musical biography about a classical composer-musician. *Song of Love* (1947), the life and times of the brilliant classical pianist, Clara Wieck Schumann (1819-1896), turned out to be a mixture of beautiful music and unintended humorous banality. The same kind of kitsch resulted in *Song of Scheherazade* (1947), about the famous Russian composer, Nicholas Rimsky-Korsakov (1844-1908).

More successful and convincing were *Song to Remember* (1945) about Frederic Chopin, *Song without End* (1960) about Franz Liszt, and *The Great Caruso* (1951) featuring Mario Lanza as the legendary operatic tenor, Enrico Caruso.

Animated Musical

Although they had done animated shorts (such as 1928's *Steamboat Willie*, the third Mickey Mouse cartoon, but the first to have synchronized sound), the first full-length animated feature film, *Snow White* (1937) marked the true beginning of the Walt Disney empire. The success of that film led to *Pinocchio* (1940), which won Oscars for Best Original Song (the beautiful "When You Wish Upon a Star") and Best Original Score. Other animated musicals followed, including *Fantasia* (also in 1940) and *Dumbo* (1941). After a decline in box-office returns through the 1950s through the 1980s, many thought that the magic of the Disney animated musical had faded, but 1989's *The Little Mermaid* started the so-called Disney Renaissance that includes *Beauty and the Beast* (1991), *Aladdin* (1992), *The Lion King* (1994), and many other features, all the way up to *Tangled* (2010) and *Frozen* (2013).

DUBBING

Movie stars are usually photogenic, but their singing voices may not be of sufficient beauty and strength to meet the demands of a musical. It would often happen, therefore, that a professional singer would "dub in" the songs for an attractive leading lady. *In My Gal Sal* (1942), *You Were Never Lovelier* (1942), and *Gilda* (1944), Rita Hayworth's vocals were dubbed in by Nan Wynn.

Vocalist Marni Nixon sang for Deborah Kerr in *The King and I* (1956), for Natalie Wood in *West Side Story* (1961), and for Audrey Hepburn in *My Fair Lady* (1964). Anita Ellis sang for Vera-Ellen in *Three Little Words* (1950); Jane Froman sang when Susan Hayward did her [Froman's] life story, *With a Song in My Heart* (1952); pop singer Gogi Grant was dubbed in for Ann Blyth in *The Helen Morgan Story* (1958).

Bill Lee was busy, too, singing for John Kerr in *South Pacific* (1958) and for Christopher Plummer in *The Sound of Music* (1965). Trudi Erwin and Jo Ann Greer sang for Kim Novak and Rita Hayworth in *Pal Joey* (1957).

Opera singers got dubbing jobs, also. Marilyn Horne dubbed for Dorothy Dandridge in *Carmen Jones* (1954), and Giorgio Tozzi for Rossano Brazzi in *South Pacific* (1958). Then in Samuel Goldwyn's lavish production of *Porgy and Bess* (1959), Adele Addison sang for Dorothy Dandridge, Inez Matthews for Ruth Attaway, and the great operatic voice of Robert McFerrin (Bobby McFerrin's father) was heard for Sidney Poitier (Ewen 1977, 583).

The practice of dubbing came back into the spotlight in late 1990 after it was discovered that R&B duo Milli Vanilli, who had won the "Best New Artist" Grammy in early 1990, didn't actually sing their songs as listed. The award was revoked, numerous lawsuits were filed citing fraud, and refunds were given to consumers who purchased Milli Vanilli's album or attended one of their concerts.

These days, many artists still lip sync to their own pre-recorded vocals, especially while on tour or during a performance that requires complicated choreography or other staging.

DIFFERENCES BETWEEN STAGE AND FILM MUSICALS

First, film loses that electrifying exchange between performer and audience. All the great stage stars have spoken eloquently about that magical and mysterious energy which comes to them from an actively engaged audience. They need it to achieve their highest levels of artistic delivery.

Second, the social ritual. Going to a movie is just not the same as "going to the theater". An elegant dinner followed by an evening at the theater is a unique experience. The film moguls knew this, so they first converted the existing grandiose theaters into movie houses, then they built their own opulent theaters which the journalists immediately, and accurately, called "movie palaces". Today, going to one of the twelve theaters in a shopping mall complex is just not the same kind of social ritual.

Third, in the old days, the "live sound" of the songs, orchestral support, and spoken exchanges was favored over the squeaky sounds of the early film tracks. Audio technology has so advanced, however, that live shows are today "miked up" in an effort to achieve the richly enhanced sounds of modern movie audio systems.

Fourth, the "close-up" is surely the most important difference. Some of the big stars of 1920s stage musicals moved easily into the new film industry, but others just could not make the change. Al Jolson is the classic example. His huge talent was just not captured on the screen. Film is "a powerful medium for understatement, with stunning emotional climaxes built on carefully accelerating, subtly observed minutiae". Eddie Cantor and Mae West understood this, but Jolson didn't. He simply assaulted the sensitive, probing camera lens, swinging from one extreme to another, and gave the camera no chance to focus on the man within and no time to assimilate his contribution to the whole" (Kobal 1983, 91).

The problem is still around, of course, and some highly talented stage performers have yet to develop a persuasive film technique.

IMPORTANT FIGURES IN FILM MUSICALS

If Al Jolson earned the title "Father" of the Hollywood musical, the King and Queen would have to be Fred Astaire and Ginger Rogers, and the Prince and Princess would be Gene Kelly and Judy Garland. These titles are arbitrary, of course, since hundreds of talented performers were involved – Ann Miller, Howard Keel, Shirley Jones, Gordon MacRae, Kathryn Grayson, Jane Powell, Mickey Rooney, Ruby Keeler, Dick Powell, Donald O'Connor, Buddy Ebsen (later, a TV star on *The Beverly Hillbillies*), Danny Kaye, Doris Day, and so many, many more.

Fred Astaire

Child dance prodigies Frederick and Adele Austerlitz were propelled into show business by their Austrian immigrant mother when she moved them from Omaha, Nebraska, to New York where they immediately captured the world of Broadway musicals. Adele married into wealth early, and retired from the grinding schedule. Fred Astaire (1899-1987) went on alone to become the most important dancer in entertainment history.

Slim and trim, 145 lbs. at 5'10" or so, Fred Astaire was a model of sophistication and elegance. With long-time adviser, Hermes Pan, Astaire invented all his own remarkable dance routines, and then taught those routines to his partners. He worked himself and everyone else mercilessly, often demanding thirty to forty re-takes until each detail was perfect.

He mastered every aspect of the art, and made a specialty out of dance routines with inanimate objects. In *Top Hat* (1935), his cane became a machine gun while his feet tapped out the rhythms of gun fire. In *Shall We Dance* (1937), he performed a drum dance, playing on assorted drums not only with sticks, but also with his agile toes. In *Carefree* (1938) he devised a golf dance, skillfully coordinating golf swings, tap dancing, and harmonica playing. In *Follow the Fleet* (1936), his solo tap dance imitated a series of close order military drills.

He danced on top of seven pianos in *Flying Down to Rio* (1933); he danced with a coat rack and then up the walls and across the ceiling in *Royal Wedding* (1951). And he always presented himself in full view, with very few close-ups of his arms, legs, or feet. His acting and vocal skills grew and developed until he was the complete Hollywood star, an absolute master of everything necessary for the art form.

Fred Astaire had come a long way from his first RKO screen test report in the 1920s: "Can't act. Slightly bald. Dances a little" (Ewen 1977, 403).

Ginger Rogers

Virginia Katherine McMath, born in Independence, Missouri, took her stepfather's last name, Rogers, to go with the "Ginger" her manager coined because of her red hair and freckles. Still in her teens, Ginger Rogers (1911-1995) sang with the Paul Ash Orchestra in Chicago, then moved to New York to try the big time. She won sufficient attention to get a movie contract. Her big moment came back on Broadway, however, when she appeared in Gershwin's *Girl Crazy* (1930).

She was teamed up with Fred Astaire for the Vincent Youmans screen musical, *Flying Down to Rio* (1933), into which "The Carioca" was inserted to give them at least one good dance number. They hit pay dirt, and went on to become Hollywood's favorite dancing team, doing eight delightful film musicals together in the 1930s.

Ginger Rogers was the ideal partner for Fred Astaire, following his lyric and poetic moves like a shadow. And her girl-next-door charm served as the right contrast to his European air. She handled his perfectionist needs with good-natured perseverance, and was always ready to do the number again after Fred had made some minor adjustments. The chemistry between them brought the Hollywood musical to one of its several high peaks of perfection.

Judy Garland

The child was stage-mothered into stardom. Veteran song-and-dance man Georgie Jessel saw her with her sisters in Chicago. She was about five years old at the time, and he said she was pretty as "a garland of flowers." When asked what her favorite tune was, she responded "Judy" (a Hoagy Carmichael tune, popular at the time). Thus Ethel Frances Gumm, from Grand Rapids, Minnesota, became the legendary Judy Garland (1922-1969).

Louis B. Mayer heard her sing, and signed her to a contract without a screen test. She went on to become MGM's most valuable property, appearing in seven films with Mickey Rooney and in dozens of musicals from the late 1930s to the early 1950s with a variety of other stars. She and Mickey Rooney became America's favorite sweethearts as they acted, sang, and danced their way through a host of classic teenage dilemmas.

A pudgy child without the shapely figure of the other movie starlets, she was put through a cruel program of study, practice, and rehearsals. To keep her weight down, the studio doctors used amphetamines, and to calm her when she couldn't sleep, they prescribed a variety of sleeping pills and other sedatives. "The stage was set for the later tragic years of dope and alcohol addiction, nervous breakdowns, attempted suicides, broken romances and marriages, and a conglomeration of emotional problems that brought about her premature death at the age of forty-seven" (Ewen 1977, 388).

As a small child in a strange hotel, her mother continually threatened to leave her – stranded alone – if she didn't do well in the next show. Her life was an endless string of pressure commitments, yet there is no hint of this in her screen personality. When the cameras started to roll, she instantly became the darling teenage beauty with the beautiful voice and the cutest pug nose in all filmdom.

Her great historical moment came when MGM couldn't get Shirley Temple to do the role of Dorothy in *The Wizard of Oz*. Judy Garland was sixteen at the time, and too old for the part, but the studio officials strapped her chest, designed dresses with a high waistline, put her hair in pig-tails, and surrounded her with tall co-stars. The result was, of course, one of the best film musicals ever, and the centerpiece of her illustrious career.

The Wizard of Oz. In his home office one early evening in May, 1898, Lyman Frank Baum was entertaining the neighborhood children with one of his charming ad-lib stories. Searching to name the wondrous land over the rainbow he had begun to describe, his eyes fell upon the filing cabinets labeled "A-N," which he rejected, and "O-Z," which he seized. Two years later, Baum was the best known author of children's literature in America, and *The Wizard of Oz* was about to alter the history of American popular music.

The show had been made into a stage musical back in 1903, but MGM producer Arthur Freed felt the need for different music, so he hired Broadway composer Harold Arlen to write a new score. Arlen's collaborator, E. Y. "Yip" Harburg, was engaged to provide lyrics, and in no time at all twelve songs were ready, among them "Over the Rainbow". Nearly everyone agreed that "Over the Rainbow" was a bad tune, including the publisher who thought that the octave leap on the opening word, "somewhere", was like some kind of "child's exercise", and that the center section, the bridge, was just simplistic (Ewen 1977, 399).

So "Over the Rainbow" was cut three different times from the final version, and each time producer Arthur Freed stormed into the front office to argue it back into the film. When the show was finally released, the tune won an Academy Award. It also became Judy Garland's signature, the tune that seemed resonant with all the longing and melancholy in her personal life.

Gene Kelly

While Fred Astaire had an air of European elegance, Gene Kelly (1912-1996) looked like a typical American college boy. No top hat and tails for him. He often danced in a short-sleeved sport shirt, casual light-colored slacks, and plain loafers. More muscular and athletic in appearance and in dancing style, Gene Kelly touched a different nerve in the minds and hearts of musical film audiences.

He was a director, too, and very good. With a partner, Stanley Donen, Kelly choreographed and co-directed three brilliant musicals, *On the Town* (1949*)*, *It's Always Fair Weather* (1955), and his greatest achievement, *Singin' in the Rain* (1952).

Kelly created several of the most memorable moments in the history of the Hollywood musical – the famous dance through the wet streets with his umbrella in *Singin' in the Rain*, the stunning "Gotta Dance" number in the same show, and the marvelous twenty-minute ballet sequence with Leslie Caron in *An American in Paris* (1951). In his later years, Gene Kelly devoted more and more time to directing and teaching.

VOCALISTS

Two very important vocalists began their careers in the big bands, then went out on their own to become film musical stars, then superstars. They rose so high in the entertainment world as to deserve special treatment at this time.

Bing Crosby

Harry Lillis Crosby (1903-1977) was called "Bing" by his high-school friends, after a comic-strip character, Bingo, who had large ears. Fond of vaudeville, he chose a career in music. Vaudeville-style singing – bellowing out over the noisy crowd – was still common in the 1920s. Crosby changed all that. Instead, he sang to his audiences in a tender, personal way, through a new device called a microphone. His style was called "crooning".

Bing Crosby used the microphone as part of his professional technique, and reduced the volume of his voice in an intimate, conversational flow of musical ideas. He also shaped the phrases of the lyrics to heighten the meaning of the words, but kept it all casual, warm, and comfortable. It was as though the microphone was listening in as Bing leaned over the piano to sing a gentle tune just for you.

His laid-back manner, witty asides, and natural charm were deceptive, to be sure. Beneath that "Average Joe", nice guy, next-door-neighbor personality was a brilliant entertainer, who worked at his profession, and got better and better throughout his fifty years at the top.

After a brief career in a duo, then a trio, then with the Paul Whiteman orchestra, Bing Crosby stepped out on his own. He was almost immediately successful. Millions and millions in record sales, weekly radio shows, then television shows, nightclub appearances, and occasional concert dates – Bing Crosby did it all. He will long be remembered for his films – *Holiday Inn, Going My Way, The Bells of St. Mary's,* and *White Christmas.*

Besides the above films where he sang half a dozen great old standards, Bing Crosby played the straight man in a series of light "road films" with his good friend, comedian Bob Hope. In these shows, Crosby and Hope always played a pair of off-beat characters who got into trouble in a foreign land – Singapore, Zanzibar, Morocco, Bali, Hong Kong, etc. In the midst of all the one-line zingers and clever bits of high camp, Bob Hope would make a pass at the ravishing beauty, Dorothy Lamour, but lose her to Bing Crosby, of course.

Bing Crosby's "White Christmas" is still the biggest selling single in history, with sales of over 50 million copies worldwide.

Frank Sinatra

Francis Albert Sinatra (1915-1998), born in Hoboken, New Jersey, has had a colorful career, to say the least. Really, two careers.

First Period. His first career began when he dropped out of Demarest High School at age fifteen to sing in amateur shows and saloons. After a brief period with The Hoboken Four, he quit to try his luck in the roadhouse taverns in New Jersey. Trumpeter and band leader Harry James hired him, and took him on a six months tour.

Tommy Dorsey offered him more money, so with James' blessing and approval, Sinatra joined the Dorsey band in 1940 as featured soloist and baritone in the Pied Pipers. A keen musician and shrewd businessman, Tommy Dorsey signed Sinatra to a contract which guaranteed Dorsey thirty-three and one-third percent of all Sinatra's earnings – for life (Moldea 1987, 57-58)! If he had any second thoughts, Sinatra didn't express them, apparently. He was ambitious, and, at twenty-eight years old, knew he was on his way to the top.

Before long, his pleasant voice, good looks, and smooth phrasing made him Dorsey's most popular attraction. Sensing that he could be more than just a pretty boy singer in a big band, Sinatra decided to go it alone. When Dorsey refused, Sinatra called on some friends to help out. Willi Moretti, a New Jersey Mafia figure, persuaded Tommy Dorsey to release Sinatra from his contract.

After several respectable, but minor, recordings and personal appearances, Sinatra's star began to rise. He stole the show at New York's Paramount Theater in early 1943. The young audience cheered him wildly, and almost ignored the Benny Goodman band. Sinatra was held over for eight weeks, while the band moved on. Hundreds and hundreds of teenage girls sat through several repetitions of the feature film just to see Sinatra again and again. Extra ushers and guards were called in to control things.

One author claims that it was all set up by publicist George B. Evans who hired the bobbysoxers, rehearsed them himself in the theater basement on how to scream and swoon, rented an ambulance to park outside, and notified the newspapers that the theater ushers were equipped with smelling salts (Tosches 1992, 145).

When Frank Sinatra came back to the Paramount Theater on Columbus Day in 1944, he had gained considerable fame and fortune. He was one of the leading singers on *Your Hit Parade*. He had a new recording agreement with Columbia Records, a movie contract with RKO Studios, a string of long and highly successful night club engagements, and he had replaced Bing Crosby in the news polls as America's best pop vocalist.

No one could have predicted the riot, though, on that October day in 1944. Before the movie theater box office opened at 8:30 a.m., "ten thousand youngsters lined up three abreast, while twenty thousand more milled around the streets in the Times Square area" (Ewen 1977, 465-466).

When the box office opened, the booth was destroyed by the onrush, windows of nearby shops were smashed, passers-by were trampled on, and some girls fainted. Times Square was impassable both for pedestrians and vehicles.

Four hundred twenty-one policemen, two hundred detectives, seventy patrolmen, twenty patrol cars, and fifty traffic cars were among the forces summoned to establish order. Fifty additional ushers were on duty. More than three thousand youngsters, mostly girls, remained glued to their seats throughout the day and evening, waving their undergarments at him, expressing their delirium, giving every indication of being under something akin to a hypnotic spell (Ewen 1977, 466).

Frank Sinatra had become the undisputed king of pop vocalists. The journalists called Bing Crosby a "crooner". They coined a new term, "swooner," for Sinatra.

By 1950, however, Sinatra's voice began to show signs of wear – small wonder, with sometimes as many as forty-five shows per week, averaging eighty to one hundred songs per day (Pleasants 1974, 185). Then too, his bobby-sox fans were growing out of their adolescence, his hair was getting thin, his marriage was on the skids, and his new girlfriend, the feisty, ravishing beauty, Ava Gardner, was driving him crazy. In 1952, he hit bottom when Columbia canceled his recording contract and his agent had no night club dates for him.

Second Period. Sinatra began his second period with the most remarkable comeback in entertainment history, with his non-singing movie role as Maggio in *From Here to Eternity* (1954). Hollywood insiders said that Sinatra's initial audition for the role was just average, and he was not called back. He needed a break, however, and he had influential Italian Mafia friends who got him a second audition.

After his Academy Award for Maggio, Sinatra appeared in *Guys and Dolls* (1955) and *High Society* (1956), then in *The Man with the Golden Arm* (1956), *Pal Joey* (1957), *The Detective* (1968), and many more, often in non-singing roles with his buddies, "The Rat Pack" – Peter Lawford, Sammy Davis, Jr., Dean Martin, and Joey Bishop.

Illustrious acting achievements aside, Sinatra's great gifts are musical. His urge was to just be the best, to work harder than anyone else to deliver the tune, but to do so in his own style. Inspired by Bing Crosby, he determined to find that style, on his own, with no teachers or coaches. In an article for *Life* magazine in 1965, Sinatra was quite clear about his intent.

> *It occurred to me that maybe the world didn't need another Bing Crosby. I decided to experiment a little and come up with something different. What I finally hit on was more the bel canto Italian school of singing, without making a point of it. That meant I had to stay in better shape because I had to sing more* (quoted in Pleasants 1974, 189).

His instinct for singing long lines, on lovely vowel colors, with judicious emotional inflection and impeccable enunciation gave his slow ballads a special warmth and beauty. At the same time, his macho, street-level code of life gave his up-tempo tunes a rhythmic, jazz-tinged sexuality that was, and still is, absolutely unique. The result was a new school of singing.

From the very beginning "all the elements that subsequently combined to make him one of the great singers of the century – a seamless legato, an intuitive grasp of phrasing, a feeling for the meaning and music of the words, and the warmth and intimacy of the voice itself, conveying a sense of sympathy and sincerity – were present then and can be heard on the first records he made with Harry James and Tommy Dorsey" (Pleasants 1974, 187).

The voice revealed the complex man. For all the controversy surrounding his personal life and questionable friends, Frank Sinatra changed the history of pop singing, and goes down in the record books as one of the true giants of the pop music business.

Italian Pop Singers

Before, during, and after Frank Sinatra's peak years, the entertainment world had a large number of Italian singers. Some of this was probably due to the fact that many of the big night clubs and resorts in America were, at the time, owned by the Mafia.

But the large number of Italian pop singers is also due to their historical and cultural gift for emotional and dramatic vocal music, the same instincts that made their countrymen the best opera composers and singers in all of Europe for three hundred years or more.

Here's a quick partial list of some of those Italian pop singers. Nick Lucas, Russ Columbo, Al Martino (Alfred Cini), Jerry Vale (Genaro Vitaliano), Frankie Lane (Frank Lo Vecchio), Vic Damone (Vito Farinola), Perry Como, Tony Bennett, Bobby Darin (Walden Cassotto), Dean Martin (Dino Crocetti), Bobby Rydell (Bobby Ridarelli), Frankie Avalon, Tony Pastor (Antonio Pestritto), Julius La Rosa, Frankie Valli (Frank Castelluccio), and Buddy Greco.

BUSBY BERKELEY

Of all the colorful personalities involved in the 1930s film musicals, choreographer Busby Berkeley William Enos (1895-1976) was certainly the most unusual and original. His trademark sequences, so unique and distinctive, were created with only one camera which recorded the most extravagant images ever put on film. His work is absolutely unmistakable, indelible, and unequaled (Thomas and Terry 1973, 15).

Francis Enos, director of the Tim Frawley Repertory Company, and his wife, Gertrude Berkeley, became parents of their second boy in 1895. Taking his wife's stage name and the names of two of his best company actors, Amy Busby and William Gillette, the proud father named the new baby boy Busby Berkeley William Enos.

Life was tough for traveling theater groups, and after a series of misfortunes during which the father and older brother died, Gertrude Berkeley enrolled her bright son, Busby, in the Mohegan Lake Military Academy, near Peekskill, New York. Upon graduation in 1914, the restless boy settled into a promising business career in a shoe company in Athol, Massachusetts. He also played semi-pro baseball, organized a dance band, and performed on stage in local shows.

After an uneventful tour of duty during World War I, Busby Berkeley drifted from one minor acting assignment to the next. He eventually became a drama director, and in that role would occasionally choreograph his own dances. Theater critics kept writing favorable reviews of Berkeley's work, and he was finally engaged to do the Earl Carroll *Vanities of 1928*. The show was a huge success, and in no time at all Berkeley was everyone's favorite choreographer-director in show business.

His dance routines consisted of intricate multi-rhythmic motions of the arms and legs of dozens of beautiful girls who formed constantly changing geometric patterns. The patterns were filmed from a distance way up in the top of the stage catwalk with a camera fixed to a giant monorail or a hydraulic lift.

For a number in *Footlight Parade* (1933), one hundred girls slid down a studio-built waterfall into a forest lake that turned into a pool with gold springboards. In *Gold Diggers of 1935,* fifty-six milk-white pianos whirled in a military drill in waltz time, an effect achieved by stagehands all in black carrying lightweight piano shells on their backs.

In "Don't Say Goodnight" from *Wonder Bar* (1934), Berkeley set up an octagon of giant mirrors so that a hundred dancers looked like a thousand. *In Ready, Willing and Able* (1934), Ruby Keeler and Lee Dixon danced across the keys of a giant mechanical typewriter, and as they jumped from one key to another, fifteen girls, lying on their backs above the dancers, snapped their legs to simulate the keys striking a piece of paper.

The image created by the beautiful girls forming ever-changing geometric patterns with their bodies was much like looking through a kaleidoscope. It is no surprise, therefore, that near the end of his productive period, Berkeley did actually construct a huge kaleidoscope. It was for *The Gang's All Here* (1943), and Berkeley described it later.

> *I built a great kaleidoscope – two mirrors fifty feet high and fifteen feet wide which together formed a design. In the center of this I had a revolving platform eighteen feet in diameter, and as I took the camera up between these two mirrors, the girls on the revolving platform below created an endless design of symmetrical forms.*
>
> *In another shot, I dropped (from above) sixty neon lighted hoops, which the girls caught and used in their dance maneuvers* (Thomas and Terry 1973), 153).

All in all, Busby Berkeley had a hand in more than fifty Hollywood musicals. He changed the art form, and brought hours of escapist pleasure to movie goers all through the Depression with stunning dance routines by hundreds of attractive young hopefuls. Many of his girls went on to big careers, including Paulette Goddard, Betty Grable, and Lucille Ball.

Chapter 12
The Blues

Beginning in the late 1800s, a major new musical style was taking shape. Although it seems to have its roots in the rural areas, particularly in the south, it quickly spread to the African-American neighborhoods of the nation's big cities. It would soon cause a cataclysmic revolution in popular music. It was called, quite simply, the blues.

The word "blues" is used here in three different, but interconnected, ways: to describe a psycho-emotional state of mind, to delineate a musical form, and to refer to a special musical culture.

BLUES AS A PSYCHOEMOTIONAL STATE

Elizabethan folks in the late 1500s said they had the "blue devils" when they felt unexplainably sad. They used the term to suggest that the sadness could not be traced to any particular event, so there was no real cure for it. They would just have to wait until the "blue devils" took flight.

It was not until the late 1800s in America, that the term "blues" came into common use. The first appearance in print may have been on December 14, 1862, when Charlotte Forten, a young black school teacher in South Carolina, returned from church, and wrote in her diary, "Nearly everybody was looking gay and happy, and yet I came home with the blues" (Oliver 1969, 8). By the late 1800s the term was common, and it is still used today to indicate a melancholy feeling of no specific origin, or, perhaps, of such a complex origin as to defy analysis and description.

BLUES AS A MUSICAL FORM

The 12-bar musical form (see p. 65) evolved from poetic declarations in the shape of a rhymed couplet, with the first line repeated. The repetition of the first line, and the musical space that follows each utterance of that first line, gives the second and final line a sense of closure. The couplet can be a complete episode in itself, or it can be a tiny chapter in an unfolding narrative.

The old timers were not conscious of this form, of course; they simply sang what felt right to them. It was often not a blues pattern at all. But, by the middle of the 1920s the 12-bar design was so common among bluesmen that mainstream jazz and Tin Pan Alley musicians took it as their model, and it fell into place as a permanent musical design in American popular music.

Blues topics seldom include the normal concerns of European poetry — trees, sunsets, bubbling brooks, birds, clouds, moonlight, rainbows, and such. Instead, blues lyrics address the deepest and most permanent of human circumstances in areas personal, financial, sexual, and social. The mixture of story-telling inclinations and musical instincts led quite naturally to the tradition now called the blues.

BLUES AS A MUSICAL CULTURE

The blues is essentially the secular half of the folk music of the American black community, the religious half being, of course, that great body of spirituals and gospel tunes. The entire field of American black music has its roots in African culture, to be sure, but it absorbed and reworked enough European traits as to become a unique art form separate from either parent.

Two major areas of blues activity arose in the early 1900s, one authentic and pure from the black culture, the other a New York pop-commercial blues from Tin Pan Alley.

AUTHENTIC BLUES

The study of authentic blues challenges even the most determined scholars because of the overlapping historical periods and performance styles. For all the complexities, though, at least three distinct styles of authentic blues can be isolated: country blues, city (classic) blues, and urban blues in two forms — small band and solo keyboard (known as "boogie-woogie"). Many blues musicians have moved through a couple of the styles, and each style can still be found somewhere in America today. Vocals are nearly always part of the art form.

Country Blues

In 1895 near Cleveland, Mississippi, in the heart of the Delta region, Will Dockery started a cotton plantation farm with hired hands and sharecroppers. By chance, many of his hired hands (who moved on to the land, family and all) turned out to be gifted musicians. One of the most important figures in the entire history of the blues, **Charlie Patton** (1887-1934), lived there from his teens until he left at age thirty-four. Often called the "Father of the Delta Blues", this "small, lean, wavy-haired young man with the powerful deep voice" began to record in his early 40s, and established a country blues style which inspired a great many followers (Oliver 1969, 31-32).

This country blues style favored spoken introductions and endings, strong "on the beat" phrasing, unamplified guitar, and much freedom in the formal structure of the songs and texts. Several regional schools arose. In Texas, **Blind Lemon Jefferson** (1897-1930) and **Alger "Texas" Alexander** (1880-1955) developed single-line guitar techniques, and were, generally, less guttural and heavy than the Delta-based Charlie Patton, Eddie James "Son" House, Jr. (1902-1988), and Robert Johnson (1911-1938) and later, Booker T. Washington "Bukka" White (1909-1977).

On the Eastern seaboard, certain white folk music traits came into the music of Blind Boy Fuller (born Fulton Allen (1907-1941)), Walter Brown "Brownie" McGhee (1915-1996), Sonny Terry (born Saunders Terrell (1911-1986)), and Joshua Barnes "Peg Leg" Howell (1988-1966). Working in medicine shows, house parties, and dance halls in Tennessee, Walter E. "Furry" Lewis (1893-1981) and John "Sleepy" Estes (1889-1977) laid down the roots of a Memphis style of country blues. In Louisiana, it was the albino Rufus Perryman (1892-1973), known as "Speckled Red", who established a regional style with his boogie piano.

Separate from any strong regional mannerisms, Huddie "Leadbelly" Ledbetter (1885-1949) fought and drank his way into the history books on his own. Scholars John and Alan Lomax got him out of prison several times, presented him in concerts and clubs, and recorded his best material for the Library of Congress. Big and strong at an early age, Leadbelly (the result, myth has it, of a gun fight) served often as the lead singer for the prison gang work songs so essential for coordinated effort in breaking rocks, digging out tree stumps, driving steel spikes, etc. Leadbelly's recordings include a variety of work songs, blues, and folk songs. Many of these tunes were adapted by British groups in the 1950s (Logan and Woffinden 1977, 34).

Robert Johnson's 1936-1937 recordings show the country blues tradition at its best:

> Despite their lack of technical polish, the songs come through with remarkable emotional intensity. Johnson's high nasal voice was made for the blues, and he drew wonderful qualities from his guitar. Through poetic lyrics he was able to speak of his buried longings, wanderlust, and torments. Through language unique to the blues, Johnson brought the imagery of the most basic human drives and fears to a height rarely achieved (Megill and Demory 1984, 16).

In groups, these country bluesmen appeared in string bands with fiddle, upright bass, occasionally mandolin or banjo, and, of course, guitar, but also with washboards, gutbuckets, kazoos, and harmonicas in what the Americans call a "jug band", and the British call a "skiffle band". Recordings of these blues patriarchs were well known all over Europe, especially in Great Britain.

City Blues

In August 1920, a Cincinnati girl, Mamie Smith (1883-1946), recorded "Crazy Blues", originally known as "Harlem Blues", in the Okeh (pronounced "okay") studios in New York. To everyone's surprise, the tune opened up a big market for a whole field of singers who soon came to be known as the "Classic Blues Singers". Victoria Spivey (1906-1976), Sippie Wallace (1898-1986), and Sara Martin (1884-1955) followed at Okeh; Alberta Hunter (1895-1984), Ida Cox (1896-1967) and Ma Rainey (c. 1882-1939) came out on Paramount; Bessie Smith (1898-1937) and Clara Smith (c. 1894-1935) on Columbia; Trixie Smith (1895-1943) on the Black Swan label.

Of the five unrelated Smith women who sang the blues, **Bessie Smith** was the most powerful and original. She recorded 180 songs for Columbia between 1923 and 1933, backed by the likes of saxophonist Coleman Hawkins, clarinetist Benny Goodman, pianist Clarence Williams, trombonist Jack Teagarden, and other big league jazzmen. Highly theatrical, tall and brown-skinned, dripping buxom good looks just this side of voluptuous, shapely as an hourglass, with a high-voltage rhythmic delivery, Bessie took charge of any musical situation, and sang like a woman "cutting her heart open with a knife" (Shaw 1986, 97). She was justly called the "Empress of the Blues".

Smith's first professional job was with a small travelling troupe of entertainers, gaining an audition because her older brother, Clarence, had been a member of the same troupe for about eight years. She was hired as a dancer, though, not a singer, since another as yet unknown singer was already a member of the group – **"Ma" Rainey** (born Gertrude Malissa Nix Pridgett). Eventually, Rainey did become a star, performing on stage with a necklace of 20-dollar gold pieces to match the many flashy gold fillings in her smile. She toured the black vaudeville circuit, and recorded some 90 titles for Paramount between 1924 and 1928. Her recording of "See See Rider" was one of the first, and the best of the more than 100 versions since. A "rider" is a sexual partner, incidentally.

Ma Rainey earned her title, "Mother of the Blues". She taught Bessie many a lesson in how to control an audience and how to handle money, booze, and sex in the rough world of black show business. Ma Rainey was the original, earthy, raw blues singer, exploiting all the possibilities of double and hidden meanings in her songs. She spent most of her career under canvas in the South, backed by jug bands and blues guitarists. While equally raw and powerful, Bessie Smith played the theaters and clubs of the North, with professional jazzmen in accompaniment, and, perhaps because of her more complex and tortured nature, delivered a more intensely personal, yet universal blues message. Ma Rainey retired comfortably in the mid-1930s and died peacefully in 1939.

With huge appetites for food, liquor, and sex, Bessie Smith eventually destroyed herself and ended up in bawdy, third-rate blues clubs, and doing vaudeville mammy routines in costume (Shaw 1986, 98). She died as a result of an automobile accident in 1937.

The city blues culture was dominated by women, but one man, **Perry Bradford** (1893-1970), caused a lot of good things to happen behind the scenes. Singer, dancer, songwriter, pianist, publisher, and astute manager, Bradford promoted Clara Smith, and wrote a dozen or so dance songs, "The Original Black Bottom" being the most famous. He was also very active in getting white record companies to hire professional jazzmen behind the blues singers.

What was recorded may not have been exactly characteristic of the field-at-large. The jazz professionals who backed up the female blues stars probably gave the music more of a "citified jazz" sound than what was the typical sound on the vaudeville circuit, in the medicine shows, at the fish fries, in the minstrel shows, and in the lower class blues clubs. Even without the professional jazzmen in back of them, however, the "city blues" women were carving out a new and different blues tradition.

Urban Blues

In 1933, a blues contest was held in Chicago. The entrants included a little lady who had the face of a librarian but the musical muscle of a longshoreman. Minnie Douglas McCoy, known as Memphis Minnie, was part of a group of bluesmen exiles from the South, who had begun as down-home singers, settled in Chicago in the 1920s and 1930s, and developed a style that became known as Urban Blues (Shaw 1986, 115).

By age 15, Lizzie Douglas (1897-1973) was singing in the streets of Memphis under the name "Kid Douglas", and a year later she joined the Ringling Brothers Circus. In 1929, she was discovered by a Columbia talent scout who gave her the stage name "**Memphis Minnie**", and was recorded extensively with her husband, Joe McCoy (given the name "Kansas Joe" by the same scout), playing a bass line on a second guitar. Settling down, she took Chicago by storm, with her formidable guitar technique and powerful, expressive voice, "the best female blues singer outside the Classic idiom." Her legendary "Blue Monday parties" became a training ground for young aspirants and a positive influence in the growth and development of Chicago's urban blues community (Oliver 1969, 110).

Many forces were at work to make Chicago the 1930s blues hot spot of the nation. Two personalities stand out. Lester Melrose, manager of Bluebird Records, Victor's new subsidiary, made Big **Bill Broonzy** (1893-1958) his resident guitarist and contractor of musicians. In addition to his own duties at Bluebird, Melrose nudged Vocalion and Decca to record a host of the blues artists newly arrived in Chicago – Georgia Tom (born Thomas A. Dorsey (1899-1993), later of gospel music fame), Jazz Gillum (born William McKinley Gillum (1904-1966)), Washboard Sam (born Robert Brown (1910-1966)), Sonny Boy Williamson (born John Lee Curtis Williamson (1914-1948)), Bumble Bee Slim (born Amos Easton (1905-1968)), Tampa Red (born Hudson Woodbridge, later Whittaker (1904-1981)), Alonzo "Lonnie" Johnson (1899-

1970), Memphis Slim (born John Len Chapman (1915-1988)), Memphis Minnie, and Bukka White.

While city blues recording sessions featured keyboard accompanists, recordings of urban blues highlighted the guitar and jug band instruments. Urban blues was a strange mixture.

> *A photograph of Washboard Sam (Robert Brown) epitomizes the ambivalence of outlook in urban blues. There he stands, attired in a neat, double-breasted suit, wearing a tie, and with spats on his feet — but he holds an ordinary washboard, mounted with two cowbells, and there are thimbles on the fingers of his right hand. The man has become a city slicker, but his instrument is a downhome contraption. He is a fusion of the rural and the urban, of country tradition and city sophistication. This ambivalence found expression in an early urban style known as "hokum"* (Shaw 1986, 117).

Broonzy led a group called the Famous Hokum Boys, one of several groups which blended the old with the new — the Hokum Trio, Harum Scarum, and the Hokum Jug Band (*ibid*). "Hokum" was the "good-natured guying of simple folkways", and hokum bands were "comic, ribbing, good-time groups who used guitars, piano, kazoo, string bass, clarinet, even, in imitation of the country string bands, but with urban sophistication" (Oliver 1969, 100). Not all urban blues groups were tongue-in-cheek hokum groups, of course.

Boogie-Woogie. Another kind of urban blues grew up among piano players in the lumber and turpentine camps of Texas and Louisiana, and soon spread to the inner-city clubs of the Mid-West, especially Chicago. It was called boogie-woogie. Leadbelly said it was called "fast western" or "fast blues" when he heard it in Texas in 1899 (Megill and Demory 1984, 47).

It's infectious music. Eighth-note ostinato patterns generate a hypnotic motor rhythm in the left hand, while the right hand embroiders a variety of highly ornamented melodies to "energize the already thick texture" (*ibid.*). A solo pianist can whip up an entire crowd of dancers with boogie-woogie, and he often did at the "rent parties" in Chicago. To raise enough cash to make their next rent payment, inner-city blacks would roll back the living room carpet, get a pianist, and invite everyone in the neighborhood for an evening of food, dancing, drinking, and socializing. At the end of the evening, the big glass jar on top of the piano would usually be filled with enough money to pay the pianist and most of the rent. Rent parties were sometimes called "boogies" (Shaw 1986, 119).

James Edwards Yancy (1894-1951) sang and danced on the vaudeville circuit from age 6 to 21, then worked in Chicago as a full-time groundsman at Comiskey Park, home of the Chicago White Sox, and as a part-time pianist at rent parties and small clubs. His home at 35th and State became a hangout for boogie-woogie pianists to whom he was a teacher and, in time, father figure. Among those young men were Meade "Lux" Lewis (1905-1964), Cripple Clarence Lofton (born Albert Clemens (1887-1958)), Pine Top Smith (born Clarence Smith (1904-1929)), and Albert Ammons (1907-1949) (Shaw 1986, 120). Since the 1920s, each generation of pop musicians seemed to discover boogie-woogie, and give its basic "shuffle rhythm" concept a fresh new treatment.

POP-COMMERCIAL BLUES

What Charlie Patton, "Father of the Delta Blues", had done for the black community, William C. Handy (1873-1958) did for the white. Although Handy himself was African-American, he created the conditions for a "white synthesis" of the black art form (Shaw 1986, 122).

Handy's father, an Alabama minister, permitted his son to study organ and theory, but was opposed to a career in music. The bright child could not resist the glamour of music, though, and behind his father's back, he began playing cornet in a local band. In 1892, Handy traveled to Birmingham to take an exam to obtain a teaching certificate, but he quit teaching shortly after he began because of the low wages, favoring instead a better paying job in a local ironworks.

In his off-hours, he started a travelling music group, called the Lauzetta Quartet. After traveling the Midwest for a short time, the quartet disbanded, and Handy ended up in Evansville, Indiana. A few years later, Handy became the bandleader of Mahara's Colored Minstrels, which traveled for three years around the country and, once, to Cuba.

He was a highly educated man and a superb musician. In no time at all he was a successful arranger, cornet soloist, and bandleader. One evening he had a quasi-conversion experience.

> He was leading his dance orchestra in Cleveland, Mississippi, when he agreed to let a local "colored" band play a few numbers. It was a three-piece band, consisting, he wrote in his autobiography, "of a battered guitar, a mandolin, and a worn-out bass... They struck up one of those over-and-over strains that seems to have no very clear beginning and certainly no ending..."
>
> But it drove the dancers wild, who responded with a steady shower of coins. "There before the boys lay more money than my musicians were being paid for the entire engagement. Then I saw the beauty of the primitive music" (Shaw 1986, 122-123).

By 1909, Handy had another band and had settled in Memphis, Tennessee. He began to orchestrate some of the local blues and pop tunes for his dance orchestra. He then wrote a campaign song for E. H. Crump's mayoralty race. Later, that tune became the famous "Memphis Blues". Several more blues compositions followed until 1914 when "St. Louis Blues" took the world by storm. In no time at all W. C. Handy was the darling of Tin Pan Alley. "St. Louis Blues" is, ironically, not in blues form, but rather in binary form consisting of an eight-measure A section (repeated) and a twelve-measure B section of blues chord progressions. It was seized upon as the real thing, however, and went all over the world. Before long, some 200 different blues titles appeared on Broadway, in sheet music and on recordings. It was a national craze, and everybody in the industry – composers, performers, producers, recording executives, and audiences – fell in love with the blues.

As a result, even the giants of Tin Pan Alley got into the act, writing a great many tunes that were either genuine blues or had a strong blues spirit: Jerome Kern, "Left All Alone Blues" and "Blue Danube Blues"; George Gershwin, "The Yankee Doodle Blues" and "Half of It Dearie Blues"; from London, Noel Coward, "Russian Blues"; Richard Rodgers, "Atlantic Blues"; Irving Berlin, "Shaking the Blues Away"; Jimmy McHugh, "Out Where the Blues Begin"; and DeSylva, Brown, and Henderson, "The Birth of The Blues".

W. C. Handy's many other blues compositions turned a profit and he formed a publishing house to take advantage of his growing skills. But it was "The St. Louis Blues" that brought him the most lasting fame. King Edward VIII asked the pipers of Scotland to play it for him, it was played at the marriage of Princess Marina of Greece, and it became the battle hymn of the Ethiopians when they were invaded by Italy in the 1930s. It is even said to be a favorite tune of Queen Elizabeth II (Ewen 1977, 221).

SUMMARY

From the early 1900s up through the 1930s, the African-American art form called the blues changed the entire concept of what an American pop tune might be. It opened a whole new musico-aesthetic territory for exploration, leading directly and immediately into its own electric extension, called "rhythm and blues", but also leading into that cataclysmic upheaval in American pop culture, the rock revolution.

More on these topics, soon. But first, it's time to see what piano players outside the blues community were doing.

Chapter 13
Ragtime and Stride Piano

On January 23, 1900, ragtime pianists from all over the nation came to Tammany Hall in New York City to participate in the competition for the Ragtime Championship of the World (Shaw 1986, 45). To "rag" a piece of music was to treat it with syncopated figures which would reverse or omit the accents normal to the meter, and to add embellishments to the basic melodic line. These pianists were judged on the inventiveness and musicality of what they could do for two minutes with one of the most popular tunes of the day, Ernest Hogan's "All Coons Look Alike to Me". Incidentally, the Hogan song did not embody the prejudicial stereotype implied by its title. It was a ballad of a broken love affair in which a woman, now possessed of a new lover who spends money on her, airily dismisses her old love with the comment, "All coons look alike to me" (Shaw 1986, 41).

Ernest Hogan (born Ernest Reuben Crowdus (1865-1905)) from Bowling Green, Kentucky, a black vaudevillian who performed the song often, once revealed that he borrowed the melody from a pianist in Chicago (Ewen 1977, 118). The huge success of the tune brought mixed feelings to its author. Although the lyrics were innocuous, blacks did not like the title, which was derisive when separated from the lyrics (Southern 1971, 316). Controversy surrounded the song, and Hogan died unhappy in the thought that his innocent novelty tune had generated so much social friction.

Ugly as the thought is today, "coon songs" permeated show business, both black and white, for thirty years or more. The songs – some of them highly syncopated, some nothing more than Tin Pan Alley pop tunes on black topics – brought a protest from Frederick A. Mills, classical violinist-turned-pop composer. He wrote "At the Georgia Camp Meeting" (1897) to celebrate, rather than denigrate, black-derived syncopation. The song became very popular, and was often performed as accompaniment to a cakewalk.

The cakewalk, too, blazed across the pop music skies in the late 1800s. A first annual Cakewalk Jubilee was held in Madison Square Garden in 1892, a three-night contest drawing dancers from all over the nation (Shaw 1986, 44). On the plantations of the South, a cakewalk was an event wherein a slave couple, dressed in hand-me-down finery, would prance around in elegant and exaggerated mockery of the high manners and dancing styles of the white folks in the "big house". After cakewalks became a minstrel show staple, they moved into Tin Pan Alley where tunesmiths turned them out by the dozens. The high-strutting style of the cakewalk was probably much like the prancing drum major in front of a marching band today.

PIANIST-COMPOSERS

Already loaded with syncopation, "coon songs" and cakewalks provided ragtime pianists with ready-made inspiration. Several pianists stood head and shoulders above the crowd.

Benjamin Robertson "Ben" Harney (1872-1938) billed himself as the Inventor of Ragtime. He was not, of course, but he was skillful and very popular. His *Rag Time Instructor* (1897) demonstrated clearly how to take ant tune and rag it (Shaw 1986, 45). In performance, he would rag pop tunes at will, and also classical works like Mendelssohn's "Spring Song" and Rubinstein's then popular "Melody in F".

Harney wrote many tunes and pop-ragtime hits, but the musical craze that swept the nation was caused by several others, among whom **Scott Joplin** (1868-1917) was by far the most influential and important. Although rags were around several years before Joplin settled in Sedalia, Missouri, it was his "Maple Leaf Rag" (1898) which created the ragtime explosion in American popular music, and Joplin became the most famous ragtime pianist-composer in the land – the "Father of Ragtime".

John Stark, Joplin's white friend and publisher, saw to it that Joplin got all his proper royalties, and soon the composer-publisher team came out with dozens more of the delightful rags, among them "Peacherine Rag", "Sunflower Rag", "Pineapple Rag", and "The Entertainer", made popular again in 1973 by Paul Newman and Robert Redford in *The Sting.* That movie and its background music were part of a genuine revival of ragtime music, with new recordings, concerts, scholarly studies, and finally a biographical movie, *Scott Joplin* (1977), starring Billy Dee Williams as the composer.

The sectional design of the rag (see p. 67), coming from European march form, put a miniaturist like Joplin at his best. His rags have a "cogency all their own, together with originality of harmonic color, a seemingly endless fund of infectious melodies, and a natural feeling for syncopation" (Ewen 1977, 160).

Among Joplin's admirers was **James Sylvester Scott** (1886-1936) whose "Frog Legs" (1906), "Great Scott Rag" (1909), and "Climax Rag" (1914) sold well for publisher John Stark. His rags have a bit more air and daylight than Joplin's, and he attracted a faithful audience to his special voice.

A white Eastern pianist, **Joseph Lamb** (1887-1960) wrote a body of rags considered equal in every way to the gifted black composers of the day. Joplin heard some of Lamb's rags, and persuaded Stark to publish Lamb's "Sensation Rag" and several others in 1908. Lamb stopped writing rags for many years, but came back with "Artic Sunset", published four years after his death. Lamb's later works show a fertile imagination and a willingness to experiment a bit with the traditional dance form.

James Hubert "Eubie" Blake (1883-1983) wrote his first rag, "Charleston Rag", at age 16, and played one of his best tunes, "Memories of You", during a Memorial Concert at the Eastman School of Music one week before his 99th birthday. In his long and distinguished career, Blake composed a variety of rags and pop tunes most of which found new life in *Eubie*, a 1978 revue. His collaboration with lyricist-vocalist Nobel Sissle (1889-1975) for the celebrated musical *Shuffle Along* (1921) was the first of many successful shows for which he composed the full musical score.

In their pure form, piano rags were played in a stately and dignified manner. Joplin and others cautioned their students to hold back, to avoid fast and flashy performances. Those words of advice were ignored often, especially on the East Coast, and a whole body of "novelty rags" appeared by the white composer **Felix Arndt** (1889-1918) – "Soup to Nuts", "Toots", the still popular "Nola", and many others.

A generation later, **Edward "Zez" Confrey** (1895-1971) followed with "Kitten on the Keys", "Dizzy Fingers", and "Stumbling". These tunes were highly entertaining, but they were a far cry from the dignified musical statements Scott Joplin and his compatriots made when they first introduced the rag to America.

DANCING

The syncopated rhythms of ragtime spawned a host of dances in addition to the cakewalk – the fox trot, turkey trot, grizzly bear, bunny hug, lame duck, camel walk, and a half dozen others. The nation was wild with dancing. In the 1910s, smart young couples would spend sunset to sunrise bouncing through various nightclubs, dancing the latest craze of the month.

Their parents, of course, were outraged. This seems to happen in America every generation or so – upper-class white adolescents pick up black folk-street musical behavior, and rework it into the latest "in thing" to do. At this specific historical moment, there was considerable "fear of racial contamination, not only from the black source of the music and dance, but also from the Jewish groups who dominated Tin Pan Alley's modernized song machine" (Maltby 1989, 42).

Even some professionals were opposed to ragtime. The American Federation of Musicians passed a formal resolution asking its members to "make every effort to suppress and discourage the playing of such musical trash" (Ewen 1977, 168).

Ivan Narodny, writing in the New York Evening Sun in 1916, said that ragtime suggested the "odor of the saloon, the smell of the backyard and subways. Its style is decadent. It is music meant for tired and materially bored minds. It is essentially obvious, vulgar, and yet shockingly strong, for the reason that it ends fortissimo" (ibid.).

As always, the pronouncements of organization officials and music critics carry little weight in the real world of show business. Irving Berlin's "Alexander's Ragtime Band", Hughie Cannon's "Bill Bailey, Won't You Please Come Home?", and Lewis Muir's "Waiting for the Robert E. Lee" continued to delight listeners and dancers right up through the First World War.

Classical composers, too, were caught up in the fever of the day – Igor Stravinsky wrote "Piano Rag Music" (1919); Paul Hindemith, "Ragtime" (1921); Darius Milhaud, "3 Rag Caprices" (1922); Erik Satie, "Rag-Time Parade" (1917), and Claude Debussy, "Golliwogg's Cakewalk", from *Children's Corner* (1908).

The dancing and ragtime fever began to diminish after World War I, and a new breed of pianists rose to fame. Many of them started out as ragtime pianists, and simply pushed the concept of "ragging" to another level of improvisation.

STRIDE PIANISTS

James P. Johnson

By all accounts, the Father of Stride Piano was James P. Johnson (1891-1955). He began playing at rent parties and Harlem night spots, then moved into making piano rolls. Duke Ellington, among many others, spoke often of the wonderful effect of hearing Johnson's powerful left hand on "Carolina Shout". The essence of stride piano is the continuous arc-like activity of the left hand delivering alternate bass notes and full chords while the right hand improvises freely in and around those chords.

The ragtime pianists did the same thing, of course, but they did not have to invent everything they did with their right hand. They played what the composer had written, most of the time.

Charles Luckyeth Roberts

Charles Luckyeth Roberts (1887-1968) held his own with the best of the stride pianists, but is remembered more for owning the successful Harlem night spot, The Rendezvous. He also wrote a great many popular songs for black musicals, one of his early ones being "Ripples of the Nile", which later became Glenn Miller's "Moonlight Cocktail" (Shaw 1986, 62).

Fats Waller

Thomas "Fats" Waller (1904-1943), a pupil of James P. Johnson's, went on to great fame as a composer, stride pianist, and comic entertainer. Fats would offer a near continuous string of sly remarks while playing passages of enormous difficulty, all without a hitch or a halt. His compositions have become jazz classics: "Jitterbug Waltz", "Squeeze Me", "Honeysuckle Rose", and the tune which became the title of the May 1978 revue, *Ain't Misbehavin'*.

Willie the Lion

William Henry Joseph Bonaparte Bertholoff Smith (1897-1973) taught many of the fine pianists of the 1930s; Joe Bushkin and Mel Powell (later, a classical composer) are best remembered. Known far and wide as "Willie the Lion", Smith backed up most of the great blues singers, and was a regular at all the best New York clubs for forty years. Duke Ellington memorialized him in a jazz symphonic work, "Portrait of the Lion".

ESPECIALLY INFLUENTIAL PIONEERS

Two of the great stride pianists moved from their early styles into the beginning of modern thinking, and their musical innovations affected not only later piano styles, but later developments in the entire field of jazz.

Jelly Roll Morton

Ferdinand Joseph La Menthe "Jelly Roll" Morton (1885-1941) listened to the legendary Tony Jackson, the best of the New Orleans ragtime pianists, and decided on a career in the same field. Thus Jelly Roll Morton set out to conquer the world of jazz and other things, for at one time or another Jelly Roll was a minstrel show comedian, a pool hustler, a hotel-club owner, a boxing promoter, a cosmetics business entrepreneur, a music editor, a recording executive, and always a dashing figure with the ladies.

But Jelly Roll Morton the pianist and composer is the one most important in American history. His huge gifts and equally huge ego were clearly evident by age 17 when he was ejected from his home for playing piano in the New Orleans bordellos. From that point on his career was non-stop achievement. He based himself in California 1915-1923, Chicago 1923-1928, then New York 1928-1935, all the time performing, composing, and recording as solo pianist and band leader.

> *The most typical features... are abundantly evident: his wealth of melodic invention and skill in variation; the tremendous swing... his feeling for formal design and attention to detail; his effectiveness of pianistic resources; the contrasts of subtle elegance with hard-hitting drive; the variety of harmony, and yet freedom from*

complication and superficial display (Ewen 1977, quoting William Russell, 137).

His Chicago recordings, valuable collectors' items now, place Jelly Roll Morton and His Red Hot Peppers among the greatest of all studio jazz groups. Several generations of jazz musicians were inspired by Morton originals "Black Bottom Stomp", "Smokehouse Blues", "Dead Man Blues", and more. His solo recordings of "Kansas City Stomp", "Frog-i-More Rag", "Grandpa's Spells", "King Porter Stomp", and "Tiger Rag" are, likewise, ranked among the great moments in jazz history.

Jelly Roll claimed that he "invented jazz". It was another of his many exaggerations, of course, but there is a bit of truth to it. He was among the first to make "arrangements" of tunes, to alter a phrase here and there, to add an interlude, and to prescribe who would do what in which order. Others did it, to be sure, but he made it central, not peripheral, to the musical offering.

And he was among the first pianists to play his eighth notes long-short, an absolute component of the genetic code of jazz from then on. Indeed, long-short, uneven eighth notes are so critical to jazz that arrangers must write in a specific instruction if they want any other interpretation. Jelly Roll had a big hand in creating this condition.

When Morton's career began to fade in the late 1930s, Alan Lomax brought him to the Library of Congress for almost nine hours of performing and reminiscing. Despite that fact that Morton's prodigious technical skills were rapidly declining and his life-long habit for hyperbole was still fully functional, he offered at that time a splendid oral history of a major chapter in the story of jazz – the story of Ferdinand "Jelly Roll" Morton.

Art Tatum

Staff pianist at Toledo's WSPD at age 17, Art Tatum (1910-1956) staggered the world of jazz with his immense pianistic invention and stunning velocity. Classical virtuosos Sergei Rachmaninoff and Vladimir Horowitz came to hear him. Once, when he heard that Tatum was in the audience, Fats Waller said, "Folks, I play piano, but God is here tonight!"

Born with cataracts on both eyes, Tatum gained limited vision in one eye after several operations. He could barely see shadows and colors with his right eye.

Myth has it that Tatum listened to piano rolls as a child, and, not knowing that some of those piano rolls were made with two pianists, set out to achieve what was necessary to enter the competitive field. And enter he did. At the "cutting sessions" in New York in the 1930s, Tatum always destroyed anyone else in the club. Many pianists refused to play when they knew Tatum was in the house.

His awesome technical speed was calculated on an early recording of "Tiger Rag" at 370 beats per minute. In a 1949 concert recording of "I Know That You Know", taken at 450 beats per minute, the eighth-note runs would approach 1,000 notes per minute (Megill and Demory 1984, 40). Such is the stuff of jazz legends.

More important, Art Tatum developed a style of "substitute chords: chords which were substituted for, or added to, the original chords of a tune, and which were more complex than those original chords" (MaCalla 1982, 56). This was a revolutionary idea, and it soon altered the entire approach to improvisation. After Tatum, all jazz musicians began to improvise not only on and around the stated melody of a given tune, but also on and around the stated chords. The use of substitute changes is a major component in modern jazz, and Tatum was one of the first, and the best, to explore that area.

SUMMARY

The ragtime pianists took the syncopated rhythms of "coon songs", cakewalks, and other minstrel-derived music, and developed a new form, the rag. They also "ragged" the pop tunes of their day. And when the stride pianists took existing rags, pop tunes, and blues compositions, and made substantial changes in the rhythm, melody, and chord sequences of those tunes, another step had been taken toward the world of modern jazz.

At the same time, a new form of black-derived music rose to claim the attention of entertainment-crazed America. Different from blues and ragtime, this new stuff was perfect for the Roarin' Twenties, a splendid complement to bearskin coats, bootleg whiskey, and flappers. It was called Dixieland.

Chapter 14
The Age of Dixieland

Legend has it that an 18th century slaveholder, Mr. Dixy, owned property in Manhattan, New York, where slavery was legal until 1827. Because he was considered a kind slave owner, "Dixy's Land" was deemed an ideal place to work. Most scholars, however, reject that charming story as totally false, and believe that the term comes from the ten-dollar notes issued by the Citizens' Bank in bilingual Louisiana before the Civil War and bearing the French word *dix* (ten) on the reverse side. Soon, New Orleans, then Louisiana, and eventually the entire South were called the Land of Dixie and later Dixieland (Flexner 1976, 124).

A certain special kind of music from the South, then, came to be called Dixieland jazz. The creation of the word "jazz" is surrounded with speculation and conjecture, incidentally. One theory is that it is a Creole word meaning "to speed up" any process or activity (Funk and Wagnalls 1959, 5202). Another theory is that "jazz" is Cajun argot for "jazz-belles," a corruption of the Biblical "jezebels" (Palmer 1976, 34). What is believed to be the most likely source though, is the now-obsolete term "jasm", slang for "spirit" and "energy", which certainly captures the essence of the music.

Whatever the derivation of the word, it was in use by the early 1900s to refer to a unique socio-musical blend of European and African elements. Some scholars call the entire field of black music "jazz". Other scholars hold that true jazz happened only in the 1920s, and everything after that – the big bands, be-bop, etc. – is really something else. Still other scholars believe that be-bop is the only jazz to reach the level of "art", and everything before and after is preparation or decline.

Best, perhaps, to consider the entire field-at-large to be African-American music, and all the various styles – ragtime, blues, gospel, Dixieland, spirituals, jazz, be-bop, fusion, funk, Motown, rap, etc. – to be different manifestations of that African-American musical genius at work under different socio-cultural and historical conditions.

SOCIOCULTURAL BACKGROUND

"Dixieland jazz" certainly sprouted in other cities – Memphis, St. Louis, New York – but not with such intensity because these other cities did not have quite the same sociocultural mix and historical roots as New Orleans.

Small Bands

In the warm outdoor society of New Orleans, every lodge, firehouse, police station, fraternal organization, and civic institution had its own little marching band to play for picnics, carnivals, funerals, weddings, fairs, parades, excursions, fish fries, and parties. These bands served a social function much like the popular high school and college pep bands of today.

New Orleans was a manufacturing center for wind instruments for several years, and as a port of embarkation for troops leaving for the Spanish-American War, it was loaded with cornets (similar to a trumpet, but with a shorter, more conical tube), clarinets, trombones, and drums in the pawn shops and second-hand stores.

Bands were the entertainment on the river boats, and bands helped advertise prize fights, department store bargain sales, and ball games (Ewen 1977, 132). The band might consist of five to ten members, with, surely, guest musicians often invited to help out.

Social Conditions

Then, too, New Orleans had a wild mix of cultures, religions, races, and ethnic communities – Spanish, French, African, English, Irish, German, Cajun, West Indian, Creole, Native American, Catholic, Protestant, and Voodoo, among others. The city was one-third black, with a rigid caste system between whites, blacks, and "creoles of color" (mulattos, quadroons, and octoroons of black/French mixtures) (Gridley 1988, 41). Famous indeed were the so-called "Quadroon Balls" where mothers would bring their beautiful daughters for the specific purpose of entering into an "agreement" with the white male guests who came to the ball. The orchestra for such an event would usually be composed of male "creoles of color" (Southern 1971, 135).

At one time in the 1800s, there were three opera companies in New Orleans. The big churches all had rich choral music traditions. A Negro

Philharmonic Society of one hundred members presented concerts and recitals, and brought in guest artists on a regular basis. Trained music teachers were abundant. Mardi Gras was (and still is) non-stop music.

Storyville

In 1897, Sidney Story, a New Orleans alderman, persuaded the city fathers to legalize and limit prostitution to sixteen square blocks specifically bordered on the north by Robertson and on the south by Basin Street. To his dismay, the area of containment came to be known as Storyville, and it flourished until 1917 when the U. S. Navy declared it illegal to operate a house of prostitution within five miles of a military institution.

Most of the brothels had piano players, "professors", who entertained the guests with ragtime selections, pop tunes, and blues. Sometimes, in more up-scale establishments, there would be a small band of three or four members.

Funeral Traditions

The New Orleans funeral tradition is frequently discussed because of its historical importance in the development of jazz. On the way to the cemetery, the band would play selections of hymns in a solemn and sacred manner. After the burial, on the way home from the cemetery, the band would often play the same hymns, but now in a wild up-tempo ecstasy, for the loved one had finally been released from all worldly sorrow, and entered heaven. This was a cause for rejoicing!

If some of the band members were on a flat-bed wagon, the trombone player would be put on the back of the wagon, pointing his instrument away from the band members and away from the children and dogs running alongside, so that his trombone slide would not bump anyone or get damaged. His was a "tailgate trombone" function as he played contrapuntal lines to complement the cornet leader's main melody. Clarinet, banjo, tuba, and drums would be the logical addition to the trombone and cornet.

IMPORTANT SOLOISTS

Because of their accomplishments and influence on later musicians, several figures tower over the hundreds of splendid musicians in New Orleans in the early 1900s. They began in New Orleans, but traveled much, and often achieved even greater fame in Chicago, New York, and Europe.

Kid Ory

Edward "Kid" Ory (1886-1973) organized his own band at age 13 and was on the road at age 15. He played saxophone, piano, banjo, bass, guitar, trumpet, clarinet, and drums, but it was as a splendid "tailgate trombonist" and band leader that he made his mark in the world of jazz. He hired and worked with the best jazz men in New Orleans. While in California for five years, he made the first jazz recording in history by a black group (1919). He later settled in Chicago and played on some of Louis Armstrong's Hot Five and Hot Seven recording dates.

Kid Ory was noted for a big, robust tone, and a strong rhythmic Dixieland trombone style. His most famous composition was "Muskat Ramble", later spelled "Muskrat Ramble", a jazz classic (Gridley 1988, 76). He is nearly always mentioned first in any list of important jazz trombonists.

Sidney Bechet

Sidney Bechet (1897-1959), one of the first great soloists in jazz history, was a profound influence on later saxophonists. Best known for his highly original soprano saxophone work, he also played clarinet. He "double-timed" with ease, playing a slow tune at twice the tempo while maintaining the same duration of time for the chord changes, sometimes for long periods, sometimes just for sections of a tune. Louis Armstrong and all succeeding great improvisers were capable of doing the same.

Bechet also created dramatic intensity by preceding certain central notes in his improvised lines with various scoops, smears, and ornaments which drew attention to those important notes. Music critics have said that Bechet's solos are "blues drenched" (Gridley 1988, 75). Bechet spent many years in France, and became a kind of national hero there.

Jelly Roll Morton

Ferdinand "Jelly Roll" Morton was a New Orleans star before he went to California, Chicago, and New York. (See page 115 for more information.)

Buddy Bolden

Charles Joseph "Buddy" Bolden (1877-1931), often called "King Bolden", is said to have recorded several cylindrical discs. Jelly Roll Morton said that on a quiet night you could hear Bolden's brilliant horn twelve miles away. Bolden spent his last twenty-four years in an insane asylum, after an episode of acute alcoholic psychosis at the age of 30.

George Lewis

George Lewis (1900-1968), clarinetist, enjoyed a second career in the 1950s and 1960s traveling around America with a Dixieland group. His raw and earthy style, with "more emotion than skill", appealed to the purists among jazz aficionados.

Tony Jackson

Tony Jackson (1876-1921), the acknowledged number one solo entertainer in New Orleans, played by ear in any key, and sang in that gentle manner that Nat Cole later made famous. Jackson played fiendishly difficult ragtime with such ease that when he sat down to perform, "all the other pianists wanted to take up drums" (Dexter 1964, 15). Jackson enjoyed the distinction of being highly praised by Jelly Roll Morton, and Jelly Roll was hard to please.

THE NEW ORLEANS STYLE

In a pattern that happened often in American music, the most famous proponents of a given style of black music, in this case New Orleans style Dixieland jazz, were white musicians. The ODJB, Original Dixieland Jass Band, later spelled Jazz, formed in Chicago, and lasted only two weeks because of personality conflicts. Regrouping with new men brought up from Louisiana, the ODJB played a few months in Chicago, opened for a famous engagement at Reisenweber's Cafe, near

Columbus Circle, in New York in 1917, then made a very successful tour of Europe in 1919.

Their 1917 recording, "Livery Stable Blues", was the first jazz recording in history. The song caught the fancy of the nation's music lovers, and the ODJB became extremely popular. Given to imitating farm animals on their horns and on-stage clowning (for which serious jazz scholars dismiss them), the ODJB made "Dixieland" style a household word.

What was that style? In brief, it was continuous collective improvisation, between and among three melodic instruments – Nick LaRocca on cornet, Larry Shields on clarinet, and Eddie Edwards on trombone – sustained by the three-man rhythm section – Russell Robinson on piano, Harry Barth on string bass, Tony Spargo on drums.

Most of the early Dixieland bands had cornet, clarinet, and trombone for melodic assignments with a rhythm section of several instruments which might include banjo, guitar, bass saxophone, string bass, piano, drums, or tuba. No one had all those instruments in the band, of course, but the rhythm section came out of that list. Many variations occurred, but the theoretical model would be cornet, clarinet, trombone, piano, string bass, and drums.

Continuous collective improvisation over a relentless 4/4 rhythmic-metrical bed was fine for shows and even recordings, but it gets a little overbearing all night long. What America calls New Orleans Dixieland (in theme parks, on television, and in the movies) is really Chicago-style Dixieland. The differences are modest but musically important.

THE CHICAGO STYLE

With the closing of the Red Light District in New Orleans in 1917 and the passage of the Volstead Act to enforce prohibition in 1919, the great days of New Orleans' cabarets, dance halls, ballrooms, saloons, cafes, and night clubs came to a close. Then, too, the boll weevil destroyed much of the cotton crop in the South in the early 1920s, and large numbers of blacks and whites were thrown out of work. Many of them moved to the mobster-controlled big cities of the North that promised full employment to waiters, bartenders, bellhops, maids, cooks, laundry workers, and musicians. By the middle of the 1920s, Chicago had replaced New Orleans as one of the entertainment centers of the nation – and that called for jazz.

In New Orleans, marching bands were strong and active all year long. In the cold and windy city of Chicago, marching bands were possible only a few months each year. The real action was in the flamboyant speakeasies (the word probably derives from the English underworld's "speak-softly shops", referring to a smuggler's home or place of business (Flexner 1976, 288)). Jazz seemed to summarize, at a subliminal level, perhaps, the collective mentality of the day.

Night life in Chicago after World War I did not have to compete with the radio and talkies (those came later), and its cabarets put on lavishly produced shows – some also featuring a jazz band, usually a large one. Chicagoans seeking entertainment frequented such spots.

Being a direct, concise expression of the times, jazz appealed not only to the prohibition gangsters, but to other Chicagoans who were caught up in a whirl of protest against a Constitutional amendment they did not like. Biting and incisive, jazz personified this protest – this direct, raw approach to life, which offended the "solid" citizen and was looked upon as sinful by pulpiteers and preachers and as cheap and tawdry by small-minded classicists (Dexter 1964, 34).

The Chicago musicians, many of them from elsewhere, opened up the New Orleans style. They prepared specific introductions and endings to their tunes, and took longer internal solos, occasionally separated by modulations and interludes. They lightened up the rhythmic-metrical density by playing much of the time in a "two-beat" delivery – that is, with piano left hand, string bass, and bass drum providing counts one and three, while the piano right hand, banjo/guitar, and smaller percussion instruments offered something strong on counts two and four. (Today's rock musicians call that a backbeat.) Then the tenor saxophone came in, and the trombone began to take on a more melodic, less strictly "tailgate", duties. A new style had materialized.

King Oliver

The dominant voice in Chicago for a while was that of Joe "King" Oliver (1885-1938). A well-known New Orleans jazz giant, Oliver was summoned to Chicago by Bill Johnson to play in the band at the Royal Gardens Cafe. Lawrence Duhe met the train hoping to persuade Oliver to play at the Dreamland Cafe. Since the clubs were within walking distance, Oliver signed on with both bands, and for a time played alternating sets in each club.

After a brief spell in California, King Oliver returned to Chicago, sent to New Orleans for Louis Armstrong to join him, and made the illustrious two-cornet ensemble the talk of the Mid-West. Musicians drove hundreds of miles to Chicago to hear Oliver and Armstrong trade jazz licks and challenge-complement each other in vigorous musical dialogue. Many years later, Armstrong confessed that he and Oliver had worked out some of those brilliant exchanges before the set. King Oliver's Creole Jazz Band made several historic recordings in 1923. Hundreds of musicians, black and white, memorized every note of those classic recordings.

New Orleans Rhythm Kings

Comparing favorably with Oliver's Creole Jazz Band was a splendid white band, NORK, the New Orleans Rhythm Kings. They were not from New Orleans, and never played there, but for several years they made Dixieland's name ring. Their 1922 Gennet recordings in Richmond, Indiana, of "Tin Roof Blues", "Tiger Rag", and "That's a Plenty" reveal a clean and inventive ensemble at work. After some changes, drummer Ben Pollack assumed leadership of the band. When NORK broke up in 1925, the business-minded Pollack formed a commercial dance band that included for brief periods such sterling musicians as Benny Goodman and Jack Teagarden.

The Austin High School Gang

In and around Austin High School, another group of white hot-bloods formed a Dixieland style band. Jimmy McPartland (cornet), Lawrence "Bud" Freeman (drums, then saxophone), and Frank Teschemacher (sax and clarinet) are best remembered. McPartland later married the gifted English jazz pianist, Marian Page, and although they have seldom worked in the same band, each has had an illustrious career.

Intermixed with the Austin High School gang were several free-lance musicians, bright youngsters still in their teens, who later went on to national fame: clarinetists Benny Goodman, Joe Marsala, and Don Murray; drummers Gene Krupa, and Dave Tough; pianists Art Hodes and Joe Sullivan; guitarist Eddie Condon; and C-melody saxophonist Frankie Trumbauer.

Wolverines

Another group, the Wolverines, remembered mostly because of their remarkable cornet player, Leon Bismark "Bix" Beiderbecke (1903-1931), made several magnificent recordings in 1924 for Gennett, among them "Jazz Me Blues", "Riverboat Shuffle", and "Tiger Rag". Beiderbecke's liquid, lyric, but firm and melodic solos are treasured jazz classics. He died of pneumonia (possibly with the contributing factor of alcoholism) at age 28, and has since become a legend – "the greatest white trumpet (cornet) player ever." Each year, thousands of jazz buffs gather in his hometown of Davenport, Iowa, for a festival to honor Bix and his style of Dixieland.

Louis Armstrong

Chicago was full of great musicians, but the giant of them all was Daniel Louis Armstrong (1900-1971), sometimes called the single "most influential jazz musician ever" (Martin 1986, 107). As a teenager in New Orleans, Armstrong was encouraged by King Oliver, and he replaced Oliver in Kid Ory's Band when the older musician went to Chicago. He soon joined Oliver in Chicago for the beginning of an illustrious career.

Lil Hardin (1898-1971), Oliver's pianist, became the second Mrs. Armstrong in 1924, and encouraged Louis to assume control of his own musical destiny. For the next six years, his musical productivity and impact changed jazz history. Recordings by studio groups called the Hot Five and the Hot Seven appear on everyone's list of the greatest jazz records of all time, largely because of Armstrong's dazzling improvisations. His solo on "West End Blues" (1928) has been transcribed and studied by several major jazz scholars as an example of a new age being created in jazz.

The High Note School. What made Louis Armstrong so different from a lot of other fine cornet players of the day were his brilliant high notes. Three and four notes above "high C" are not so unusual today, but in the 1920s they were just electrifying.

After he switched to trumpet, the effect was even more pronounced. When he appeared in Paris, the trumpet players in the symphony orchestra went backstage to examine his horn. They thought it was a trick, that his horn and mouthpiece had been modified for those special high notes.

Following Armstrong's inspiring example, generations of trumpet players have made high note virtuosity part of their professional equipment – Cat Anderson, Roy Eldridge, Dizzy Gillespie, Maynard Ferguson, Bill Chase, and many others. The purists in this crowd, especially Cat Anderson and Maynard Ferguson, came to be known as "screech" trumpet players. Armstrong was the first to open up this whole musical territory.

The Low Note School. Armstrong also played the trumpet in the poetic lower register, and delivered a blues-flavored lyric sound of broad emotional warmth. Ruby Braff, Warren Vache, Art Farmer, Chet Baker, Bobby Hackett, and a host of others followed this path of musical expression.

A wide range of colors, then, plus the remarkable invention of always new motivic figures which grow out of previous ideas, made Armstrong one of the greatest trumpet players of all time. Add to all of these musical gifts an infectious smile, an appealing stage manner, an endless string of cute verbal remarks, and the result is one of the most famous and best-loved American jazz musicians in history.

Earl Hines

Earl Kenneth "Fatha" Hines (1905-1983) from Duquesne, near Pittsburgh, Pennsylvania, first came to national recognition when he settled in Chicago and recorded with Louis Armstrong in the late 1920s. He's on Armstrong's famous "West End Blues", for instance. Soon after, he began an eleven-year engagement at the Grand Terrace Ballroom, and with network remotes, his fame increased immeasurably. Two generations of jazz pianists heard and were inspired by Hines' radio broadcasts – Teddy Wilson, Nat "King" Cole, Art Tatum, Billy Kyle, Bud Powell, and others (Gridley 1988, 63).

Hines trained rigorously in classical piano studies, and it shows in his wide technical innovations. He could play stride piano with the best of them, and occasionally did for select passages, but he seldom remained in any specific mode for long. His fertile mind propelled him into brilliant horn-like phrases, complete with what seem to be breathing spots, in powerful right-hand octaves that could cut through the musical fabric of the moment. Some writers call this his "trumpet style" derived from his close musical association with Louis Armstrong. Then with flowery embellishments and bursts of double-time over walking-tenth left hand support, plus occasional explosions of off-balance bass rhythms, Hines stunned a good many jazz piano hopefuls in the radio audiences of the 1930s. He remained active and popular right up to his final days.

SUMMARY

The 1920s were exciting times for jazz, and the activities in Chicago and New Orleans appeared in nearly every major city in America. Kansas City and New York, especially, had active jazz movements which set the stage for the next major shift in America's dominant popular music, the Age of the Big Bands.

Chapter 15
The Big Bands

At the end of World War I, America had gone on an entertainment binge – booze, gambling, marathon dance contests, sitting on flag poles, swallowing goldfish, smoking in public, radio, recordings, Dixieland jazz bands, sexual innuendos on the silent movie screens in eighteen thousand theaters, Miss America contests, automobile racing, miniature golf, Broadway shows, professional sports, and all those activities summed up so nicely in the phrase, "The Roarin' Twenties."

But on October 28 1929, "Black Friday", the whole structure came tumbling down with the crash of the stock market. Nearly twenty-five thousand banks failed, thirty thousand businesses folded, and, by 1931, there were ten million jobless workers waiting in bread lines, soup kitchens, and free milk depots. The Great Depression had begun.

Record sales plunged; nightclubs and dance halls closed. Concert ticket sales dropped to an all-time low. The entertainment and recreation industries suffered more than the industries devoted to life's necessities, of course, but all of America was in serious economic trouble.

In this new socioeconomic environment, a big band popular music style took shape. The new style was called swing, and it came partly from blues and ragtime traditions, and partly from earlier dance music as played by society syncopators.

SOCIETY SYNCOPATORS

Big bands were not completely new. In 1924, Fate Marable's Society Syncopators featured nine pieces – piano, drums, banjo and tuba in the rhythm section, and trumpet, trombone, tenor saxophone, and two alto saxophones in the front line. Several musicians "doubled" on violin or mellophone (a piston-action instrument shaped like a French horn). Louis Armstrong performed on the steamboats in the Fate Marable organization for a while as did many of the New Orleans jazz musicians who worked their way up the Mississippi to settle in Chicago.

"Society syncopators" was a common term for bands, black and white, which played popular music in the restaurants, nightclubs, and dance halls of the day. The tradition goes all the way back to the 1860s. "Old Man" Finney established a musical dynasty in Detroit, and he often had a half dozen bands out working for upper class "society" functions. Finney's Quadrille Orchestra(s) were filled with sons and daughters and spouses. The same conditions pertained in all the major cities of America, and still can be found today – the Lester Lannin and Peter Duchin bands out of New York, for instance.

These society bands made no pretense of playing creative jazz, but held firm to the reason they were hired, which was to play a wide variety of dance versions of the popular tunes of the day. This would mean, almost by definition, that there would be no "featured solos" and dramatic musical moments, but rather a near continuous string of well-known tunes for dancing, conversation, and general socializing.

There were hundreds of bands. New Orleans had the Halfway House Orchestra, with clarinetist Leon Rapollo, soon to join NORK; the Owls Orchestra at the Gruenwald Hotel; Fate Marable's Capitol Revue, before he went on the Streckfuss steamboats; Johnny Bayersdoffer's Band at Tokyo Gardens; Brownlee's Orchestra; and Armand J. Piron's Novelty Orchestra at Tranchina's Restaurant, Spanish Fort.

Chicago had the Midway Dance Orchestra, led by Elmer Schoebel; Merrit Brunies and his Friar's Club Orchestra; Joe Jordon's Sharps and Flats, and the Art Sims Creole Roof Orchestra. New York had Guy Lombardo and His Royal Canadians, Ben Bernie, Rudy Vallee, Fred Waring and His Pennsylvanians, and dozens more.

Notice that the word "jazz" does not appear in the name of any of the bands mentioned above. A few of the band leaders did include the word jazz, to indicate that they had certain gifted improvisers among their "side men", and that the leader, often, would dazzle the crowd with an inspired and creative solo. They would not, however, neglect their obligation to provide plenty of high-grade, energetic dance music.

BIG BANDS

By the middle of the 1920s, several bands revealed an attitude and intent significantly different from the society syncopators. These bands were driven by the jazz aesthetic. They still provided music that could be, and was joyously, danced to, but deep at work in the mind of the leader was a different concept of what the endeavor was all about.

Various mixtures appeared, but generally a big band consisted of piano, string bass, guitar, and a set of drums in the rhythm section; three trumpets, with one playing the "hot" or jazz solos; two trombones; and two alto and two tenor saxophones, with one of the tenors as soloist. This instrumentation settled down to become the generic model by the middle 1930s.

Add to the above, a beautiful girl singer and a handsome boy singer ("band vocalists" as they were called), a small vocal ensemble (like the Modernaires), a comic singer out of the trumpet section (like Ishkabibble with the Kay Kyser band), a small Dixieland band out of the big band (like Tommy Dorsey's Clambake Seven). Top it all off with a brilliant virtuoso-leader, and an entire evening could be filled with top-quality danceable music interlaced with comedy and specialty offerings. Not all bands had all of the above components, of course, but every band leader was prepared to fill up the evening with interesting fare.

Fletcher Henderson

Often called the "Father of the Big Bands," James Fletcher Henderson (1897-1952) arrived in New York from Georgia to be a research chemist and to pursue graduate studies at Columbia University. He took part-time work in W. C. Handy's publishing house, then later accepted a pianist's position with Henry Pace's Black Swan Phonograph Co., named after the famous black operatic soprano, Elizabeth Taylor Greenfield, called the "Black Swan".

At Pace's suggestion, Henderson formed a band to tour with Ethel Waters to promote her slow-selling Black Swan discs. After the tour, he returned to New York and a full-time career as pianist-arranger-leader. He hired the best musicians in the business, often college graduates who could read music fluently and who played several instruments. He rehearsed them carefully on his interesting modern arrangements. "Each section of the band played intricate figures with a precision and swing that astounded other musicians and spawned imitators everywhere" (Dexter 1964, 62).

Henderson and his lead alto saxophonist and fellow arranger, Don Redman, invented the vocabulary, grammar, and syntax of the big band. Over a throbbing four-four rhythmic pulse, the brasses and reeds would exchange musical passages, often followed by unison riffs behind improvised solos, all wrapped up perhaps in a final, swinging, full-band final chorus. Sprinkle in a few quick modulations and clever interludes, and the result is a powerful and exciting new style of jazz which soon became America's prevailing popular music.

Fletcher Henderson was a marvelous musician, but a little casual in the business details of running a big band. Then he suffered serious injuries in an automobile accident in 1928, and never did quite return to his youthful vigor and productivity. At John Hammond's urging, Benny Goodman put Henderson on the payroll as staff arranger. Many of Goodman's huge hits came from the imaginative pen of Fletcher Henderson: "Sometimes I'm Happy", "King Porter Stomp", "Blue Skies", "Down South Camp Meeting", and others.

Duke Ellington

Born Edward Kennedy Ellington (1899-1974) in Washington, D.C., Ellington had loving parents and a stable, comfortable home life. His boyhood chums called "Duke" because of his stylish dress and debonair manner. He carried the nickname all his life, and it always seemed appropriate to the man and to his career.

He dropped out of high school in his senior year to start a sign-painting business. For several years, he had been a part-time pianist, too, and before long music took over his full time and energies. By the early 1920s he was well known in his home town as a promising pianist and band leader.

He went to New York, and, from 1923 to 1927, his Washingtonians packed the Hollywood Club at Broadway and 39th Street. When he moved to the Cotton Club in 1927, he increased the band to fourteen members and garnered international fame with his imaginative arrangements and original compositions. Because of his importance and influence, scholars sometimes consider his career in three stages, with considerable overlap, of course.

First Period. During the first ten years or so, Ellington explored the instrumental colors of the jazz orchestra. He hired theatrical musicians who specialized in exotic sounds, and then he gave them free reign. Soon all the kids in America were trying to copy the muted trumpet growls of Bubber Miley and later Cootie Williams, the liquid beauty of alto saxophonist Johnny Hodges, and the clever licks of trombonist Joe "Tricky Sam" Nanton.

These new sounds caught the fancy of journalists who quickly called them "jungle sounds". Publicity material for the exotic and erotic Cotton Club floor shows frequently used the term "jungle music" to excite the white folk who flocked to Harlem for its fashionable thrills. Right in the center of all this, "the Duke would rise from behind his pure white grand piano as impeccably and expensively dressed as any of the society patrons wildly applauding him" (Dormen 1976, 39). And, of course, a New York music teacher, Arthur Cremin, attributed the rise of sex crimes to Duke Ellington's music (Ephland 1989, 22).

Second Period. Ellington's next creative endeavors were during the 1930s and early 1940s when he wrote hundreds of great pop-flavored jazz tunes. He composed everywhere – in taxis, trains, and air terminals – and always seemed to have a tune about half ready to be tried by the band. He would enter a rehearsal, pass out a few slips of papers, and finish the tune in a matter of minutes. After a job, when the band members might go out for some after-duty night life and an early breakfast, Ellington would go back to his quarters (where he always had a piano), and work on music, often until sunrise.

Among his 952 copyrights are three large sacred works, twenty-one suites, three complete shows, three movie scores, a ballet, and hundreds of great songs like "Sophisticated Lady", "Mood Indigo", "Solitude", "Don't Get Around Much Anymore", "Satin Doll", "Perdido", "I'm Beginning to See the Light", and "It Don't Mean a Thing If It Ain't Got That Swing". Listed as co-author on many of the tunes was Ellington's white manager and publisher, Irving Mills, who, until their separation in 1940, received 45 percent of Ellington's proceeds.

Third Period. During the last twenty years of his illustrious career, Ellington turned to large orchestral works – *Black, Brown, and Beige*; *Liberian Suite*; *A Drum Is a Woman*; *The Golden Broom and the Green Apple*; and dozens more. In these extended compositions, Ellington stretched the traditions of jazz, and moved into symphonic concepts of programmatic (story-telling and picture-painting) music. These big works always contain some free space for jazz improvisation, however.

During the final months of his life in 1974, Ellington, dying of lung cancer, was hard at work at the piano in his hospital room, composing an opera, *Queenie.*

No one has surpassed Ellington's singular gifts. Other big bands may have been more popular, perhaps, because the Duke would often neglect the current pop hits of the day in favor of his own more substantial tunes, but Edward Kennedy Ellington goes down as one of the most important personalities in the entire history of jazz.

Paul Whiteman

A competent viola player, and a shrewd businessman, Paul "Pop" Whiteman (1890-1967) was known and loved for 50 years in American popular music. His approach was always symphonic in scope and intent. He played mostly concerts and theaters, not so often dance halls and nightclubs. His groups were large, much like the Boston Pops Orchestra of today, but he interlaced the sections with outstanding jazzmen – Jimmy and Tommy Dorsey, Bix Beiderbecke, Frankie Trumbauer, Joe Venuti, Jack and Charlie Teagarden, and similar first-string improvisers.

Known as the "King of Jazz," he said, "I want to make a lady out of jazz," and he did. He presented jazz in its more favorable and complementary nature, and appeared with his huge orchestra in many movies. One of his best moments occurred when he premiered George Gershwin's *Rhapsody in Blue* in 1924, at Aeolian Hall in New York, with the composer at the piano. Whiteman's chief pianist, and the man who orchestrated *Rhapsody*, was Ferde Grofé (1892-1972), who later went on to compose film scores and symphonic works, among them the *Grand Canyon Suite.*

Most of the famous big band musicians of the 1930s and 1940s were touched directly or indirectly by Whiteman. A man with great respect for the jazz talent he gathered in his orchestra, Paul Whiteman earned a listing among the important and influential big band leaders of the time.

Benny Goodman

One of the most brilliant soloists of all time, Benjamin David Goodman (1909-1986) became the symbol of the superstar "swing" musician. By his early teens, he was well known as a promising clarinetist in the Chicago area, and by his late teens, his skills were in demand all over America. When he was eighteen years old, Melrose Music Corp. published a book, *125 Jazz Breaks*, which Goodman had transcribed (Baron 1979, 81). His first real jazz band employment came when he joined the Ben Pollack Band in California in 1925, as did Glenn Miller, about the same time. The two Bens, Goodman and Pollack, often played extended drum-and-clarinet improvisations. Goodman left Pollack, and settled in New York as a free-lance studio and theater musician. He then decided in 1934 to form a band to audition for a radio network show, *Let's Dance*.

The National Biscuit Co. sponsored the radio show on NBC on Saturday nights, from 10:00 p.m. to 1:00 a.m., and they wanted a sweet band, a rhumba band, and a hot band to alternate sets. Goodman's band was hired to be the hot band. They rose to the occasion, and were soon a favorite among America's considerable dance audience. In 1935, the Benny Goodman Band was selected by the authoritative jazz journal, *Metronome*, as the "Best Swing Band of 1935". Soon the newspapers began to refer to Goodman as the "King of Swing".

With his reputation growing, Goodman went on tour in 1935, and it was just so-so. A bit conservative by nature, Goodman may have taken the safe road, and played what he thought the middle-of-America dancers would want. At the Palomar Ballroom in Los Angeles, however, Goodman threw caution aside, and brought out some of his hot arrangements. The response startled the band. Many of the kids stopped dancing, and pressed toward the front of the stage in benumbed awe at the exciting new sounds. The musicians then caught the meaning of what had happened, and played with renewed inspiration. If "swing" as a national craze had a moment of truth, it was on that night, August 21, 1935.

Big band "swing" was the passion of the 1930s adolescents in much the same manner as rock was for kids in the 1950s and 1960s. In March 1937, Benny Goodman was hired to play five separate thirty-minute sets between the all-day movie runs at the Paramount Theater in New York. The theater opened at 10:00 a.m., but when the band arrived at 7:00 a.m. for rehearsal, teenagers had already formed a ticket line all around the block. By 10:00 a.m., four thousand youngsters had skipped school to catch the Benny Goodman Band. As soon as the band started to play, the fans bolted out of their seats, danced in the aisles, and jumped up on stage with the band to Jitterbug with and for their friends. A few years later, in Philadelphia, fans killed a Philadelphia policeman's horse as they swarmed to buy tickets to a Goodman concert.

Many of the big band leaders began to lament that they (and their agents and managers) had created a monster. Fellow clarinetist and band leader, Artie Shaw said, "When you start making music into a commodity and selling it to the masses, you've lost something very precious" (Palmer 1976, 152).

Still, there was no holding back. On January 16, 1938, Benny Goodman coordinated a giant concert of jazz musicians at Carnegie Hall. Arranged by MCA, with Sol Hurok's reluctant blessing, the concert was a smash success. Later in 1938, twenty-five thousand listeners went to Randall's Island, New York, for a seven-hour concert by twenty-six bands. On November 18, 1940, a mammoth show was put together at the Manhattan Center with twenty-eight bands playing for fifteen minutes each.

"Swing" dance bands were at once idolized and hated. "Swing dancing" (Jitterbugging) was banned from all school dances in Chicago. In 1939, two San Francisco sociologists warned girls not to marry musicians. In 1943, a U.S. Senate committee investigating the recording industry concluded that "if the ban on recording wipes out Jitterbug music, jive, and boogie-woogie, it might be a good thing for America all around" (Ephland 1989, 27).

Count Basie

Of all the hundreds of big bands, the one that most consistently pleased the musicians of the day was the band of William "Count" Basie (1904-1984). To fully understand this, it is necessary to realize that the word "swing" has two meanings. One, the musical style which Fletcher Henderson and Don Redman created (see page 131). Two, a sensation that occurs when each member of the band plays every note with such buoyant accuracy at exactly the same millisecond in the rhythmic flow, that the whole band feels a kind of spiritual unity and elevation. The euphoric sensation is so potent that listeners, too, are drawn into its magical zone.

The Basie band could create a "swinging" sensation almost at will, while other bands might reach this level of pure joy only rarely. If the rhythm section – piano, bass, drums, and guitar – generates this "swinging" condition, the horns will pick it up immediately, but the horns cannot create it on their own. If the rhythm section doesn't quite "have it together", the band will just not "swing".

Later generations of jazz musicians replaced the term "swinging" with "cooking" and "grooving", and "smokin'". Rock musicians say that the band is really "tight" when everything is going well.

The secret of Basie's success was that he had the best rhythm section in all jazz history – Basie, himself, on piano; Walter Page (1900-1957) on bass; Freddie Green (1911-1987) on unamplified guitar, and Jo Jones (1911-1985) on drums. They played with a relaxed and infectious exuberance at all tempos. Their medium and up-tempos were especially memorable. The throbbing 4/4 pulse is known as the Kansas City Style, and a special kind of hippity-hoppity rhythm, sure to be used on five or six tunes in the course of an evening, is sometimes called the Kansas City Shuffle.

Page developed the new "walking bass" style into an art form, and delivered a strong, ringing tone, not the dull thud so common among string bass players of the day. Green choked off the second and fourth strokes of his 4/4 strumming pattern to create a crisp, metallic complement to Jo Jones' fluid and subtle drumming, much of which was done on the "high-hat" (also called the "sock cymbal"), saving the bass drum for accents.

But the essential ingredient was Basie's punctuation and editorial remarks from the piano. He was the first jazz pianist to "comp". Probably short-hand for "accompaniment", "comping" is the judicial interjection of sparse chords and motives between and among the phrases of the horns, solo or in ensemble. Basie's "comping" was so selective and skillful that it would inspire the soloists or the horn sections to increased energy and application. His final remark on many songs – a delightful "plink-plank-plunk", kind of a "that was fun" closing – is well-known in the jazz world. So familiar is it, that arrangers need not write it out for a pianist, but if they simply say, "Basie ending," any professional jazz pianist will automatically play the "plink-plank-plunk".

Basie was from Redbank, New Jersey, and, touring as pianist with a show, he was stranded in Kansas City, Missouri, in 1927. He played piano in a movie-theater pit, then in Walter Page's Blue Devils, and finally in Bennie Moten's band. When Moten died in 1935, Basie formed a band of his own consisting largely of Moten alumni, and featured the great blues singer, Jimmy Rushing, often called "Mister Five by Five" because of his girth.

One night in Chicago in 1936, John Hammond went up and down the AM radio dial, when he picked up the faint sounds of the Basie band over Station WXBY coming from Kansas City's Club Reno. He asked his good friend, and later brother-in-law, Benny Goodman to run out to Kansas City to hear the band in live performance. Goodman did, and confirmed Hammond's hunch that the band had promise. The rest, as is often said, is history.

Hammond arranged for bookings in Chicago and New York, then a national tour, then recording contracts, and before long, the Basie band was one of America's favorite first-rate jazz ensembles, much in demand in dance halls, theaters, colleges, and hotels. A booking into the Famous Door, a tiny jazz club in New York, from July 1938 to January 1939, with almost nightly national network broadcasts, made Count Basie one of the most popular band leaders in America.

Basie's huge success was threefold. First, he was willing to play for an average listener. "He had an uncanny sense of knowing just how far to go – in tempo, in volume, and in harmonic complexity" (Simon 1967, 87). He played many of the pop tunes of the day, filtered, of course, through his own mentality so the tunes had electrifying new jazz nuances to them. Second, he caught the fancy of the jazz buffs because the many open spaces in his arrangements were filled over the years with some of the greatest soloists in jazz history – trumpeters Emmet Berry, Joe Newman, Clark Terry, and Thad Jones; and tenor saxophonists Lester Young, Hershal Evans, Don Byas, Illinois Jaquet, Frank Wess, Eddie "Lockjaw" Davis, and Frank Foster. Third, he took care of business. The band appeared on time, did the job with enthusiasm, and conducted themselves as professional musicians. Club owners and bookers were always confident that Basie would deliver.

His nickname came, incidentally, during a radio broadcast in 1936 from the Reno Club in Kansas City. The announcer thought that Basie should have a title to put him up there with "Duke" Ellington and "Earl" Hines. A band member suggested, "Make him a Count" (Shaw,1986, 150). And they did.

Jimmie Lunceford

During disc jockey Martin Block's Marathon of Big Bands, November 18, 1940, at Manhattan Center, each band was scheduled for fifteen minutes from eight in the evening until four in the morning. Twenty-eight bands were there – Benny Goodman, Glenn Miller, Count Basie, Les Brown, Glen Gray, and such of equal caliber. The routine went well until about midnight when the Jimmie Lunceford band broke it all wide open. The fans would not let them leave the stage, yelling, "More! More!" Finally, the stage manager asked Lunceford to play several additional selections.

What was it the kids liked? Showmanship! The same kind of showmanship that Berry Gordy put into each of the Motown groups thirty years later. The Lunceford trumpet players would throw their horns into the air, and catch them in time to play the next phrase. The trombonists would weave left and right while opening and closing the bell of their horns with derby hat mutes. The saxophones would do little dance steps without missing a beat. Mix in some novelty vocal trios – complete with hand clapping, wise cracking, and good-natured banter between and among singers and musicians – and a formula for huge success took shape. The band's infectious spirit communicated goodwill and rollicking fun at all times.

James Melvin Lunceford (1902-1947) earned a B.A. in music at Fisk University in Nashville, and, while coaching sports and teaching music at Manassa High School in Memphis, put together a school band that quickly became a local sensation. Two years later, that band went professional. After short appearances around the Mid-West, the band settled in New York to become a favorite at the Cotton Club, no less. Recordings and radio broadcasts soon put Lunceford up with the most popular and successful big bands of the day.

Much credit goes to Melvin James "Sy" Oliver (1910-1988), trumpeter and arranger for the band. Oliver's fondness to "two-beat" rhythmic support gave his intricate arrangements an open feeling of relaxed energy. His special touch is clean and clear on "For Dancers Only", "My Blue Heaven", "Lonesome Road", and "Swanee River" which became a giant hit for Tommy Dorsey when Oliver later moved into that band.

Oliver's previous duties with the Lunceford band were then capably handled by William "Bill" Moore and Edwin Wilcox who developed complex and sophisticated saxophone ensemble choruses into a Lunceford signature. Lunceford was a superb teacher and disciplinarian, giving his musicians a great sense of confidence, security, and enthusiasm for their work. It was one of the most exciting of all the many powerhouse big bands of the day.

Glenn Miller

In his brief eight years as a band leader, Alton Glenn Miller (1904-1944) became one of the most famous of all. "Moonlight Serenade" and "In the Mood" are among the most popular tunes in the history of American entertainment, still performed in theme-park revues as moments that instantly transport the listener to the 1930s and 1940s. The Glenn Miller Band is still touring the nation, seventy years after his death.

He started as a trombonist with an interest in arranging, and worked with the best – Ben Pollack, Red Nichols, the Dorsey brothers, and Ray Noble. By 1937, he was yearning to try his own hand as a band leader. He put together a Dixieland group, made a few recordings, worked a few jobs, and gave it up. Everything went wrong with bookings, schedules, musicians, weather and road conditions, personality conflicts, and morale. A straight-ahead, no-nonsense professional, Miller decided that it was much easier to let someone else take all the grief while he continued to play in the trombone section and make arrangements. He was, after all, very successful and secure.

But, in true American "rags to riches" tradition, he hankered after some kind of artistic fulfillment he couldn't quite explain. It was not, as the 1954 movie suggested, a "sound" that would make the hair tingle on the back of his neck. He had used that high clarinet lead on several arrangements for Ray Noble, and it was nothing new to anyone in the industry.

So, without knowing exactly why, Glenn Miller formed another band in 1938 to play in the ballrooms on the Boston-New York-Philadelphia corridor. He changed personal managers, and this new band began to click. His big break came when he was booked into the famous Glen Island Casino in the summer of 1939. He took the job, even at a financial loss, because he wanted the national exposure of the well-known nightly network radio broadcasts, called "remotes".

"Remotes" were fifteen-minute live radio shows from theaters and ballrooms that were at a remote location, not the station's home studios. The signal was sent back to the local affiliate, then on up the line to the network for immediate national broadcast. "Remotes" helped make heroes out of many musicians, especially the big band leader-virtuosos of the 1930s.

For Glenn Miller, remotes worked. Soon after the Glen Island engagement, the band broke attendance records at the Capitol Theater in Washington, D.C., the Hippodrome in Baltimore, and in several other big city ballrooms and theaters. Each time the kids screamed for "In the Mood", which had become the national anthem of the Jitterbug crowd. The band had finally arrived in the big leagues, and was there to stay. More evidence came when the Miller band was chosen to share a Carnegie Hall concert with the well-established Paul Whiteman, Benny Goodman, and Fred Waring orchestras.

The schedule was hectic, but they somehow managed three radio shows per week, dance jobs of five and six hours per night all week long, and five programs each day between movies at the Paramount Theater. In the midst of all this, the band recorded thirty songs during the first two months of 1940. Understandably, Miller hired several arrangers to help out, among them Bill Finnegan, Jerry Gray, and Billy May who went on to big careers.

Glenn Miller had become an entertainment factory, and he wasn't exactly happy about it, and he said so to George T. Simon, his drummer, friend, and, later, biographer.

> *So many people are asking me to do so many things, and I really do want to do some of them, but I just don't have the time. It's murder. I find myself doing things I'm ashamed of doing, and yet I know people would never understand if I told them the plain, simple truth. I'm just not the kind of guy I want to be any more* (Simon 1967, 358)

In 1941, the Glenn Miller band appeared in two motion pictures, *Sun Valley Serenade* and *Orchestra Wives*. Glenn had recently hired the Modernaires to add musical and visual variety to the band. In September of 1942, Miller enlisted in the military. Too old to be drafted, he still felt an obligation to serve. He took a captain's commission, and made big plans to change the old fashioned band traditions throughout the entire military. He was stopped at every turn by massive bureaucratic protocol. Finally he gave up in disgust, and volunteered to go overseas to form an entertainment unit for the European theater.

He began auditions in New Haven, Connecticut, and, for nearly a year, hired and rehearsed the musicians, and also put on a series of weekly coast-to-coast Air Force recruitment radio broadcasts. Besides all the music, the broadcasts included sketches by a resident drama group headed by the young and promising Broderick Crawford, later of *Highway Patrol* television fame.

Finally, in the spring of 1944, the entire company went to England – twenty string players, five trumpets, four trombones, one French horn, six reed players, two drummers, two pianists, two bassists, a guitarist, three arrangers, a copyist, five singers, two producers, an announcer, two clerical administrators, two instrument repairmen, Warrant Officer Paul Dudley, and 1st Lt. Don Hayes, Glenn's personal manager from civilian days (Simon 1967, 365).

This magnificent battery of America's best entertainers performed all over England for six months, and broadcast over the BBC several times a day for the troops in Europe. Among the arrangers, and the guy who led one of the small jazz groups out of the big ensemble, was the brilliant pianist-composer, Mel Powell. Years later, Powell became director of the California Institute of Arts and an active classical composer.

On December 15, 1944, a pilot, an Air Force colonel, and Major Glenn Miller set out for Paris in a single-engine Norseman utility transport to prepare details for the relocation of the entertainment company. The small plane took off into a dense fog, started flying over the English Channel, and vanished. As of this writing (2014), it has still not been found.

Glenn Miller's brief, but memorable and important, career moved into the history books as one of the illustrious chapters in the age of the American big bands.

Artie Shaw

Arthur Jacob Arshawsky (1910-2004) was a brilliant freelance sax and clarinet player in New York when he changed his name and decided to perform one of his own compositions with a string quartet at a jazz concert in 1936. Shortly later, he formed a dance band with brass instruments, a rhythm section, and only one saxophone. It failed. He then put together a conventional big band which succeeded, especially with "Begin the Beguine" in 1938.

In no time at all, he was a celebrated big band name, favorably compared and contrasted with Benny Goodman. A man of mercurial temperament, Shaw quit the band business at the height of his fame and fortune. He went to Mexico for a few months, then came back to form another band, and released an immediate hit, a blockbuster called "Frenesi", recorded with a traditional fifteen piece big band, plus French horn, oboe, bass clarinet, and thirteen strings.

He was a restless spirit, loaded with talent, always searching for musical perfection. He formed a small group, the Gramercy Five, with Johnny Guarnieri on harpsichord. He quit the music business, several more times, became a farmer, moved to Spain to be a translator, became a theatrical producer, wrote several novels, and an autobiography, *The Trouble With Cinderella*. Among his eight wives were movie stars Ava Gardner and Lana Turner, and novelist Kathleen Winsor.

For all his controversies, Artie Shaw created some of the most memorable big band recordings of all time. His special treatments of "Dancing in the Dark" and "Stardust" are among the best ever of all big band statements.

Woody Herman

As a nine-year old, Woodrow Charles Herman (1913-1987) sang in vaudeville, then took up saxophone at eleven and clarinet at fourteen. After a brief stint at Marquette University, he started working in various dance bands, and soon landed a job with the well-known Isham Jones in Chicago. When that band broke up in 1936, several of the ex-members formed a cooperative band with Woody Herman as their designated leader. Calling themselves "The Band That Plays the Blues", they found work at the Roseland Ballroom in Brooklyn, then at Frank Dailey's Meadowbrook.

Herman turned out to be a natural leader, capable of decisions that were good for the individual members and for the band-at-large. He also had a knack for dealing with club owners, booking agents, mobs of dancers, and recording executives. Before long, the band expanded its repertoire to include pop tunes, novelty vocals, and a lot of great jazz. Around 1940, music journalists began to refer to the band as the Herman Herd, probably because of its muscular approach to everything.

That big, strong, college-football personality of the band derived partly from the only saxophone section in big band history with no alto saxophones. Some writers have said it was because Herman himself played alto sax. But so did Jimmy Dorsey, Hal McIntyre, and many others, and they still put alto saxophones in their front line.

For whatever reason, Woody seemed attracted to that robust sound, and made it his own special voice. The "First Herd" (1940-1946) recorded "Caldonia", "Your Father's Mustache", "Apple Honey", and several other unbridled jazz-novelties. The "Second Herd" (1947-1949) contained and recorded Jimmy Giuffre's "Four Brothers" — tenor saxophonists Stan Getz, Zoot Sims, Al Cohn, and baritone saxophonist Serge Chaloff. Giuffre followed later with "Four Others" and "Four Mothers" to feature the trombones and trumpets in the band.

Woody Herman survived the be-bop revolution, and continued to put together a series of bands filled with bright young musicians from the better music schools of the nation. In the 1950s and 1960s, jazz writers ignored any first, second, or third designation, and began to refer to the band as "the '50s Herd" and "the '60s Herd" then finally as "Woody Herman's Thundering Herd."

In March 1946, at Carnegie Hall, Woody Herman played the *Ebony Concerto*, composed and conducted by Igor Stravinsky. More successful was a later jazz-rock adaptation of Aaron Copland *Fanfare for the Common Man*. Such interests were consistent with Herman's native musical curiosity. He always kept up with the times, and often featured complex jazz-rock compositions by the youngsters in the band, saying, "And now, ladies and gentlemen, some 'space music' for the kids in the band."

In his final days, Herman suffered income tax problems from an unsavory business manager. The jazz community rose, as one, to help out with contributions, and with a special request to Congress for a compromise to reduce and satisfy the huge debt. It was a testimony to Herman's position in the jazz world.

Sometimes called, fondly, "The Godfather of the Road Bands", Woody Herman was loved by his men and admired by the public as one of the most successful leaders in big-band history.

Stan Kenton

In his early days, Stanley Newcomb Kenton (1912-1979) played piano with many of the local bands on the West Coast, with a kind of restless discontent that began to appear in his special arrangements. At age twenty-nine, he formed his own band, and got booked into the Rendezvous Ballroom in Balboa Beach, California. Next came the Hollywood Palladium, then the Roseland Ballroom in New York. Some fans and jazz critics found the band too loud and hard to dance to. Kenton boldly declared that his kind of "progressive jazz" was not meant to be danced to.

From that point on, his public was equally divided among those who saw him as the man who would save the big bands from boredom and death, or the man who would destroy the big band tradition by his ruthless experiments with ugly new sounds. He was neither, of course. He was a man driven by a vision of the American big band as something other than a machine for ballroom dancing.

He was, in fact, responding to a whole new set of sociocultural conditions. He felt, intuitively perhaps, that things were different for him than they had been for Benny Goodman, Jimmie Lunceford, and Glenn Miller. He became popular with the college crowd, and played for their dances, but always with some reluctance and reservation. He gave up music for a while, and toyed with the idea of going into psychiatric medicine.

In 1950, at age thirty-eight, however, he came back into music. He pushed the big jazz band concept to new levels of complexity and aesthetic challenge. He brought in a full string section for a while, and wrote jazz-fused symphonic works. He went on the road, almost yearly, with a large group of musicians and singers, playing concerts billed as "Innovations in Modern Music". He helped form the Los Angeles Neophonic Orchestra to promote and perform modern music. Everything he did seemed to generate controversy because of his fondness for powerful music driven by large brass sections.

Less controversial, and perhaps more important in the long run, was the establishment of a nation-wide series of summer jazz camps, competitions, and recording opportunities for high school and college musicians. Many talented youngsters attended those Stan Kenton Jazz Workshops on scholarship awards, and spent a week or two with the big-league professionals Kenton would bring in to teach and coach.

In 1977, Kenton suffered a skull fracture after a fall, and never quite fully recovered. He died in Hollywood in 1979. His six-foot six-inch frame was filled with restless energies, and his career revealed a unique creative pianist-composer-teacher at work with a missionary zeal to expand the horizons of that special jazz instrument called the big band.

WHY 1930 TO 1945?

The seeds were planted in the 1920s, but the big bands matured and bloomed in the 1930s and early 1940s because conditions were just right. Prohibition was repealed in 1933, and nightlife moved out into the open. With a twenty-five cent admission fee, an evening of ballroom dancing became a favorite enjoyment for the Depression-era adolescents whose fathers and brothers were out of work. And "late-night listening became especially popular; tuning in for free to dance bands broadcasting from celebrated night clubs [and ballrooms] partly compensated for the loss of more costly leisure pursuits" (Maltby 1989, 102). Marshall McLuhan says that radio "tribalizes" a culture by erasing regional distinctions in favor of, and in search of, common experiences.

The common experiences of poverty, fear, and sadness were offset by the imaginary common experiences of wealth, security, and happiness. "Pennies from Heaven", "Who's Afraid of the Big Bad Wolf?", "Brother, Can You Spare a Dime?", and similar tunes were collective commiseration and therapy devices. And in romantic film comedies, an heiress might fall in love with a reporter, while, across the street, Walt Disney's dream factory bathed its audience in warm fantasies where things turn out OK in the end. America needed to believe in itself, and the pop arts rose to the occasion. It's not a coincidence that Kate Smith, General Motors, the New York Yankees, the Superman comic strip, the Hollywood musical, the Sears and Roebuck catalog, the singing cowboy movie hero, and Benny Goodman all reached the peak of their fame and productivity during the same fifteen-year stretch of American history. The arts – and the pop arts are quickest to react – always reveal and express the deepest collective subliminal needs and desires of the tribe.

America needed teamwork, and heroes who would lead the team to do the work. And the big bands were wondrous teams, creating assembly-line music for their hero-leader. "The music's synchronized control reinforced a shaken sense of [social] order by echoing and embodying that order in its full but conventional harmonies and regular, mechanical rhythm. One day, the big bands suggested, if everyone was compliant, life would be as 'full' as these sounds" (Maltby 1989, 103).

Meanwhile, America's theater responded to the Depression with escapist works, of course, but also with some of the most powerful and important musicals ever created. Curt Sachs, preeminent German music historian, wrote that in times of social upheaval – pestilence, famine, flood, war, economic disaster, earthquakes, etc. – there is often a great outpouring of creative energies.

After the Great Depression, the entire field of popular music took a dramatic turn toward being more a "business" than a field of "entertainment", but not before the Second World War was cleared out of the way. And what a remarkable effort that war generated! The entire world of pop music seemed unified in its propaganda mission.

Later wars – Korea, Vietnam, the Persian Gulf, and elsewhere – were terribly controversial and unpopular with certain people in America, but not World War II.

Nothing today could possibly come close to the unanimous spirit so prevalent during World War II. It was a war that had to be fought. It was justified, and no one doubted its purpose or style. Time for a quick survey of popular music during that historic event.

Chapter 16
Pop Music Goes to
World War II

The unprovoked attack on Pearl Harbor by Japan on December 7, 1941, swept America into a dreadful war. Congress declared war on Japan on December 8th, and on Germany and Italy two days later.

Instantly, the songwriters of the country sprang into action. "We Did It Before (and We Can Do It Again)" was written within hours after Pearl Harbor. Two days later it was interpolated into a Broadway musical, *Banjo Eyes*, starring Eddie Cantor. Within a few weeks, all America was singing "Remember Pearl Harbor" and "Goodbye Mama, I'm Off to Yokohama".

Navy Chaplain William Maguire filled in for a fallen team member on one of the big gun installations at Pearl Harbor, and when they shot down an attacking Japanese plane, he said, "Praise the Lord, and pass the ammunition." Broadway composer Frank Loesser wrote a hit pop tune on that phrase, and for several years thereafter Father Maguire had misgivings about being associated with the famous slogan (Ewen 1977, 429).

As the war developed, three basic song types began to appear: sentimental ballads of loneliness, separation, and longing; militant anti-enemy songs; and comedy, nonsense, and novelty tunes that served as diversion from the fear and agony of the war mentality.

The entertainment industry collected its energies in three major productions: stage musicals, film musicals, and concert tours. The entire world of pop music hurriedly got into the war effort. Nothing quite like it ever occurred before or since.

SONG TYPES

Sentimental Ballads

"You'll Never Know (Just How Much I Miss You)" expressed the emotion so common to mothers, wives, and sweethearts whose men were scattered all over the globe. The same holds true for "Sentimental Journey" (1944) sung by Doris Day, "When the Lights Go On Again (All Over the World)" crooned by Vaughn Monroe in his best nasal delivery, Dinah Shore's treatment of "I'll Walk Alone", and Frank Sinatra's masterful reading of Jule Styne's "Saturday Night Is the Loneliest Night In the Week".

Not intentionally, "White Christmas" (1942) became wartime favorite, second only to "Silent Night" among Christmas classics. Including all versions of the song, it has sold over 100 million copies worldwide. The most famous version, performed by Bing Crosby, holds the world record for best-selling single of all time, with over 50 million copies sold. According to the trade journal, *Variety,* it is "probably the most valuable copyright in the world" (Ewen 1977, 430).

Militant Tunes

Roy Acuff's "Cowards Over Pearl Harbor", Red Foley's "Smoke On the Water", Tex Ritter's "Gold Star In the Window", and Bob Wills' "White Cross On Okinawa" expressed America's shock and anger at being drawn into a war they wanted to avoid.

Surprisingly, American entertainers exercised considerable restraint in fierce, anti-war, musical rhetoric. The large immigrant population of Germans and Italians may have tempered things a bit.

Comedy, Nonsense, and Novelty Songs

Spike Jones' treatment of "Der Fuehrer's Face", with his rubber "razzer" creating a Bronx cheer, put the bandleader-comic in the big time to stay. In a rare vocal display, Bette Davis sang "They're Either Too Young or Too Old", lamenting on the men available for romance, in the movie called *Thank Your Lucky Stars* (1943). The Andrews Sisters added "Don't Sit Under the Apple Tree (With Anyone Else But Me)" to their long list of blockbusters.

Several novelty tunes from the 1930s came back – "Three Little Fishes", "Flat Foot Floogie", "A-Tisket, A-Tasket", and "The Music Goes 'Round and 'Round" among them. The big hit, however, was Milton Drake's "Mairzy Doats", which derived from his four-year-old daughter's playroom patter ... "cowzy tweet and sowzy tweet and liddle sharksy doisters" (Ewen 1977, 433).

STAGE MUSICALS

Within a few months after Pearl Harbor, the celebrated Broadway composer-lyricist Irving Berlin repeated his World War I success (*Yip! Yip! Yaphank!*, 1918) by writing and producing *This Is The Army*, another stage musical of, by, and for the military. He spent several weeks at Camp Upton to gain firsthand material for his routines, songs, and production numbers from the normal activities in the classroom, training field, service club, canteen, mess hall, and PX (Ewen 1977, 430). The result was a brilliant musical revue brought to life by a few professionals and a host of gifted amateurs.

The show opened on Broadway in July of 1942, and was so successful that its initial run of four weeks was extended to twelve weeks. It soon went on tour, was made into a movie, and sent to Great Britain. It closed two years later, having earned ten million dollars for the Army Relief Fund and three-hundred and fifty thousand dollars for British War Charities. Ex-president Ronald Reagan and ex-senator George Murphy were in the movie, incidentally. As he had twenty-five years earlier, Irving Berlin declined any financial gain from the entire project, but retained copyright ownership of all material.

The above all-soldier revue served as a pattern for Moss Hart's *Winged Victory* (1943), an Air Force musical similar in design, intent, and focus. The music for *Winged Victory* was written by David Rose who later went on to fame as composer of "Holiday for Strings", "Our Waltz", and the themes for twenty-two television shows, among them *Highway Patrol* and *Sea Hunt*.

Cole Porter had two war-theme musicals. *Let's Face It* (1941), featuring Danny Kaye as one of three Camp Roosevelt inductees recruited as gigolo lovers for three society women on Long Island, contained the fine cabaret tune, "Ace in the Hole". *Something for The Boys* (1943) put the fabulous Ethel Merman on stage as Blossom Hart, a onetime chorus girl who, because of the war, has become a defense worker. "Hey, Good Lookin'" was the big pop tune from this show (Ewen 1977, 439).

With music by Phil Charig, *Follow the Girls* (1944) presented Gertrude Niessen as Bubbles La Marr, a striptease queen who sacrificed her career to work in a servicemen's canteen. In the role of Goofy Gale, Jackie Gleason drew praise for his comic talents.

Leonard Bernstein's *On the Town* (1944), based loosely on the Robbins-Bernstein ballet, *Fancy Free*, opened new territory for a musical. Three sailors spend most of their 24-hour shore leave pursuing three girls. Nothing new here, except that the characters dance their way through the plot all around New York – in the Museum of Natural History, Central Park, Times Square, and Coney Island. This dance-driven musical established Jerome Robbins as a major force in the world of stage musicals.

In an interesting effort to invoke the war theme, producer Billy Rose and lyricist Oscar Hammerstein II updated and reworked George Bizet's 1875 opera *Carmen*. In the new stage show, Carmen becomes a worker in a parachute factory in the South, and her love affair is with Joe (Don Jose), an Army corporal. Cindy Lou (Micaela) is a country girl who loves Joe, and Husky Miller (Escamillo, the bullfighter) is a professional boxer who wins Carmen away from Joe.

The famous music doesn't come off, somehow, when transferred to World War II America – "Dat's Love" for "Habanera", "Dis Flower" for "The Flower Song", and "Stand Up and Fight" for the vigorous "Toreador Song". The movie version (1959) of *Carmen Jones* suffered the same aesthetic difficulties.

Still, for all their limitations, the stage musicals of the war made a contribution to the overall spirit of the day. As always, the arts reveal – in symbolic gestures – the prevailing collective mentality of their age.

FILM MUSICALS

The story is very much the same for wartime film musicals as it was for wartime stage musicals. On one hand, the industry made a highly focused and unashamed effort to generate strong patriotic emotions. On the other hand, the industry created escapist films, to enable movie-goers to forget about the war, at least for an hour or so. The Jewish movie moguls, mostly of liberal political persuasion, had some misgivings about any war, to be sure, but they had to be careful that the government didn't move into their monopoly by making its own propaganda films in the name of national security. What happened was that "messages about the war were conveyed in the familiar idioms of advertising and movies, and predigested information and ideas were presented to a public already familiar with this form of address" (Maltby 1989, 114).

In stark contrast with the European film industry, American filmmakers have always avoided deep philosophical and political statements. In its early days, Hollywood turned out some heavy shows which were financial disasters. After that, the veterans would caution, "We're in show business – Western Union is for sending messages!"

One of the first big wartime film musicals, *Buck Privates* (1941), contained the runaway hit, "Boogie-Woogie Bugle Boy", sung by the Andrews Sisters. The movie featured Universal's top comedians Bud Abbot and Lou Costello as tie salesmen who flee the police by entering a movie theater recently turned into an Army induction center. In no time at all, they are put in the military. The rest of the show is one sustained humorous routine about Army life. "The War Office couldn't have wished for a better eighty-four minutes of recruitment propaganda..." (Hirschhorn 1981, 185).

Universal's follow-up attempt, *In the Navy*, again with Abbott and Costello and the Andrews Sisters, starred crooner Dick Powell, who joins the navy to escape the incessant advances of his adoring fans. Much less successful than *Buck Privates*, the navy show still made a few dollars for the studio, and presented the war in non-threatening terms.

Inevitably, Universal finished up 1941 with Abbott and Costello in the air force, this time with Martha Raye playing twins, in *Keep 'Em Flying*. A splendid blues-based tune, "Pig Foot Pete (The Boogie-Woogie Man)", enjoyed great popularity, but the movie itself was only modestly appealing.

Hollywood delivered the predictable, of course, in several wartime film revues. With a negligible plot, the screen was filled with a monumental parade of talent for no other purpose than to be there for the military boys to see when the film went all over the world. In addition to Irving Berlin's *This Is the Army*, there are several that film historians always mention: *Thousands Cheer* (1943) with Judy Garland, Eleanor Powell, Mickey Rooney, Gene Kelly, Lena Horne, Ann Sothern, Kathryn Grayson, Red Skelton, Margaret O'Brien, Frank Morgan, Lucille Ball, Jose

Iturbi, and the bands of Kay Kyser, Bob Crosby, and Benny Carter; *Thank Your Lucky Stars* (1943) with a similar long line of superstars; *Two Girls and a Sailor* (1944); *Stage Door Canteen* (1943); and *Hollywood Canteen* (1944) with no less than thirty-nine big name entertainers, including Roy Rogers' horse, Trigger.

Not related to the war topic in any way, a few absolute masterpiece pop tunes appeared in various wartime musicals: "The Boy Next Door" and "Have Yourself a Merry Little Christmas", sung by Judy Garland in *Meet Me in St. Louis* (1944); "One For My Baby" and "My Shining Hour", sung by Fred Astaire in *The Sky's the Limit* (1943); "You'd Be So Nice To Come Home To", sung by Don Ameche and Janet Blair in *Something to Shout About* (1943); "Long Ago and Far Away", dubbed by Nan Wynn for Rita Hayworth in *Cover Girl* (1944); and many, many more.

TOURS

Quicker, cleaner, and more directly patriotic were the tours to military installations by all the big names in the world of entertainment. A promoter would pick a superstar as the central figure, then surround that superstar with several secondary acts – a juggler, acrobat, a new Hollywood starlet, a jazz trio, a magician, a trained dog act, a beautiful singer, etc. – and send that entire company of talent on a tour.

The most famous and durable of these operations was the Bob Hope Annual Christmas Tour. Beginning in World War II and continuing for more than fifty years, comedian Bob Hope went on tour each Christmas with a big band, the latest Hollywood sex goddess, and a few other assorted entertainers. In recent times, those tours were videotaped for later showing in America. Most of the top entertainers in America followed his model, and many of them are still doing it.

In addition to the tours, many entertainers performed at the wartime USO Clubs all over America. At the outbreak of the war, the government set up the United Service Organization, with the goal of establishing "clubs" for the off-duty hours of the military men. Every medium-size city had a USO Club, and the big cities had several. Staffed mostly by volunteers, the USO Club provided quiet rooms for reading, a canteen for soft drinks, coffee, and light meals, a game room for checkers, chess, ping pong, and card games (no gambling, though), a room for arts and crafts, and a dance floor often with a stage. On Friday and Saturday nights, the girls from local colleges would go to the USO Club to dance and socialize with the military boys.

The USO clubs in Hollywood, Chicago, New York, and other major cities would get free talent of world-class caliber. Even the most famous of the movie superstars – Bette Davis, Joan Crawford, Henry Fonda, Bing Crosby, Frank Sinatra, and others – were known to volunteer for brief appearances when their schedules would permit. Actors and actresses from dinner theaters and neighborhood theaters all over America would put on free mini-dramas. Mothers, wives, and girlfriends volunteered as waitresses, short-order cooks, and clerical staff to handle all the details of the USO Club. The American Federation of Musicians sent famous big bands, soloists, and small combos to the USO clubs, and paid the musicians out of the AFM Trust Fund.

All in all, America's music-and-entertainment establishment rose to the occasion and provided the military men with first-class recreational diversion during their off-duty hours. It was a splendid example of a very high level of patriotism and civilian support of the war effort, perhaps, even, a "finest hour".

Chapter 17
The Golden Days of
Traditional Pop Singing

The human voice is the oldest, most personal, and most expressive instrument in the world, and the one most often recorded. Before the days of rock and roll, there were hundreds of "pop singers" who were held in high esteem. It is now time to highlight a few of those famous and important vocalists.

They came from all directions – vaudeville, dance bands, country music, musical comedy, and out of the churches – but they soon settled into a mainstream pop career that eventually separated them somewhat from their musical roots. A few of the early singers have already been mentioned in this book, but they will be listed again, so this chapter might serve as a single location for quick reference to America's traditional pop singers.

THE REPERTOIRE

Traditional pop songs took shape during the 1920s when the Mighty Five (see page 38) and others began to take over stage musicals, pushing out the vaudeville tunesmiths. At the same time, jazz groups, dance bands, radio shows, recording artists, and film musicals created a voracious appetite for these new, more artistic pop songs.

Under these circumstances, a popular tune, "Star Dust", for example, would earn millions of dollars for its composer and performers in live performance, radio, movie, and recording royalties. One tune, one good traditional pop tune, was indeed a valuable piece of copyright merchandise.

Pop songs are different from the songs found in rock, jazz, operetta, gospel, and the blues. First, they are almost always romantic and gentle in their language. "Blue Moon", "Embraceable You", "Tenderly", and other traditional ballads are declarations of dreams and desires as revealed in the courtship behavior of American adolescents during, roughly, the early 1920s through to the late 1960s.

"They don't write songs like that anymore" is absolutely true because those sociocultural conditions don't exist anymore. For fifty years, however, those standard pop tunes were the secular psalms of the land, compressed expressions of the collective social and cultural values and attitudes of the nation.

Second, the songs have memorable chords and melodies which lend themselves to imaginative instrumental treatment. The tunes were raw material which musicians arranged and re-arranged for singers, for dance bands, for movie scenes, and for nightclub floor shows.

Third, the delivery of the great pop songs was always moderate and refined. In the entire history of pop music, no one ever screamed out, "A kiss is just a kiss, a sigh is just a sigh!" (Hemming and Hajdu 1991, 3). Nor has anyone ever shrieked and bellowed out the charming words to "Moon River".

THE TRADITION

Pop singers take great care to convey the lyrics, the words to the song. They want the listener to connect with the song, and draw emotional meaning from it (Hemming and Hajdu 1991, 3). To accomplish this, they enunciate clearly and try to obey the "oratorical rhythms and emphases" of the English language (Pleasants 1974, 16).

Unlike jazz singers, pop singers often sing and record songs they are not especially fond of. They lean toward tunes they like, of course, but they are quite willing to answer requests for light-weight ditties. And once into the tune, they will give it their best reading. They think of themselves as professionals who can and should work with all kinds of "material". They are pleasantly surprised, to be sure, when a throw-away tune on the B-side of one of their singles turns into a giant financial success.

Pop singers move easily in and out of allied fields. The world of entertainment is a business for them, and they surround themselves with agents, accountants, and lawyers who take care of that business. These business associates often push their talented singers into radio, television, and the movies. It is a logical progression of their careers. The singers handle the English language well, and consider themselves performers, so they sometimes turn into top-level radio personalities, movie stars, and television hosts.

It happened from the 1920s well into the 1960s. Kate Smith, Bing Crosby, Frank Sinatra, Dinah Shore, Merv Griffin, Mike Douglas, Ginger Rogers, Andy Griffith, Doris Day, and hundreds of others were singers before they became movie stars and television celebrities.

FIFTY YEARS OF POP SINGERS

What follows is a survey of traditional pop singers – those who became household names by virtue of their personal renditions of the standard popular tunes of the day – from the 1920s to the late 1960s, from Tin Pan Alley to Woodstock. After Woodstock, the pop music industry became very specialized, as performers more and more sang only their own tunes, which other performers often avoided. By that time, traditional pop singing of traditional pop songs was history, and an age had ended.

In rough chronological order, the following pop singers were at one time very important and influential, inspiring hundreds of imitators. Some listed below enjoyed only a brief period of fame and fortune. Others had better luck, and survived for long and successful careers. Pop singing, like professional sports, is often a difficult, unpredictable, brief occupation.

Louis Armstrong

Surely one of the best pop singers, ever, was Louis Armstrong (1901-1971). It went on for fifty years, and no one seemed to mind that his voice was raspy and gritty. The secret was in his phrasing, in the way he altered an interval now and then to deliver the text more to his inclination of the moment.

He was also the first of the jazz "scat" singers, singing improvised phrases on neutral syllables, no words. And no matter what he was singing – fast or slow, great song or average pop tune, strong words or inane lyrics – he always "swung", which is to say, that he sang his words with such rhythmic emphasis that the beat was noticeable and pleasurable at all times. (For more about Louis Armstrong's career, see page 126.)

Al Jolson

For information on Al Jolson's career, please see page 56.

Rudy Vallee

In contrast to Al Jolson's energetic singing, Hubert Prior Vallee (1901-1986), sang through a cheerleader's megaphone in a soft, gentle, conversational singing style called "crooning". His first band, the Yale Collegians, consisted of two strings, two saxophones, and a four-man rhythm section. After graduation in 1927, Rudy Vallee and the Connecticut Yankees became the most famous pop group in the nation during a long engagement at the Heigh-Ho Club in New York. His signature greeting, "Heigh-ho, everybody!" opened each evening of dancing, and the band was heard on four radio stations each week.

Girls shrieked and swooned when he sang. He was the first in a long line of American teen heartthrobs, and (like Frank Sinatra and Elvis Presley years later) most men and nearly all music critics hated him. His blue eyes, Ivy League manner, boyish charm, and shrewd business instincts took him to the top of the industry, however.

He sang in four languages, and for ten years had his own radio show, *The Fleischmann Hour*, America's first network radio hour. He was an amiable and affable host, with a natural flair for comedy that would later play an important part in carrying him through a long career in show business (Hemming and Hajdu 1991, 34). He co-wrote several of his most famous songs, "I'm Just a Vagabond Lover", "My Time Is Your Time", "Life Is Just a Bowl of Cherries", and "Say It Isn't So". As a Yale graduate, he had to sing "The Whiffenpoof Song" (the theme song for Yale's senior male a cappella group) nearly every time he appeared in public, of course.

Bing Crosby

Rudy Vallee is said to have predicted the demise of his own style with the rise of Bing Crosby, who possessed a microphone technique unnecessary when Vallee began (Clarke 1989, 1993). (For more information regarding Bing Crosby's career, see page 92.)

Kate Smith

Known as the "Songbird of the South", Kathryn Elizabeth Smith (1909-1986) began her career as a vaudeville song-and-dance performer. Short and rotund, she drew applause when she sang and danced the Charleston. She moved into Broadway musicals, but always as the object of jokes made about her size.

A chance guest appearance on Rudy Vallee's radio show attracted the interest of Columbia Records executive, Ted Collins. He became her fan, then manager, then husband. In a short time, Kate Smith was a very famous female pop singer. In 1933, at age twenty-four, she earned three thousand dollars a week, at that time the highest paid woman in America.

Her late 1930s radio show, *The Kate Smith Hour*, was a mixture of pleasant songs, motherly responses to her fans' letters and unabashed words of patriotic encouragement to all the poor and lonely in America's Depression-era society. At its peak in 1939, the program had twenty-three million listeners per day, and Kate Smith received three million letters that year.

Her voice was in the mezzo-soprano range and color, and she used it effortlessly to convey the standard pop tunes of the day. Her radio theme song, "When the Moon Comes Over the Mountain", was her biggest hit until an Armistice Day program in 1938. She wanted a patriotic tune, and asked Irving Berlin to provide one. Berlin dusted off a tune he had deleted from a 1918 wartime musical, *Yip! Yip! Yaphank!*, and gave her "God Bless America".

"God Bless America" swept the nation, to say the least, and all profits still go to the Boy Scouts and Girl Scouts of America. Every now and then, there is a movement to make the song America's national anthem.

Nat "King" Cole

In the twenty-one years he was at the top, Nathaniel Adams Coles (1919-1965) sold fifty million records (the "s" in his name was dropped in his teens). His resonant baritone voice was rich, relaxed, and hauntingly warm. He had a marvelous way of "caressing a word, of wrapping his voice around it" (Pleasants 1979, 226).

In 1943, at age twenty-four, he recorded "Straighten Up and Fly Right" with his piano-bass-guitar jazz trio. The vocal caught everyone by surprise. Up to that time, he had been considered only as a rising jazz pianist in the style of a modern

Earl Hines. He gradually moved away from jazz piano, and became one of the most famous singers in the industry.

His giant hits – "Mona Lisa", "Nature Boy", "The Christmas Song", "Route 66", "Sweet Lorraine", and "Too Young" – were brought back into America's memory when his daughter, Natalie, released an album, with her singing her father's songs. The first single from the album was an ingenious electronic work of wonder, "Unforgettable", which allowed her to sing a "virtual" duet with her late father. This revealed just how sophisticated and beautiful Nat Cole's vocal quality and style were, and still are.

Frankie Laine

Born in Chicago, Francisco Paolo LoVecchio (1913-2007) knocked around as a machinist, car salesman, and bouncer in a beer parlor. He changed his name to Frankie Laine and began working in the local nightclubs. Hoagy Carmichael heard him sing "Rockin' Chair", and got him a job at the Vine Street Club in Hollywood, California, for seventy-five dollars per week.

A big, rugged type, Frank Laine sang with great passion and masculine intensity. Mercury Records picked him up, and his first release, "We'll Be Together Again", took off. It was followed by "That's My Desire" in 1947, and nearly seventy more Top 100 hits over the next ten years, among them "Mule Train", "Jezebel", "That Lucky Old Sun", and "Jealousy". He was also known for the theme song to the TV show *Rawhide*, as well as the theme song for Mel Brooks' western comedy, *Blazing Saddles*.

Kay Starr

With thirty hits to her credit, Kay Starr, born Katherine Laverne Starks (b. 1922) in Oklahoma, held her own with the best. After a brief career in country music, she moved to the big bands of Bob Crosby and Glenn Miller. Her first big hit, "Bonaparte's Retreat" (1948), was followed by "Wheel of Fortune" (1952), which was No. 1 in the nation for ten weeks.

Her buoyant enthusiasm and bell-like clarity gave each song a professional sparkle. "Oh Babe", "Side by Side", "I'll Never Be Free", and the charming "Rock and Roll Waltz" (1955) made her a household name all through the 1950s.

Rosemary Clooney

Born in Maysville, Kentucky, Rosemary Clooney (1928-2002) got her start on Cincinnati radio station WLW at age thirteen singing with her sister Betty. The girls then traveled with the Tony Pastor big band for three years, after which Rosemary went on to a huge solo career.

"Beautiful Brown Eyes" was a modest hit, but "Come-on-a My House" (1951), with an unusual harpsichord accompaniment, sold over a million copies, and made Rosemary Clooney a star overnight. She went on to record a dozen giant hits, among them "Tenderly", "Half as Much", "Hey, There", and "This Ole House". In 1956, the "Rosemary Clooney Television Show" was carried by over one hundred TV stations.

In several movies (including the classic *White Christmas)*, on the Palladium stage in London, and in the best supper clubs of the nation, Rosemary Clooney charmed audiences with her careful interpretations of great tunes, with her musical sophistication, and with her radiant good looks.

Although she struggled with bipolar disorder and depression, as well as an addiction to prescription drugs into the 1970s, she had a comeback of sorts beginning in the early 1990s and she continued to tour until late 2001, when she was diagnosed with lung cancer, which she died of six months later.

Dinah Shore

Frances Rose Shore (1919-1993) picked up her stage name, "Dinah", from the theme song of her program on hometown radio station, WSM, in Nashville, Tennessee. She then went to New York and began a steady climb to the top of the business. In January, 1939, she joined Leo Reisman's band, and shortly after recorded with Xavier Cugat's orchestra.

She appeared on *Your Hit Parade*, and was named the "new star of radio" for 1940. Eddie Cantor put her on his popular radio program in 1942, and for three years she enjoyed fame as everyone's favorite female pop singer.

Her records sold in the millions – "Yes, My Darling Daughter", "Blues in the Night", "Buttons and Bows", "Shoo-Fly Pie and Apple Pan Dowdy", "Doin' What Comes Natur'lly", "Lavender Blue", "Dear Hearts and Gentle People", and "The Anniversary Song" are best remembered.

In the late 1940s, she appeared in several movies, then did a fifteen minute NBC television show from 1951 to 1956, and finally hit her peak of fame in 1957 with her own prime-time TV variety show, complete with celebrity guests, comedy skits, and big production numbers. The show was an American favorite well into the 1960s.

She had a gentle manner with people, and treated friends and coworkers with a natural mixture of energy, generosity, and gracious Southern charm.

Judy Garland

For information on Judy Garland's career, please see page 90.

Ella Fitzgerald

One of the most accomplished singers in jazz history, Ella Jane Fitzgerald (1917-1996) won the admiration of mainstream pop music fans on her first big hit, "A-Tisket, A-Tasket" (1938). She later recorded a series of two-record "songbooks", each devoted to a different songwriter or songwriting team. Her clean, clear, warm tones gave everything a distinct elegance and sophistication, and her delivery was faultless at all times.

She would sing "Into Each Life Some Rain Must Fall" in the pure manner described above, and her pop fans would be very happy. The very next tune might be "Perdido", and she would scat and swing in the highest of jazz traditions. Her instinctive approach was to honor the composer's intent on every tune, and that pleased both pop and jazz fans.

Frank Sinatra

See page 93 for more information on Frank Sinatra's career.

Tony Bennett

Anthony Dominick Bennedetto (b. 1926), born in Queens, New York, got his first break at age twenty-four on *Arthur Godfrey's Talent Scouts* show, under the name Joe Bari. At the time he was working as an elevator operator, and singing free for anyone who would listen.

Bob Hope heard him in a guest appearance on Pearl Bailey's show at a Greenwich Village nightclub, suggested a name change, and took him on a national tour. When the tour ended, Mitch Miller at Columbia Records took interest, and selected "The Boulevard of Broken Dreams" as a trial record. It clicked.

Then came "Because of You", "Cold, Cold Heart", "I Won't Cry Anymore", "Rags to Riches", "Stranger in Paradise", and later his 1962 blockbuster, "I Left my Heart in San Francisco". He's been at or near the top of the pop music industry ever since.

Perry Como

Pierino Como (1912-2001) was born in Canonsburg, Pennsylvania. He worked as a barber just out of high school, then auditioned for Freddie Carlone's band. He stayed for three years, but joined the Ted Weems orchestra in 1937. When Ted Weems got drafted into World War II, Como went back to Pennsylvania to resume his career as a barber.

Too many people had heard that resonant, dark, and very musical baritone voice, however, to forget him. Victor Records offered a demo record, and "Goodbye Sue" in 1943 became the first in a long line of hits. Especially memorable were his elegant treatments of "Till the End of Time", "Prisoner of Love", "Long Ago and Far Away", "If I Loved You", "I'm Always Chasing Rainbows", "Catch a Falling Star", and "I Wonder Who's Kissing Her Now".

From 1944 to 1958, Perry Como had forty-two songs in the Top Ten. He had his own television show for eight years, and enjoyed a sixty-five-year reputation as one of the most highly respected singers in pop music history.

Doris Day

Doris Mary Ann Kappelhoff (b. 1922), born in Cincinnati, Ohio, wanted to be a dancer, but broke her leg in an auto accident at age fourteen. While recovering, she took voice lessons from Grace Raine, who taught her to "make the lyrics mean what they say" (Hemming and Hajdu 1991, 153). Her first singing job was with bandleader Barney Rapp who coaxed her into changing her name to Doris Day.

By age sixteen, she was working in New York with Bob Crosby, then moved to the Les Brown band for six years of success and great recordings, among them "My Dreams Are Getting Better All the Time" and "Sentimental Journey".

She broke into the movies in 1948 singing "It's Magic" in *Romance on the High Seas*, and immediately became America's favorite girl next door – blonde, blue-eyed, with freckles, a cute smile, a pug nose, and a trim figure. She eventually made thirty-nine movies (including some that didn't feature her singing, and co-starring leading men such as Cary Grant and Jimmy Stewart). She was twice named the number-one audience attraction nationwide, only the fourth actress in movie history to be so named. Her giant hit from Alfred Hitchcock's *The Man Who Knew Too Much,* "Que Será, Será (Whatever Will Be, Will Be)", won the Academy Award for Best Original Song in 1956.

Meanwhile, her third husband embezzled and lost $20 million of her savings. She turned her attention to television, and had her own successful sitcom from 1968 to 1972. By this time, her singing career was over, but she will always be remembered for a marvelous mezzo-soprano voice, clear and clean, with an adolescent sensuality produced by subtle inflections in the way she delivered the text.

Billy Eckstine

William Clarence Eckstein (1914-1993) changed the spelling of his last name when an agent suggested that the spelling "Eckstein" looked too "Jewish" in print, and perhaps might limit his bookings. A little odd, it seems, these days.

Billy Eckstine's African-American roots were deep in jazz as a trumpeter, occasional guitarist, and valve trombonist, and his place is secure in jazz history as one of the most successful and innovative big bandleaders in the age of be-bop. But it was his rich, deep, resonant baritone voice, his suave personality, and his movie-star good looks that launched him into a career as a romantic pop singer.

From 1949 to 1952 he was at the top of the pop charts with "My Foolish Heart", "I Apologize", "I Wanna Be Loved", and several others. His jazz-tinged phrases were long and lyrical, and his vocal sound was almost operatic, at times. He justly deserved the complimentary title, the fabulous "Mr. B."

Dean Martin

Handsome and care-free, Dino Paul Crocetti (1917-1995) from Steubenville, Ohio, had two careers, both very successful and profitable. The first was as one-half of the comedy team of Martin and Lewis; the second was as a pop singer, movie actor, television star, and lovable Hollywood playboy.

When he broke away from the talented Jerry Lewis in 1956, everyone thought he would disappear from show business. It turned out that he had a knack for playing himself – a charming, laid-back, irreverent, skirt-chasing, scotch-on-the-rocks style, Italian night club singer. Indeed, he often did his night club routine with a drink in one hand, a cigarette in the other, and a gorgeous young starlet not too far away.

Elvis Presley was greatly impressed, and tried to copy Dean Martin's vocal style and hip manner – especially that relaxed, gently slurred articulation of the lyrics, as, for example, in Martin's treatment of "Memories Are Made of This".

The critics were never much impressed with Dean Martin's singing, but the fans kept him up in the Top 40 for many years. "That's Amore", "Everybody Loves Somebody", and "Volare" show him to be a master of the casual manner with a pop tune. His charter membership in Frank Sinatra's "rat pack" and his friendship with well-known Mafia club owners gave Dean Martin a guaranteed career from the 1950s through to the early 1980s.

Lena Horne

Surely one of the most beautiful pop singers ever was Lena Mary Calhoun Horne (1917-2010), born in Brooklyn, New York. She began her career as a chorus girl at the famous Cotton Club in Harlem, then moved to Broadway's first all-black stage revue, *Shuffle Along*, and later to featured vocalist with the Charlie Barnet big band.

She was twenty-three years old, and had arrived at the top of the business. A three-week booking at Barney Josephson's famous racially-integrated Café Society in New York's Greenwich Village turned into an engagement of seventeen months, during which time her sensational voice and dramatic intensity made her one of the most famous singers in America. At the end of the 1940s, she was earning $12,500 per week in Las Vegas, the highest fees paid to anyone up to that time.

She appeared in fifteen movies, *Stormy Weather* (1943) being most memorable. She played Glinda the Good [Witch] in the movie *The Wiz* (1978), and finally, in 1981, at age sixty-four and still a ravishing beauty, created her own one-woman show, *The Lady and Her Music*, a masterpiece which ran forty-two weeks in New York, then went to London, then into home video production.

Harry Belafonte

Born in Harlem, New York, Henry George Belafonte (b. 1927) moved to Jamaica at age eight, then returned to New York at age thirteen. His first big break came in the film *Bright Road*, followed by a Broadway musical, *Almanac*. A recording contract with RCA in 1955 lifted him to a new level of fame.

With a pure baritone voice, marvelous diction, and striking handsome features, Harry Belafonte became a national sensation when RCA released "Jamaica Farewell", and "Banana Boat Song (Day-O)". From then on, he was considered a calypso specialist, but he continued to perform and record a wide variety of songs from the blues to Broadway show tunes.

He was also very active as an actor, record and film producer, and has received many honors, awards, and honorary degrees for his musical gifts and for his vigorous work for civil rights and humanitarian causes.

Nancy Wilson

Nancy Wilson (b. 1937) was born in Chillicothe, Ohio, and sang in school and church as a child. She went on tour with the Rusty Bryant jazz group at age nineteen. Jazz giant Cannonball Adderly heard her, and got her a recording contract with Capitol Records. They moved her from jazz to pop, and her career took off.

She brings a jazz musician's sensibilities to pop music, and gives every text a bittersweet, soulful reading. Her treatment of "Guess Who I Saw Today" is an absolute masterpiece of dramatic suspense.

She has a gift for storytelling, and frequently sings the verse to a song in a conversational manner, before settling into the beat-oriented refrain. As a theatrical device it works every time. "You Can Have Him" and "Happiness Is a Thing Called Joe" are on one or more of her fifty-three albums which encompass standards, Broadway show tunes, blues, and jazz.

In the mid-sixties, she had her own television show during which she established herself as a top-quality professional in every way. Certain aspects of Nancy Wilson's style can be heard in the recordings of Regina Belle, Anita Baker, and Whitney Houston.

POP GROUPS

Before the days of rock, there were several groups that performed the standard tunes of the day, sometimes providing their own instrumental accompaniment, but often just adding their voices to an already established band. These ensembles, mostly trios and quartets, paved the way to the future.

The Golden Gate Quartet

In the 1930s and 1940s, one of the most successful black groups was a gospel-pop crossover quartet from Virginia. Co-leaders Willie Johnson and William Langford called their special style "jubilee" singing, a term that had also been used for spirituals back in the late 1800s.

They began recording for Victor Records in 1937, and appeared in John Hammond's famous "Spirituals to Swing" concert at Carnegie Hall in 1938. They signed with Columbia Records in 1941, and were in the movies *Star Spangled Rhythm, Hollywood Canteen*, and *Hit Parade of 1943* (Erlewine 1991, 414).

Their 1938 version of "Stormy Weather" is an early example of what later came to be called doo-wop. Several of the famous Motown groups seem to have copied the musical style and stage mannerisms of the Golden Gate Quartet.

The Ink Spots

Jerry Daniels formed the Ink Spots in 1934 with Charles Fuqua, Ivory Watson, and Orville "Hoppy" Jones. When they returned from England after their first tour, Bill Kenny replaced Daniels, and they began to establish their signature style – an opening chorus with Kenny in a lovely high falsetto, followed by Hoppy Jones' dramatic recitation in a rich, resonant, baritone voice, and then a four-part conclusion to the tune.

Legend has it that the group got its name during a conference in their New York manager's office when an overturned inkwell spattered a blotter with ink spots (Shaw 1986, 183).

"If I Didn't Care" (1939) put them into orbit, and they appeared with Glenn Miller at the New York Paramount Theater. They soon became a featured attraction at the Apollo Theater in Harlem. For a while they were so much in demand that after their show at the Apollo, they would race downtown to do a late show at the Famous Door, a jazz club on 52nd Street. To get through the Manhattan traffic, they rented an ambulance and crew (Shaw 1986, 183).

Among their memorable hits were "We Three (My Echo, My Shadow, and Me)", "Do I Worry", and "Java Jive" in 1940; "I'm Making Believe" and "Into Each Life Some Rain Must Fall", with guest Ella Fitzgerald, in 1944; "The Gypsy" and "To Each His Own" in 1946; and "For Sentimental Reasons" in 1947. Their beautiful 1939 treatment of "My Prayer" inspired the Platters to do a similar version in 1956.

In 1954, the original Ink Spots broke up, and, since then, there have been over 100 other groups calling themselves the Ink Spots, with no connection to the original group or rights to the name, touring both in America and in Europe.

The Mills Brothers

As famous as the Ink Spots, well into the 1950s, were the Mills Brothers from Piqua, Ohio. Their father, John Mills, Sr., a barber and concert singer, got them started early. Donald was just ten years old, Harry twelve, Herbert thirteen, and John Jr. fifteen when they landed a job on radio station WLW in Cincinnati (Ewen 1977, 284).

John Jr. died at age twenty-three in 1936, and John Sr. filled in until his retirement in 1956, after which the group continued on as a trio with a guitar accompanist.

Imitating instruments by cupping their hands over their mouths, the Mills Brothers developed a unique and appealing style. After their first giant hits, "Tiger Rag" and "Nobody's Sweetheart" in 1931, they went on to record more than one thousand songs over the next forty years.

Most of their million-selling records were made in the 1940s and 1950s – "Paper Doll" (1943), "You Always Hurt the One You Love" (1944), "Lazy River" and "'Till Then" (1946), "I've Got My Love To Keep Me Warm" (1949), and "Glow Worm" and "Be My Life's Companion" (1952). They had a modest hit in 1958 when they covered the Silhouettes' "Get a Job". The Mills Brothers' last pop hit was "Cab Driver" in 1968. Their recording of "Daddy's Little Girl" has become a perennial father-daughter dance favorite for weddings.

***

Major stars of radio, recordings, and film, the Mills Brothers, the Ink Spots, and the Golden Gate Quartet established that special genre, the black male quarter, and opened the door to the future for all the doo-wop groups soon to appear in American pop music history.

The Boswell Sisters

In the early days of radio, the Boswell Sisters – Connee, Martha and Helvetia – made themselves a household name in the South singing pop songs on a New Orleans radio station. Their purity of intonation and their bluesy, infectious, swinging harmonies established the model for several later female trios (Erlewine 1992, 313).

Brunswick Records signed them in the 1930s, and they were backed by the famous Dorsey Brothers Band for many excellent recordings. "When I Take My Sugar to Tea" is their most famous trio number. They became regular guests on *The Kraft Music Hall* on NBC, appeared in the movies *The Big Broadcast of 1932, Moulin Rouge*, and *Transatlantic Merry-Go-Round*, and toured Great Britain in 1933 and again in 1935. They disbanded in 1936, and Connee went on to a distinguished solo career, even though she was confined to a wheelchair by childhood polio.

Connee Boswell was one of the first female pop singers to change notes and rhythms in her treatment of a song. This jazz technique created a different feeling from the stiff-music style so common up to that time. "They Can't Take That Away from Me", "I Cover the Waterfront", "That Old Feeling" were among the seventy-five million records she sold before her death in 1976.

The Andrews Sisters

The most popular female trio in the 1940s was comprised of sisters Patti, Maxine and LaVerne Andrews. They left Minneapolis, Minnesota, in their teens, and hit the big time in New York with a recording of "Bei Mir Bist Du Schoen", a bouncy Yiddish folk song given new lyrics by Sammy Cahn.

They went on to record many more giant hits, to appear in a half dozen movies, and to become the favorite vocal group of the American military forces during World War II. They were frequent guests on the radio shows of Bob Hope, Bing Crosby, and others because of their exuberant delivery and smart musical arrangements.

"Rhumboogie", "Booglie Wooglie Piggy", and "Boogie-Woogie Bugle Boy" caught the boogie-woogie fever sweeping America in the 1940s. "Rum and Coca-Cola" (banned in Boston), "Pistol Packin' Mama", "I'll Be With You In Apple Blossom Time", and "The Beer Barrel Polka" earned the Andrews Sisters lasting fame and fortune.

The McGuire Sisters

The McGuire Sisters – Chris, Dotty and Phyllis – sang for local hometown functions in Middletown, Ohio, and moved up quickly when they appeared on the national radio show, *Arthur Godfrey's Talent Scouts*. Decca Records agent Milt Gabler signed them to a contract, and asked them to cover the Spaniels' "Goodnight, Sweetheart, Goodnight" and the Moonglows' "Sincerely".

The group rapidly diversified and had great success with a series of film songs, including "Something's Gotta Give", the theme from the movie *Picnic*, and "Sugartime" (Hardy and Laing 1990, 508). Through the 1950s, they had seventeen Top 40 hits. Their nice blend and sweet style is remembered fondly by Americans who grew to maturity in the 1950s.

When Chris and Dotty retired, Phyllis continued as a solo artist, appearing regularly in Las Vegas clubs in the 1970s. She was Chicago mobster Sam Giancana's steady girlfriend for a long time, and when Sam was killed, she hired a twenty-four hour armed bodyguard for her personal safety and to watch over her enormous collection of priceless jewels.

THE HIT PARADE

From 1935 to 1959, the barometer of success for pop songs was a radio show called *Your Hit Parade*, sponsored by Lucky Strike cigarettes over the CBS network. On Saturday nights, the top ten pop songs were performed by a staff of professionals. Decisions as to which songs would appear were based on the number of performances the tunes had received that week over the radio, on jukeboxes, in sheet music and record sales, and among the dance bands around the country.

The exact method of calculation was a carefully guarded secret, and was the work of the accounting firm Price, Waterhouse and Co. Each Friday before the broadcast rehearsal, a Brinks armored truck collected information from several unidentified national locations and delivered it to the producers of the radio show. The top three tunes were not even disclosed even to the singers until the last possible moment (Ewen 1979, 295).

Many of the great pop standards appeared at one time or another on the show. The all-time hit, appearing thirty-three times on the show, ten times in the first position, was Irving Berlin's "White Christmas". Next, appearing thirty times, was "People Will Say We're In Love", from Rodgers and Hammerstein's *Oklahoma*. Finally, appearing twenty-nine times, was "Harbor Lights", a 1937 English pop song by Kennedy and Grosz which captured America's fancy in the 1940s.

CONCLUSION

There were many other fine pop singers and groups in the field, of course – Eddie Fisher, Vic Damone, Georgia Gibbs, Teresa Brewer, Johnny Mathis, Al Martino, Dick Haymes, and the King Sisters, the Four Aces, the Letterman, the Four Freshman, and hundreds more.

By the end of the 1960s, though, pop singing had changed beyond recognition. *Your Hit Parade* had already died a decade earlier because the traditional pop singers (Frank Sinatra, Doris Day, and the others) could not quite capture the style and spirit of the rock tunes that were sweeping the charts. Besides, the fans didn't want to hear anyone else sing their favorite rock star's new hit.

The industry had become so specialized and fragmented that there no longer was any single best pop tune of the week. Rather, we now had a best rock tune, a best country tune, a best soul tune, and soon a best heavy metal tune, a best disco tune, a best adult contemporary tune, etc.

The age of traditional pop standards was all but gone. It's not surprising, though. Songs are symbolic expressions of the dreams and desire of a nation, and America was a decidedly different nation in the 1960s than it had previously been, with changes in business, science, and education, and with the changes that occurred because of the civil rights and women's movements and the onset of the Vietnam War. There are still a few acts these days that fit in the traditional pop singer mold, though – Harry Connick, Jr., and Michael Bublé, for instance.

Chapter 18
Early Country Music

Country music lay buried in the mountains and flatlands of the Southeastern pocket of America until the early 1920s, when Ralph Peer (1892-1960), recording director for Okeh (the same recording director who captured so many of the early blues performances, see Chapter 12), began to roam around with his new-fangled equipment in search of folk performers. Francis Child and Cecil Sharp had studied and catalogued this Anglo-Celtic (Welsh, Irish Gaelic, and Scottish Gaelic) music, but Peer was not interested in scholarly investigations, and it is unlikely that he even knew about the work of Child and Sharp. Businessman Ralph Peer wanted to be sure that he got in on the new market for white folk music. A new market it was, indeed, and the flames of profit were being fanned by the new technologies of radio and recordings.

RECORDINGS

The Victor Talking Machine Company led the way, but soon the entire industry was involved. Victor had country fiddlers Eck Robertson and Henry Gilliland doing "The Arkansas Traveler" and "Sally Goodin"; Columbia had recorded a blind singer, Riley Puckett, doing "The Little Old Log Cabin in the Lane" and "Rock All Our Babies to Sleep"; and Okeh had recorded the singer-fiddler John Carson doing "The Old Hen Cackled and the Rooster's Going to Crow" with his treatment of "The Little Old Log Cabin in the Lane" on the reverse side.

The record companies were not sure what to call this music. They suspected, correctly, that the word "hillbilly" had some negative resonance, so they coined "hill country tunes", "songs of the hills and plains", "old familiar tunes", "old-time music", and other self-conscious terms. John Edwards of Cremorne, Australia, the world's foremost scholar before his death in 1960, called these early days "The Golden Age of Hillbilly Music" (Malone 1968, 44). But even today, the word "hillbilly" brings a mixed reaction. It is used, occasionally, by real country music insiders as a term of endearment, but citified outsiders would be wise to be very selective about when and where they use the word.

Mainstream entertainers took notice. Wendell Hall, "the red-headed music maker" of vaudeville fame, accompanied himself on ukulele, and with his own text to an old folk melody, came up with giant hit, "It Ain't Gonna Rain No More". Light opera singer Marion Try Slaughter recorded under forty different pseudonyms for nineteen different labels before he hit it big using the name Vernon Dalhart (1883-1948). Taking the names of two towns in Texas (Vernon and Dalhart), he recorded hundreds of folk and quasi-folk tunes and became country music's first millionaire. Two of Vernon Dalhart's biggest hits were "The Death of Floyd Collins" and "The Prisoner's Song".

But it was in August of 1927, in Bristol, Tennessee, that country music history was to be made. After a few years of recording blues tracks for Okeh Records, Ralph Peer left the company and, formed his own publishing firm, Southern Music Publishing Company, and started lining up talent for the big record companies, mostly Victor, in return for copyright ownership of all the music recorded. He put advertisements in local newspapers, set up a temporary recording location, and "it worked like dynamite" (Malone 1968, 86). Peer was now one of the most successful talent scouts in the industry.

Lured by Peer's newspaper ads in the Bristol area, several dozen acts appeared, two of which became the most influential forces in early country music, and "provided it with two of its basic styles" (Malone 1968, 63).

Mountain Music

The Carter Family produced a special kind of white folk music best described, perhaps, as "mountain music". Mountain music tended to be more conservative, relying on traditional songs and instruments, and it was performed in Appalachian high-nasal harmony. Today's bluegrass groups owe much to this tradition.

Alvin Pleasant "A. P." Carter (1891-1960) married Sara Dougherty (1898-1979) in 1915, and their home in Maces Spring, Virginia, soon became a neighborhood hangout for local music fans and performers. When Maybelle Addington (1909-1978) married A. P.'s brother, E. J. Carter, in 1926, she brought superb skills on autoharp, banjo, and guitar into the family. The Carter Family was well prepared to record when Ralph Peer arrived in Bristol, Tennessee (Malone 1968, 64).

Over the years they recorded some three hundred compositions on a dozen or more labels, becoming one of the most influential acts in country music history. Sara sang lead, Maybelle sang alto, and A. P. sang bass-baritone. That disposition of harmony parts is still common in "Southern Gospel" trios today. Maybelle's guitar style and some of her specific "licks" (short melodic motives) can be heard in almost any modern guitarist's version of "Wildwood Flower", one of the Carter Family's special numbers. Many of today's country guitarists, Chet Atkins among them, acknowledge indebtedness to Maybelle Carter's pioneer style.

A. P. Carter freely altered some of the modal lines in the many regional variants of the traditional folk songs they recorded so the three-way harmony felt more comfortable and up-to-date. He wrote a good number of tunes for the group, also, and, after they moved from Victor to Columbia and Decca, he secured copyrights on both his own works and the public domain traditional songs – many of which were deep fundamentalist Christian songs and the remainder of which were secular songs on topics of intense grief and despair. Those sad songs are still a big part of country music today – somebody-done-somebody-wrong songs, or "country weepers", as they are sometimes called.

In later years, Maybelle's three daughters Helen (1927-1998), June (1929-2003), and Anita (1933-1999) joined the Carter Family, and even after the elder Carters divorced, the group held together. After a while, Mother Maybelle and her three daughters continued on by themselves until Maybelle's death. June eventually became the second Mrs. Johnny Cash and the family music tradition continues with many Carter relatives in Virginia.

Pop Country

Jimmie Rodgers' style, simply called "country music", stressed more solo singing accompanied by instruments from the world of mainstream popular music, and he often drew on his early experience with black blues and work songs. Today's mainstream country industry has its historical roots here.

Jimmie Rodgers (1897-1933), known and loved by all as the Father of Country Music, had a sad career in many ways. His mother died when he was four, and he was discovered to have tuberculosis in late adolescence. With no formal schooling, Jimmie followed his father around the railroad gangs from one job to another. It was here that he learned blues and work songs from the black railroad men, and learned to play banjo and guitar.

He worked as a railroad brakeman and part-time entertainer for fourteen years until his tuberculosis sapped his strength. In the final eight short years of his life, he established the single most important career in the entire history of country music.

He wrote many of his own tunes with the assistance of his sister-in-law, Elsie McWilliams, a trained musician and poet. His repertoire included railroad songs such as "The Southern Cannonball" and "Waiting for a Train", rounder tunes like "Frankie and Johnny" and "My Rough and Rowdy Ways", risqué numbers like "Pistol Packin' Papa", lullabies like "Sleep, Baby, Sleep", cowboy tunes like "When the Cactus Is In Bloom", hobo melodies like "Hobo Bill's Last Ride", and a large number of sentimental songs depicting semireligious, nostalgic, and romantic themes (Malone 1968, 96).

But it was for his blue yodels that he was idolized. In that mournful utterance at the end of stanzas, he somehow tapped the deepest regions of a collective country mentality. Scholars argue about the derivation of the yodel – a kind of cross between a Swiss yodel and a black field holler – but they agree on its profound effect. John Greenway goes so far as to claim that the whole history of country music in Australia is clearly attributable to Rodgers' compositions, themes, and styles. And one of Greenway's correspondents reported seeing a large collection of Jimmie Rodgers records in an Inuit hut near Point Barrow, Alaska (Malone 1968, 92).

Although he often posed in a cowboy suit or railroad brakeman's attire for pictures, he seldom appeared on stage that way. For performances, he usually wore a light tan suit and a straw hat. He would put his foot on a chair, cradle his guitar across his knee, and captivate his audiences with a selection of tunes taking no more than twenty minutes (Malone 1968, 93).

In a voice unmistakably southern, he kidded his audiences in a whimsical fashion and beguiled them with songs that seem to catalogue the varied memories, yearnings, and experiences of small-town and rural America: nostalgia for the departed mother or "the old southern town" of childhood; pathos for the homeless hobo dying in a boxcar or trying to bum a South-bound freight; unrequited

memories of the sweetheart who proved unfaithful; laughter for the
rakes and rogues who "loved and left them" in every town; and a
variety of other experiences with which most people could identify
(Malone 1968, 93-94).

His gentle guitar and rough nasal tenor gave his tunes a kind of plaintive sincerity that is mentioned by everyone he touched. Professional musician friends, railroad workers, truck drivers, laborers, farmers, and housewives all felt that he was one of their own, and that he was singing directly to them. It made the bleak early years of the Great Depression somehow more bearable.

At his peak, he made $100,000 per year, but spent it on extravagance and medical bills. During his last recording session, he was so weak that a cot was placed in the studio. He would sing a selection, then rest on the cot, then sing another selection. Two days later he died. His body was transported by train to his home in Meridian, Mississippi, where today there is a Jimmie Rodgers Museum of personal papers, music, and memorabilia.

***

A great many entertainers made it big in records. A surprising number of them were household names in the South, but almost completely unknown in the big cities of the North. Uncle Dave Macon, the masterful comedian and banjo picker, had a large crowd of faithful fans, as did Ernest "Pop" Stoneman and the Dixie Mountaineers, Gid Tanner and his Skillet Lickers, the Carolina Tar Heels, Byrd Moore and His Hotshots, Dr. Humphrey Bate and the Possum Hunters.

Record sales of the 78 rpms outdistanced anyone's wildest dream. It is said that rural folks would go to the general store to buy a loaf of bread, a pound of butter, and the latest Jimmie Rodgers recording. Sears, Roebuck, and Co. and several other big mail-order companies carried their own line of records, as did many of the "five-and-dime" stores such as the Woolworth and Grant national chains.

The major record companies came out with special series numbers and with subsidiary labels to handle certain areas of music. Back then also, as now, the companies were buying each other, consolidating or hiring new production teams, and stealing each other's executives, performing talent, and engineers.

NETWORK RADIO

Equally important to the sudden growth of country music in the 1920s was another new engineer's toy called radio. Experimental at best before World War I, radio soon captured the entertainment fancy of America, and moved into nearly every home by the end of the decade.

WSB in Atlanta, Georgia seems to be first to broadcast country music, followed soon by WBAP in Fort Worth, Texas, which enjoys a claim to being first in the production of a "barn dance" format. The broadcast power (wattage) of these early stations was unregulated, and their signals often traveled to Canada, New York, Haiti, and Hawaii.

The most important weekly barn dance program for a while was the **National Barn Dance** from WLS in Chicago. Owned by Sears, Roebuck, and Co., with call letters for the World's Largest Store, WLS broadcast its first group of country fiddlers from a small mezzanine in the Sherman Hotel, April 19, 1924, alternating with the popular Isham Jones dance band from the College Inn.

The surprising response pleased the station executives, and they quickly formed the *WLS Barn Dance*, which changed names shortly thereafter to *National Barn Dance*. Mixing pop entertainers with country music acts, the show grew to be a huge success, moving to Chicago's Eighth Street Theatre in 1932. It was picked up for national distribution by NBC in 1933. In addition to the regular country music stars, the *National Barn Dance* presented a number of personalities who went on to various careers in show business: Gene Autry, Correl and Gosden ("Amos 'n' Andy"), Jim and Marian Jordan ("Fibber McGee and Molly"), "Lonesome George" Gobel, and many others.

George D. Hay (1895-1968), journalist-turned-announcer, had been a strong member of the WLS team in Chicago, and he was hired away to be station director for WSM (We Save Millions), in Nashville, Tennessee, owned by the National Life and Accident Insurance Company. He created the *WSM Barn Dance*, and served as its announcer-host. Following Walter Damrosch's *NBC Music Appreciation Hour*, George D. Hay, "The Solemn Old Judge", announced one early Saturday evening in 1926, "For the past hour we've been listening to music taken largely from grand opera, but from now on we will present the *'Grand Ole Opry.'*" The name caught everyone's imagination, and the program is still broadcast weekly, the oldest continuous radio program in media history.

To house the ever increasing number of performers, WSM constructed Studio A, and installed a large plate glass window so spectators could view the show. Then came permission for fifty people to be in the studio, then a small auditorium was built to hold five hundred, then later the Hillsboro Theater was rented. The show then moved to a large church in East Nashville, then to the War Memorial Stage, then to a converted tabernacle called Ryman Auditorium for thirty years or so, then to the Opryland theme park. Although Opryland closed in 1997 and was converted into a mall, the *Grand Ole Opry* building was separate and is still used today.

For a long time, an appearance on the *Grand Ole Opry* was absolutely essential for any credibility in the country music business, much like a Carnegie Hall debut for an aspiring classical musician. These days, however, the recording industry can create a big career separate from the *Grand Ole Opry*. It is still a strong emotional tie for the traditionalists, however.

Through radio and recordings, country music penetrated the urban-controlled popular music industry in the 1920's.

Chapter 19
The Western Influence
in Country Music

In the 1920s, largely through radio and recordings, country music had entered the world of popular music – that is, music created and delivered for commercial gain. It still sounded, however, very much like the authentic folk music of its origin. The topics of the songs, the instrument used, the manner of performing, the style and character of the "concerts", and the music itself were all just a cut above the level of non-commercial folk culture.

As country music moved into the 1930s, several substantial changes occurred. Two new traditions took shape – the cowboy and his music, and Western Swing as a special style category – and two old traditions came back strong – the "mountain culture" with its music and concerns, and a self-deprecating, "corn-ball" brand of humor.

THE SINGING COWBOY

During the Great Depression, waves and waves of poor folk traveled across the United States to find employment. John Steinbeck's *Grapes of Wrath* (1939) treated this subject with great compassion. As they moved across the nation's Dust Bowl, the poor farmers, share-croppers, and mountaineers from the East and central Mid-West encountered groups of unfortunates with similar social problems – cowboys, ranch hands, oil-rig workers, and other assorted drifters. They, too, had a rich musical heritage, and before long the two musical cultures merged into what journalists and scholars called for twenty years or so "country and Western music". Today, there seems to be a tendency to refer to this whole big mixed body of music as country music, and to designate specific sub-categories when necessary, such as Tex-Mex, old-timey, honky-tonk, cowboy, folk, Appalachian, bluegrass, flatland, etc.

Cowboy ("Western") music first came into the world of professional entertainment (including the vaudeville circuit) with Otto Gray and the Oklahoma Cowboys. Their radio broadcasts and personal tours were well received through the 1930s and 1940s.

The very first cowboy recording may have been made by Carl T. Sprague, "When the Work's All Done This Fall" (1924). Goebel Reeves (the Texas Drifter), Jules Verne Allen, and others became popular "cowboy entertainers" in the 1920s, mostly though the great power of radio and recordings.

Gene Autry

America's favorite, and historically most important, singing cowboy – Gene Autry – was created not by recording and radio, however, but by the movies.

Born on a tenant farm in Tioga, Texas, Orvon Grover Autry (1907-1998) learned guitar from his mother, but also played saxophone as a teenager in the Field Brothers' Marvelous Medicine Shows. At age seventeen, he took a job as a telegraph operator for the Frisco Line in Sapulpa, Oklahoma. While working the midnight shift at the telegraph office, Autry had plenty of time to practice.

One night, a man entered the office to send a wire. He saw the guitar, and asked Gene Autry to play and sing a tune. Autry did. The stranger then returned the favor, singing a version of the old folk classic, "Casey Jones". After he left, Autry saw that the wire was signed by "Will Rogers". The famed humorist came in several times thereafter, and encouraged Autry, saying, "Work hard at it, and you may get somewhere" (Shelton 1971, 157).

Shortly thereafter, Autry made several recordings in New York, then took a steady job (1930-34) in Chicago on the *WLS Barn Dance* as "Oklahoma's Singing Cowboy". The Sears organization took notice of his growing popularity, and promoted his records on the Silvertone (Sears) label, along with a Gene Autry "Round Up" Guitar and assorted songbooks and guitar instruction books in the Sears-Roebuck catalogue.

In 1934, at age 27, Autry went to Hollywood for a screen test. He was good looking with a winning smile, and Republic Studios' president, Herbert Yates, wanted to cash in on the new craze for "musicals". Yates told his chief producer, Nat Levine, to find a "tuneful cowpuncher". Then, too, the National Legion of Decency was cracking down on films with "morally objectionable" content, and all the studios were searching for a new style of clean family entertainment.

Thus came the phenomenal rise of a new American hero, "the singing cowboy". Gene Autry became a household name. He made over one hundred films, wrote alone or with a partner some three hundred songs, and created a huge market for western style clothing, especially hats, boots, and fancy shirts. Autry made an asset out of his limited acting skills. Audiences loved that "shy cowboy" manner in everything he did.

Autry's B-movie "horse operas", as the critics called them, moved the cowboy film musical three large steps toward mainstream middle-class pop art.

First, the songs were nicely integrated into the narrative. Instead of interrupting the story, the songs pushed the plot forward. Autry's songs could sway a mob like a Marc Anthony speech. In one picture, he sang a message to a pal in prison. In another, he used a ballad to unmask some crooks. He could sing good citizens into fury, and villains into desperation (Shelton 1971, 159).

Second, his instrumentation moved toward mainstream pop. With the introduction of the piano accordion, pedal steel guitar, and occasionally a clarinet or muted trumpet, country music absorbed instrumental colors and textures from the world of Hollywood pop music.

Third, the tunes grew more sophisticated in their melodic contours and chord progressions. Autry's giant hit, "Back in the Saddle Again", is a big step away from the plaintive simple ballads of the 1920s. The same can be said for his most popular recording, "Rudolph the Red-Nosed Reindeer". It is a pop tune, not a country tune, in every regard.

Rudolph the Red-Nosed Reindeer. Robert L. May, an office worker for Montgomery Ward and Company, wrote "Rudolph" as a children's story, and persuaded the company to publish the work and offer it for sale in Christmas of 1939. It was a great success. Veteran New York music man, Johnny Marks, wrote the tune ten years later, and asked Gene Autry to record it. Autry's 1949 recording became the second biggest seller in pop music history – up to that time – exceeded only by "White Christmas". Before it began marketing toys, clothing, movies, and became a television production, "Rudolph the Red-Nosed Reindeer" had sold one hundred thirteen million recordings in four hundred different versions in thirty-seven languages.

But Autry's career was already international before "Rudolph". All over the world, he was, as his publicity material declared, "America's Number One Singing

Cowboy". During his visit to Dublin, Ireland, in 1939, seventy-five thousand fans crowded into the streets. In 1941, the town of Berwyn, Oklahoma, changed its name to Gene Autry, Oklahoma. In 1953, Autry purchased the Placeritas Ranch, near Newhall, California, where many Westerns had been filmed. He renamed it "Melody Ranch" and used its seventy-two buildings and extensive acreage as headquarters for his radio and movie production facilities.

In several movies, Autry paired up with his friend, Smiley Burnette, a comedian, hillbilly singer, and songwriter. Burnette provided the comic relief from the relentless good-guy image of Autry's movie persona.

Through brilliant investments, Gene Autry built an enormous financial empire in real estate, radio and television stations, film production studios, Western-style clothing stores, sports organizations, and recording and music publishing companies. As often happens in American show business, the "inventor" of a "new thing" – if surrounded by competent business team – becomes not only active and famous, but wealthy beyond measure.

Sons of the Pioneers

Canadian Bob Nolan (1908-1980) formed a guitar-vocal group, The Pioneer Trio, with Tim Spencer (1908-1974) from Missouri and Leonard Slye (1911-1998), from Cincinnati, Ohio. After the addition of brothers Hugh and Karl Farr, the trio became the Sons of the Pioneers, and went on to a big career in the country music industry.

Bob Nolan wrote several of the group's big hits, "Tumbling Tumbleweeds" and "Cool Water" among them, and shaped the close-harmony style which was their trademark. Their three- and four-part vocal style drew more from mainstream pop music than it did from genuine country music traditions. They were smooth and precise in delivery, careful to blend their matched vowel colors, skillful in their phrases, and more "in tune" than the country folk groups preceding them.

The Sons of the Pioneers set performance standards that later groups would have to meet – the Jordanaires, the Eagles, Alabama, and others.

Roy Rogers

Leaving the Sons of the Pioneers to strike out on his own, Leonard Slye changed his name to Dick Weston, and appeared in a few minor movie roles. In one of those minor parts, he gets into a film fight with Gene Autry, and Autry forces him to sing at gunpoint. This minor part in *The Old Corral* boded well for the young and handsome Dick Weston.

When Gene Autry left to work for Columbia, Republic changed Dick Weston's name to Roy Rogers, and launched his career as "King of the Cowboys". He became Gene Autry's only true rival for fame and fortune. After a short period of understandable competition, they became good friends and colleagues. Roy Rogers and his beautiful horse, Trigger, held their own with Gene Autry and his steed, Champion.

Roy Rogers teamed up with, and soon married, a former big-band vocalist, Dale Evans (1912-2001), who appeared in many of the one hundred or more movies which eventually materialized. One of his most endurable recordings was Johnny Mercer's western standard, "I'm an Old Cow Hand". Roy Rogers and Dale Evans backed out of show business gently, and began to devote more and more time to their investments, to their "Roy Rogers" restaurant chain, and to humanitarian concerns.

Tex Ritter

Born in Texas, Woodward Maurice "Tex" Ritter (1905-1974) aspired to a career in law at Northwestern University, but abandoned it for the Broadway stage, eventually appearing in five productions in the early 1930s. He made frequent radio appearances, and was largely responsible for the "vogue for cowboy songs that seized New York in the early 1930s" (Ewen 1977, 392). He went on to sixty films and a full-time passion for promoting the music he so dearly loved. An articulate and highly intelligent man, Ritter ran for the U.S. Senate in 1970, but lost and returned to the world of entertainment. His most famous recordings were "You Two-Timed Me One Time Too Often", "There's a New Moon Over My Shoulder", "Hillbilly Heaven", and "The Ballad of High Noon" (also known as "Do Not Forsake Me, O My Darlin'").

***

The singing cowboys brought country music to America's mainstream musical preferences. The melodic contours of the songs, the harmonies, the rhythms, and the whole "feel" of the musical experience had moved from Appalachian bibbed overalls to Hollywood and New York.

A classic "theoretical model" cowboy band took shape in movies to weave the musical fabric of the new style. Give or take an instrument, the model consisted of guitar, piano accordion, string bass, fiddle, Dobro or steel guitar, and perhaps a clarinet or muted trumpet. How the delicate mechanical parts of the piano accordion and clarinet could still function after three weeks of dust, cattle stampedes, fights, and barroom brawls was never explained in the plots of the movies. Nor was the fact that the cowboys just happened to have a bulky string bass with them up in there in the mountains of Montana. That's Hollywood.

WESTERN SWING

The second big development in country music during the 1930s was a strange mixture of cowboy music with big band swing. Move the singing cowboy away from the campfire, put him on stage in the main ballroom of a huge hotel in Dallas, mix in several ingredients from mainstream 1930s big bands, and the result is "western swing".

Bob Wills

By all accounts, one of the best western swing bands was that of James Robert Wills (1905-1976) from Limestone County, Texas. With guitarist Herman Arnspiger, the 24-year-old Bob Wills began to play for dances in the Fort Worth area. Adding vocalist Milton Brown, the team changed into the Light Crust Doughboys when they were hired to promote Light Crust Flour on station KFJZ.

After several moves and modifications fraught with legal battles with former advertising sponsors, Bob Wills and His Texas Playboys settled into a long career based in Tulsa, Oklahoma. They recorded with Brunswick, broadcast often over station KVOO, and played regularly for throngs of ballroom dancers at Carn's Academy.

Known as the "Father of Western Swing", Bob Wills had thirteen musicians in the 1930s and eighteen musicians in the 1940s. It was a true mixture of country and big band musical characteristics – country ballads, blues and riff-based dance-band jazz, saxophones and fiddles, trumpets and trombones, piano, bass, drums, guitar, steel guitar, boy singer, girl singer, vocal group, and all fronted by the talkative and personable leader.

Spade Cooley

Of Scotch-Irish and Cherokee heritage, Donnell C. Cooley (1910-1969), from Oklahoma, acquired the name "Spade" from an exceptional run of spades he once held during a poker game. At his peak, he was Bob Wills' chief rival for popularity and influence.

Billing himself often as the "King of Western Swing", Spade Cooley became a Hollywood extra, a business man with his own gigantic ballroom headquarters in Santa Monica, a radio star, and a successful band leader. His music was a mixture of good jazz, country, and commercial dance-band arrangements. He came up in the late 1930s and remained very popular through the 1940s.

A man of strong emotions, Spade Cooley killed his second wife in a quarrel. The story is still cloudy and controversial, but there were some reports at the time that his wife had a secret lover. In any event, Cooley went to prison for eight years, and, three months before he was to be released on parole, he died of a heart attack while on a 72-hour furlough to play a benefit concert in Oakland, California.

A WORD ABOUT STYLE CHANGES

Looking back with hindsight at the whole history of country music, the style changes now in seem tame. Back then, however, these were matters of fierce conflict. The old time country musicians hated the fancy cowboy singers with their rhinestone shirts, ridiculous ten-gallon hats, and "cheap" manufactured "popular" tunes. They were sure that America was losing its moral fiber, and the new "music" – if it could be called "music" – was just another example of how some people would sell their soul to the devil just to make a dollar. The cowboy singers and western swing musicians dismissed the traditionalists as a bunch of old fogies who were getting in the way of real progress.

When Bob Wills came to play on the *Grand Ole Opry*, he appeared with a set of drums among the instruments. The *Opry* officials were outraged, and would not let him perform with those "wicked" drums. He said he could not play without drums as they were central to his whole style of music, western swing. Finally, they compromised. Wills could perform as scheduled, but the drummer and his flashy gear would be placed behind a curtain. Wills would be able to hear the drums, but the audience would be spared the indignity of looking at those evil things.

Being an expression of profound subconscious values and attitudes, music generates strong opinions, and, generation after generation, the "new thing" is considered an insult to the "establishment". And the establishment leaps quickly from "insulting" to "evil". Things haven't changed much since Plato and Aristotle spoke about the dangers of undesirable music.

MOUNTAIN MUSIC RETURNS

The third big development in country music during the 1930s was an unexpected return to the original stuff. As if to grasp and celebrate the past, several talented personalities rejected the modern trends. It was probably not a specific, conscious effort; it was just natural for them to do what they did best.

Roy Acuff

A Baptist preacher's son, Roy Claxton Acuff (1903-1992) was born in Maynardsville, Tennessee, and spent his early years on a tenant farm in the foothills of the Smokey Mountains. Moving to Knoxville, he won thirteen athletic letters at Central High School, and was invited by the New York Yankees to their training camp in Florida. A serious sunstroke and its lingering complications ended his athletic career, so he began to develop his latent fiddle and vocal skills. Before long, he was good enough to join Doc Hower's medicine show for an extended tour of Tennessee. He then settled in the Knoxville area and landed a job on radio station WROL and later WNOX with his own band, called the Crazy Tennesseans.

To avoid any thought of being derogatory to his native state, Acuff changed the name of his string band to The Smokey Mountain Boys. Although he played fiddle quite well, Acuff put the spotlight on the other instruments – string bass, rhythm guitar, five string banjo (played in the old-fashioned frailing style), and the Dobro guitar – while he entertained his audiences with vocals, gentle comments about the music and the life style it symbolizes, and a variety of stage delights (tricks with his yo-yo, balancing the fiddle bow on his chin, etc.).

Beecher Ray "Pete" Kirby (1911-2002), known on stage as "Bashful Brother Oswald", played an unamplified Hawaiian-style Dobro guitar. Invented by the Dopera brothers in 1925, the Dobro has a metal vibrating disk which resonates acoustically to magnify the sound without any electrical amplification. The Dobro is played flat like a pedal steel guitar. It is, in fact, the historical ancestor of the modern pedal steel guitar. Kirby's masterful Dobro work was the main factor in the unique sound of the Smokey Mountain Boys for forty years or more.

In 1936, Acuff recorded the first of his most famous works, "The Great Speckled Bird". Set to the melody of "I'm Thinking Tonight of My Blues", with an initial text by a little known preacher named Gant, "Speckled Bird" pictures the church as a group of persecuted individuals who will gain eternal salvation as a reward for their earthly travail. It is drawn from the ninth verse of the twelfth chapter of Jeremiah: "Mine heritage is unto me as a speckled bird, the birds round about are against her."

"The Great Speckled Bird" became a favorite in some of the Pentecostal Holiness churches. Folklorist Vance Randolph heard it sung in Pawhuska, Oklahoma, as an Assembly of God hymn, and historian W. J. Cash claimed that it was an official hymn in the Church of God (Malone 1968,203).

Acuff's second hit, "The Wabash Cannon Ball", recorded at the same 1936 session, dips into hobo lore to describe a mythical train that will carry the hobo to the land of fantasy. During this tune, Acuff used to imitate a train whistle, but some dental work put an end to his train whistle in the 1960s. He sang "The Wabash Cannon Ball" every time he appeared on the *Grand Ole Opry* for at least forty years.

Given the title "King of Country Music" by Dizzy Dean, the famous baseball pitcher, Acuff kept his focus on sacred and mountain-style music. He believed so deeply in the songs and their meaning that he sometimes wept openly during performance. In 1942, he formed, with pianist-composer Fred Rose, the first publishing house to specialize in country music, Acuff-Rose Publications, Inc. The company was an enormous success and made both founders millionaires many times over.

Like Gene Autry, Roy Acuff became an international star. During World War II, he garnered more votes than Frank Sinatra in a popularity contest among the American troops in Europe. His open declaration of traditional American verities – home, motherhood, God, patriotism, truth, and justice – made him famous, indeed. Attacking an American military position on the remote island of Okinawa during

World War II, the Japanese banzai charge shouted a battle cry meant to be the ultimate insult: "To hell with Roosevelt, to hell with Babe Ruth, to hell with Roy Acuff!" (Malone 1968, 206).

Even though Hollywood was creating its own western-pop form of the art, Roy Acuff was among hundreds of singers and instrumentalists who remained faithful to the mountain-culture roots of country music during the 1930s and 1940s.

RADIO PROGRAMS

All over the Mid-West, country music prospered on radio programs in its mountain-culture form and in its western-pop form. Often the two styles were mixed without any tension at all during the same performances. Each individual group had its own special personality, of course.

John Lair started his *Renfro Valley Barn Dance* in Music Hall, Cincinnati, Ohio, November 4, 1937, then moved it to Renfro Valley, Kentucky, in 1939. His basic group, the Cumberland Ridge Runners, and a wide variety of guests were broadcast over WLW in Cincinnati for many, many years.

Performing on WLW was, at the time, a big deal. From 1934 to 1942, WLW was known as "The Nation's Station", as it was the only station in the U.S. to broadcast at 500,000 watts, meaning WLW programming could be heard across most of North America, and, depending on atmospheric conditions, even as far away as Europe. (To give a bit of perspective, current stations can only broadcast at 50,000 watts, per Federal Communication Commission regulations put in place because WLW's signals were so powerful they effectively "blocked" other stations trying to transmit on the same wavelength.)

The *WLW Boone County Jamboree* broke records in 1941 playing to one hundred sixty-nine thousand persons on sixty-three programs in seven states during the summer fair season from July to October. Later known as the *Midwestern Hayride*, the organization featured the Willis Brothers, Bonnie Lou, Zeke Turner, the Geer Sisters, Kenny Price, and others in a its forty years of stage, radio, and television performances.

The same kind of record holds for the *WWVA Jamboree* from Wheeling, West Virginia, first heard in 1933 over its sponsoring radio station WWVA. Marshall Lewis "Grandpa" Jones was a big star in Wheeling for many years.

The Louisiana Hayride, broadcast first in 1948 over station KWKH, from Shreveport, served as training ground for Hank Williams, Webb Pierce, Jim Reeves, Floyd Cramer, Elvis Presley and several other big league entertainers.

The *Iowa Barn Dance* in 1939 had the four Williams Brothers. One of them, Andy, went on to a fine career in popular music. Kansas City had the *Bush Creek Follies*. In Fort Wayne, Indiana, radio station WOWO aired its *Hoosier Hop* for many years.

Dave Macon

Known occasionally as "The Dixie Dewdrop", "The King of the Hillbillies", and "The King of the Banjo Players", David Harrison Macon (1870-1952) remained an amateur entertainer until, at age 48, he tried to get out of a request appearance by asking the outrageous price, at that time, of fifteen dollars. To his surprise, the fee was paid. He promptly abandoned his mule-and-wagon transport company, and entered show business full time.

"Uncle Dave" became a celebrity with his own radio show, recording contracts, and personal tours. He was known for his slightly off-color stories, for his powerhouse banjo playing, for stomping his feet and cackling while he played, for drinking much whiskey, and for the many gold fillings in his broad and infectious smile.

Pop Stoneman

Ernest "Pop" V. Stoneman (1893-1968), his wife, Hattie, and their thirteen children were an industry unto themselves. From 1924 to 1929, Pop recorded over 200 songs for Okeh, Victor, and other record labels.

The Great Depression, however, cut that part of his musical career short, as the family lost their home and most of their possessions. In 1947, though, the Stoneman Family won a talent contest at Constitution Hall in Washington, D.C., which gave them local exposure. In 1956, the Blue Grass Champs, a group consisting mainly of Stoneman children, won another talent contest, this time on the CBS television network. That win lead to tours and a recording contract from 1962-1970.

The Stonemans were known for authentic mountain-culture music on sometimes home-made instruments, with great attention to the story-telling character of all that they did. Theirs was pure string music with occasional judicious amplification.

COUNTRY HUMOR

The fourth big development in country music in the 1930s was the emergence of humorists as a central part of the country music entertainment industry.

All through the history of country music, there has been a fondness for self-parody, gentle insults, and puns. The earliest pioneers laced everything with incidental remarks before, during, and after the songs. Even their names revealed an inclination for the absurd: Gid Tanner and the Skillet Lickers, The Gully Jumpers, Uncle Eck and His Hillbillies, Cousin Emmy and Her Kinfolks, The Fruit Jar Drinkers, etc.

It seems almost as though the country folk realized how "corny" their life-style and its music must have been to middle-class America. They had two choices: try to pretend it didn't exist, or go along with it and use it for a gain in entertainment appeal. They chose the latter, and several gifted singers and musicians drew away from their musical stills to devote themselves to comedy full time.

Minnie Pearl

Born in Centerville, Tennessee, Sarah Ophelia Colley (1912-1996) began her career as a dancer fresh out Nashville's prestigious Ward-Belmont College, a liberal arts school for wealthy Southerners. Shortly before her marriage to businessman Henry R. Cannon, she took an appointment as a drama coach in Atlanta, Georgia. To entertain her friends, she would sometimes pretend to be a little country girl, Minnie Pearl. Her witty remarks caught everyone's interest, and she was recommended to the *Grand Ole Opry* officials for a brief appearance.

She was an instant success, and immediately became one of America's favorite comics. From the make-believe small town of "Grinders Switch", she offered wry suggestions to the ladies in the audience on how to "ketch fellers". Her wide-brimmed hat with the sales tag still affixed and her old-fashioned mountain-wife dress became as familiar to Americans as Charlie Chaplin's tramp suit (Shestack 1974, 198).

Whitey Ford

Known as "The Duke of Paducah", Benjamin Francis "Whitey" Ford (1901-1986) toured as a banjo player with a Dixieland group in the 1920s before hosting NBC's *Plantation Party* on WLW in the 1930s. Always ready with one-line zingers and clever remarks, Ford usually closed his act with a rousing banjo solo followed by his tagline, "I'm going back to the wagon, folks, these shoes are killing me." The jokes leading up to that line were standard, good, clean vaudeville fare.

Lulu Belle and Scotty

Husband-wife teams are favorites in country music, and one of the earliest and most successful was that of Myrtle Eleanor Cooper (1913-1999) and Scott Greene Wiseman (1908-1981). They became *National Barn Dance* regulars before moving to Cincinnati for a stint (1938-1941) on the *Boone County Jamboree*. Scotty wrote "Mountain Dew" (based on an earlier version of the song by Bascom L. Lunsford), "Have I Told You Lately That I Love You?" (not to be confused with "Have I Told You Lately" written by Van Morrison), and several others. While in Chicago, their big hit was "Does the Spearmint Lose Its Flavor on the Bedpost Overnight?", written by Billy Rose, Ernest Breuer, and Marty Bloom.

In the 1940s they returned to Chicago, and continued working into the late 1950s. After their retirement, Scotty got a master's degree in education and fulfilled a lifelong ambition by becoming a college professor. Lulu Belle served a couple of terms in the North Carolina legislature.

Homer and Jethro

Guitarist Henry "Homer" D. Haynes (1920-1971) and virtuoso mandolin player Kenneth "Jethro" C. Burns (1920-1989) discovered that their parodies gained more recognition that their straight music, so they made a career out of spoofing major hits from the world of popular music. "Baby It's Cold Outside", "That Hound Dog in the Window", "Hernando's Hideaway", "The Battle of Kookamonga", and "I Want to Hold Your Hand" grossed millions for the duo and RCA Records.

***

The country music comics of the early years poked fun at themselves and the culture they represented, and they launched an industry still profitable and productive today in the radio and television industry. *Hee Haw*, which ran from 1969 to 1992, is probably the most famous (and durable) example, but Jeff Foxworthy, with his redneck jokes, and Larry the Cable Guy are more recent cases.

Chapter 20
Country Music Moves Uptown

The Second World War changed country music in much the same way as it changed black music, and because of similar circumstances: population shifts, an emerging pride in being "from the country", new purchasing power, technological advances in the recording industry, and economic changes in the music business.

The Appalachian white community and its closely related equivalents – agrarian, poverty level, working-class folks – across Mississippi, Louisiana, Arkansas, Missouri, Oklahoma, and Texas had to overcome strong resistance from America's mainstream middle class. It was not racial prejudice, of course, but class prejudice.

In the early 1940s, these country folks moved up from the South to work in the war-related industries of the North. With their new purchasing power, they wanted to buy recordings of the kind of music they had known back home.

As they had for black musicians, the independent record companies reached out eagerly to address the recording needs of the country musicians, especially Sun Records in Memphis and King Records in Cincinnati. The officials of BMI did the same – they signed up hundreds of country musicians and small publishers who had been neglected, often rejected outright, by ASCAP.

And the boundary lines between country and mainstream pop began to blur a little in the 1950s. Country stars were recording pop tunes and pop stars were recording country tunes. The tunes moved in and out of categories more easily than the surroundings, however. When Tony Bennett sang Hank Williams' "Cold, Cold Heart", he did it at a large supper club in New York. He did not put on a cowboy hat and boots.

TRUCKERS AND RADIO

During and right after the war, the trucking industry had begun to muscle out the railroads for dominance in moving material goods around the nation. And truckers, being spiritual descendants of the wagon masters of old, were and still are, strong country music fans.

The new independent record companies, the "indies", made sure that they got their recordings played on the powerful megawatt all-night radio stations that could reach out hundreds of miles. All across the Mexican border, untouched by American regulations, radio stations geared up to 500,000 watts to be heard as far away as Nova Scotia, Seattle, and other distant points. In mainland America, 650 radio stations had country music programmed sometime during the week.

At the end of the 1950s, eighty-one big market radio stations moved to a full-time country music format, and the number rose to three hundred twenty-eight by 1966 (Malone 1968, 265). Country music was clearly on its way to being what it is now – the second most lucrative music style in America.

MAJOR PERSONALITIES

Hank Williams, Sr.

Hiram King Williams (1923-1953) captured the hearts and minds of hundreds of thousands of country music fans in his brief career. He was a tenant farm boy, raised in poverty, untutored, unlettered, and terribly serious. By age twelve, he had decided to be a singer-entertainer. He was largely self-taught, but seems to have learned much in a few guitar lessons from an elderly black musician named Rufe Payne, known as Tee-Tot, in the streets of Montgomery, Alabama (Malone 1979, 233).

From age fourteen to twenty-four, Hank Williams knocked around in the life of a typical small-club, honky-tonk musician. He formed a band called the Drifting Cowboys, fell off a horse and hurt his back, got married at twenty-one, and yearned desperately to be somebody – all while abusing his body with alcohol and pills, and writing songs.

But finally things fell in place, musically. His first hit was "Lovesick Blues"(1949), written in 1922 by Irving Mills and Cliff Friend and previously recorded in 1925 by yodeler Emmett Miller and again in the middle 1930s by Rex Griffin. But Williams gave the tune an especially poignant treatment, and it made him a star overnight. From then, nearly everything he did in music turned to gold, and everything he did in his private life turned into tragedy.

He was always scribbling words on brown paper bags, envelopes, and assorted bits of scrap paper. The story goes that Fred Rose was suspicious when he first looked at some of Williams' tunes. Doubting the authorship, Rose challenged Williams to write a tune about a rich girl in a big house who rejects a boy living in a modest cabin down in the valley. Legend has it that Williams came back twenty minutes later with "Mansion on the Hill", a tune which sold in the millions just a few months later.

His tunes were dead serious declarations of his tormented view of life, and he sang them with an intense and passionate conviction. The titles are revealing: "My Bucket's Got a Hole in It", "I Just Don't Like This Kind of Livin'", "Half as Much", "I'll Never Get Out of This World Alive", "Your Cheatin' Heart", "Take These Chains from My Heart", and on and on.

This lonely, tragic, gifted man died, not quite thirty years old, of alcohol and pills in the back seat of a Cadillac on his way to a New Year's Eve performance in Canton, Ohio. His son, Hank Williams, Jr., also musically gifted, carries on the family name, fame, and life style.

When Tony Bennett, the Boston Pops Orchestra, and even the Muzak Corporation began recording many of Hank Williams' tunes, it was obvious that country music had taken a giant step toward the middle of America's pop music industry and that it was here to stay.

Eddy Arnold

Born near Henderson, Tennessee, Richard Edward Arnold (1918-2008) sold more than sixty million records in the 1940s and 1950s. His smooth, rich, resonant baritone voice earned him the nickname of "the Country Como", for the similarity in tone and style to mainstream superstar Perry Como.

Although he began singing and playing guitar in his teens and worked for several years with Pee Wee King, he didn't make a recording until 1944 at age 26. But his style was so immediately appealing that RCA promoted him heavily, and he soon captured a large pop audience in addition to his country fans. "It's a Sin", "I'll Hold You in My Heart", "Bouquet of Roses", "Anytime", "Just a Little Lovin'", and many more carried Arnold to the top of the field, and he became a regular guest on the television shows of Milton Berle, Perry Como, Arthur Godfrey, Dinah Shore, and Bob Hope.

Chet Atkins

Guitarist supreme Chester Burton Atkins (1924-2001) first appeared in 1942 as an eighteen-year-old fiddler on station WNOX in Knoxville, Tennessee. He toured with Archie Campbell and Bill Carlisle, but failed an audition with Roy Acuff. In 1944, he worked at station WLW in Cincinnati for a while, then moved to Nashville to take a job with Red Foley. He teamed up for a while with Mother Maybelle Carter and her three daughters, and during that time his singing was as important to the group as his instrumental work.

Gradually his guitar playing became his strong suit. He appeared at the Newport Jazz Festival, was a featured soloist with several major symphony orchestras, and played occasional solo recitals on the Library of Congress chamber music series.

In addition to his top level guitar skills – never cheap and flashy, always wonderfully musical – he carried himself with quiet dignity and reserve. This "Mr. Nice Guy" demeanor made him a logical candidate for a position of leadership, and before long he became RCA's chief talent scout and record producer. His huge reputation and keen musical mind gave him instant credibility with the inexperienced country musicians and with the mainstream recording stars who came to Nashville – Perry Como, Al Hirt, and others.

The Nashville Sound. With pianist Floyd Cramer, drummer Buddy Hartman, bassist Bob Moore, and guitarists Grady Martin and Hank Garland, Chet Atkins produced and performed on most of the RCA country recordings aimed at the pop market. These instrumentalists spent their spare time hanging out and playing jazz at the Carousel, a favorite Nashville nightclub. They brought those musical instincts to their work in the recording studio.

By the early 1960s, music trade journals were using the term "Nashville Sound" for Chet Atkins' recording sessions. Country music had moved another step toward Middle America. The arrangements were relaxed and open, the delivery was free from tension or strain, the sound was clean and clear, the traditional country fiddle and steel guitar were not used much at all, and the general jazz-flavored feeling was upbeat and positive. It was still country music, but a comfortable, happy, and appealing kind of country music – a perfect extension of Chet Atkins' personal and musical characteristics.

Backup vocals were provided by the Jordanaires, the Anita Kerr Singers, and the Glaser Brothers all of whom sang in a decided "pop-country" tone and manner. Many of them were trained singers. Floyd Cramer's trademark "slip-note" piano licks were found on an estimated twenty-five percent of all the hits which came out of Nashville in the 1950s, including Elvis Presley's "Heartbreak Hotel" (Malone 1979, 254).

Since those innocent days of the 1960s, country music has absorbed large chunks of the rock mentality. But back when Chet Atkins was the reigning influence, country music experienced one of its finest periods of musical sophistication and financial success.

Johnny Cash

For mainstream America the most visible country music star in the 1950s and 1960s was a dirt-poor Arkansas cotton farmer's boy named John R. Cash (1932-2003), fifth of seven children. Older brother Roy had a group called the Delta Rhythm Ramblers, but Johnny was too young to get into the act. It was only while he was stationed in Germany during the early 1950s that Johnny Cash started playing guitar and singing his own brand of urban-country songs.

Upon discharge in 1954, Cash married Vivian Liberto and settled in Memphis as an electrical supply salesman. He teamed up with guitarist Luther Perkins and bassist Marshall Grant to perform free on station KWEM. He auditioned for Sam Phillips' Sun Records, and came up with a regional hit, "Cry, Cry, Cry", backed with "Hey Porter". But the big break was "Folsom Prison Blues" in December of 1955 which got him on KWKH's *Louisiana Hayride*. After that, there were several major tours, the *Grand Ole Opry*, and a few movie roles.

His career peaked with a television variety show (1969-71), when he became a household name. He had earlier problems with popping pills, chasing skirts, drinking too much, and trashing motels. All that seemed to clear up with his marriage to June Carter, however, in March of 1968. He returned to his deep religious roots, quit the bottle, and stabilized his personal and professional life.

Cash's special kind of urban-hobo-country ballads sung out in front of a sparse honky-tonk rhythm section caught rock and country fans by surprise. Like many of the great stars in country music, Johnny Cash sang with such deep conviction about topics so dear to his heart that specific musical considerations became secondary to the emotional experience. His appearance with Bob Dylan at the Newport Folk Festival (1964) and a guest spot on Dylan's *Nashville Skyline* were no accident. Dylan and Cash were spiritual brothers in the rock-flavored pop-folk business.

Kitty Wells

The first of the female stars in country music, Kitty Wells (1919-2012) was born Muriel Deason in Nashville, Tennessee. She took her stage name from a Carter Family hit "I'm A' Goin' to Marry Kitty Wells". She raised a family while making records, touring, and singing at the *Grand Ole Opry*.

She was called the "Queen of Country Music", and loved by all who heard her Tennessee accent and country vibrato. She answered Hank Thompson's "Wild Side of Life" with "It Wasn't God Who Made Honky Tonk Angels" and Lefty Frizzell's "If You've Got the Money, I've Got the Time" with "I Don't Want Your Money, I Want Your Time". Her strong professional skills and high personal integrity opened the door for all future female country singers.

Patsy Cline

One of the first country singers to cross over into pop was Patsy Cline, born Virginia Petterson Hensley (1932-1963) in Winchester, Virginia. Her career began at age four as a tap dancer. She sang in local clubs in her teens, and got her first big break on the *Arthur Godfrey's Talent Scouts* show in 1957 singing "Walking After Midnight". The tune entered both the country and pop charts. She divorced her first husband, Gerald Cline, and married Charlie Dick at about the same time.

With her 1961 release of "I Fall to Pieces", she challenged Kitty Wells for the title of Queen of Country Music. "Crazy", "Who Can I Count On", and several more tunes soon followed, which established her at the top of the industry.

Though she died in 1963 in the same airplane crash that killed Hawkshaw Hawkins and Cowboy Copas, her business manager kept her name in the field through regular reissues up into the 1980s. In 2002, Country Music Television named Cline as No. 1 on their list of *40 Greatest Women of Country Music*.

Patti Page

Born Clara Ann Fowler in Oklahoma, Patti Page (1927-2013) began her career on KTUL in Tulsa singing on a fifteen-minute program called *Meet Patti Page*, named after a spokeswoman for the Page Milk Company. Taking the name with her, the singer moved to Chicago to be on Don McNeill's *Breakfast Club* morning radio show on ABC.

At the age of nineteen, she made her first big recording for Mercury, and pioneered the technique called "overdubbing", singing a duet with herself and a four-voice background harmony, all of which parts she had also sung. By the time of her New York night club debut in 1940, she was on top of the industry, at age twenty-three.

Her big hits up to this time were "With My Eyes Wide Open" and "Confess", and she had to sing those tunes for every audience. Nothing prepared her for the next event in her life, however.

In 1950, she needed a "B-side" tune for a recording date single. Many of her pop music friends were experimenting with country tunes, and she thought she would also give it a try. She picked out Pee Wee King's "Tennessee Waltz", recorded it in her trademark style, as a duet with herself, and went about her normal career commitments.

Within two weeks, the "Tennessee Waltz" blazed up the charts and became the giant hit of the day. It was the first tune ever to be No. 1 in every industrialized nation in the world! It changed her whole life. Country music professionals suddenly realized the potential of their field, and from then on things would never be the same in Nashville.

Les Paul

One of the most important guitarists in all pop music history, Lester William Polsfuss (1915-2009), from Waukesha, Wisconsin, began his career as a country musician, harmonica player, and comedian. Calling himself Hot Rod Red, and later Rhubarb Red before settling on Les Paul, he toured for a while with Rube Tronson and His Texas Cowboys.

Moving out of country music into pop and jazz, Paul spent five years with bandleader Fred Waring's organization, then moved to Los Angeles where he teamed up with and married Iris Colleen Summers (1924-1977). Summers had worked as a guitarist and vocalist with Gene Autry, Jimmy Wakely, and others. She changed her name, and soon Les Paul and Mary Ford recordings were finding their way onto the pop music scene.

A self-taught electronics inventor, Les Paul developed the solid body guitar, improved multi-track recording procedures, and a whole "New Sound", as it was called, in jazz-flavored country pop. "How High the Moon", "Lover", "Caravan", and "The World Is Waiting for the Sunrise" went to No. 1 for Capitol in the 1940s and 1950s. Shortly thereafter, two generations of rock superstars took pride in their original Les Paul model solid-body guitars.

George Jones

One of the most important vocalists in country music history, a central stylist, George Jones (1931-2013), grew up in Saratoga, Texas, where he sang in church while his mother played piano. His intense delivery and special brand of pain-wracked slipping and sliding from one note to another has been much copied. He is of the same cloth as Hank Williams, Sr., Merle Haggard, and Lefty Frizzell in the perpetuation of a style called "honky-tonk" singing. Honky-tonk singers favor "country weepers", the "somebody done somebody wrong" songs so loved by the true fans and so ridiculed by the sophisticates. "Why, Baby, Why", "White Lightening", "Window Up Above", and "She Thinks I Still Care" may be sung by others, but Jones' authentic stamp can never be removed from the concept of the songs.

His drinking and cocaine problems and his stormy marriage to Tammy Wynette kept George Jones in the newspapers all through the early 1980s, as he lived the kind of life so poignantly detailed in his sad recordings. In 1980, after six years without a chart-topping single, he recorded the poignant "He Stopped Loving Her Today", which shot to No. 1 on the country charts and stayed there for eighteen weeks. Although he had his last number one hit in 1983, his last album was released in 2013, and he continued touring until twenty days before his death at age 81.

BLUEGRASS

While Chet Atkins and others were moving country music toward the center of the American pop music, a movement in the opposite direction was taking shape. It was called bluegrass for reasons not entirely clear. Since Bill Monroe, from Kentucky, pioneered the style and his group was called the Blue Grass Boys, most scholars believe that fans and disc jockeys just made a leap from the specific group to the generic style, and called all the music of that basic manner "bluegrass".

The roots of bluegrass, and all country music for that matter, are found in the British Isles. In the 1920s this British music entered America's entertainment industry by way of radio, recordings, and tours. Bluegrass, specifically, harkens back to the string bands so common at that time – Dr. Humphrey Bate and the Possum Hunters, Al Hopkins and his Buckle Busters, Gid Tanner and the Skillet Lickers, the Coon Creek Girls, and hundreds more. But the real thing, modern bluegrass, starts with Bill Monroe.

Bill Monroe

William Smith Monroe (1911-1996) was born in Rosine, Kentucky, the youngest of eight children and a descendent of President James Monroe. Poor eyesight caused Bill to avoid the rough and tumble activities of his siblings, and he became rather shy and introverted. He took to music, though, and by age thirteen was playing guitar behind his crippled uncle, Pendleton Vandiver, a virtuoso fiddler.

At age eighteen, he joined brothers Birch and Charlie in daytime manual labor in East Chicago, Indiana, while playing for dances and parties at night. Before long they were hired as regulars on WLS in Chicago. Birch dropped out, but Charlie and Bill went on to a successful career as the Monroe Brothers.

After Bill and Charlie separated in 1938, Bill organized his famous Blue Grass Boys, and landed a spot on the *Grand Ole Opry*. His big hit from this period was "Mule Skinner Blues". Always searching for new and exciting sounds, Monroe added Sally Ann Forester on accordion and banjo player David "Stringbean" Ackerman in the early 1940s. The music was in a direct line with the 1920s string bands mentioned above.

A whole new concept arose, however, and a totally new sound emerged when Monroe hired Earl Scruggs, a twenty-one year old banjo player, in 1945. The new thing, now banjo-driven, changed the history of country music. The core instruments were fiddle, guitar, mandolin, banjo, and string bass, and the energy and spirit were high at all times.

Earl Scruggs

Born in North Carolina, Earl Eugene Scruggs (1924-2012) grew up in a large crowd of banjo players. For some reason, his part of the North Carolina developed a special "three-finger" style (now called "Scruggs style"), in contrast to the traditional two-finger clawhammer or frailing styles. By the time he was barely into his teens, Scruggs had surpassed all his peers in accuracy, velocity, and imagination.

After working with several regional groups, Scruggs got a call from Bill Monroe. Considering Monroe's fame, Scruggs of course accepted, and took his place in the group with Lester Flatt on guitar, Chubby Wise on fiddle, Cedric Rainwater on bass, and leader Bill Monroe on mandolin. This was the quintessential bluegrass band of the day, and the one which scholars and fans alike consider to have defined the style for all time. "Blue Grass Breakdown", "Will You Be Loving Another Man?", and "Blue Yodel No. 4" were among their best offerings.

Lester Flatt

Lester Raymond Flatt (1914-1979), ten years older than Scruggs, came from Overton County, Tennessee, where he learned all the strings. He worked with the Happy-Go-Lucky Boys and other groups before signing on with Charlie Monroe. He detested traveling, and soon dropped out to drive truck and work at a radio station.

Then Bill Monroe called, and Flatt joined the band on the *Grand Ole Opry* singing high tenor. He had to work on his guitar to keep up with the Blue Grass Boys, and legend has it that he developed the "Lester Flatt G Run" to catch up and finish the musical phrases on time with the rest of the band (Palmer 1977, 87).

Flatt and Scruggs

In 1948, within weeks of each other, Flatt and Scruggs resigned from Bill Monroe's Blue Grass Boys to escape the constant traveling. They teamed up to do a few radio shows, and before long decided to make it a permanent arrangement. They recruited Jim Shumate on fiddle, Cedric Rainwater on bass, and Mac Wiseman on guitar, and called themselves the Foggy Mountain Boys.

This is the group that got so famous with the 1960s college folk-song crowd. Their tunes had an infectious vitality and ringing brilliance delivered in large part by Scruggs' technical speed and inventive subtleties. All-time favorites include "Foggy Mountain Breakdown", "Roll in My Sweet Baby's Arms", "Old Salty Dog Blues", and "Earl's Breakdown".

"Foggy Mountain Breakdown" was heard in the background during the famous auto chase in the 1967 movie *Bonnie and Clyde*. Flatt and Scruggs also performed "The Ballad of Jed Clampett", written and composed by Paul Henning for *The Beverly Hillbillies* television show.

In 1969 Flatt and Scruggs separated. Flatt went back to his traditional roots, and Scruggs threw his net out into the deep waters of modern rock with his sons Randy, Steve, and Gary in a new group called the Earl Scruggs Revue.

Bluegrass caught the fancy of American, European, and even Asian music lovers. In fact, the Lost City Cats, five young Japanese musicians from Kobe, came to America in the late 1960s. They played all the great bluegrass standards note-for-note with stunning precision and virtuosity, and they learned it all by listening to the American records. They could not speak a word of English, but they brought the house down when they concluded their shows with a rip-roaring version of "Orange Blossom Special", led by their classically trained fiddler, Shige Kawa.

TWO INFLUENTIAL PERSONALITIES

A great variety of country music stars contributed to the growth and development of the industry along with Hank Williams, Sr., Chet Atkins, Bill Monroe, and the others listed above. Each had an individual musical gift and a personal way with a tune, and each had adoring fan clubs scattered across the nation. They sold records by the millions – Ernest Tubb, Hank Snow, Marty Robbins, Roy Clark, Conway Twitty, Roger Miller, Loretta Lynn, Tammy Wynette, Barbara Mandrell, Kris Kristofferson, Glen Campbell, Charlie Rich, and hundreds more.

Two careers stand out above the crowd for their special consequence on the business of country music in America.

Buck Owens

As a young man, Alvis Edgar "Buck" Owens, Jr. (1929-2006), hauled produce from Arizona to the West Coast, all the while playing guitar and writing songs on weekends. He finally settled down to cultivate a career in the night clubs and television studios of Bakersfield, California. He signed with Capitol Records in 1956, and within a few years began to attract a national following. In 1969, he created and co-hosted a hit television show called *Hee Haw*, bringing country music and humor to millions who had never paid much attention.

When CBS canceled *Hee Haw*, Owens bought it and put it on three hundred local stations himself. Between its cornball jokes and preposterous skits, the TV show offered the best of the established and rising talent in America.

In Bakersfield, Owens founded a publishing company, a record company, several radio stations, a record shop, a booking agency, and several other music-related businesses, and he was well known to help out country musicians in need of counsel and encouragement.

Owens' special mixture of country honky-tonk and rockabilly came to be known as the Bakersfield Sound, and fans liked to call the city "Buckersfield", the Nashville of the West. "Together Again", "Let the World Keep On Turnin'", "Who's Gonna Mow Your Grass", and "Before You Go" inspired many later singers, Dwight Yoakam among them. "Act Naturally", written by Johnny Russell and Voni Morrison was Owen's first No. 1 hit. The song was later covered by the Beatles in 1965 on *Help!*

Buck Owens retired in 1992, with twenty No. 1 hits to his name. He changed the direction of country music, expanding its coverage while maintaining its essential traditions. He was inducted into the Country Music Hall of Fame in 1996.

Willie Nelson

King of the Outlaw movement in Austin, Texas, Willie Nelson (b. 1933) grew up listening to his grandparents' gospel music. By age ten, he was writing songs and playing in a polka band. At age eighteen he joined the Air Force, but was released shortly after with a bad back.

From Waco to Fort Worth to Tacoma to Houston to Nashville, Nelson worked as a salesman and part-time disc jockey by day, while he played in local

204

rough honky-tonk clubs by night. During this time he wrote dozens of songs, "Family Bible" and "Night Life" among them.

Finally, he landed a job playing bass in the Ray Price band, and Price used "Night Life" as his theme song for a while. Nelson then wrote "Hello Walls", recorded by Faron Young, "Crazy" recorded by Patsy Cline, and soon "The Party's Over" which he recorded himself. These songs are somber and haunting melodies, true "white man's blues" (Green 1977, 163).

While making eighteen albums for RCA, he traveled far and wide, featuring black singer Charlie Pride on his show in the Deep South during the racially sensitive 1960s. He left RCA to sign with Atlantic, then moved to Columbia, all the while determined to make it without the Nashville old-boy network.

Settling in Austin with his third wife, he began his famous Fourth of July Picnics, which lifted him to cult status, and gave him a kind of hard-nosed authenticity in country music. Always a little off center, he recorded an album titled *The Troublemaker*, an audio revival meeting, with Sammi Smith, Dee Moeller, and Larry Gatlin. The hero of the title track is Jesus Christ.

Later he recorded *Red-Headed Stranger*, a semi-autobiographical concept album, which contained the Fred Rose chestnut "Blue Eyes Crying in the Rain". His most requested tunes are "Mamas, Don't Let Your Babies Grow Up to Be Cowboys", "On the Road Again", "If You've Got the Money, I've Got the Time", and "Always On My Mind" (later turned into a synthpop dance track by the English duo, the Pet Shop Boys).

In the late 1970s, moved by the death of Bing Crosby, Willie Nelson came out with *Stardust*, an album of all mainstream pop tunes. Its success surprised everyone, and "Georgia" became a giant hit. The album revealed an impressive grasp of pop-song phrasing, interpretation, and vocal nuances.

In the 1980s, Nelson, along with fellow musicians John Mellencamp and Neil Young, organized Farm Aid, a huge benefit concert to help struggling American farm families that became an annual fund-raising event. Nelson is politically active in other ways, too. He's co-chair of NORML (National Organization for the Reform of Marijuana Laws), a partner in a bio-diesel fuel company, a crusader for the better treatment of horses, a supporter of the LGBT movement, and an advocate for renewable energy.

He's had brushes with the law in the past, though, both for marijuana possession and non-payment of income tax (it was later discovered that his accountants hadn't paid his taxes for years). These incidents, as well as some of his song choices, garnered him the moniker "outlaw", which also applies to Waylon Jennings, Mickey Gilley, and a few other country performers. The term "outlaw", incidentally, seems to derive from their pronounced anti-establishment inclinations and from their determination to get control over their records. The big companies had buried these singers in layers of clutter – overproduced string arrangements, extra instruments – destroying any specific or unique musical identity. When the outlaws finally got control of things, they stripped the music down to essentials, and breathed new life into country music.

Another aspect of their "outlaw" status was that they built their careers without assistance from the Nashville old-boy musical fraternity. They ignored the conventional wisdom of a neat country-style stage image, and did their shows in dirty jeans and rumpled shirts, with earrings and bandannas, looking more like San Francisco hippies than country singers.

This all appealed to the then twenty-something music fans who were weary of the same old mainstream pop rock. The result was the emergence of "country rock", or, as some journalists called it, "red-neck rock", paving the way for the Eagles, Pure Prairie League, and others.

Willie Nelson is a country boy down to his toes, but through his hundreds of blues-tinged compositions and the symbiotic jazz-pop inflections in his vocals, he took country music into a new and productive age of expansion.

***

While Willie Nelson, Waylon Jennings, and Mickey Gilley were leading an outlaw movement in Texas, a different group led a different kind of outlaw movement in New York. These outlaws were black jazz musicians, not country music millionaires, but they, too, wanted control of their own musical destiny. It caused a musical revolution.

Chapter 21
The Be-Bop Revolution

At the end of World War II, the black jazz community was disillusioned. They had dutifully enlisted in the military, and had served with distinction. They didn't get the news coverage that Glenn Miller got when he took that big entertainment company over to England, but then no one could match Glenn Miller's popularity in those days. Everyone understood that.

What really disappointed and hurt the African-American musicians was the high degree of racism they encountered when they returned home. The war had temporarily removed some of the more obvious and degrading racist traditions, and things looked promising. But conditions soon returned to pre-war circumstances.

Bookings were hard to get in the better white locations. When they did get work, they had to go in and out of some of the clubs through the back service entrance, and they had to eat with the workers in the kitchen. Roy Eldridge told of touring with a big white band during which time his name was in bright lights on the marquee above the front door of the night club, "...featuring Roy Eldridge, World's Greatest Jazz Trumpeter." When he arrived to perform, he was not permitted to enter the club through the front door.

Record companies still favored white groups, and routinely cheated black musicians on royalties and copyright entitlement, and with dishonest sales figures. When the black musicians challenged the company, they were told to take what was offered or there would be no more recordings at all.

If black jazz musicians appeared in a film musical, those sections of the movie were deleted when the film was shown in the South. Lena Horne suffered that kind of fate, often. She was beautiful, famous, and a marvelous singer, but her scenes were edited out when Southern audiences saw the films.

Lena Horne was especially bitter over one incident shortly before the war. She was the featured singer in the famous white band of Artie Shaw. Shaw was well known for his insistence that his mixed bands would all enter through the front door, eat together in the main dining room (not out in the kitchen), sleep in the same kind of rooms as the white guests, and be treated with dignity and respect. He hired the best musicians in the business, and he would not tolerate their mistreatment.

On this particular tour, Lena Horne had her three-year-old daughter traveling with her. It was a big resort with elaborate recreation facilities. One afternoon, the child fell into the swimming pool. A teenage swimmer quickly saved the child, and the incident was a minor affair. It became a major affair, however, when a half-hour later, the resort manager had the pool drained and scrubbed out.

This is the kind of social setting the blacks found when they returned from the war. They quite understandably turned inward with their music, hoping to prevent more of the decades-old tradition of racism so painfully evident in their careers.

SOCIOECONOMIC CAUSES

It wasn't just racism, however. There were many other factors that caused the be-bop revolution, including the same population migration which triggered the rise of inner-city rhythm and blues and country music, for one. The downtown sections of the major cities were bustling with blue-collar black and white laborers, but the middle-classes began to move out of downtown, looking for more space, cleaner air, better schools, and safer playgrounds.

Out there in the village-like suburbs there were no huge hotels with giant ballrooms and spacious supper clubs. There was no Trianon Ballroom or beautiful Hall of Mirrors in Suburbia, U.S.A. Instead, there were little cocktail lounges with a trio or a quartet of musicians being quite sufficient for the evening's entertainment.

The Brunswick Corporation invented the automatic pin-setter, which allowed bowling alleys to stay open into the wee hours of the morning. (Prior to that invention, they would have had to send their teenage workers – boys who used to set the pins by hand – home at midnight.) Bowling alley managers offered all-night bowling at reduced prices. And many bowling alleys had good restaurants and first-class cocktail lounge entertainment to attract a wide variety of patrons.

Television drew dancers away from the large ballrooms, too. Fast food establishments suddenly appeared, and with a station wagon full of kids, the young married couple didn't feel like going out to dance on Friday night, especially since dad had to coach the Knothole Tigers at 9:00 a.m. the next morning, and mom had to get Susan to ballet lessons by 9:30 a.m.

The social revolution is well documented in history and sociology books as the "Move to Suburbia" or "The Beginning of the Baby Boom Generation". Roughly seventy-five million babies were born in the fifteen years right after the war. Those children became the flower children of the 1960s, and are now the famous aging "Baby Boomers".

MUSICAL RESULTS

As a result of the above social and economic changes, the big bands folded. In December 1946, at the end of the tax year, the big bands of Benny Goodman, Woody Herman, Harry James, Tommy Dorsey, Les Brown, Jack Teagarden, Benny Carter, and Ina Ray Hutton dissolved. Some of them came back later, but the great days of the glorious big bands were permanently gone.

The musical energies of the most restless and creative musicians were now turned toward a new art form – small combo jazz ("combo" being verbal shorthand for "combination"). The jazz quintet became the standard – five men (very few women at that point in time, and it hasn't changed much at all) on piano, bass, drums, and two horns, most often trumpet and saxophone. This was the model.

Melody

Be-bop melodies were angular, intellectual, and complex. And they often demanded great technical skill to execute. This new art was no place for the timid or inexperienced. Only the most dedicated and gifted would survive.

The practice of writing a new tune over an existing tune, but keeping the original set of chord changes, developed. Called the "silent theme" by Yale music theorist Frank Tirro, it became a universal habit in the jazz community. James Hanley's "Back Home Again in Indiana" was turned into "Donna Lee", "Tiny's Cow", and "Ice Freezes Red". Cole Porter's "What Is This Thing Called Love" became "Hot House" and "Subconscious-Lee". George Gershwin's "I Got Rhythm" was a kind of training ground for young hopefuls. It was turned into "Shaw 'Nuff", "Anthropology", "52nd Street Theme", "Oleo", "Cheers", "Kim", "Merry Go-Round", and several more.

Harmony

The be-bop musicians pushed harmony to its upper limits, extending their chords from sevenths to ninths to augmented elevenths and thirteenths. Then they improvised on these upper extensions, and a whole fresh new feeling entered jazz. The old swing musicians were distraught and the jazz public puzzled, but the inner circle of jazz performers knew exactly what they were doing.

They also substituted new chords for existing chords. To go from D-minor to G-seventh to C-major was for them dull and boring. They went, instead, from D-minor to D-flat augmented eleventh to C-major. Or, sometimes, they just altered chords to provide new sonorities for color and mood.

Rhythm

No longer charged with the responsibility of delivering a clean and clear beat for dancers, the rhythm section found new freedom. The drummer didn't have to pound away in a 4/4 pulse all the time, so he offered his comments on what was happening among the soloists.

Kenny Clarke and Max Roach were especially influential, and the young drummers coming up would copy them as they punctuated the musical narrative with "kicks" and "bombs" on the bass drum, "chatter" on the cymbals and snare drum, and an endless cushion of sound on their "sizzle cymbal".

The piano players didn't have to attend to the beat, either, so they began to join in the dialogue between soloist and rhythm section. Led by Bud Powell and Al Haig, pianists now began to "comp" (from, perhaps, "ac/*comp*/any" or "*comp*/lement") behind the soloists. They played short chords and motives which were answers to, suggestions for, and comments on what was happening up front.

Upright acoustic bass players now amplified their instruments and began to play a smooth "walking bass line" which outlined the chords. That strong rhythmic bass line soon became the center of gravity for the be-bop combo, along with the drummer's left foot on high hat cymbals on beats two and four.

Tempos were faster in be-bop than in swing, because no one tried much to dance. It became almost a mark of superiority for be-bop musicians to play tunes at blinding speed. It also kept the amateurs in their place, since they could seldom hold their own in such velocity contests.

Three beats, six beats, and occasionally five beats per measure entered the world of jazz during the be-bop revolution, but not all that often, generally.

Form

Not surprisingly, when the above three ingredients were so dramatically modified, musical forms remained relatively untouched. The traditional binary and ternary pop tune forms were still common. The twelve-bar blues came back into vogue, but few major innovations occurred in the design construction of jazz tunes.

During their improvised solos, however, the be-boppers stretched and pushed formal design. They would often enter to solo four to six measures after the basic design had begun, partly to wait for the preceding soloist to acknowledge applause from the audience and to return to a background location, and partly because they wanted some time to tell their story. Also, they would blur the edges of the form by planting musical ideas in early choruses which they would develop in later choruses. And it often took them nine or ten choruses to fully deliver their emotional statement of the moment.

Tone Color

This is one area where the traditional jazz fans were most unhappy. The be-boppers spoke in a different voice. Gone was the big, rich, robust sound of Coleman Hawkins' tenor saxophone and the sweet pulsation of Louis Armstrong's trumpet. Instead, crisp, tight, dry sounds came from the major instruments.

And gone, completely, never to return in jazz, was the bell-like, crystal clear sound of Benny Goodman's clarinet. A new day had arrived.

THE BIG THREE PIONEERS

Charlie Parker

Charles Christopher Parker, Jr. (1920-1955), called "Bird", is the second most important figure in jazz history, Louis Armstrong (1900-1971) being historically first.

Several stories are told about the nickname "Bird". He was in and out of jail frequently for narcotics problems, thus "jailbird". On tour in Kansas, his car accidentally killed a chicken – which the hungry musicians promptly picked up and roasted during their next stop. When he first settled in New York, he worked in a chicken shack. He played with all the poetic fluidity of a bird in flight. Take your pick.

In any event, Bird was the most influential of the be-bop pioneers. His speed, imaginative improvisation skills, and expanded sense of harmony were copied by everyone in the field. Horn players, guitarists, and pianists memorized motives that Bird threw out in a moment of spontaneity. His performances were electrifying, and his fame – in the jazz world, not in general society – spread until he had disciples all over the world playing his solos, note-for-note, from the latest recordings.

Every working jazz soloist on any instrument today routinely spins out a bundle of musical threads which Bird first wove into the new be-bop cloth of the late 1940s and early 1950s. Charlie Parker's improvised fantasies became part of the common language of mainstream jazz.

Dizzy Gillespie

John Birks Gillespie (1917-1993) was called Dizzy because of his comic behavior. He was the last of nine children, and he undoubtedly learned how to attract attention to himself. Whatever the source of his persona, the name Dizzy stuck, and the stories of his bandstand pranks are legendary – throwing spitballs at the band leader, stuffing toilet paper in a soloist's trombone, putting the valves in a friend's trumpet in the wrong order, making faces behind the back of a singer, and similarly harmless but disturbing things.

At his core, however, Dizzy Gillespie was a compassionate, brilliantly gifted, and extremely intelligent musician with astute business skills and leadership qualities. A colleague once said, "Dizzy, yeh. Dizzy like a fox!" He meant the remark as a compliment.

Dizzy patterned his trumpet style after Roy Eldridge, but soon found his own voice. With an astonishing wide range, and with velocity superior to anyone in the trade, Dizzy's solos are a marvel of poetic energy and savage beauty.

His home life was in direct contrast to his stage personality. He was married to his wife Lorraine for fifty-three years, and was never known to use alcohol or drugs. Strange, that this solid citizen appeared on the cover of *Life* magazine in the early 1950s in dark glasses, goatee, and a soft felt tam to represent the edgy world of be-bop.

Thelonious Monk

Thelonious Sphere Monk (1917-1982) lived in the same house in the San Juan Hill section of Manhattan for over forty years, first with his parents, then with his wife, Nellie, and their two children.

At age eleven, he played piano to accompany his mother's vocals at church. He quit high school at age sixteen to become a professional jazz musician, and soon won several amateur contests playing in the difficult stride style of Fats Waller and James P. Johnson.

As years passed, his piano style became more economical, more dissonant, and more rhythmically irregular and percussive. Lightning bolts of jagged notes would flash across an otherwise traditional musical passage, along with "odd phrases, unexpected pauses, tempo changes, and melodic quirks that always came together at the end to make a coherent, memorable statement" (Erlewine 1992, 1045).

His compositions have a stamp of their own. "Straight, No Chaser", "Well You Needn't", and "'Round Midnight" have become jazz classics. In spite of his obvious gifts, jazz fans sometimes found his music difficult and irritating, and his professional co-workers found his eccentric behavior embarrassing and unexplainable. On the bandstand he might suddenly get up from the piano to dance around the stage by himself. Or he might play something completely different from what anyone could reasonably anticipate.

In 1984, A&M Records released *That's The Way I Feel Now: A Tribute To Thelonious Monk*, featuring covers of Monk's music by musicians Peter Frampton, Todd Rundgren, Joe Jackson and others. In the 1988, a documentary film about his life, *Thelonious Monk: Straight, No Chaser*, was created after a large cache of archived footage of Monk was found. Big name musicians today still have strong words of praise for him.

DISTINCT STYLES

East Coast Be-bop

In New York and surrounding environs, the be-bop style was hot and energetic. Complex harmonies and melodies were driven by angular rhythms at ferocious speed. Dizzy Gillespie, Bud Powell, Max Roach, Charlie Parker, Sonny Stitt, J. J. Johnson, Tal Farlow, and several others led the way.

West Coast "Cool" Be-bop

In Los Angeles, the be-bop style was equally intellectual and complex, but the general mood and atmosphere was more laid back, or "cool" as they said. Miles Davis, for one, stopped playing like Dizzy Gillespie, and began to listen to his own (Miles') inner voice. The result was a style with fewer notes more delicately placed, slower tempos with more open spaces in the musical landscape, and a general feeling of relaxed control.

Miles' Capitol recording *The Birth of the Cool* (1949-1950) set the mood and gave the movement its name. Shortly thereafter, baritone saxophonist Gerry Mulligan formed a quartet with no piano. With two horns, bass, drums, and no piano, the quartet established clearly that be-bop need not be hot and heavy.

Progressive Be-bop

A kind of academic school of be-bop emerged, too. Dave Brubeck studied classical composition and brought those sensibilities to his jazz performances. He took his quartet on a tour of colleges, and found himself on the cover of *Time* magazine. Critics complained that Brubeck's brand of be-bop was a little too clinical, at times.

With similar training in classical composition, John Lewis enjoyed a career as a be-bop pianist and leader. His sparse lines and gentle touch contrasted nicely with Milt Jackson's blues-tinged and more aggressive vibraphone solos in The Modern Jazz Quartet, one of the premier groups of the be-bop age.

Third Stream Jazz

About the same time, classical composer-conductor-scholar Gunther Schuller advocated a "third stream" of American music that would be a merging of the two powerful rivers, classical music and jazz, into something truly different. He wrote several remarkable compositions to show what he meant – his "Concertino for Jazz Quartet and Orchestra", written for John Lewis and the Modern Jazz Quartet, for example. But the third stream movement never really took hold of the minds and hearts of American music fans.

CONCLUSION

By the early 1960s, the be-bop revolution had lifted jazz out of the realm of pop music into the world of high art. No one danced to be-bop, because the music demanded careful attention. Fans gathered in small clubs, and listened with discerning ears to the astonishing complexity of this new jazz style. Jazz was no longer America's premier "pop music".

Where would the art form go now? How would the flower children of the 1960s respond to this complex new jazz language? For their parents and grandparents, jazz had been a light-hearted form of adolescent rebellion. What would happen to jazz in the hands of really serious social rebels like the Woodstock generation?

As it turns out, not every member of the Woodstock generation was a social rebel. There were many serious young men and women who loved rock, but also loved the complex arrangements they played in their local high school jazz bands. In addition, there were many college music majors who were unfulfilled by the aimless meanderings of psychedelic rock that dominated the airways. The future of jazz was transformed by these talented youth, who longed to combine the jazz they loved with the rock and roll they heard all around them. They would combine the two genres and create a new one, fusion, which will be discussed in Chapter 29.

Chapter 22
Rhythm and Blues

World War II changed America's economic and social conditions dramatically, and, as always, the new socioeconomic circumstances were revealed in new musical behavior. The new music was not immediately available throughout America, however, because the giant record companies, the "majors" – RCA, Columbia, Decca, Capitol, MGM, and Mercury – thought that it was too much of a risk. Big corporations go for guaranteed profit, so they continued with their usual fare – Bing Crosby, Frank Sinatra, Jo Stafford, Doris Day, and the other established winners.

The majors produced the recording sessions, manufactured the recordings, pressed them out in their own factories, and distributed them through their own network of wholesale outlets. Included among the established winners were some black stars like the Ink Spots, Nat "King" Cole, the Mills Brothers, and Lena Horne. Their music was not representative of real black life in America, however. They were black stars, marvelously talented and very professional, but they were creating a white musical product for a white audience. They were not indifferent to the plight of their race, and they often used their fame and wealth to improve things. Still, they were part of the "white" pop music establishment.

Meanwhile, in the genuine black community, a revolution was taking shape – a monumental upheaval which would lift black music up and put it in the absolute center of mainstream American pop music. Five war-related circumstances were responsible for this revolution: population shifts, an emerging black pride, new black purchasing power, technological advances in the recording industry, and economic changes in the music business.

POPULATION SHIFTS

Large numbers of human beings moved all over the globe during World War II. Eighteen to twenty-five year old men by the thousands volunteered for the

216

military. They took with them the folk and pop music of their home territories – country music from Texas and Tennessee, blues from the fields of Alabama, standard pop tunes from Oregon and Wisconsin, etc. They lay on their Army cots listening to the music of other servicemen, sometimes hearing, for the first time, tunes far different from what they had heard in their childhoods.

Entire divisions of military personnel were airlifted from one continent to another in a few weeks, and boys who had never been very far away from home found themselves on duty overseas. Civilians, too, especially the blue-collar laboring class, left the Deep South and the rural Mid-West for employment in the big cities.

Nearly a million Southern blacks moved to work in the shipyards and airplane factories of the West and in Northern industrial centers. "This migrant black population contained not only a significant number of talented performers, but also a vast potential audience seeking entertainment of the kind they had grown familiar with 'back home'" (Futrell 1982, 8).

Entertainment back home included, of course, authentic black music, not the pop music being turned out by the white major labels. Soon the music of black inner-city nightclubs and bars took on the highly charged vocal emotionalism of down-home blues and storefront gospel, mixed with the throbbing rhythms of the boogie-woogie pianists and the famous black big bands. Thus, by the late 1940s, the big industrial centers with large black populations – Los Angeles, Detroit, Chicago, New York, Philadelphia, Boston, and elsewhere – exploded with the new music, called "jump blues" for a while, but soon universally known in both black and white circles as rhythm and blues, and later, as R&B.

BLACK PRIDE

America's black citizens had fought valiantly in World War II, and had carried out their patriotic duties on the home front right alongside the whites with bond rallies, scrap metal collections, paper recycling, gas rationing, touring entertainment shows, and the like.

Despite wartime promises, however, when the country returned to business as usual, it was discrimination as usual, with blacks still being excluded from white areas of entertainment.

They were compelled to turn for entertainment to their own ghettos where the jukebox, whose use greatly expanded during the wartime shortage of live music, had become the instrument for listening and dancing (Shaw 1986, 187-188).

The black community took great pride in the accomplishments of Louis Armstrong, Fletcher Henderson, Duke Ellington, and Count Basie, but they knew full well that Benny Goodman, Glenn Miller, Tommy Dorsey, and the other white bandleaders had become famous and wealthy partly because of their marvelous talents to be sure, but also just because they were white, and therefore favored by the white corporations in control of the music industry.

With the new rhythm and blues style (henceforth abbreviated R&B), they were determined to avoid being exploited again by unscrupulous white agents and record companies. The same mixed feeling of "rage, resentment, and pride in black musicians' commercially undervalued artistry and creativity" was the basis, incidentally, of the be-bop revolution which was taking shape elsewhere in the black community (Shaw 1986, 188).

NEW BLACK PURCHASING POWER

Brutal as the hard-core black poverty was in the cities of the North, it was still an improvement over share-cropping in the South. The good salaries paid in the war-related industrial plants of the North created small business opportunities for black-owned clothing outlets, grocery stores, auto repair shops, dry cleaning services, household goods, neighborhood restaurants, bars, dance halls, apartment buildings, and such.

The result was a new experience for the blacks – what economists call "disposable income" – and part of the disposable income that went for entertainment found its way into the new black-owned record stores. These record stores were not in the old-boy white business network, and therefore not beholden to the majors for their inventory. They were eager to stock the recordings which the new black-directed radio stations were playing.

TECHNOLOGICAL ADVANCES

Recording Techniques

The records being played over the black-directed radio stations were supplied by small independent record companies, the "indies" as they are called by historians. The indies went out into the night clubs, set up their equipment, and made acceptable master tapes for conversion to vinyl discs. In the space of a few days, they could record a local group, and get that record played on the radio, and put it on all the jukeboxes in the neighborhood.

All this was made possible by the development of the magnetic recording process. Developed by the Germans to guide their radio-controlled V-2 bombs and then quickly modified for the mass distribution of Hitler's propaganda speeches, the magnetic tape recorder revolutionized the music industry.

Recording was no longer confined to those gigantic and elaborate studios owned by the majors in a few big cities. Tolerably decent recordings could now be made anywhere, at any time of the day, by untrained personnel who knew very little about engineering or acoustics.

Around the same time, hi-fi 45-rpm (45 revolutions per minute) technology exploded on the scene. Peter Goldmark, head of CBS Laboratories for many years, had invented high fidelity, "hi-fi" as it came to be called, and the 33-1/3 revolutions per minute process way back in the 1930s. He was designing phonograph equipment to handle the remarkable new product when the war broke out. Everything was therefore put on hold for a few years.

After the war, when CBS made its move to 33-1/3 rpms, RCA countered with a 45-rpm record, and immediately invented a little economical 45-rpm playback unit. CBS then caught up by making a three-speed turntable with an adapter for the 45-rpm option. The result of this corporate warfare was a huge jump in pop singles. And it was in the world of 45-rpm singles (two sides, the favored one called the A-side, and the throw away gesture called the B-side) that rhythm and blues had its first great moment in pop music history.

Musical Instruments

By the middle of the 1940s, nearly all guitar players were using amplification. Primitive as the contact microphones, amplifiers, and speakers were, they still created a new and exciting sound, with untold possibilities in lyrical expression, tone modification, percussive effects, and gradations of volume.

Upright "stand up" string bass players soon joined the guitarists in amplifying their instruments, and before long most bands were putting a microphone somewhere down in the piano. Horn players then moved to play into the singer's microphone, and soon the entire band was amplified. A new sound-style had been born.

About the same time, a remarkable invention appeared, the Hammond B-3 Organ. The basic sound was created by small discs rotating through a magnetic field. That sound was amplified through a slowly revolving Leslie speaker. The player's right foot controlled the dynamics (loud and soft) with a large pedal about the size of an accelerator on a big truck. Down near the player's left foot was an octave pedal board.

The overall variety of funky sounds available on the Hammond B-3 was absolutely singular to inner-city R&B for at least twenty years. The instrument later made a comeback in the 1990s.

Another special instrument appeared at the same time, the Fender Rhodes electric piano. Pianist and do-it-yourself electric tinkerer Harold Rhodes invented the piano when he needed more instruments for therapeutic music lessons he was giving to wounded military men. He took some spare hydraulic parts from an old B-17 bomber, and fashioned a working piano for himself. The first ones fit on a hospital tray so the men could practice without getting out of bed. The Rhodes electric piano has a classic blues-tinged sound that also made a comeback in the 1990s.

ECONOMIC CHANGES IN THE MUSIC BUSINESS

With new technology came new business practices, of course. Three major changes in the industry moved R&B into a position of considerable influence and financial gain: the rise of independent record companies, the formations of BMI, and the emergence of Top 40 radio.

The Indies

The big establishment record companies, the majors, were now in trouble. They had controlled "race music" before the war with their subsidiaries created specifically for the black market. But faced with shellac quotas and other stringencies during the war, the majors had scaled down their black music and devoted themselves to white mainstream merchandise (Shaw 1986, 188). The resultant void was filled by a new breed of maverick entrepreneurs.

Although some members of this new breed entered the field because of a fondness for black music, most of them just sensed that there was a lot of money to be made. They saw the rising demand for R&B records, they saw the big corporations stumbling around instead of addressing the demand, and they saw hundreds of black musicians and singers out there who knew absolutely nothing about, and had no lawyers to advise them on, the intricacies of copyright royalties, contracts, performance rights, recording residuals, and related matters. These new record company owners were among the most flamboyant and slippery businessmen in the history of America pop music, and several of them had mobster friends.

Some four hundred new record companies were started in the 1940s, and by the 1950s one hundred or more were still around, strong and productive (Chapple and Garofalo 1977, 29). Each company would create several subsidiary companies partly to separate their various artists and target markets, but also to get around the radio stations reluctance to play too many songs from the same label.

> George Goldner, for example, launched Rama in New York and hit paydirt when his fifth release, the Crows "Gee", crossed over to go top twenty on the pop charts early in 1954. Had he followed up this success with another potential winner on Rama, he might have found airplay limited.
>
> He therefore set up subsidiary logos – Gee, End, and Gone. He could then count on airplay for the Teenagers (on Gee), the Imperials (on End), and the Dubs (on Gone), ostensibly three separate [labels] but in fact, all housed under one roof (Futrell 1982, 9).

Goldner was also a compulsive gambler, and he kept selling his subsidiaries to Morris Levy to pay off big debts. Levy owned Roulette Records and Birdland, the New York jazz nightclub, and was well known in the industry for his Mafia connections.

Jerry Wexler formed many subsidiaries, too. He split Atlantic Record's product among various distributors. It just made good business sense, he said.

> *Suppose you have ten records, all with good potential. It would be a lot to expect one distributor to make them all go. But divide them into two groups of five [records] each, with each group given to a different distributor, and you've got a considerably better chance* (Chapple and Garofalo 1977, 34).

Also to be considered were tax laws which favored the creation of many separate corporations, for each new corporation could claim office rent, telephone bills, headquarters needs, company automobiles, executive salaries, travel expenses, and dozens more deductible operation expenditures on paper, when in fact they were all under one roof and one owner.

There were independent record companies all over America, but three cities stood above the crowd because they were the central magnet for three different migration paths which produced three distinct sub-styles of R&B:

1) Chicago received the bulk of the blacks who came up the Mississippi River from Arkansas, Alabama, and that region which produced a delta-blues-flavored kind of R&B,

2) Los Angeles received a large crowd of bluesmen from Oklahoma, Texas, and the Southwest region which produced a kind of honky-tonk, jazz-tinged R&B, and

3) New York received a large number of bluesmen from the Carolinas, Florida, Georgia, and the Piedmont area which produced a pop-gospel kind of R&B.

The above generalizations are highly over-simplified, and there are major exceptions everywhere. Still, for purposes of this survey textbook, the large view will be helpful.

CHICAGO

Chess Records

In the 1930s and early 1940s, Polish immigrants Phil and Leonard Chess operated several after-hours clubs in Chicago, the last being the Macomba, a South Side jazz and blues club at 39th and Cottage Grove. One of their blues singers, Andrew Tibbs, was getting a lot of attention from local talent scouts. There were only a few record companies at the time in Chicago, so the shrewd businessmen decided to record Tibbs themselves.

The bought into the existing Aristocrat label, changed the name to Chess, and set up shop in a street-level store front at 71st and Phillips. The inventive Leonard Chess hung an open mike in their tiny toilet room (for resonance) and suspended a ten-foot section of sewer pipe from the ceiling (for reverberation) (Shaw 1978, 289).

Andrew Tibbs' record – the new company's first – "Union Man Blues" backed by "Bilbo's Dead" (banned in the South), carried the catalog number 1425, the number of the house on South Karlov Avenue in Chicago's Jewish section where the Chess brothers lived. For distribution, they drove around the South Side, peddling their finished records from the trunk of their car. "Every porter, Pullman conductor, beauty operator, and barbershop owner in town was selling records in those days" (Shaw 1978, 289).

From that modest beginning, Chess Records (and its subsidiaries Checker and Argo) became a huge force in R&B, eventually recording Muddy Waters, Howlin' Wolf, John Lee Hooker, the Moonglows, Chuck Berry, the Monotones, Little Walter, Sonny Boy Williamson, Bo Diddley, the Flamingos, and jazzmen Ramsey Lewis, Ahmad Jamal, and Wes Montgomery.

Chess Records gets into the history books, of course, for two reasons: (1) one of its early releases by Muddy Waters in 1950, "Rollin' Stone", served as the inspiration for the name of the British rock group and also the name of the rock counterculture news journal, and (2) its biggest star, Chuck Berry, is considered by most rock historians to be the "Father of Rock and Roll".

LOS ANGELES

Specialty

Second-generation Hungarian Art Lupe formed this company, and set out to find out what would sell. He bought $200 worth of records from several different black record stores in the Watts area, and with a stop-watch, analyzed the recordings for the length of introductions, choruses, vocal solos, instrumental interludes, etc. Among his most talented stars were Lloyd Price, the Soul Stirrers (Sam Cooke's training ground), and the wild and unpredictable Little Richard Penniman.

Imperial

Lewis Chudd, founder of Imperial Records, had an eye on the Mexican market for his Imperial label, but he also wanted to record R&B, so in 1949 he went on a recruiting trip to the Deep South. Arriving in New Orleans, he met one of Imperial's talent scouts, Dave Bartholomew, who had previously played trumpet for Duke Ellington. Bartholomew took Chudd to the Hideaway Club to see a big guy who had been playing piano with Bartholomew's band. Chudd signed Antoine "Fats" Domino that night.

Besides Domino, Chudd recorded a variety of first class musicians, the most famous of whom were R&B legend T-Bone Walker and the more rockabilly Ricky Nelson.

NEW YORK-NEW JERSEY

Atlantic

In the East Central area, several labels dominated things. Atlantic, formed in 1947 by Ahmet Ertegun, the Turkish ambassador's son, recorded a lot of top level R&B talent – Joe Turner, Ruth Brown, LaVern Baker, Clyde McPhatter, Ray Charles, Ivory Joe Hunter, the Coasters, and Aretha Franklin.

Jubilee

Jerry Blaine's company struck gold with the Orioles' "Cryin' in the Chapel" in 1953. With the help of Herb Abramson, a dentist and part-time talent scout, Jubilee recorded the Royaltones, the Cadillacs, the Four Tunes, and Edna McGriff.

Savoy Records

Formed in 1942 by Herman Lubinsky, Savoy had the teenage Little Esther Phillips, Big Maybelle, and Varetta Dillard – and Lubinsky "paid scarcely ever a dime in royalties" (Dannen 1990, 31).

Rama

George Goldner's Rama, as a subsidiary of Tico, had the Crows, Little Anthony and the Imperials, Frankie Lymon and the Teenagers, and the Chantels. When Morris Levy bought Rama and its talent from Goldner, he, too, found ingenious ways to avoid paying the performers their rightful earnings.

ELSEWHERE

Of the dozens of other companies in dozens of other cities, two deserve special mention.

Sun Records

Sam Phillips' career as a radio announcer was just dull. Bored with mediocre country music and the polite dance bands he handled night after night, Phillips opened up his own Memphis Recording Service. In no time at all, his keen instincts led him to record a number of territorial bluesmen – B. B. King, Bobby Bland, Howlin' Wolf, Walter Horton, and several others.

Sun was just a production studio, however, and Phillips leased his aluminum masters to Chess Records in Chicago. When he saw the enormous money being made, he formed his own full company.

One of his first releases was "Bear Cat", by Rufus Thomas, an answer to Big Mama Thornton's "Hound Dog". The record took off, and Sam Phillips was on his way. During those early few years, he often said, "If I could only find a white man who had the Negro sound and the Negro feel, I could make a million dollars" (Shaw 1978, 502).

One day in 1953, a white kid in his late teens came in to cut a couple of songs for his mother's birthday. Nearly a year went by before Phillips and the young man met again, this time to record some country tunes. The hillbilly youngster was singing in the style of Dean Martin, who was quite popular in the 1950s.

According to legend, the nervous teenager was fooling around between takes, doing an exaggerated version of Big Boy Crudup's "That's All Right Mama". Phillips' secretary heard it, and ran to get Sam. He listened for a few seconds, and said, "Quick, turn on the recorder!"

The kid's name was Elvis Presley. Sam Phillips had found what he wanted. Phillips also recorded Johnny Cash, Jerry Lee Lewis, Carl Perkins, and many others who made the big time, but it was Elvis who put Sun Records in the history books.

King

Formed in 1945 by Sydney Nathan, King and its subsidiaries, DeLuxe, Federal, and Queen, recorded a host of important musicians and singers in gospel, R&B, and country music. Geographically well-placed in the Mid-West (Cincinnati, Ohio) and recording touring groups in several musical styles, King had a large hand in turning out R&B versions of country tunes like Bullmoose Jackson's "Why Don't You Haul Off and Love Me", originally done by country singer Wayne Raney.

In R&B, Nathan had the Royals, the Platters, the Midnighters, the Dominoes, the Five Royales, Otis Williams and the Charms, Wynonie Harris, Bullmoose Jackson, Bill Doggett, Big Jay McNeely, Earl Bostic, and many more.

To reach the country music market, Nathan had Moon Mullican, Cowboy Copas, Grandpa Jones, the Delmore Brothers, Hawkshaw Hawkins, and Hank Penny.

Syd Nathan's superstar, often called Soul Brother No. 1, was James Brown from Macon, Georgia. Brown established his own special kind of gospel-drenched R&B which caught on, to say the least.

THE FORMATION OF BMI

Broadcast Music, Inc. (BMI) was founded on October 14, 1939, in reaction to an earlier announcement by the American Society of Composers, Authors, and Publishers (ASCAP) that on January 1, 1941, all revenues from radio airplay would be increased from 5% to 15%. The broadcasters were prepared, and for nearly a year no ASCAP music was heard on the air. In November of 1941, ASCAP settled for 2.8%. BMI had broken the ASCAP monopoly.

From its first day of existence, BMI aggressively sought out country music, ethnic folk music, and the new and exciting development called rhythm and blues. Hundreds of new publishing companies were formed, devoting themselves to BMI composers, and independent producers appeared everywhere to record BMI's music catalog.

Pop music historians have observed that the ASCAP-BMI fight was more than just a squabble over percentage points on airtime royalty payments and good music as opposed to bad music. By 1940, the many movie studios had bought up the rights to top ASCAP writers and music publishing firms. Warner Brothers, for example, had the rights to all the songs of Victor Herbert, Jerome Kern, Cole Porter, Noel Coward, George Gershwin, Sigmund Romberg, and Rodgers and Hart.

The showdown in 1940 was really between the multimillion-dollar movie-controlled publishing business and the threat posed by the growing radio entertainment empires (Chapple and Garofalo 1977, 65).

TOP 40 RADIO

The transistor radio, developed by Bell Laboratory in 1947, appeared on the market in the early 1950s. About the same time, the car radio became an affordable option in the automobile industry, especially appealing because of the increased pleasure of high-fidelity. Then too, television was taking away radio's special shows, and the radio men were looking for something to fill their airtime.

Several innovations in radio programming arose. The first change occurred to station owner Todd Storz and his program director, Bill Stewart, one afternoon when they were at a bar in Omaha. They had been talking shop all afternoon, and were irritated that the same song kept coming up on the jukebox.

After a brief silence, the cocktail waitress went over to the jukebox, and played three times in succession the very song that was driving Storz and Stewart mad! By the third hearing, they found the tune less irritating, and they suddenly realized the persuasive effect of repetition. It could create a favorable response to an otherwise decidedly mediocre tune! Top 40 radio was born at that moment (Chapple and Garofalo 1977, 59).

Top 40 became the new radio format. The same forty tunes would be repeated every twenty-four hour radio cycle, with the top ten of those getting more frequent play than the bottom thirty. In addition, Top 40 radio integrated short new spots into the music offering, inserted contests and promotional gimmicks at will, and offered frequent station identification spots by talkative disc jockeys speaking the language of the growing teenage listener market.

Bill Drake later (in the 1960s) refined Top 40 and tightened it considerably, but it remained essentially the same broadcast strategy that Storz and Stewart had designed. It also created a perfect environment for corruption, because getting a record into the Top 40 playlist became the single most important factor in the possible success or failure of a tune. More about that corruption, called payola, in later chapters.

Why forty tunes? Because the Wurlitzer jukeboxes, which flooded the industry at the time, contained forty recordings.

MAJOR PERSONALITIES

Certain personalities are historically more important than others because of their innovations, their extensive recordings, and their influence on white country musicians in the South and on the British youngsters who were enraptured by the whole R&B culture. Here is an overview of a few of them.

Louis Jordan

Sometimes called the "Father of Rhythm and Blues", Louis Jordan (1908-1975) changed the image of black musicians by appealing to the white market without losing his authentic black musical style. His group, the Tympany Five, recorded extensively so everyone in the music business was familiar with his infectious shuffle rhythms.

His million-seller "Is You Is, Or Is You Ain't My Baby?" in 1944 became a catch phrase among adolescent lovers all over America. And "Caldonia" was everyone's favorite gal. Through the 1940s, Jordan's records were seldom off the "Harlem Hit Parade", as black charts were then called in *Billboard* (Shaw 1878, 63).

Jordan began his career as a top-level alto saxophone player in Chick Webb's band in the 1930s, and was highly respected. He soon tired of "jazzmen playing for themselves" all the time, and made a specific effort to reach out to a market larger than the inner circle of jazz aficionados.

His approach was to treat African-American folk traditions, language patterns, and cultural nuances in a humorous manner – which somehow did not offend his black fans. Jordan was no Uncle Tom. He didn't try to attract white followers with any kind of self-effacing gimmick. He just dealt with the things that came out of his own background, things he was comfortable and familiar with.

In the 1950s, Mercury Records signed Jordan as a solo artist. With arrangements by Quincy Jones and others, Jordan re-recorded some of his earlier hits. He then formed a big band, but eventually went back to the Tympany Five format for the remainder of his career. He was the first cross-over personality to work in three areas – jazz, R&B, and pop.

Muddy Waters

McKinley Morganfield (1913-1983) was discovered in Mississippi by Alan Lomax. Lomax recorded him for the Library of Congress, but those recordings were soon forgotten as Muddy Waters moved to Chicago in 1943, at age twenty-eight.

Waters changed his country-style blues to inner-city R&B when his uncle bought him an electric guitar. With his half-brother, Otis Spann, on piano, Jimmy Rogers on second guitar, and Little Walter on harmonica, Muddy Water's band put out a succession of classic hits, including "I've Got My Mojo Working", "Tiger in Your Tank", "I'm a Man", and his giant hit, "Rollin' Stone".

Waters' influence on the British R&B groups can be seen at every turn in the road, and his stature in the world of R&B put him in the spotlight on hundreds of concerts in the 1960s and 1970s. Eric Clapton took Muddy Waters with him on the 1979 tour.

There seems to be no real way to know if his mother called him Muddy Waters because he spent so much time playing in the muddy creeks around his home. All the R&B historians mention it, though, as the gospel truth.

T-Bone Walker

Aaron Thibeaux Walker (1910-1975), nicknamed "Tibou" (from his middle name), which somehow got corrupted to T-Bone, played an electrically amplified guitar before almost anyone else in the field, and inspired B. B. King, Chuck Berry, Lowell Fulson, and many others. T-Bone's virtuoso technique enabled him to play jazz solos right along with Dizzy Gillespie, Lawrence Brown, and Gerald Wilson — fellow members of the Les Hite Band in the early 1940s.

Way back in the 1930s, T-Bone was also playing guitar in the acrobatic and provocative sexual manner that later made Elvis Presley and Jimi Hendrix so popular. His "Stormy Monday", "Mean Old World", and "I Gotta Break, Baby" were well known by the British blues crowd in the 1950s and 1960s. His horn-like improvisations put him in the company of Oscar Peterson and Clark Terry for some big concert dates sponsored by Norman Granz.

His top level guitar work and rich, deep blues singing kept him busy with European tours, recording dates, and special appearances right up to 1975 when he died of pneumonia.

B. B. King

Riley King (b. 1925) was known at radio station WDIA in Memphis as the "Beale Street Blues Boy", shortened to "Blues Boy", then to "B. B.". Ike Turner, talent scout for Modern Records, signed B. B. King to a contract in 1950, and before long he had a string of hits "Three O' Clock Blues", "You Know I Love You", and "Every Day I Have the Blues" among them.

King does not, perhaps cannot, play and sing at the same time. He alternates powerful vocal lines with dazzling guitar licks. It is, of course, the well-known call and response pattern, and it works well for King.

He calls his guitar "Lucille", and wrote a tune of the same name. His career received a substantial boost when he appeared at Fillmore West in 1966. A whole generation of white bluesmen and blues fans suddenly discovered B. B. King.

King routinely worked three hundred dates per year, and spent the other days in the recording studio, sometimes with strings, as with "The Thrill Is Gone" (1969), which held at No. 15 on the American charts for several weeks. He performed with U2 in their 1988 movie, *Rattle and Hum*. Even though he had his "farewell" world tour in 2006, he still makes appearances at events, such as the New Orleans Jazz Festival in 2013.

Bo Diddley

Ellas Bates (1928-2008) was adopted by his mother's cousin, Gussie McDaniel, who changed his name to Ellas McDaniel. At age twenty-three, he moved from street corners into the 708 Club, and began to record for Chess Records. Some say Phil Chess called him "Bo Diddley" which is fractured Yiddish-Polish for storyteller. Others say that as he came up with guitars of strange shapes, his friends called him "Bo Diddley" after the diddley bow, a single-stringed instrument of African origin played by blacks in the South.

Bo Diddley is one of the most copied musicians in pop music history – "I'm a Man" (Yardbirds), "Mona" (Rolling Stones), "Bo Diddley" (Animals), and more. In 1963, he toured the United Kingdom with the Everly Brothers and the Rolling Stones (who dropped all of Diddley's songs from their part of the act, out of respect for him).

Bo Diddley was known for a special kind of busy beat with a lot of things going on between drums and maracas at all times, even through the breaks. This unique beat was used by Buddy Holly on "Not Fade Away", by Johnny Otis on "Willy and the Hand Jive", and by U2 on "Desire". The Animals recorded a tribute to him, called "The Story of Bo Diddley", in which they give him much of the credit for starting rock and roll.

Fats Domino

Antoine Domino (b. 1928), one of nine children, was taught to play piano in his early teens by his brother-in-law, Harrison Verrett. "Fats" (5'5" and 230+ lbs.) was discovered by Imperial Records talent scout, Dave Bartholomew, and played with Bartholomew's band at the Hideaway Club in New Orleans in 1949. Domino soon had several hits near the top of the American R&B charts – "Goin Home", "Please Don't Leave Me", "Ain't That a Shame", and finally, "Blueberry Hill".

His first language was French, and it gave his blues-tinged vocals a trace of accent that was immediately likeable. Add to that a masterful boogie-woogie piano style with his trademark triplet figures, then some honking R&B horn riffs, and the result is thirty-six records in the Top 40 charts in eight years. A former Duke

Ellington trumpet player, Bartholomew played and arranged for Fats, and eventually became his manager, producer, and songwriting partner.

In the 1990s, Fats Domino spent most of his time at home in New Orleans with his wife and eight children enjoying the rewards of his talent and good fortune. Hurricane Katrina changed all of that in 2005.

Living in an area that was heavily flooded, Domino and his family were rescued by a Coast Guard helicopter, but they lost all of their possessions. Domino and his family moved to Harvey, Louisiana, and work to gut and repair their home in New Orleans began in January 2006. Since then, he has made a few appearances (including portraying himself on the HBO drama *Treme*) and has received numerous honors, including induction into the Louisiana Music Hall of Fame and the Delta Music Hall of Fame.

Little Richard

Richard Wayne Penniman (b. 1932), born in Macon, Georgia, pranced across the pages of pop music history as no other figure could or would. He was one of the first performers to become famous for outrageous stage behavior, and he served as a model for Jerry Lee Lewis, Elvis Presley, Elton John, Mick Jagger, Prince, and others.

Singing in the streets and in local churches at age seven, Little Richard's whole life was a constant battle between his simple but deep religious convictions and his wild passion for drugs, several varieties of sex, and the devil's music – rhythm and blues.

During a break in a 1955 Specialty recording session that was going nowhere, Little Richard went to the piano and blurted out a raucous and off-color tune, which he called "Tutti Frutti". The producer, Robert Bumps Blackwell, called in local songwriter Dorothy La Bostries to clean up the lyrics, and before the afternoon was out, they had a giant hit (Stuessy 1990, 56). Little Richard's gospel-flavored boogie-woogie piano and his rip-roarin' "woo-woo" vocal style carried through "Long Tall Sally" (1956), "Slippin' and Slidin'" (1956), and "Good Golly, Miss Molly" (1958).

In 1957, Little Richard renounced pop music, married a Washington, D. C., secretary named Ernestine Campbell, and entered Oakwood, a Bible college, in Huntsville, Alabama. In the early 1960s, he recorded many gospel tunes for

Mercury in recording sessions produced by Quincy Jones. While at Oakwood, he earned a B. A., and became an ordained Seventh Day Adventist minister.

By 1962, however, Little Richard, without a wife, was back in the entertainment business touring the United Kingdom with the Beatles and, later, with the Everly Brothers and the Rolling Stones (they were his opening acts).

Although he never again achieved the same success on the charts as he did in the late 1950s and a hip issue now prevents him from showcasing some of the stage antics he first became famous for, Little Richard continues to make appearances at award shows, benefit concerts, on tour, on television and in the movies.

Ray Charles

Wrapping the glorious sounds and rhythms of black gospel music around traditional secular lyrics made Ray Charles (1930-2004) one of the most influential musicians of the 20th century. What was probably just a marketing phrase for Atlantic Records when they released *The Genius of Ray Charles* (January 1960), turns out, after over fifty years, to be more than just hyperbole.

Very simply, what Ray Charles did was change the history of American pop music. Everything he touched, he changed. It was partly instinctive and emotional; he just felt it should be. But it was also partly calculated and cerebral; he thought it might succeed. And it did.

He used jazz-style horn riffs in many of his arrangements. He was among the first to use the Fender Rhodes electric piano. He formed a female backup group, the Raelettes, and they did things the Supremes would do years later.

Everything he did was charged with electrical energy and emotional intensity. And he was fearless in stepping into new territory. In 1962, he recorded *Modern Sounds in Country and Western Music* in, of all places, New York City and Hollywood, California. From that album, "I Can't Stop Lovin' You" topped the charts in three categories: country, soul, and pop. This was unthinkable, but he did it.

He was bold enough to risk the anger of the fundamental religious community by changing the lyrics of "Talkin' 'Bout Jesus" to "Talkin' 'Bout You" and "I Got a Savior" to "I Got a Woman". He was sometimes called the greatest gospel singer alive, and he never recorded a straight-ahead gospel song.

Ray Charles Robinson, born in Albany, Georgia, lost his sight at age seven, with a rare form of childhood glaucoma. He studied music in Florida at the St.

Augustine School for the Blind, and when his parents died, left school at age sixteen to make it on his own as a musician. After some modest success, he took off for Seattle, Washington, to get as far away from the South as he could, and still be in America.

He formed a jazz-blues trio patterned after Nat "King" Cole, and soon landed a recording contract with Swingtime Records. To avoid confusion with Sugar Ray Robinson, he dropped his surname to become Ray Charles. From his first entry into the profession, Charles had a strong and unmistakable style of his own – a raspy, passionate, gospel-soaked, oratorical delivery that turns every song into an emotional event. His versions of "America the Beautiful" (1972) and "Georgia on my Mind" (1979) are considered classics in every sense of the word.

He served as a role model and musical inspiration to Otis Redding, Sam Cooke, James Brown, and a host of other soul singers. He overcame a dreadful heroin habit, and landed on his feet stronger than ever. He won every conceivable honor and award in the industry, and performed all over the world to huge throngs.

His final public appearance, less than two months before his death in June 2004, was in Los Angeles, when the music studio he had built in 1964 was designated as a "Cultural and Historic Landmark".

James Brown

By the late 1950s, another personality emerged to take his place among the stars, and by the early 1960s, the term "soul" came into favor to describe his special style. It was more than just a casual change of terms; it was a new declaration of a second wave of black pride.

The term was used in jazz and elsewhere to indicate that someone or something possessed an honest black authority and authenticity. John Coltrane's *Soultrane* and Lou Donaldson's *Swing and Soul* made the point, as did the most important Soul Brother of all time, James Brown (1933-2006).

After a delinquent childhood in Augusta, Georgia, James Brown formed a gospel style R&B group called the original Flames, then the Famous Flames. In April of 1956, a King Records subsidiary, Federal, released Brown's "Please, Please, Please". It was a regional R&B hit, and showed great promise. In 1958, "Try Me" was sufficient to get Brown signed to Universal Attractions booking agency.

For the next decade or more, King released a single every two or three months to satisfy the demand for Brown's recordings, a demand caused by the near continuous touring of The James Brown Revue. The Revue – forty singers, dancers, and musicians in stunning silk concert stage attire – was programmed to perfection in a mixture of calculated theatrical hysteria and absolute musical discipline. Backup musicians were fined if they played any wrong notes, and every stage mannerism of the frontline musicians and singers was rehearsed to brilliant precision.

Brown's dancing became the model for future stars like Mick Jagger and Michael Jackson. Brown ended each show, sweat pouring off his face, as he sank to his knees and collapsed on stage, and then had to be carried off stage covered with a beautiful cape – only to return for another round of "Please, Please, Please", and more collapses and capes. He earned his reputation as the "Hardest Working Man in Show Business".

Musically, Brown established a special soul-funk style all his own, bits and pieces of which were sampled by rap entertainers in the 1980s through to the present day.

Typically, the horns would punctuate Brown's phrases with short bursts while the bass and drums played tight rhythmic patterns to generate the momentum. The band would often just "vamp" as Brown delivered his preacher-like declarations, and then at the right time change chords to establish a new set of riffs, then finally bring the whole thing back home (Stuessy 1990, 218). It was simple, but effective, and it shifted all the focus to Brown and his dazzling footwork.

Brown's passionate style and strong black identity carried him to the edge of politics at times. The funky "Say It Loud – I'm Black and I'm Proud" gave hope to thousands of his fans. In concerts, Brown urged his crowd, "Don't terrorize, organize!" and "Don't burn, learn!" (Stuessy 1990, 218).

Between 1967 and 1972, Brown had thirty songs in the Top 40 charts, many of them No. 1 hits in R&B and at the same time in the Top Ten of the pop category. He became a worldwide symbol of blackness. In Africa, people would come out of mud huts carrying James Brown albums, even though they had no electricity or phonograph equipment (Stuessy 1990, 218, quoting Leon Austin).

Brown's style was pushed to the side in the late 1970s as disco flashed across the horizon. He did have one final Top 10 hit – "Living in America", which was featured in the movie *Rocky IV*, in which Brown had a cameo. In general, though, the world passed him by, and he began to suffer financial and legal difficulties. He was arrested at various times for speeding, drug, weapons, and domestic violence charges throughout the rest of his life. He died in 2006 of congestive heart failure, a complication of pneumonia.

Chuck Berry

The "Father of Rock and Roll", as rock historians have begun to call him, Charles Edward Anderson Berry (b. 1926) was born in San Jose, California, and moved to St. Louis, Missouri, while in his early teens. He worked as a hairdresser and beautician by day and a jazz-blues guitarist with his own trio by night. With Johnnie Johnson on piano and Ebby Harding on drums, Berry took the trio to Chicago to audition for Chess Records.

Thus, at age 29, Chuck Berry was already a veteran night club entertainer when he converted "Ida Red" ("Ida May" (?) – see Lazell, 1989, 42) a country tune done years earlier by Bob Wills, to a giant hit, "Maybellene", or in some writing, "Maybelline". In return for being listed as co-author, disc jockey Alan Freed promoted the record on his Cleveland radio show, and it rose to No. 1 in R&B and No. 5 in the pop charts (Stuessy 1990, 62).

It was classic Chuck Berry, and it established his basic guitar style which several scholars have said is the single most influential style in the early days of rock and roll (Stuessy, Lazell, Helander, and others). His introductions, double-note solos, and alternating accompaniment chords were widely imitated guitar techniques in the industry for a long time. Not until Jimi Hendrix came along did Berry's influence begin to wane.

"Maybellene" also established Berry's poetic skill with lyrics treating topics high in the minds of America's new teen culture, both black and white: cars, girl-boy problems, school, music, growing up, parents, etc. He put his arm around the kids and said, "Yeah, life can be a drag sometimes, but we all get through it OK. Hang in there!" (Stuessy 1990, 63). Shaw says that Chuck Berry is the most important rock poet this side of Bob Dylan (1982, 35).

Berry led an interesting private life, filled with dramatic contrasts. For example, in June of 1979, he appeared by special request at the White House, and in July of 1979 was sentenced to four months in jail for income tax evasion.

For all his inconsistencies, "Sweet Little Sixteen", "Roll Over Beethoven", "Back in the U.S.A.", "Johnny B. Goode", "School Days", "No Particular Place to Go", "Nadine", and several others lift Chuck Berry head and shoulders above most of the early rock and roll pioneers. His innovations in music and in lyrics "are ingrained in rock's collective conscience" (John Floyd, in Erlewine 1992, 44). It was with complete confidence that the selection committee chose him among the first to be installed in the Rock and Roll Hall of Fame.

CONCLUSION

There were many others, of course, whose careers sparkled brightly in the firmament – Sam Cooke, Lloyd Price, Willie Mae Thornton, Clyde McPhatter, Otis Redding, Charles Brown, Ruth Brown, Hank Ballard, Johnny Otis, Jackie Wilson, Arthur Crudup, and many more. By its very purpose, however, history must be arbitrary and selective. A different historian might offer a different view of the same facts, but the above biographies of major personalities in the field of rhythm and blues will have to suffice for now. These ten were not chosen entirely randomly, however. They have been credited – by their peers, by historians, and, most importantly, by those they influenced who later went on to "make it big" themselves – with laying the groundwork for the rock and roll revolution, to be discussed in the next chapter.

Chapter 23
The Birth of Rock and Roll

The world of rock and roll has two large historical divisions – before Woodstock, when it was called rock and roll (and rock & roll, and rock 'n roll, and rock n' roll, rock'n'roll, and even rock-'n'-roll), and after Woodstock, when it gradually came to be called just rock. The reduction of the term is of little consequence, except that today's scholars and critics can call up a host of impressions by the use of the earlier term "rock and roll" to suggest a kind of innocence and purity as compared with the later days of "rock", a less innocent genre that has associations with the seedier parts of life – sex, drugs, drinking, and violence.

DISC JOCKEYS

Exactly when disc jockeys (sometimes abbreviated deejays or DJs) came into existence is a matter of conjecture. Up until the 1940s they were just called "announcers". They introduced the programs, read the commercials, and announced the titles of the record selections being played.

But the idea of playing records and offering remarks goes way back. One Christmas Eve in 1906, Reginald A. Fessenden, an engineer for Edison, transmitted Handel's "Largo" [probably from the opera *Xerxes*] out of his laboratory in Massachusetts. As early as 1910, Doc Herrold played recordings over his own San Jose radio station which acquired the call letters KQW in 1929. In 1932 Al Jarvis played recordings and offered ad lib remarks on a noonday program over KJWB in Los Angeles (Ewen 1997, 287).

The first really famous national disc jockey was Martin Block, whose *Make Believe Ballroom* over WNEW in New York was picked up and rebroadcast by hundreds of stations all over America through the 1930s and 1940s. The first black disc jockey of national influence was Jack L. Cooper. From the early 1930s to the

1950s, Cooper and his wife, Gertrude, played black music and offered black-oriented radio programming over station WSBC in Chicago.

By 1947 there were three thousand disc jockeys filling the radio airwaves with pleasant sounds and chatter. They became late-night companions to truck drivers, second-shift factory workers, and to the growing teenage high school and college market. The stage was now set for one of those DJs to reach out to the new music of the day, rhythm and blues.

Alan Freed

The story is well known, now, that radio announcer Alan Freed (1921-1965) took a dramatic career turn when he went to Cleveland in 1951 to take a job with the independent station WJW. Trained in trombone and music theory, Freed was quite successful with his early evening classical music program. But, as he passed a local record store on his way to work each day, he saw groups of white teenagers jumping around to the sound of black jazz-blues musicians Red Prysock and Al Sears (Szatmary 1987, 20). He decided to try to reach that young audience with this new energetic music.

An ambitious young man, Freed got permission from the station owner to follow his classical program with a program of this rhythm and blues (hereafter abbreviated as R&B). As his theme song, he chose a King Records release by Todd Rhodes, "Blues for Moondog", and he called his show *The Moondog House*. He even began to call himself "Moon Dog". Shortly thereafter, a blind New York street musician named Moondog sued the station, and after a $5000 settlement, the name of the show was changed to just plain [Alan Freed's] *Rock 'n' Roll Party* (Ewen 1977, 552).

Because he feared the term rhythm and blues would drive away his white audience, Freed pick up the phrase "rock and roll" from one of the R&B recordings. Whether or not he knew that the term was used in the black community as early as the 1920s as a euphemism for sexual activity has never been established by rock scholars.

Already thirty years old, Freed was an unlikely candidate to launch a teenage revolution, but he certainly did. He would often shout "Yeah, yeah, yeah!" and "Go, man, go!" into the microphone while he pounded on a telephone book in rhythm to the music. He also drank a lot, but the kids had no way of knowing that. They loved him. He was a kindred spirit. He too, thought their parents were stuffy and old fashioned. They just knew it, you could tell by the little remarks he made between the records.

Freed became a celebrity of the highest order. He sponsored concerts which featured Charles Brown, the Orioles, the Moonglows, the Dominoes, and many other R&B acts. In March of 1953, he sold eighteen thousand tickets for an auditorium that had only nine thousand seats. When eighteen thousand screaming teenagers appeared, he had to cancel the show, and police vans hauled away the rioting youngsters to cool them off in jail for a few hours.

In 1954, at age 33, Freed went to WINS in New York, and was soon making nearly a million dollars a year – not only playing, but selling records over the air, along with dozens of other teenage commodities made by his sponsors. He became a very famous spokesman for the new teenage subculture, and soon appeared in three movies, *Don't Knock the Rock, Rock Around the Clock* and *Rock, Rock, Rock.*

Freed eventually got summoned before Congress, indicted for accepting bribes from record companies to push their recordings, and spent the last few years of his life a broken man.

Bill Randle

In Cleveland at about the same time as Alan Freed was veteran disc jockey Bill Randle (1923-2004), who already had a very successful career going.

> *Like most disc jockeys, Randle was possessed of a powerful ego, but unlike most others, Randle had, and still has, a daunting intelligence to back it up.*
>
> *The afternoon time slot and Randle's more mature audience made him a far more powerful figure to record company executives than Freed in the early going* (Smith 1989, 183).

With 65 percent of all of the radios in Cleveland tuned to him from 6:00 to 7:00 p.m. each day, Bill Randle had the highest rating of any DJ in the country in 1954. In November of the same year, he signed on with WCBS in New York to do a weekend stint for four hours each Friday night, in addition to his work at WERE in Cleveland, where he was a stockholder as well as an employee (Smith 1989, 183).

At the suggestion of Marks Music executive Arnold Shaw, Sam Phillips of Sun Records sent his brother, Jud, up to Cleveland with a several records by an unknown "hillbilly" singer named Elvis Presley. Most of the Cleveland disc jockeys rejected the records, but Bill Randle – with a keen musical ear and a shrewd businessman's killer instinct – knew he was listening to pure gold. He played one of the Elvis recordings every fifteen minutes that weekend, and changed the history of pop music in America.

It was monumental. Randle telephoned Shaw,

> *"I don't know what those Presley records have, but I put them on yesterday, and, Arnold, the switchboard lit up like Glitter Gulch in Las Vegas. He hits them [the kids] like a bolt of electricity. My phone hasn't stopped ringing and I haven't been able to stop playing those records"* (quoted in Ewen 1977, p. 558).

Randle was no stranger to success. Earlier, in 1951, he made a hit out of Mantovani's symphonic pop version of a beautiful old waltz, "Charmaine", demonstrating that repeated air play had become a major factor in the new world of popular music.

> *Among his other coups was Johnnie Ray, whom he had heard singing in a Cleveland nightclub and championed on the air, making him a star.*
> *Randle was also the mentor of a male quartet that was known as the Canadaires when he found them. He clipped their hair, changed their names to the Crew-Cuts, and lined them up with Mercury Records where their tunes "Crazy 'Bout You, Baby" and "Sh-Boom" became rock-'n'-roll classics* (Smith 1989, 185).

Bill Randle took a break from radio in the 1960s to pursue other interests (including an undergraduate degree, multiple graduate degrees, and a career in law), but returned to radio in the 1970s now and again until his death in 2004.

There were disc jockeys all over America who rose to fame and fortune on the strength of the new music called rock and roll – Rufus "Bear Cat" Thomas, Bill "Hoss" Allen, Bob "Wolfman Jack" Smith, Dick "The Screamer" Biondi, Douglas "Jocko" Henderson, Zena "Daddy" Sears, Murray "The K" Kauffman, and hundreds more.

241

They "were to the airwaves what Holden Caulfield and 'Catcher in the Rye' were to literature and Marlon Brando and James Dean were to the movies – sources of identification for the stirring teenage rebellion of post-World War II" (Smith 1989, 26).

The disc jockeys were colorful and popular characters, and they often talked and acted like the pubescent teenagers who made them so famous. Many took payola in the forms of money, drugs, and sex. They promoted local concerts and traveling tours, and got carried away with the power they seemed to have over their teenage listeners. A few of the DJs were frustrated entertainers, and got a break, leaving radio for careers as performers. Some went on to open record stores and businesses related to the entertainment world. Some are still around today, hosting "Golden Oldies" programs on the nation's airwaves.

ROCK AND ROLL PIONEERS

Bill Haley

His mother was a piano teacher, his dad played mandolin, and he liked country music. So Bill Haley (1925-1981), from Chester, Pennsylvania, by way of Detroit, was drawn into the entertainment business first as a country yodeler, then as a disc jockey, then as leader of The Four Aces of Western Swing, later called The Saddlemen. They played "country and western" music.

In 1951, Haley did a cover of Jackie Brenston's blues release, "Rocket 88", and though the recording sold only a few copies, Haley's live performances of the tune drove white teenage dancers wild. He renamed his group Bill Haley and The Comets, and set out to create a new R&B image for his band. He signed with Decca Records in 1954, then covered Sunny Dae's 1952 treatment of "Rock Around the Clock" and Joe Turner's early 1954 classic "Shake, Rattle, and Roll".

As was the case for nearly all cover records, the sexual references in the original black version were muted, modified, or deleted. The black artists delivered all those sexual innuendoes in jest, with whimsical good humor. But the white record executives took the remarks seriously, missing the light-hearted intent.

A chubby married man in his late twenties with several small children, Bill Haley did not look like a promising rock and roll star, but he became the first really big one. "Rock Around the Clock" was of only modest interest until it appeared in the movie *The Blackboard Jungle*. It went to No. 1 in America for seven weeks, and stayed in the Top Ten for forty weeks.

As always, the movie moguls could see big dollars in the making, and soon came out with a movie called *Rock Around the Clock*, the story of how Bill Haley and his band were discovered and put on national TV by Alan Freed, who played himself in the picture (Chapple and Garofalo 1977, 37).

Haley made a specific effort to capture a black feeling in his band. His pianist said, "We'd begin with [Louis] Jordan's shuffle rhythm ... and build on it" (Szatmary 1987, 34). The result was an appealing mixture of country music and R&B, which even Haley did not call rock and roll until he had been playing it a year or so.

Elvis Presley

Of the twin sons born to Gladys and Vernon Presley of Tupelo, Mississippi Jesse was stillborn. Elvis Aron Presley (1935-1977) survived, healthy and strong. His childhood was as normal and uneventful as that of most children of poor southern white day laborers. After high school, he started driving a truck for Crown Electric, and decided to make a recording for his mother at Sun Records. He caught the interest of the owner, Sam Phillips, who brought in Scotty Moore and Bill Black from a neighborhood club band to practice with him and coach him a little on style and stage presence.

Before long, Presley was on his way to local fame. Encouraged, Sam Phillips got him on Nashville's *Grand Ole Opry*. He sang "Blue Moon of Kentucky" to a mostly silent audience who were polite but did not quite know what to make of the young man shaking his hips during the instrumental part of the song. Jim Denny, talent scout for the *Opry*, suggested that Presley take up truck driving again (Lazell 1989, 384).

When former carnival barker "Colonel" Tom Parker (1909-1997) took over as Presley's manager and agent, things began to move in a hurry. Before Elvis, Parker had great success in promoting country singers Eddy Arnold and Hank Snow. Parker knew the business, there is no doubt about that. He talked Elvis and his parents into signing a management deal that gave the Colonel complete control over the singer's career and an incredibly high percentage of his income – as much as fifty percent in some instances.

[Incidentally, there was no real "Colonel Tom Parker". In actuality, he was born Andreas Cornelis ("Dries") van Kuijk in Breda, the Netherlands, and, although he did enlist in the U.S. Army, he did so under the assumed name "Tom Parker". He served two years in Hawaii, obtained an honorable discharge, and reenlisted shortly thereafter in Florida. This time, he was charged with desertion and was punished with solitary confinement. His time in solitary induced a psychosis, which garnered him a medical discharge from the Army. Although he later married an American wife and would also have been eligible as a U.S. Army veteran, Parker never applied for U.S. citizenship. As his true identity was not discovered until the 1980s, there has been much speculation as to whether the "Colonel's" lack of citizenship (and therefore, the lack of papers needed for international travel beyond the U.S. and Canada) was the reason that Elvis never toured overseas.]

In November of 1955, Presley signed a contract with RCA records, and before long Elvis was doing guest shots on the television shows of the Dorsey brothers, Milton Berle, Steve Allen, and finally on *The Ed Sullivan Show*. Parker then formed Elvis Presley Music, Inc., to issue all the folios of printed music made famous by Elvis.

There was no end to Tom Parker's ingenuity. After that he licensed Special Products, Inc., of Beverly Hills, California, to market all the commodities bearing the name Elvis – jewelry, soft drinks, guitars, book ends, dolls, greeting cards, diaries, pillows, stuffed hound dogs, cosmetics, girls' underwear, pens, pencils, hair curlers, combs, belts, big buttons that said "I Love Elvis", big buttons that said "I Hate Elvis", and so on. "The Colonel" took a sizable portion of the immense profits from all of these ventures for himself, of course.

Elvis altered the history of popular music in America, to say the least, and things were never the same after he arrived at the top of the world of pop culture in late 1958. It was Parker's idea for Elvis to serve in the regular Army. Presley wanted to go into the special entertainment division. Parker persuaded him it was better for his image to go in as a buck private. Like an obedient child, Elvis did.

No matter, perhaps, because by March of 1959, Elvis Presley's real contributions had been made – he absorbed, internalized, and delivered the mixture of country and black musical traditions so effectively as to create, along with Chuck Berry, a whole new art form. Presley wanted more, however. He wanted to be a giant movie star in the manner of James Dean, Marlon Brando, and Dean Martin.

But the Colonel would have no part of it. Parker examined all movie scripts submitted, and rejected anything not in that narrow vein of the hillbilly singer who always gets the prettiest girl at the end of the show. Although Parker did get Elvis into 32 B-movies, some rock scholars believe that Elvis had enough raw talent to grow into a substantial movie career, but Parker had limited vision.

After his Army duty, the rest of Elvis Presley's monumental career was simply a matter of astute business management designed to break every existing record in every existing category of achievement in popular music – highest paid Las Vegas act, most records sold in various styles, biggest crowds in history at all the huge stadiums, first satellite global concert to a billion viewers, and on and on and on. He did it all, and he did it well.

Parker's control was absolute. He even chose the date, the site, and the guest list for Elvis' wedding to Priscilla Wagner in 1967 – and he excluded many of Presley's body guards and drinking buddies, the so-called Memphis Mafia.

But Elvis' image of who and what he was never grew. Without saying a word, the Colonel reminded him every day that he was just a hillbilly singer in the hands of a smart businessman. His personal life crumbled. Off the road, his weight ballooned up to two hundred pounds. He would then go on a crash diet with amphetamines and lose thirty pounds to go back on tour. His marriage went sour. He was mobbed every time he went outside his mansion, Graceland. For recreation, he would sometimes rent an amusement park or movie theater from midnight to six in the morning, then invite his friends to join him in what had to be an artificial kind of fun.

It was all a magnificent, but shallow, existence, which served only to delay the inexorable decline of both personal identity and musical gifts. He yearned to be more than a sexy hillbilly singer. He wanted a bigger role in American society. He wanted to put his talent (his value to the world) in a greater frame of reference. But the Colonel knew better, each time, and Elvis turned inward to drugs, sex, and motorcycles.

Elvis Presley's final years were sad, indeed, as the good natured country boy tried to make some kind of sense out of the strange and difficult world of pop superstardom Colonel Tom Parker had created for him. He died at age 42, officially due to a heart attack, but with the contributing factor of multiple drug interactions.

Jerry Lee Lewis

Another country boy who rose quickly in the world of rock and roll was Jerry Lee Lewis (b. 1935), born into a deeply religious family from Ferriday, Louisiana. When he revealed musical talent, his father mortgaged the family home to buy a piano. Jerry Lee taught himself in a few weeks, and by age twelve he was being hauled around town, piano and all, as the father tried to encourage the boy to a musical career.

At age fifteen, Jerry Lee was expelled from a Bible school in Waxahachie, Texas. At age sixteen he married a preacher's daughter, Dorothy Barton, and, when he went on tour, Lewis knowingly committed bigamy when he married Jane Mitcham at a shotgun wedding attended by her brothers.

At age twenty-one, he got a break and recorded "Whole Lotta Shakin' Goin' On" backed by "Crazy Arms". His career was beginning to look up as he became better known. In December of 1956, Jerry Lee Lewis joined Elvis Presley and Carl Perkins at Sun studios for an impromptu recording session called the "Million Dollar Quartet". Johnny Cash was the fourth member, and, although he appears in the famous picture, he left the session before it started, at the insistence of his wife who wanted to go shopping (Lazell 1989, 298).

Called "The Killer" because of the savage way he attacked the piano and because of his success with the ladies, Lewis was on his way, and his recordings were selling very well. After getting the Barton marriage dissolved, but while he was still married to Jane Mitcham, Jerry Lee again committed bigamy when he secretly married his bass player's daughter, Myra Gail Brown, who was only thirteen years of age at the time and who was also Lewis' cousin. His other cousins, country singer Mickey Gilley and evangelist Jimmy Swaggart, made no comment about the marriage, but Lewis' faithful fans were outraged.

In England, he was booed off stage, and thirty-four out of his next thirty-seven scheduled concerts were canceled. He took out a five-page ad in one of the trade journals to notify the world that he had properly divorced Jane, and then he immediately re-married Myra Gail in an impeccably official and legal ceremony (Lazell 1989, 298).

Late in 1957, Sun Records released "Great Balls of Fire", written by Jack Hammer and Otis Blackwell who had provided Elvis with "Don't Be Cruel" and "All Shook Up." Hammer and Blackwell also wrote "Good Golly, Miss Molly" for Little

Richard. Lewis appeared on the Steve Allen television show and in a movie called *Jamboree*. He was riding high in the charts and all looked well.

In 1958, however, he began to lose his place in the sun. "High School Confidential", the title song from the MGM movie (1958), was his last significant hit. Somehow he could never regain the musical authority and popularity he had before he married his young cousin. The remainder of his professional life was just average. He continued to generate enormous energy and enthusiasm on stage, and made a good many more tours, recordings, and guest appearances, but the magic was gone.

His personal life became an endless string of bad luck – four more wives (for a total of seven), two of whom died tragically, several arrests for drunken and disorderly behavior, major troubles with income taxes, the loss of two sons in freak accidents, hospitalization for bleeding ulcers, law suits with former friends and record companies, and an occasional moment of joy with a few second-generation British rock stars who remembered his great early days.

For all the complexity of his personal and professional life, Jerry Lee Lewis was a superb bluesman. He sang with a natural sense of the meaning and power of the text. He was the white Little Richard of the late 1950s, and he earned his place in the history books.

Buddy Holly

Charles Hardin Holley (1936-1959) was born in Lubbock, Texas. He took violin lessons, but switched to guitar in his early teenage years. By age thirteen, he was being called "Buddy" and was performing country music with school chum Bob Montgomery. They soon had their own radio show on station KDAV in Lubbock. Soon after, the "e" disappeared from his last name.

A talent scout recommended Holly to Decca Records in 1956, and he went to Nashville three times that year to record under veteran producer Owen Bradley. The recordings did not make the charts, but Holly's ambition was now on fire.

He formed The Crickets, and went to record with producer Norman Petty in Clovis, New Mexico. They hit it off well because they were kindred spirits, greatly interested in every aspect of the recording process. The Crickets set the model – two guitars, bass, and drums – and established the precedent for the self-contained rock band, writing their own material and choosing what and how to record (Helander 1982, 255).

Holly and Perry continued to experiment in the studio, utilizing different forms of echo ("Peggy Sue"), double-tracking ("Words of Love"), and close-miking techniques, now commonplace in the industry (Erlewine 1992, 136).

Holly's distinctive "hiccupping" vocal style, his skinny build, and his black horn-rimmed glasses gave him an immediate identity. He could not be confused with the other rock pioneers.

On February 2, 1959, following a concert at Clear Lake, Iowa, Buddy Holly, at age twenty-two, died when his chartered plane crashed shortly after takeoff. Also killed were Richie Valens and J. P. "The Big Bopper" Richardson. Bassist Waylon Jennings had been bumped from his seat, and therefore was not on the flight. Dion and The Belmonts, also on the tour, had made alternate travel arrangements.

Other Rockabillies

That "rockabilly" style – an energetic mixture of R&B, Country and Western, honky-tonk, boogie-woogie, and gospel – served well for Carl Perkins ("Blue Suede Shoes"), Roy Orbison ("Ooby Dooby"), Eddie Cochran ("Summertime Blues"), Gene Vincent ("Be-Bop-A-Lula"), the Everly Brothers ("Bye, Bye, Love"), and many, many other pioneers of rock and roll all through the 1950s and 1960s.

Chapter 24
Ownership and Control

By the late 1930s, certain business aspects of the popular music industry were taking shape. With vast sums of money being generated, it was natural that all parties would maneuver for power and control.

From its first flash across a composer's mind to its finally being enjoyed by an audience, a popular tune goes through various stages of ownership and performance-related profit sharing. Movie scores, television background music, excerpts from classical works, and many other forms of a musical "product" are frightfully complex, of course, but certain basic patterns are at work in the industry.

For the purposes of this general overview, many important ownership and copyright concerns will not be treated – foreign record deals, recording artist contracts, album covers and liner notes, union labor agreements contracts with agents and promoters, foreign publishing rights, Muzak versions, etc.

Then, too, big stars, established companies, and strong agents demand more freedom and a greater percentage of the financial gain than the newcomers in the industry. Indeed, many of the considerations listed are, like baseball players' contracts, highly individual and constantly negotiable matters which seem to be dependent on raw potential, past performance, and a promising future.

In sweeping generalizations, then, the following principles pertain in the world of popular music.

COPYRIGHT

After Gutenberg invented movable type in 1453, there were many maps, booklets, pamphlets, articles, and such printed and sold without regard to who wrote the work or who first published it.

In 1556, Queen Mary I of England (also known as Mary Tudor, the Catholic daughter of the Protestant Henry VIII) decided things had gotten out of hand. Actually what bothered her was not that printers were ripping off authors, but that some of the printers were publishing articles and pamphlets critical of her, and that Protestant pamphlets and other materials were still being published, making it difficult for her to return England to its Catholic roots. So Parliament passed the Licensing Act that licensed publishers and created the Stationers' Company, with a Royal Charter from the Queen. The Act limited who could print books and other materials and gave the Stationers' Company the legal right to seize materials that violated Church and State content standards, effectively creating a means of censorship for the Crown. It worked. The number of critical pamphlets dropped dramatically (Althouse 1984, 12-13).

When the Licensing Act expired in 1694, the unauthorized printing and pirating of all types of publications began anew. Parliament responded again, this time for more democratic reasons, with the 1710 Statute of Anne granting authors protection of their works for fourteen years (Althouse 1984, 13).

In the early days of America, each colony had its own copyright statute, so when the new nation came into being, one of its first tasks was to set up adequate protection for creative people. Thus, the first United States Copyright Act of 1790 appeared "to promote the Progress of Science and useful Arts, by securing for limited Times to Authors and Inventors, the exclusive Right to their respective Writings and Discoveries." Subsequent revisions increased the coverage to include musical works (1831), photographs (1865), and dramatic works (1870) (Althouse 1984, 13).

In an effort to keep up with the times and technology, Congress passed another Copyright Act in 1909, with a renewable twenty-eight year period established as the duration. Then, fearing that the wealthy piano roll industry and the rapidly growing phonograph companies would buy up all the popular tunes, Congress created, in that same 1909 bill, a "compulsory mechanical license", giving anyone the right to prepare separate, different copies of the basic tune as first recorded for a fee of two cents for each additional recording made, payable to the copyright owner.

Today, under the Copyright Act of 1976, creative works are protected for the life of the author plus fifty years, and each of the modern possibilities for a "copy" is separate and distinct – publishing rights, of course, but also movies rights, stage rights, television rights, commercial ("jingle") rights, mood (Muzak) rights, and so on.

There is also a common law copyright. "Common law copyright springs into being without formality, registration, or notice, immediately upon the creation of a musical or literary work" (Shemel and Krasilovsky 1971, 110).

Shemel and Krasilovsky make no mention of the urban myth about getting a common law copyright by mailing the song to yourself, registered mail, preferably across state lines. In these days of corporate control and manipulation of the supply and demand of tunes, talents, and markets, holding a common law copyright on a given song has become fairly meaningless.

Statutory copyright comes when the composer sends a complete copy of the tune, with the appropriate application form and the registration fee, to the U.S. Copyright Office. The tune is registered with its own copyright number, and fully protected as the composer's exclusive personal property. What happens more often is that the composer permits a publisher to own the copyright as part of their basic agreement. And then, a strange condition arises, as it did with the Beatles, that the publishing house merges with a bigger firm or gets sold. Because John Lennon and Paul McCartney did not have the majority ownership in their publishing company, Northern Songs, they lost their copyrights to almost every song they wrote for the Beatles when Northern Songs was sold to ATV Music Publishing. ATV held the copyrights until 1984, when they were sold to Michael Jackson (who, ironically, had been told by Paul McCartney that the way to really make money in the music business was to own publishing rights) for $47,500,000.

PERFORMANCE RIGHTS ORGANIZATIONS

The idea of "permission to perform" was first applied to plays and operettas in Europe. Prior to that time, a play was written, copyrighted, printed, and sold, and it then became public property. Playwrights might have to compete with other companies doing their (the playwrights') shows which the other companies had legally purchased.

In the United States, "performance rights" were not protected until 1897. Before that, when a Gilbert and Sullivan show would tour the United States, for example, "American producers purchased quantities of opening night seats for stenographers who transcribed the dialogue." [Then] with a legally purchased copy of the musical score and a transcribed dialogue, a producer could put on, a few weeks later, his own production of that operetta – all without any payment whatsoever to Gilbert and Sullivan. All of this was completely lawful and quite common until 1897 (Althouse 1984, 41).

ASCAP

Finally, in 1897, Congress recognized public performance rights as part of the principle of ownership, and in 1909 it authorized the creation of ASCAP (the American Society of Composers, Authors, and Publishers), a not-for-profit agency that would collect fees from venues where music was performed. The story is long, complex, and filled with human drama. Litigation went all the way to the Supreme Court, but ASCAP finally emerged in 1914 as a duly sanctioned collection agency.

ASCAP promptly hired a group of men to go out to collect fees from restaurants, dance halls, night clubs, and theaters, and to listen, log, and report back about whose music was played how often in which location. When radio, recordings, and the movies came along, there was a quantum leap in the amount of money involved and in the complexity of the judgments to be made on the "facts" gathered.

Consulting with insurance actuaries and other experts in the field of statistical extrapolation, ASCAP came up with workable procedures, imperfect of course, but reasonable and practical ways to decide which of their members should get how much.

By the late 1930s, ASCAP concluded that their member composers, authors, and publishers were not getting a fair share of the profits "out there in the industry", and they (ASCAP) increased their "pay to play" fees substantially, meaning record companies, radio stations, theaters and such had to pay more to press a record, broadcast a song over the air waves, or feature a song in a live show.

BMI

In protest, the National Association of Broadcasters bolted out of ASCAP to form their own performance rights organization which they quite logically called BMI (Broadcast Music, Inc.)

In the long run, this was a very good thing for increasing the diversity of music available in America. ASCAP had been largely populated by industry insiders – musical comedy composers, classical composers, Tin Pan Alley tunesmiths, and composers of movie music. They had neglected the development of black and country music through the 1920s and 1930s. Jelly Roll Morton and Gene Autry, for example, had great difficulty getting admitted into ASCAP, even though their own publishers were members of ASCAP (Ryan 1985, 62-64).

Therefore, BMI attracted hundreds of song writers who were hungry for attention and financial recognition. In no time at all, BMI became a formidable competitor to ASCAP for performance rights coverage in the industry.

For quite a while, all the big stars in early rock and in country music were affiliated with BMI. Bob Dylan, Johnny Cash, and many others eventually moved to ASCAP, however. In recent times, BMI and ASCAP seem to be equally strong in coverage of pop music.

SoundExchange

Created in 2000 as part of the Recording Industry Association of America (RIAA), a trade organization that represents record labels and distributors, SoundExchange became a stand-alone non-profit organization in 2003. It collects royalties on behalf of copyright owners (record labels and artists), mainly from satellite and Internet radio transmissions, such as SiriusXM and Pandora.

SESAC

SESAC, originally called the Society of European Stage Authors and Composers, was founded in New York in 1930 by Paul Heinecke as a way for European stage authors and composers to collect the copyright fees owed them by American performers and publishers.

Over time, SESAC's headquarters moved to Nashville, Tennessee, and it began focusing more on building relationships with composers, writers, and publishing companies (regardless of where they were located), and dealing with all aspects of the music business, including creation of the works, licensing for all manner of circumstances, and general administration.

SESAC is smaller than ASCAP and BMI, and there's one other major difference between it and the other three performance-rights organizations – SESAC is a for-profit corporation. SESAC is also more exclusive. While anyone who is a songwriter or publisher can join either ASCAP or BMI, only a select few are invited to join SESAC. One of those select few was Mariah Carey, who signed with them in July 2014.

***

The above four performance rights organizations track royalties for most of the music in the land. They have fixed fees which they collect from night clubs, restaurants, theaters, sports arenas, colleges, radio stations, Internet channels, and anywhere else copyrighted music may be played. The amount of royalties these establishments pay to the performance rights organizations depends on many things, including how big of an audience is reached, what a broadcaster's revenues from advertising are, and how many times a specific song is played. Broadcasters are constantly fighting to keep the fees down so they can increase their profits, and performance rights organizations are constantly fighting to increasing the fees, so the copyright holders are equitably paid for their work. It's all terribly complex, and in a continuous state of legal maneuvering and lawsuits.

MECHANICAL RIGHTS

Deriving from the piano roll industry, when copies of the music were in fact mechanical, "mechanical rights" are those concerning records, tapes, compact discs (CDs), and movie and television soundtracks.

Since it would be extremely difficult for individual composers and publishing houses to know when the songs they own are being recorded or distributed, organizations grew up in the recording industry to handle all such details.

Harry Fox Agency

Since the late 1920s, most of the leading publishers have used the Harry Fox Agency in New York as their agent-trustee to collect mechanical fees from the recording industry. For its services, the agency charges a certain percentage of the fees it collects on behalf of the publishers. The agency may handle each recorded song in a separate contract, or it may work with a record company in a blanket agreement covering all the singles and albums released by that company. With changes in the industry, HFA developed Songfile® (an online mechanical licensing tool to allow the public to purchase a license for a song they didn't write that they

254

want to record or distribute) and Slingshot (which helps digital music providers manage their licenses). HFA is also the designated YouTube administrator for many music publishers.

American Mechanical Rights Agency

Formed in New York in 1961, the AMRA works much like HRA, and seems to specialize in attending to the interests of American composers and publishers in foreign countries.

SYNCHRONIZATION RIGHTS

Named when music was synchronized with the action of a movie are "synchronization rights." The mechanical rights organizations named above also handle synchronization rights for their clients, although some major publishers have separate departments to look after their music when it is used in the film industry.

The many functions and occurrences of music in films make the legalities of synchronization rights complex indeed. Music may be composed specifically for a film, or old standards may be used in the background, or an ancient classical work may be heard throughout the film. Then, too, a song from the film may have pop super hit potential, or the movie cast album might be promising, or the soundtrack by itself could turn into a best-selling record.

Synchronization rights are so interlaced with movie profits that all the major motion picture companies simply purchased outright, or gained controlling interest in, the important record companies. Those very same record companies had earlier, for the same reasons of self-interest, purchased or gained control of the important publishing houses. So, even if it is complex, much of it is in house or, at least, in the family circle.

VIDEO RIGHTS

In their infancy, videos looked like a truly new art form, but by the late 1980s and early 1990s, they seemed to degenerate into a kind of meaningless early-adolescent visual Muzak on one hand, and aggressive promotion for movies, tours, and recordings on the other hand. Still, there are some marvelously imaginative videos that appear now and then, such as those by Peter Gabriel.

For a while, video rights and their prolonged legal battles got a lot of newspaper coverage. But now things have settled down quite a bit – perhaps because the giant international firms own all the companies along the way, and thus control all the copyrights, performance rights, mechanical rights, movie rights, television rights, video rights, even foreign rights to all the above.

HOLOGRAPHIC RIGHTS

There is no doubt that holographic images and their attendant sounds will be a part of living room entertainment in the future. When it happens, holographic rights will be negotiated for profit by those who control the product. Popular music is big business, and it is perfectly reasonable and predictable that powerful law firms and special focus corporations would emerge to distribute the billions of dollars involved.

Chapter 25
The Expansion and
Mutation of Rock and Roll

NEW YORK

By the late 1950s, the new pop music called rock and roll was showing signs of cultural fatigue. The folk music trend was taking shape. The California beaches were attracting a unique crowd of surfers, and Berry Gordy was not happy as a body trim specialist at the Ford plant in Detroit.

Then, too, several major stars were taken out of action. In 1957, Little Richard renounced rock and roll to go into the ministry of the Seventh Day Adventist Church. In 1958, Elvis Presley began a two-year tour of duty in the U.S. Army in Germany. In 1959, Buddy Holly, Richie Valens, and the J. P. "The Big Bopper" Richardson were killed in a plane crash and Chuck Berry was sentenced to two years in the federal penitentiary at Terre Haute, Indiana. In 1960, Eddie Cochran died in an auto accident in England.

At the time, four major record companies – RCA Victor, Columbia, Decca, and Capitol – had begun to gobble up the small companies, and these four companies sold seventy-five percent of the recordings in America (Szatmary 1996, 54). By their size and bureaucratic design, big corporations knew how to market and distribute "product". To discover and nurture "talent", which leads to a product, is a slightly different skill. Two brilliant young men appeared on the late 1950s pop music scene to do just that.

Dick Clark

Richard Augustus Clark II (1929-2012) showed an early interest in business matters, and his high school class voted him the "Man Most Likely to Sell the Brooklyn Bridge". He went to Syracuse University to study advertising and radio. At age twenty-two he worked for a short time for his father who was station manager at WRUN in Utica, New York.

After several modest jobs in radio and television, Clark got his big break. He took over the WFIL *Philadelphia Bandstand*, changed the name to *American Bandstand*, and did his first big program on August 5, 1957. The show aired for 90 minutes each weekday afternoon and on Monday nights from 7:30 to 8:00 p.m. One hundred fifty teenagers were in the audience, many of them getting up to dance and offer opinions about the music. With smooth patter and impeccably good taste, Clark would mingle with the kids, and then interview several guest artists before they got up to lip-sync their most recent hits.

> Clark's business savvy transformed a local telecast into a national phenomenon. To get sponsors for the show he traveled the advertising agency circuit on Madison Avenue and eventually snagged the lucrative Beechnut Spearmint Gum account (Szatmary 1996, 55).

In no time at all, Clark became famous and very wealthy. He was one of the most influential disc jockeys in the nation – most of whom were suspected of taking bribes (called "payola") from the big record companies to play certain records more often than others. Congress held hearings to investigate that matter, and President Eisenhower ordered the Federal Trade Commission to bring formal charges against the offending record companies (Ewen 1977, 528). Clark was never accused of taking payola, but his personal investments in music publishing and recording companies were considered a conflict of interest, so he had to divest himself of those companies.

Beneath the boyish good looks and charming stage demeanor was a very astute business mind. For nearly ten years, *American Bandstand* was a primary force in the creation of a whole outlook on teenage life – hair styles, fashions, dances (the Mashed Potato, the Frug, the Watusi, Walking the Dog, and others), dating issues, and all the other adolescent concerns about behavior and social values.

Dick Clark launched the careers of Fabian Forte, Frankie Avalon, Bobby Rydell, the Dovells, and Chubby Checker. Often called America's oldest living teenager, Dick Clark gave rock and roll a wholesome image, and he did a lot to persuade parents that their children were not all that bad just because they were addicted to the music.

In later years, Dick Clark added to his financial empire with a strong move into independent television production. His companies have created and/or produced numerous television series television specials, and movies, including the *Golden Globes*, the *Billboard Music Awards*, *Dick Clark's New Year's Rockin' Eve*, and the *American Music Awards.* In the 1990s he opened a chain of *American Bandstand* restaurants to capitalize on his fame with the aging Americans who remember him from their formative adolescent years back in the 1960s.

Clark remained active in the entertainment industry until 2004, when he suffered a stroke. He made infrequent appearances after that, as his ability to speak had been affected. He died in 2012 due to complications from surgery.

Don Kirshner

Five years younger than Dick Clark, but driven by equally keen business instincts, was a songwriter named Don Kirshner (1934-2011). The son of a Bronx tailor, Kirshner began to shape a dream in his late teens. His dream was to develop new rock songwriters the way Max and Louis Dryfuss (Chappell Music Publishers) had developed Tin Pan Alley songwriters – the Gershwins, Rodgers and Hart, and others – a few decades earlier (Szatmary 1996, 61).

At age twenty-four, Kirshner made his move when he and pop guitarist Al Nevins of the Three Suns formed Aldon Music in 1958. They even rented space in 1650 Broadway, a few doors down from the famous Brill Building (1619 Broadway at 49th, where many big band publishers had their offices in the 1930s and 1940s) and a few blocks north of the historic Tin Pan Alley. Kirshner and Nevins succeeded beyond all expectation in creating a world of "publisher-manufactured" rock and roll (Shaw 1982, 55). Since 1650 Broadway and the Brill Building were both essentially manufacturing centers for music, rock industry insiders began to call the tunes "Brill Building Rock", with a mixture of admiration, disrespect, and envy.

At his peak, Don Kirshner had thirty-five young men and women tucked away in little one-room studios composing simple tunes with simple lyrics about teenage concerns. Just as it was in Tin Pan Alley in the 1920s and '30s, many of the composers and lyricists were Jewish and young. Journalists said that Tin Pan Alley had become Teen Pan Alley, all because of the giant publishing octopus called Aldon Music, Inc. (Szatmary 1996, 67).

SONGWRITING TEAMS

Sedaka and Greenfield

The child of a Turkish cab driver who was a competent pianist, Neil Sedaka (b. 1939) took to music at an early age. By thirteen he was a brilliant pianist and writing pop songs for school productions with his friend Howie Greenfield (1936-1986) doing the lyrics.

Sedaka went to the Juilliard School of Music, and was on his way to a promising career as a classical pianist. He got deflected, however, by his rock composing skills, and soon gave up his Juilliard scholarship to concentrate on pop tunes, again with Howie Greenfield. Sedaka's piano and vocal demos were so well received that he went on to a huge career as a performer, as well.

Together they wrote "Stupid Cupid", "The Diary", "Calendar Girl", "Fallin'", "Breaking Up Is Hard To Do", "Stairway to Heaven", "Happy Birthday, Sweet Sixteen", and "Oh! Carol", dedicated to Sedaka's then girlfriend, Carole Klein (later to be known as Carole King). She responded with "Oh! Neil", but it didn't make the charts.

Mann and Weil

Barry Mann (b. 1939) began composing at age twelve, but went to the Pratt Institute to study architecture. He dropped out of college, and set his sights on a career in pop music. Early in his career as a songwriter and demo pianist, he married lyricist Cynthia Weil (b. 1940) who was trained as an actress and dancer.

"It was insane," recalled Barry Mann. "Cynthia and I would be in this little cubicle about the size of a closet, with just a piano and a chair. No window or anything. We'd go in every morning and write songs all day.

In the next room Carole [King] and Gerry [Goffin] would be doing the same thing, and in the next room after that Neil [Diamond] or somebody else.

All of us... were so insecure that we'd never write a hit again that we wrote constantly in order to prove we could" (quoted in Szatmary 1996, 65).

Barry Mann and Cynthia Weil cranked out tunes 9 a.m. to 5 p.m. just like factory workers. Over fifty years later, Mann and Weil still work together in their own publishing house, Dyad Music. Between them, they have over 600 song credits to their names, including the Grammy winning "Somewhere Out There" from the movie *An American Tail* (1987), "You've Lost That Lovin' Feelin'" (co-written with Phil Spector, 1964), and "On Broadway" (co-written with Jerry Leiber and Mike Stoller, 1963).

King and Goffin

Carole Klein (b. 1942) played piano at age four. While in high school, she changed her name to Carole King and formed her first band, the Co-sines. At Queens College, she began to write songs with her new boyfriend Gerry Goffin (1939-2014). They married, and became a prolific songwriting team, turning out a wide variety of hits – "Will You Still Love Me Tomorrow?" (The Shirelles), "Take Good Care of My Baby" (Bobby Vee), "The Loco-Motion" (Little Eva), "Up On the Roof" (The Drifters), "Go Away Little Girl" (Steve Lawrence), "Crying in the Rain" (The Everly Brothers), "Halfway to Paradise" (Tony Orlando and Bobby Vinton), "Just Once In My Life" (Herman's Hermits), and many more first-rate pop tunes.

By 1968, the King-Goffin partnership was over. They divorced and went their separate ways, but each continued to be quite successful in the world of big time pop music.

King moved to California, where she would later collaborate with other notable musicians, such as James Taylor and Joni Mitchell. Her second solo album, *Tapestry*, released in 1971, went to No. 1 on the album chart and held the spot for 15 weeks. Over 25 million copies of the album have been sold worldwide. In 2014, "Beautiful: The Carole King Musical", which chronicled her beginnings in the music business, debuted on Broadway. The actress who portrayed King, Jessie Mueller, won the 2014 Tony Award for Best Leading Actress in a Musical.

Goffin began writing with other composers, including Michael Masser, with whom he co-wrote the theme from *Mahogany* (sung by Diana Ross and for which Goffin and Masser received an Academy Award nomination), "Saving All My Love for You" (recorded by Whitney Houston), and "Tonight, I Celebrate My Love for You" (recorded by Roberta Flack and Peabo Bryson).

Leiber and Stoller

Composer Mike Stoller (b. 1933) and lyricist Jerry Leiber (1933-2011) were one of the most active and influential writer-producer teams in the field. Their parents had moved to Los Angeles during World War II and the boys were introduced by Lester Sill of Modern Records. In 1951, at age 18, they had their first commercial tune, "Real Ugly Woman", recorded by bluesman Jimmy Witherspoon.

For the next twenty years they carved out their place in rock and roll history, leading the way with innovations that soon became standard operating procedures. Every aspect of their recording sessions was carefully pre-planned, and there were times when they did sixty takes and agonized through much editing before they approved the final master (Clarke 1990, 696).

They were among the first to give their songs a mini-drama character, "little playlets", Leiber called them – like "Riot in Cell Block No. 9", "Smokey Joe's Cafe", and "Searchin'". They were among the first to become independent producers. It was a natural extension of their instincts. "We don't write songs," they said, "we write records." And they did, "tightly plotted and paced, and as relentlessly rehearsed, as any evening at the theater" (Palmer 1995, 39).

Leiber and Stoller blazed a new trail in 1960 by putting Latin rhythms into an arrangement of "Save the Last Dance for Me", then followed with "Spanish Harlem", making a solo star of the Drifters' lead singer, Ben E. King (Stambler 1977, 303). They used strings on "There Goes My Baby". Their young assistant, Phil Spector, took all their techniques to the maximum when he stepped out on his own.

When Leiber and Stoller moved back to New York, part of the West Coast music group called the Robins went along. Since they went from one coast to the other, they called themselves the Coasters. They immediately became a kind of rock and roll repertory company for Leiber and Stoller, acting out the story line during live performances of "Yakety Yak", "Along Came Jones", and other tunes.

One of the giant early hits of Leiber and Stoller was a textbook demonstration in the changing sociology of pop music.

"Hound Dog" was written by the white team of Leiber and Stoller, a couple of Jewish kids from the East Coast. They gave it to Johnny Otis, a white R&B bandleader who often passed for black. Otis, in turn, claimed that he had written the song and given it to blues singer Big Mama Thornton, who recorded it in a bluesy style.

Then along came Elvis, the white hepcat, who shot "Hound Dog" full of rock-'n'-roll and made it classic, only to have some claim that he had merely covered a "black" song (Smith 1989, 28).

For all its troublesome complexity, the revolutionary new music, rock and roll, did a great deal to bring black and white musicians, record producers, and audiences much closer together than they had been during any previous musical style. Dick Clark would later remark that he saw "rock and roll as the most subtle form of integration that ever existed" (quoted in Smith 1989, 17).

Phil Spector

Co-writer of Ben E. King's "Spanish Harlem" and Gene Pitney's "Dream for Sale", Bronx-born Phil Spector (b. 1939) started out playing guitar and piano as a teenager when his parents moved to Los Angeles. He formed the Teddy Bears with schoolmates Annette Kleinbar and Marshall Leib, and at age 18 wrote "To Know Him Is to Love Him", which had been inspired by the inscription on his father's tombstone.

He moved back to New York, and worked as a freelance studio assistant for Leiber and Stoller and several other established composers and producers. Finally, at age 21, he teamed up with Lester Sill, and, combining their names, they formed a new record label called Philles.

He was obsessed with studio techniques, and soon was recording with triple rhythm sections – three drummers, three bass players, and three pianos – plus several guitars and horns. The singers became almost interchangeable, and Spector would often lay down the monster instrumental track even before he hired the singers.

Spector would boil all this instrumentation down into a massive mono mix, a great, grandly textured "wall of sound". The idea was not to hear individual instruments, but... to hear a sound that was deliberately blurry, atmospheric, and of course HUGE – Wagnerian rock and roll with all the trimmings (Palmer 1995, 40).

The records were unusual, to say the least, and they were commercially successful, especially the Ronettes' "Be My Baby", "Walking in the Rain", and "(The

Best Part of) Breakin' Up". He also had big hits with the Crystals' "Uptown", "He's a Rebel", and "Da Doo Ron Ron". He even scored with the Righteous Brothers' version of "You've Lost That Lovin' Feelin'" (co-written by Barry Mann and Cynthia Weil).

The "wall of sound" stunned everyone in the middle of the 1960s. It got a little weary, though, with the same gigantic sounds always creating rather the same effect – and it was very expensive! In 1967 Spector sold the label and hired himself out as a freelance celebrity producer, eventually working on such projects as the Beatles' *Let it Be* album.

Although he was largely inactive in the music business in the 1980s, 1990s, and 2000s, Spector was inducted into the Rock and Roll Hall of Fame in 1989 (as a non-performer) and the Songwriters Hall of Fame in 1997. Things took a bit of an interesting turn after that, however, as he was convicted in 2009 of second-degree murder. He is now serving a prison sentence of nineteen years to life in California.

THE FOLK PROTEST MOVEMENT

As if to get some pure musical roots back into the pop music industry, a wave of folk song groups washed over the land. Some, like Leonard Cohen, Richie Havens, and Phil Ochs followed the legendary Woody Guthrie (1912-1967), who spent his whole life as a spokesman for poor people. Guthrie could formulate the most complex political argument in simple terms, within the framework of traditional folk-country tunes. He was the absolute archetype of all later American singer-songwriters (Logan and Woffinden 1977, 100).

Others, like the Kingston Trio, John Denver, and Tom Paxton, followed a more pop-rock approach and sang the songs of others with sweet harmony in a gentle, entertaining manner. Many of these singers were not real folkies, but urban middle-class kids who massaged the traditional folk style into what came to be known as folk-rock.

Here, then, is a brief overview of some of the biggest names in folk music.

Pete Seeger

His father, Charles Seeger (1886-1979), music specialist at the Library of Congress, studied and catalogued thousands of folk songs from all over the world.

Little did the father suspect that his son, Pete, would use that great body of folk songs as the raw material for a huge career in protesting all manner of establishment abuses of power and position.

Just like Woody Guthrie, Pete Seeger (1919-2014) was deeply concerned with peace, love, honor, and social compassion. He, too, was outraged when big corporations violated all principles of decency and democracy by hiring mobsters to beat up union organizers. He, too, wanted workers to get a reasonable share of company profits. Like the Hutchinson Family Singers (see page 33) had done one hundred years earlier, Seeger traveled around the country lashing out at what he saw as the major social problems of the day – greed, prejudice, corruption, and such.

In 1941, Seeger formed the Almanac Singers. In the great tradition of folk singers all through history, they took well-known tunes and performed them with new, original protest lyrics. In 1948, Seeger formed the Weavers, establishing a more pop-flavored style of folk singing, featuring strong harmonies and geared more toward entertaining and less fiercely political in nature.

Joan Baez

As the daughter of a Mexican-born physicist and a Scotch-Irish mother, dark-skinned Joan Baez (b. 1941) felt a lot of nasty discrimination growing up in Clarence Center, New York. She marched on Washington, D. C., in 1963 along with Bob Dylan, Odetta Holmes, Harry Belafonte, and Peter, Paul, and Mary. She helped organize the Free Speech Movement and founded the Institute for the Study of Nonviolence (Szatmary 1987, 72).

In and out of jail frequently for demonstrating against the Vietnam War in the 1960s, Baez continues her musical activism today. The subdued passion of "Birmingham Sunday", "We Shall Overcome", and "What Have They Done to the Rain" inspired thousands of American adolescents to challenge the political status quo.

Bob Dylan

Certainly the most influential of all the folk-song activists was Robert Allen Zimmerman (b. 1941) who named himself, so the story goes, after poet Dylan

Thomas. Dylan denied the story in some interviews (Charlton 1990, 139), but offered no other explanation.

Woody Guthrie's accusatory, righteous stance as the guitar-picking People's Sage was copied lock, stock, and cracker-barrel (even down to the harmonica rack) in Bob Dylan's early career – except that Dylan spoke about adolescent alienation instead of the displaced hobos, drifters, and Great Depression homeless who had been Guthrie's main concern (Logan and Woffinden 1977, 100).

Dylan's singing and guitar playing have often been ridiculed as amateurish and unintelligible, but no one has ever doubted the power and significance of his poetic-philosophical declarations. "Blowin' in the Wind" and "The Times They Are A-Changin'" carried the folk-protest movement to new heights of sensitivity and awareness.

Dylan was discovered by John Hammond, at the time a volunteer executive at Columbia Records. (Volunteer because his mother was a Vanderbilt, and he didn't need the job or the money.) Hammond had a long list of discoveries – Count Basie and Billie Holiday among them – and he heard Dylan's promise. All the other executives at Columbia spoke of Bob Dylan as "Hammond's Folly".

A few months after his audition, Dylan's self-titled album was released (1962). His second album, *The Freewheelin' Bob Dylan*, contained "Blowin' in the Wind" and "Masters of War". Dylan was on his way. With his next album, *The Times They Are A-Changin'* (1964), he became a major star, indeed *the* major star of the folk movement.

He is certainly one of the most peculiar superstars in American pop music. He rejected all the parties, glitz, and glamour of his fame to live the life of a recluse. He embraced Christianity, but turned back to Judaism when his oldest boy approached the age of bar mitzvah. Then, there are some who say that a motorcycle accident in July of 1966 did not really happen, but rather, that Dylan was doing battle with his manager, Albert Grossman, trying to regain control of his wealth and his career (Eliot 1989, 117).

> *Dylan's Witmark [publishing] contract expired in 1965, at which time Dylan agreed, at Grossman's urging, to start his own publishing company, Dwarf Music. The move... doubled Grossman's take to 50 percent of all Dylan's publishing income. This was in addition to his managerial piece, said to be 20 percent of everything,*

including Dylan's share of his own publishing income (Eliot 1989, 115).

Whatever may be the cause, Dylan's career has been a continuous string of oblique shifts that surprise and disturb his fans. The most famous instance came at the Newport Folk Festival in 1965. He appeared, much to his followers' dismay, with an electric guitar and the highly amplified Paul Butterfield Blues Band, leaving the stage after only three songs because of the hissing and booing, ostensibly because he "went electric". (Some say the hissing and booing occurred only after the announcement that Dylan could only play a short set, and that it had nothing to do with the non-acoustic delivery.) Irwin Silber, longtime activist and fan, editor of the radical folk magazine *Sing Out*, said, "I would not have minded so much if he had sung just one song about the war!" (Szatmary 1987, 74).

Peter, Paul, and Mary

Owning such a big chunk of Bob Dylan's creative rights, Albert Grossman was eager to get those songs recorded. In due time, all the acts in Grossman's stable of performers would have hits with Dylan tunes – Judy Collins, Manfred Mann, the Byrds, the Animals, Sonny and Cher, the Turtles, and Peter, Paul, and Mary.

They were just as political and serious as the unpolished "authentic" folk singers, but Peter Yarrow (b. 1938), Paul Stookey (b. 1937), and Mary Travers (1936-2009) distinguished themselves from the others by their clear enunciation and carefully shaded harmonies. They became enormously popular, scoring nineteen hit singles between 1962 and 1970. Most of their songs were written by others – "Leaving on a Jet Plane" (John Denver), "Blowin' in the Wind" (Bob Dylan), and "If I Had a Hammer" (the Weavers, Pete Seeger, and Lee Hays) were among their biggest hits. Yarrow's "Puff, the Magic Dragon" and Stookey's "I Dig Rock and Roll Music", however, revealed strong compositional skills in the group.

Although they went through a brief period in the early 1970s where they were not working together, Peter, Paul, and Mary continued to tour on and off until Travers' death in 2009.

Arlo Guthrie

Woody Guthrie's son, Arlo (b. 1947), carries on his father's anti-establishment social and political views, and has added a classic put-down to the repertoire of folk-song protests. It's called "Alice's Restaurant Massacree", and it became a giant hit at the Newport Folk Festival in 1967.

The tune is a long, droll, comic tale of Arlo's troubles with the police and the draft board. After Thanksgiving dinner at Alice's Restaurant, Arlo and his buddy offer to take some garbage to the city dump on their way home as a friendly gesture to Alice (owner of the aforementioned restaurant). The police arrest the boys for littering, for which they have to pay a $50 fine. The song then goes on to describe Guthrie's interactions at the draft board, during which he discloses the prior littering incident. To make a long story short, Guthrie is eventually dismissed with the reproach "We don't like your kind." It's a hilarious spoof of the establishment mentality so prevalent in the late 1960s.

Arlo Guthrie went on to a modest film and TV career when *Alice's Restaurant* was made into a movie, and he still continues to write and record music today.

Joni Mitchell

After growing up in Saskatchewan, Canada, Roberta Joan Anderson (b. 1943) went off to the Alberta College of Art in Calgary, but soon dropped out to sing folk songs in the local coffee houses. She moved to Toronto, married and divorced a cabaret entertainer, Chuck Mitchell, and soon made a name for herself composing and singing poignant ballads.

By the end of the 1960s, she was something of a cult heroine, with a strong crowd of fans devoted to her whole approach to life. Her characteristic view, expressed in "Both Sides, Now", "Let the Wind Carry Me", and "Woodstock", is a mixture of social commentary and personal moods, feelings, and scenarios. "Joni exorcises her demons by writing those songs," said Stephen Stills, "and in so doing she reaches way down and grabs the essence of something very private and personal to women" (quoted in Ewen 1977, 643).

She continued to write and record through the mid-2000s, but she officially retired in 2010 for health reasons.

Simon and Garfunkel

In 1957, Paul Simon (b. 1941) and Art Garfunkel (b. 1941), fifteen year old classmates at Forest Hills High School in New York, began a rocky but illustrious career in urban-folk music. After several years of ups and downs, including an appearance on Dick Clark's radio show as "Tom and Jerry", they began to click. In 1964, their first major album, *Wednesday Morning, 3 A.M.* (Columbia Records), contained some Bob Dylan tunes and several originals of their own. One of the tunes, "The Sounds of Silence", was remixed and reissued with bass, guitar, and drums. It shot up to No. 1 in the nation on New Year's Day, 1966. A month later, an album of the same name was released, with a surprise hit, "I Am a Rock".

A third album in 1966, *Parsley, Sage, Rosemary, and Thyme*, sold over a million copies with masterful tunes like "Homeward Bound", "Scarborough Fair/Canticle", and "The 59th Street Bridge Song (Feelin' Groovy)", and "7 O'clock News/Silent Night, Holy Night", with a newscaster's voice describing the death and destruction that day, while the famous Christmas carol is heard in the background.

For the next three years, Simon and Garfunkel led a charmed musical life. They became the spokesmen for adolescent angst in America – delivering a message of "literate protest against the pangs of youth, the pathos of old age, and the matter-of-fact hypocrisies of the middle-aged and the middle class in between"(Josh Greenfield, quoted in Ewen 1979, 651).

After the movie soundtrack for *The Graduate* (1967), with the classic "Mrs. Robinson", they went on to record a number of hits, but one masterpiece stands out – "Bridge Over Troubled Water", which was eventually recorded by two hundred different singers over the next four decades.

After a breakup in 1969, Simon and Garfunkel broke up. Garfunkel went into acting and continued to do solo work in music. Simon continued to write songs, perform, and produce, winning the 1987 Grammy for Album of the Year for *Graceland*. The duo has reunited on and off since the early 1970s, making appearances at benefit concerts and the occasional tour.

Hootenannies

As always happens, big money can be made by packaging and marketing sentiments. And sure enough, by the middle of the 1960s, ABC Television took the folk-protest, anti-war mood of America's college students and dropouts, and put together a squeaky clean, non-threatening weekly TV show that derived its name from a Scottish folk party, called a "hootenanny".

In the 20th century revision of the word, a hootenanny became the term for a gathering of union men, working-class poor, folksingers, and intellectuals sympathetic to the cause. They gathered to sing old and new songs and to cement their emotional bond. The ABC show, of course, turned out to be something completely different.

Joan Baez refused to appear when she learned that Pete Seeger had been turned down for his left-wing political views. Others did appear, though, and, generally speaking, the show was not all that objectionable.

Fiercely proud and confident, Pete Seeger summed it up succinctly when the ABC-TV *Hootenanny* finally went off the air.

> *"It was just a bunch of white college kids all clapping inanely, no matter what song was sung, big smiles all over, and never a hint of controversy or protest. In the six months the show was on, it almost ruined the word "hootenanny". I was pleased when they moved on to make money out of something else"* (quoted in Palmer 1976, 207).

DANCING

Back in the 1950s, hardly anyone ever danced to Elvis Presley, Jerry Lee Lewis, or Little Richard. By the 1960s, however, because of Dick Clark's *American Bandstand*, dancing was coming back into fashion.

In August of 1960, Ernest Evans, known as Chubby Checker (b. 1941), caused a dance craze with his treatment of Hank Ballard's release of March 1959 called "The Twist". It began a huge movement of dances. Checker then followed up with "Let's Twist Again" and "Slow Twistin'".

The Isley Brothers offered "Twist and Shout", covered later by the Beatles. Sam Cooke recorded "Twistin' the Night Away". Gary U.S. Bonds came out with "Twist, Twist, Señora", and Jimmy Soul with "Twistin' Matilda". Santo and Johnny released "Twistin' Bells", and the Marvelettes came up with "Twistin' Postman". Bill Black's combo recorded "Twist-Her".

Of course, Hollywood saw dollar signs, and moved in with *Twist Around the Clock*, in 1961, with Chubby Checker introducing "Twistin' U.S.A.". At the same time came the film *Hey, Let's Twist!* Then in 1962, *Twist All Night*, with jazzman Louis Prima, and *Don't Knock the Twist,* again with Chubby Checker.

New York's Peppermint Lounge became the favorite hangout of the Jet Set as Joey Dee and the Starliters played their hit, "The Peppermint Twist", all night long. Among the frequent twisters were English playwright Noël Coward, gossip columnist Elsa Maxwell, American playwright Tennessee Williams, Judy Garland, and a variety of East Coast politburo types. Checker's business advisers, no doubt including Dick Clark, introduced Chubby Checker T-shirts, jeans, dolls, Twist skirts, Twist raincoats, and Twist nighties.

The Twist spawned other dances, most with their own special tune – "The Loco-Motion" by Little Eva, "The Mashed Potato" by Dee Dee Sharp, "Limbo Rock" and "Popeye (the Hitchhiker)" by Chubby Checker, "The Wah-Watusi" by the Orlons, "Hully Gully" by the Dovells, "Walkin' the Dog" by Rufus Thomas, along with more generic dances without specific songs, including the swim, the jerk, the shake, the pony, the Frug, and others.

History was repeating itself, with modifications. A wave of colorful dances sweeps through America every fifteen years or so. In the 1920s parents were puzzled by the strange attraction their teenager children had for the Shimmy, the Charleston, the Black Bottom, the Sugar Foot Strut, and the Varsity Drag – and then in the late 1930s the Lindy Hop, the Jitterbug, the Bunny Hop, the Samba, the Tango, the Mambo, the Conga, and dozens more.

The urge to shock their parents with "undignified" dancing seems to be a necessary phase for each generation of teenagers on their way to adulthood. The 1980s found teenagers imitating hieroglyphics with the Bangles' "Walk like an Egyptian". The rage of the 1990s was the Macarena. More recently, South Korean K-pop musician Psy introduced the world to "Gangnam Style".

Chapter 26
More Expansion and
Mutation of Rock and Roll

The 1960s were filled with exciting changes in the world of rock and roll. Three new styles began to take shape: music about surfing and hot rods in Los Angeles, authentic black rock in Detroit, and psychedelic rock in San Francisco. Los Angeles and Detroit will be explained now, and San Francisco will be addressed in Chapter 28.

LOS ANGELES

About the same time the Twist captured the East Coast, a different style of music grew up on the beaches in southern California with Dick Dale and the Del-Tones, the Surfaris, Jan and Dean, the Belairs, the Beach Boys, and similar groups.

Dick Dale and the Del-Tones

From Beirut, Lebanon, by way of Quincy, Massachusetts, Dick Dale (born Richard Monsour in 1937) became a West Coast legend when he combined his love of surfing and playing guitar.

> *There was a tremendous amount of power I felt while surfing and that feeling of power was simply transferred into my guitar when I was playing surf music. It was that good rambling feeling I got when I was locked in a tube with the whitewater caving in over my head. I was trying to project the power of the ocean to the people* (quoted in Szatmary 1996, 71).

Musically, that translated into a powerful style of sharp, short chords heavily reverberated, and "rapid-fire, double-stroke picking... with long Middle Eastern melodies slithering along atop shimmering Spanish-inflected chording, punctuated by slamming slides up the neck" – and everything at high decibel levels (Palmer 1995, 41).

The style caught on, and surfers drove hundreds of miles to Balboa to hear Dick Dale and the Del-Tones. "The Rendezvous Ballroom held well over 1000 people, and Dale's sound was, in a word, awesome!" (Pete Johnson, quoted in Szatmary 1996, 71).

"Let's Go Tripping" (1961), "Surfing Drums" (1961), and "Miserlou" (1962) led Dick Dale to a Capitol recording contract in 1963, and he was soon known as the "King of the Surf Guitar".

Duane Eddy

Using some of Dick Dale's guitar techniques, but playing nearer the bridge to make the sound even more brittle and metallic, Duane Eddy (b. 1938) arrived at his special voice, called the "twangy guitar". It was similar in raw energy to the surf sound of Dick Dale, but it seemed to have more commercial possibilities. Recording most of his material at Audio Recorders in Phoenix, Arizona, Eddy often sent the master tape to Gold Star Studios in Hollywood to add a jazz saxophone track. Very soon, Duane Eddy and the Rebels attracted a cult following in both America and England.

Shy and handsome, he appeared in movies, had a few hit releases which pleased his crowd immensely, and enjoyed a solid career in the music business. In 1986, he recorded a remake of his earlier hit, "Peter Gunn" (written by Henry Mancini), with British synthpop group The Art of Noise, for which they won a Grammy for Best Rock Instrumental.

His "Movin' and Groovin'", "Cannonball", and "Your Baby's Gone Surfin'" are still heard on Golden Oldies programs today.

Jan and Dean

Their football lockers were next to one another at Emerson Junior High School, so Jan Berry (1941-2004) and Dean Torrence (b. 1940) became classroom buddies. Their common interest in cars and surfing led them into the music business where they struck gold by singing about those topics.

An appearance on *American Bandstand* lifted them to national fame, and they hit the big time when "Surf City" entered the charts in July of 1963. They sang of the same concerns as the rest of the California surf music crowd, and soon recorded "Ride the Wild Surf", "Sidewalk Surfin'" (about skateboarding), and others.

They collaborated with the Beach Boys on several albums, and had a strong career going. It all came to a sudden stop in 1966, however, when Jan Berry was involved in an automobile accident and suffered severe brain damage. While Berry recovered, Torrence turned his attention to graphic design, specializing in album covers and poster art, which he continued to do until 1980. Berry's recovery was incomplete, but eventually Jan and Dean were able to perform again on stage beginning in the late 1970s. The duo continued performing on and off up until Berry's death in 2004.

The Beach Boys

The supergroup of the surfing craze first called themselves the Pendletones, a musical play on "Pendleton", a plaid flannel shirt-jacket popular among surfers. Then they called themselves Carl and the Passions, then Kenny and the Cadets for their first recording. There was no one in the group named Kenny, but their first tune was "Barbie" (1961) when the Ken and Barbie dolls were just getting popular (Charlton 1990, 111).

Brothers Brian (b. 1942), Carl (1946-1998), and Dennis (1944-1983) Wilson joined with their cousin, Mike Love (b. 1941), and a friend, Al Jardine (b. 1942), in Hawthorne, California, for what became a long and occasionally irregular, but very successful career. Unpredictable and high-strung (he was later diagnosed as mildly bipolar with schizoaffective disorder), Brian was the musical leader of the group, and for a long time he made all the important decisions for everything.

He wrote some appealing tunes about surfing, hot rods, and California girls – kind of like a white Chuck Berry – then the Beach Boys sang them in four-part harmony, like the Four Freshman, the Hi-Los, and other jazz-tinged male vocal groups of the 1950s. Finally he added Dick Dale's surfing sound – greatly toned down in volume, complexity, and fire. The resultant musical mini-sagas of sex, surf, and sun caught on with America's teenagers, to say the least. The Beach Boys even displaced the Beatles as the World's Best Group in the 1966 music critics' poll (Lazell 1989, 30).

One of their hits, "Surfin' U.S.A." (1963), was musically identical to Chuck Berry's "Sweet Little Sixteen" (1958), and a long legal battle developed when lawyers for the record companies went to court. After some hesitation and honest confusion in his mind, Brian finally gave credit to Chuck Berry.

Rock historians consider the concept album *Pet Sounds* (1966) to be the Beach Boys' highest musical achievement. The album addresses the eternal problems of youth growing up with hopes, dreams, and fears. With Tony Asher's strong lyrics, Brian composed a group of songs that reached a new level of sophistication for pop rock. Especially memorable are "Wouldn't It Be Nice", "God Only Knows", and "I Just Wasn't Made for These Times".

"Good Vibrations", however, is their biggest hit. It came out in late 1966, as a single off of the *Smile* album. It cost $50,000 – ninety hours of studio time over six months to create eleven versions of the song – before a version that satisfied everyone involved was finally released.

Without knowing it, the Beach Boys and the Beatles were working toward the same kind of mutation and expansion of the new music called rock and roll, involving longer and more serious tunes, tempo changes, modulations, better lyrics, more imaginative recording studio procedures, guest musicians, strings, reverberation techniques, and echo chambers.

As often happens, the group went through drug problems, internal personality warfare, contract disputes with record companies, nervous breakdowns, and all the predictable stresses of artistic and creative people. Although Carl and Dennis Wilson have since died, Brian Wilson, Mike Love, and Al Jardine reunited for the album *That's Why God Made the Radio* in 2012, along with Bruce Johnston (b. 1942), who had joined the group in 1965, and David Marks, who had been an active member of the group in the late 1960s and in the 1990s. Some of the personality clashes apparently resurfaced, though, as Love announced in late 2012 that he would tour in 2013 with Johnston, but without Wilson, Jardine, and Marks.

Hot Rods

In addition to surfing, the vast shoreline of Southern California offered endless stretches of roads – ideal for automobile travel, and for the competitive instincts of adolescent males. Technology spun-off from World War II research led to wondrous new engines that could be modified by any teenage mechanic. An automobile life style emerged.

Music historian David Szatmary describes this late 1950s' California subculture in his sociological study of rock.

> *Rather than a staid station wagon, they cast their eyes upon "asphalt eaters" (dragsters) such as 'Cudas (Plymouth Barracudas) or GTOs (Grand Turismos) propelled by such huge engines as the rat motor (a 427 cubic inch Chevy engine) or the Chrysler Hemi (a 426 cubic inch engine equipped with hemispherical combustion chambers)* (Szatmary 1996, 76).

The adolescents also developed their own language to describe the life they were leading.

> *Like cowboys on their horses in a California of another era, teens with greased hair and tight black pants drove their machines to seldom-used roads and waited for a competitor to drag (race). They anticipated the flash of light, "dropped the hammer" (released the clutch quickly) and sped away, "shutting down" (defeating) an opponent* (Szatmary 1996, 76).

The entertainment industry took notice, of course, with pop tunes like "Drag City", "Car Crazy Cutie", "Don't Worry, Baby", "Shut Down", "Hey, Little Cobra", "The Little Old Lady from Pasadena", and "G.T.O.", and the albums *Hot Rod Alley, Boss Drag at Hot Rod Beach, Drag City*, and many others.

The movie moguls got into the action, too, with *Hot Rod Girl, Dragstrip Girl, Hot Rod Gang, Dragstrip Riot, Teenage Thunder*, and a host of films peddling sex, speed, sun, and teenage tans.

DETROIT

Meanwhile, half way across America in the streets of Detroit, a different but equally powerful new style of rock and roll caught the nation's teenagers by surprise – Motown. It happened in December of 1960 with the release of "(My Mama Told Me You'd Better) Shop Around", with words and music by William "Smokey" Robinson and Berry Gordy, Jr. In the early months of 1961, it was in the Top Ten charts. It was a strong opening for a brand new musical group and a brand new record company.

Berry Gordy, Jr.

As young man, Berry Gordy, Jr. (b. 1929), tried his hand at boxing, factory work, running a jazz record shop, and many other things, including writing pop songs. He had a knack for a good melody and interesting lyrics. He wrote "Reet Petite (The Sweetest Girl in Town)" (1957) and "Lonely Teardrops" (1959) for Jackie Wilson. The success of those tunes led him to finally quit his job on the Ford assembly line and give the music business his full attention for a while.

In 1959, the same year that Don Kirshner started Aldon Music, Berry Gordy borrowed eight hundred dollars from his family and rented an eight-room house at 2648 West Grand Boulevard. He told his sister, Esther, "I'll live upstairs, I'll have my offices down in the front part, and I'll have a studio out back where I can make demos and masters to sell to record companies" (quoted from Szatmary 1996, 130).

He succeeded beyond his wildest dream, and started a pop music revolution that changed American history. He first called his new company Hitsville U.S.A., then changed the name to Motown in recognition of Detroit's fame as the Motor City. Among the several subsidiaries of the main label were Tamla, Gordy, and later Soul, VIP, Mowest, and Melody. The publishing company was called Jobete, after Gordy's daughters Joy, Betty, and Terry.

> *Through the period of racial unrest and riots in the Sixties, Motown artists sang of love and other human concerns with which people of all races, religions, and political beliefs could identify. Gordy cultivated in his performers a sophisticated image, and helped bring respect and self-esteem to black Americans, who saw the Motown performers as role models* (Charlton 1990, 91).

Gordy kept tight control over everything and everyone who worked for him. Without his approval, there was not the slightest change in any act. A strong sense of pride, loyalty, and love was needed to survive Gordy's rules. Yet the corporation was, for many, one big happy family. Smokey Robinson married Claudette Rogers, a fellow member of the Miracles. Marvelette Wanda Young married Miracle Bobby Rogers. Marvelette Katherine Anderson married the Temptations' road manager, Joe Schaffner. Marvin Gaye married Gordy's sister, Anna (Stuessy 1990, 226).

It all worked, and almost overnight, Berry Gordy changed the face of pop music in America. In his seventh year of business (1967), he sold more singles than any other record company in the world, independent or major, and his empire was profiled in *Fortune, The New York Times*, and in several other major publications. It is estimated by some rock scholars that an astronomical 75% of all Motown releases ended up somewhere in the Top 40! That was unheard of in the pop music business!

The Motown Formula

Gordy mixed the elements of previous black and pop styles to arrive at a product that would appeal to the white market – classic saxophone-driven big band riffs, gospel tambourines and hand-clapping backbeats, lush orchestra strings from the Detroit Symphony for the slow tunes, and strong bass lines laid down below exotic Latin- and jazz-tinged rhythm patterns.

The studio musicians – soon called the Funk Brothers – were mostly jazzmen who enjoyed the new financial rewards of working for Motown Records: Benny Benjamin on drums, Earl Van Dyke or Joe Hunter on keyboards, Dave Hamilton on vibraphone or lead guitar, James Jamerson or Carol Kaye on bass, and Robert White on rhythm guitar. Secretaries and friends filled in on tambourines and handclapping. To get more backbeat, a studio carpenter had bolted a couple of 2"x 4"s together with a hinge. It could make a strong and crisp smack on counts two and four of the meter.

This layered big-band mix was captured at different times on two homemade eight-track tape recorders.

Producers could bring in the rhythm section, horns and strings, back-ground singers, and lead vocalists all at different times while recording, and this made all the difference in the final product.

A young electronics wizard named Michael McClain built these eight-track facilities, said to be the first in the country (most other companies were still using two- and four-track systems) (Taraborrelli 1986, 4).

The Motown Team

Gordy molded the talented youngsters from the projects of Detroit into a musical force of unparalleled importance. The musicians and singers who came to him had almost no exposure to the white world at all, so he formed a school called International Talent Management, Inc. (ITMI) to train them in the social skills they would need when they got wealthy and famous.

Maxine Powell. Berry Gordy hired modeling school director Maxine Powell (1915-2013) who taught the young performers how to make small talk at cocktail parties, how to hold their silverware at a banquet, how to move and act with grace and style, and how to dress so they didn't look like kids from the streets of Detroit. Equally as important as body language and clothes, Maxine Powell taught the youngsters to remove the abusive tone and aggressive manner from their speaking voices. She often said, these young men and women were "diamonds in the rough who needed polishing. We were training them for Buckingham Palace and the White House, so I had my work cut out for me" (quoted in Szatmary 1996, 133).

Cholly Atkins and Maurice King. Gordy also hired Cholly Atkins (1913-2003), dancer and choreographer in the legendary 1930s Cotton Club revues, and Maurice King (1911-1992), music director for big name jazz acts at Detroit's famous Flame Show Bar. Old pros Atkins and King put class into every Motown act, and wouldn't let the acts perform until they had learned their stage lessons.

Holland-Dozier-Holland. Brothers Brian (b. 1941) and Eddie (b. 1939) Holland and good friend Lamont Dozier (b. 1941) wrote and produced all of the Supremes hits between 1964 and early 1968. They also wrote for the Isley Brothers (from 1965-1968) and Marvin Gaye (during the early part of his career), as well as writing most of the material recorded by the Four Tops, several tunes for the Miracles, and a lot of songs for Martha and the Vandellas.

Typically Eddie Holland worked with the vocal leads in the various groups, Lamont Dozier helped with vocal backgrounds and instrumental tracks, and Brian Holland handled the overall composition and assisted with backup vocal tracks (Stuessy 1994, 225).

Strong and Whitfield. Barrett Strong gave up a singing career to write songs for others. He and writer-producer Norman Whitefield had a string of hits for Gladys Knight and the Pips, the Temptations, Jimmy Ruffin, Edwin Starr, and Motown's biggest hit of the 1960s, "I Heard It Through the Grapevine", originally recorded by Marvin Gaye (Charlton 1990, 92).

Holland-Dozier-Holland and Strong-Whitfield often took a portion of a song's refrain (chorus) to use as an introduction – "Stop! In the Name of Love" (1965), for example. They also used modified A-A-B and A-B-B forms as well as the standard A-A-B-A tradition. Then, too, they often modulated up a semitone about two-thirds of the way through the arrangement to give their tunes a psychological lift going out (see page 68).

MOTOWN'S STARS

Smokey Robinson

William "Smokey" Robinson (b. 1940) was one of Berry Gordy's teenage friends. Long before Motown, they dreamed of success. So when Gordy finally made the move, the first group he put on the payroll was Smokey Robinson and the Matadors. Changing their name to the Miracles, they plunged in to make the idea of Motown work. So obvious was Robinson's talent and business skill that Gordy named him vice president in 1961, well before the corporation had any major success at all. The Miracles eventually rose to the top of the industry with dozens of Top 40 hits, including five songs in the Top Ten.

Smokey Robinson did it all – gifted vocalist, songwriter, producer, adviser, business executive, talent scout, premier backup singer, and emotional anchor of Motown. Among his compositions are dozens of the best in the field: "My Guy", "Shop Around", "I Second That Emotion", "My Girl", "Cruisin'", and "The Agony and The Ecstasy".

Marvin Gaye

A handsome young man with enormous musical gifts, Marvin Gaye (1939-1984) had a budding career as a doo-wop singer and drummer with the Marquees and with Harvey and the Moonglows before he joined the Motown family. He paid his dues as a session drummer and backup vocalist, then got a solo release in 1962, "Stubborn Kind of Fellow".

Through the 1960s he placed seventeen songs in the solo Top 40 charts and a dozen more in the Top 40 duet category with Kim Weston, Mary Wells, Diana Ross, and Tammi Terrell. His two giant solo hits were "How Sweet It Is to Be Loved by You" (1964) and "I Heard It Through the Grapevine" (1968).

In the mid-1960s he married Gordy's sister, Anna, who was seventeen years older than he, and his career seemed to be stable. Things started to go downhill a bit in 1967, though, when his favorite duet partner, Tammi Terrell, age 24, collapsed in his arms during a stage performance. Terrell was later diagnosed with a brain tumor, which caused her death in 1970.

Filled with grief and disillusioned with the music business, Gaye withdrew from the public for six months. Then in a bitter scene, he divorced Anna and married Janis Hunter, whom he met in 1973. His strange double album, *Here, My Dear* (1978), aimed at Anna, is filled with irony, contradictions, and angry sarcasm (Stuessy 1994, 224). The album was clearly the work of a disturbed man.

The next few years were up and down, with periodic fits of depression during which time he threatened suicide. Finally, during a violent argument at his home, Gaye was shot by his father, Marvin, Sr., an apostolic preacher, who had for years been ashamed of what he saw as the dreadful decay of his sons' value system.

Stevie Wonder

Born in Saginaw, Michigan, and blind since birth, Stevland Judkins (b. 1950) was taken to Motown by Ronnie White, a member of the Miracles. He amazed Berry Gordy by singing and then playing piano, organ, drums, harmonica, and nearly every other instrument in the studio. He was signed that day, and within a few months went on tour with the Motown regulars, billed as Little Stevie Wonder. Gordy was convinced he had found the new Ray Charles.

That Motown Review tour had big names – Marvin Gaye, the Supremes, the Miracles, and Mary Wells – but the new kid held his own. In fact, one of his seven-minute blues-drenched live appearances so stunned the Motown executives that they released it in two parts in 1963 and "Fingertips – Part 2" went to No. 1 on the charts.

In 1970, Stevie Wonder cut a deal to make all his own decisions on music, production techniques, and styles. Motown would distribute the recordings, but Wonder would have absolute control of his own career. He married, moved to New York, and made significant changes in his musical output.

Since then his music has branched out considerably. He addressed social issues in "Living for the City" (1973), gave a jazz history lesson in "Sir Duke [Ellington]" (1977), and paid tribute to Bob Marley's style of reggae with "Master Blaster" (1980). He sang with Paul McCartney on "Ebony and Ivory" (1982), and with Dionne Warwick, Gladys Knight, and Elton John on 1986's "That's What Friends Are For", which raised money for AIDS charities. An advocate for civil rights, Wonder was instrumental in getting Martin Luther King, Jr.'s birthday recognized as a national holiday in 1980. He also appeared as a "warm-up" act for Barack Obama as he stumped from state to state during his presidential campaigns in 2008 and 2012.

Starting with *Talking Book* (1972), every studio album by Stevie Wonder from 1972 to 2005 went into the Top 5 on the US R&B charts, and nine of them were in the Top 5 on the US album charts. His *Songs in the Key of Life* (1976) regularly makes it onto "Best Albums of All Time" lists, and many performers, particularly British pop star George Michael, have covered Wonder's songs. He has received twenty-two Grammys for his work, the most ever awarded to a male solo artist.

The Jackson Five

When the Jackson Five signed with Motown in 1969, Michael was only eleven years old. He became the instant darling of the group and of the entertainment business. Joe Jackson, father and manager of the Jackson Five, stayed with Motown for a while, but then tangled with Berry Gordy over professional and financial matters. He then pulled his boys out to sign with Epic in 1976.

Gordy owned the name, however, so the group had to go out as "The Jacksons", but they still received 2.7% of all profits Gordy received from the old or any new "Jackson Five" recordings (Lazell 1989, 251). The name change also reflected a personnel change – brother Jermaine Jackson stayed with Motown, having married Berry's daughter, Hazel.

Michael Jackson's illustrious solo career will be discussed later in this book.

The Supremes

With a string of five consecutive No. 1 singles, the Supremes brought Motown into the major leagues in a hurry. Formed in 1959 to be a sister group to the Primes (who later became the Temptations), the new group was called the Primettes, consisting of Florence Ballard (1943-1976), age 16, Mary Wilson (b. 1944), age 15, and Betty McGlown-Travis (1941-2008), age 17. Paul Williams of the Primes brought in Diana Ross (b. 1944), age 15, to strengthen the trio's sound, and for a short time it was really a quartet singing three-part harmony.

Betty Travis left in 1960 and was replaced by Barbara Martin (b. 1943). The group dissolved soon thereafter when the parents of Florence Ballard and Barbara Martin insisted that the girls concentrate on their high school studies (Lazell 1989, 494).

Mary Wilson and Diana Ross carried on as a duo until the second iteration of the quartet re-formed to audition for Diana's neighbor, Smokey Robinson. Robinson took the girls to Berry Gordy who showed no interest, but gave them some occasional backup vocals behind Marvin Gaye and others. When Barbara Martin pulled out of the group again, Gordy decided to sign the trio, but insisted on a name change.

As the Supremes, they struggled for two years, getting no higher than No. 30 on the charts, but they struck gold in August of 1964 with "Where Did Our Love Go?" by Holland-Dozier-Holland. The tune had been written for, but rejected by, the Marvelettes.

By December of 1966, the Supremes had registered nine more No. 1 hits – "Baby Love", "Come See about Me", "Stop! In the Name of Love", "I Hear a Symphony", "Back In My Arms Again", "You Can't Hurry Love", "You Keep Me Hangin' On", "Love is Here and Now You're Gone", and "The Happening", all by Holland-Dozier-Holland (Elrod 1994, pp. 238-247).

By 1967 Diana Ross was becoming a star, and Florence Ballard started missing performances due to an increasing dependence on alcohol. When Ballard finally left to try a career on her own with ABC Records, Cindy Birdsong (b. 1939) was called in to fill the Ballard's vacancy. Florence Ballard's new career did not go well, and she died nine years later of heart failure at age thirty-three.

Diana Ross left the Supremes and began a huge career with a solo stage show in Framingham, Massachusetts, in March of 1970. Despite their many changes and issues over the ten years they were in existence, the Supremes remain, even today, as the "gold standard" for girl groups. Hundreds, if not thousands, of other groups have followed in their footsteps, with varying degrees of success. A loosely-based, fictionalized account of the Supremes' rise to stardom was dramatized in the Broadway musical (later to become a movie), *Dreamgirls* (1981).

The Marvelettes

In addition to the Supremes, there were the Marvelettes, whose "Please Mr. Postman", "Beachwood 4-5789", and "Too Many Fish in the Sea" confirmed that Motown's musical formula would work. Just high school girls from Inkster, Michigan, they didn't even win the school talent show, but their teacher took them to audition for Motown.

They went on to a total of nine Top 10 tunes over the next several years, but were passed around from one producer to another and therefore never developed a specific sound or personality. Of the constantly changing personnel, Wanda Rogers (b. 1943), Gladys Horton (1945-2011), and Katherine Anderson (b. 1944) are the three who are on most of the hits.

Martha Reeves and The Vandellas

When she heard Della Reese in Detroit's New Liberty Baptist Church, a young Martha Reeves (b. 1941) decided to be a singer. She formed her own singing group, the Delphis, and auditioned for Berry Gordy. The group failed the audition, but Martha Reeves was hired as a secretary at Motown. She also did handclaps and backup vocals on many studio sessions.

Finally in 1962, Gordy signed Martha's vocal trio, now called the Vandellas, using the name of her inspiration, Della Reese, as part of the trio's name. Reeves hired and fired her singers, and there were many changes in names and faces. In 1964, the group consisted of Reeves, Rosalyn Ashford (b. 1943), and Betty Kelly (b. 1944), and they did most of the famous tunes. They had a good number of Top 10 hits – "Heat Wave", "Dancing in the Street", "Quicksand", "Nowhere to Run", and several others.

In 1972, the group disbanded, but a few years later Martha Reeves hired some new singers and started again. After serving on the Detroit city council from 2005 to 2009, she is still traveling around with a first-class stage show, bringing classic Motown harmony to the nation.

Gladys Knight & the Pips

Already an established act when they signed with Motown's Soul label in 1965, Gladys Knight & the Pips had a strong musical style and a firm professional agenda of their own. But their career was in a slump, and they were eager to get with a winning company.

Gladys Knight (b. 1944) had been a child prodigy. Her parents sang in the Wings Over Jordan Gospel Choir in Atlanta, Georgia, and by age seven Gladys was on tour with the Ted Mack Original Amateur Hour stage show. At age eight she was lead vocalist in a family group consisting of her brother Merald ("Bubba"), her sister Brenda, and her cousins William and Elenor Guest. Another cousin, James "Pips" Woods became their manager and persuaded them to turn professional. Soon thereafter, they toured with Sam Cooke, B. B. King, and Jackie Wilson as Gladys Knight and the Pips.

Brenda Knight and Elenor Guest soon left the group to get married. They were replaced by another cousin, Edward Patten, and an outsider, Langston George, who left a year or so later. The basic quartet was now firm, and their style began to solidify – and it was a special style all their own. With Gladys out front on red-hot lead vocals and the guys (William, Edward, and Bubba) on crisp, sassy harmonies, the group was tight, energetic, sharply-choreographed, and unlike any other act at Motown.

They never did manage to win Berry Gordy's full favor, of course. Few ever did. Insiders always complained that Motown was a small inner circle devoted mainly to the Miracles and the Supremes – and even deeper, to mega-talent Smokey Robinson, mega-star Diana Ross, and mega-executive Berry Gordy. Everybody seemed to feel it at one time or another.

Still, from 1965 to 1973, Gladys Knight & the Pips did their thing. "Just Walk in My Shoes", "Take Me In Your Arms and Love Me", and "Everybody Needs Love" got on the charts in England, and a re-make of the Miracles' "I Heard It Through the Grape Vine" went to No. 1 on the American soul charts and No. 2 on the pop.

After several more fine recordings – "Help Me Make It Through the Night", "If I Were Your Woman", "Neither One of Us (Wants To Be the One To Say Goodbye)", and "I Don't Want to Do Wrong", for example – the stress of trying to fit into a Motown mold got to be too much, so Gladys Knight and the Pips moved to Buddah Records in 1973.

The move was a masterstroke. Within months they had a platinum album, *Imagination*, and four hit singles: "Midnight Train to Georgia", "I've Got To Use My Imagination", "Where Peaceful Waters Flow", and "The Best Thing That Ever Happened To Me".

The group went on to host their own television series, record a soundtrack for the film *Claudine*, and enjoy the just rewards of their unique talent. Although the Pips officially retired in 1988, Gladys Knight continued to tour until 2009 and she released a solo album in 2013.

The Four Tops

It's almost unheard of in pop music, but the same four men were the Four Tops for forty-four years – Levi Stubbs (1936-2008), Lawrence Payton (1938-1997), Renaldo "Obie" Benson (1936-2005), and Abdul "Duke" Fakir (b. 1935). While still teenagers, they opened in Las Vegas for the famous jazz vocalist Billy Eckstine and elsewhere for Count Basie and Della Reese.

Nothing much happened through five record labels, however, until Berry Gordy took them into the Motown family and turned them over to Holland-Dozier-Holland. In July, 1964, their first release, "Baby, I Need Your Lovin'" entered the Top 40. A year later, their "I Can't Help Myself" (a.k.a. "Sugarpie Honeybunch") was No. 1 in America. And then in October of 1966 they hit No. 1 again with "Reach Out I'll Be There".

The ingredients of success for the Four Tops were the beautiful and expressive voice of lead singer Stubbs and the rich, jazz-tinged harmonies. Several times Berry Gordy tried to get Stubbs to go out on his own, but to no avail. The last time was in 1971 when Gordy sent a telegram to Europe asking Stubbs to audition for a perfect film role. Stubbs declined, and the role went to somebody else. Stubbs did eventually make a film debut of sorts, as the voice of Audrey II, the carnivorous plant in 1986's *Little Shop of Horrors*.

Although the lineup of the group was eventually forced to change as members died, the Four Tops, including original surviving member Duke Fakir and Payton's son, Lawrence Payton, Jr., were still touring in 2014.

The Temptations

Using the classic gospel-group formula of a light, high tenor lead vocal against earthy, gutsy background voices, the Temptations were one of Motown's hottest R&B groups from 1965 to 1975. Even with continuous changes of personnel, co-anchors Melvin Franklin (1942-1995) and Otis Williams (b. 1941) always managed to present a first-class stage show.

Motown's premier composer-producer Norman Whitfield became their musical godfather, and their success owes much to his studio skills. Berry Gordy was an unforgiving executive, so when the Temptations went with Atlantic Records (1977) and returned to Motown (1980), Smokey Robinson smoothed everything out both times. Their giant hits include "My Girl", "Beauty Is Only Skin Deep", "(I Know) I'm Losing You", "All I Need Is You", "You're My Everything" and many more.

The group released its final album with Motown, *Legacy*, in 2004.

The Commodores

The Commodores met as freshman in 1968 at what is now Tuskegee University in Alabama, and hit the big time in 1971 when they opened for the Jackson Five on a world tour. They signed with Motown, and took off on another tour, this time with Stevie Wonder and the Rolling Stones.

Their disco-funk "Machine Gun", "Slippery When Wet", and "Brickhouse" were balanced by Lionel Richie's (b. 1949) beautiful love songs, "Sweet Love", "Easy", "Three Times a Lady", and others.

The group was not the creation of Motown, however, and when Lionel Richie went out on his own in 1982 with his eponymous solo album, the group no longer enjoyed Berry Gordy's keen interest and fulltime support.

Although there have been many personnel changes over the years, the Commodores still continue to tour.

BUSINESS MATTERS

In 1971, Berry Gordy moved Motown to Los Angeles to try his hand at really big money. Diana Ross was Motown's most valuable property, and Gordy wanted to make her a movie star. He did. The film reviews were mixed, but the biopic about Billie Holiday, *Lady Sings the Blues*, starring Ross, Richard Pryor, and Billy Dee Williams, held its own against *The Godfather* and *Last Tango In Paris* in 1972. Gordy went on to direct Ross again in 1975's *Mahogany*.

Gordy sold Motown to MCA and Boston Ventures in 1988, and the company has since been acquired by other companies, mostly as part of Universal subsidiaries.

Chapter 27
The British Invasion

While the American baby boom generation was "turning on, tuning in, and dropping out" all over the land, a similar situation was taking place in Great Britain. The English baby boomers were called "The Bulge", and they, too, were crammed into schools short on facilities and trained teachers. Hundreds of thousands of youngsters left secondary school at age fifteen or sixteen, and roamed the streets looking for gainful employment. As often happens, these idle working-class youths began to form gangs, partly out of boredom, and partly out of a need to feel like they belonged to someone, if only to each other. The two main gangs were the rockers and the mods.

THE ROCKERS

The rockers wore black leather jackets, tight-fitting pants, and pointed boots or blue suede shoes. They greased back their hair in pompadour style, put on beatnik sunglasses, and roared around the streets on motorcycles. They loved American white rockabilly and black R&B.

The Beatles were among the rockers. As a boy, John Lennon joined a rocker gang which "went in for things like shoplifting and pulling girls' knickers down." Paul McCartney spent hours styling his pompadour and choosing clothes that fit into rocker fashion. McCartney's father "over and over again said that he [Paul] wasn't going to have tight trousers, but he just wore me down." George Harrison would sneak upstairs to his mother's sewing machine to "tighten up his trousers." His dad found out and demanded that George "unpick them." "I can't, Dad," George said. "I've cut the pieces completely off" (Szatmary 1987, 87-88).

In their early days, the Beatles wore black-and-white cowboy shirts with tassels dangling from the pockets, leather jackets, and pointed cowboy boots. They wanted the rockabilly sound, and they tried to look the part. When Malcolm Evans, later their road manager, first heard them, he said they sounded a bit like Elvis, who was their inspiration – sound, image, and all.

In 1959, George Harrison changed his stage name, temporarily, to Carl Harrison, after one of his heroes, Carl Perkins. For a while, the Beatles called themselves the Foreverly Brothers, in honor of the Everly Brothers. Then a change came. As John Lennon told reporter Jim Steck, "I was looking for a name like the Crickets [Buddy Holly's band] that meant two things. I went to Beatles... When you said it, people thought of crawly things; when you read it, it was beat music." (Szatmary 1987, 88).

THE MODS

The modernists, called "mods" for short, favored Italian teenage styles. Pete Townshend (b. 1945) of the Who, himself a mod, said,

> *"You needed short hair, money enough to buy a real smart suit, good shoes, good shirts, and you had to able to dance like a madman... You had to have plenty of pills all the time, especially Drynamil [amphetamines known as purple hearts], and your scooter had to be covered with lamps...* (Szatmary 1987, 83)

> *Not only were we young, but we were lower class young, no higher than garbage men, you know, but we had to find enough money to buy a Sunday best... And the outfit might change, so you had to change the whole lot next week. But it was an incredible feeling. It covered everybody. Everybody looked the same. Everybody acted the same. Everybody wanted to be the same. Any kid, no matter how ugly or screwed up, if he had the right haircut and the right clothes and the right motorbike, he was a mod. He was a mod!"* (Szatmary 1987, 83).

When Peter Meadon was manager of the Who in 1963, he stressed their mod image. When Kit Lambert and Chris Stamp later assumed control of the group as co-managers, they sent the band to Carnaby Street for pants, bulls-eye T-shirts, and jackets cut from the British flag, and then booked them for sixteen consecutive

Tuesdays at London's Marquee Club, a mod hangout owned by Ziggy Jackson. To complete the mod image, Townshend wrote "My Generation", one of his best, which became the battle cry of the mod gangs in England (Szatmary 1987, 85).

AMERICA IN THE EARLY 1960s

America's teen subculture in the early 1960s churned with conflicting passions and dreams. Some kids bathed in the innocent joys of rockabilly, the Twist, surfing music, and the doo-wop sounds of the street-corner groups. Others got angry along with the folk singers who cried out against U.S. involvement in Vietnam and against police brutality during the civil rights demonstrations.

In August of 1963, Martin Luther King, Jr., told 300,000 Americans that he had a dream, and the whole world knew that the handsome young president, John F. Kennedy, was going to be a big part of that dream. But three months later, that promising young president was gunned down in Dallas, Texas. The nation staggered in disbelief during the relentless television repeats of the gruesome final moments, the close-ups of Jackie's blood-splattered suit, and then the funeral proceedings in Washington, D.C. Then came a truly bizarre television event – Kennedy's alleged assassin, Lee Harvey Oswald, was shot and killed right there on live daytime TV!

People looked at each other with tear-stained cheeks and asked, "What is wrong with America? How could this happen?" A huge blanket of self-doubt covered the nation, accompanied by a yearning for release, for something to believe in, for something gentle, non-threatening, and non-political. That something came in the form of four lovable musicians from Great Britain.

THE BEATLES

Shortly after she gave birth to John Winston Lennon (1941-1980), his mother, Julia, ran off with a man. Her sister and brother-in-law, Mimi and George Smith, raised the child as their own. George died suddenly when John was fourteen, and the boy immediately became a problem. His grades dropped, he turned into a rocker, formed the Black-Jacks skiffle band, and made his Aunt Mimi very unhappy with his new anti-establishment personality.

Skiffle bands were big at the time – comprised of a guitar or banjo (or both), a washboard played with thimble-capped fingers, and a broom handle washtub bass. The American version was called a jug band because it often contained an earthen jug player among the other instrumentalists. These bands go way back to the early 1900s.

Left-handed guitarist James Paul McCartney (b. 1942) joined up, and they changed their name to the Quarrymen (after John's Quarry Bank High School). For a year or so, with different youngsters in and out of the band, they played around Wooton under such names as Johnny and the Moondogs, the Rainbows, the Moonshiners, and the Nurk Twins.

Lennon dropped out of high school, and, at his aunt's insistence, enrolled in the Art Academy. Skiffle was losing fashion as another guitarist, Paul's friend George Harrison (1943-2001), joined the group. John's schoolmate at the Academy, Stu Sutcliffe, a rank beginner, bought a bass and joined up. The again renamed Long John and the Silver Beetles now had three guitarists and a bass. Finally they picked up a temporary drummer, Pete Best, and for the moment the group was complete.

Their first manager, Liverpool club owner Alan Williams, agreed with changing the "e" to an "a" in their name, and then got them a two-month engagement at a club called the Indra in Hamburg, Germany. It was their first test in the world of real entertainment. The Indra was located in the Reeperbahn, Hamburg's red-light district, a place where alcohol, drugs, and sex were readily available to those willing to pay. The Beatles not only survived the challenge, but eagerly joined in the colorful activities of the area during their off-duty hours.

Stu Sutcliffe left the group to study art, so Paul moved over to bass. When they returned to the Cavern Club in Liverpool in 1961, John, Paul, George, and Pete developed a loyal crowd of fans who came to hear them night after night. They worked some three hundred nights from 1960 to 1962.

Brian Epstein

In 1961, a wealthy young Jewish businessman, Brian Epstein (1934-1967), had several requests for Beatles recordings at his dad's record shop, North End Music Enterprises. He took pride in being able to find any recording for anybody, and was irritated when couldn't locate a single recording by the Beatles. Since the Cavern Club was only a few blocks from his record store, he went to hear the boys.

The Cavern Club was very low class, not exactly Epstein's kind of hangout, but he went back several times. After a few informal meetings, he became the band's manager. He was bored running the music store, and they were bored playing the same old stuff for the same old crowd in Liverpool.

Epstein moved quickly. He destroyed their rocker image by putting them in neat suits and ties, and made them shave regularly and cleanup for shows. They were a scruffy crowd and had some bad habits that needed to be broken. They smoked, ate, talked, belched, and pretended to hit each other as they played. Pete Best said, "He [Epstein] forced us to work out a proper program for the evening, playing our best numbers, not just the ones we felt like playing at the moment (Szatmary 1987, 89-90).

George Martin

When Decca Records rejected the Beatles, Epstein went to George Martin, recording engineer with Electrical and Musical Industries, Ltd. (EMI) and landed a routine new act contract – one year and four songs, for one cent per single and six cents per album, should that unlikely development occur.

EMI was a huge conglomerate much like RCA in America and George Martin was buried at EMI's subsidiary label, Parlophone (which produced spoken comedy and light music recordings), very low on the totem pole of the EMI corporate empire. Martin, too, was bored with the current conditions in his life. He had been trained in classical music, and was eager to do something interesting.

In September of 1962, Epstein listened to the first joint effort between Martin and the Beatles, liked what he heard, and hired Tony Barrow, a veteran publicity man from Decca, to arrange for marketing and distributing the release. Epstein always got the best people in the industry to handle specific tasks.

That recording, "Love Me Do", and its B-side, "P.S., I Love You", modestly succeeded, reaching No. 17 on the British pop charts. Encouraged, Epstein and Martin set up another recording session for November. Martin had musical knowledge, a discerning ear, and burning ambition. He insisted that Pete Best, a poor drummer in Martin's eyes, be replaced by a studio drummer for the new recording dates. Already contemplating that issue, the Beatles gave Epstein permission to fire Best.

The Final Component

Richard Starkey (b. 1940), not flashy but a rock-solid drummer, was hired away from Rory Storm and the Hurricanes to join the Beatles after Best was fired. Starkey had been thrown out of school at age fifteen, grew a beard, started wearing many rings (thus, "Rings", which was later changed to "Ringo"), and used to run around with the Beatles during their off-duty escapades in Hamburg. Ringo was not a capricious choice for the Beatles. He had fundamental drumming competence, and they knew he would fit in socially with them. Ringo settled in as their permanent drummer. The six magic components of an unparalleled musical team were now in place – John Lennon, Paul McCartney, George Harrison, Ringo Starr, Brian Epstein, and George Martin.

Before long, the Beatles skyrocketed to the top of British pop music. Back in 1961 when they were sitting around dreaming of fame and fortune, Lennon would yell out, "Where are we going, fellas?" They would shout back, "To the top, Johnny!" He would ask, "What top?" And they would return, "To the toppermost of the poppermost, Johnny!" (Szatmary 1987, 90).

George Martin wisely followed "Love Me Do" with *Please Please Me*, a full-length album of newly recorded songs from the Beatles' live performance repertoire. It was a mix of Lennon-McCartney songs (for example, "I Saw Her Standing There" and "Do You Want to Know a Secret") and cover versions of American tunes (most notably the Isley Brothers' "Twist and Shout").

Epstein busily arranged radio, television, and tour appearances, not only to publicize the group and its record releases, but to insure adequate revenue should the record successes prove to be of the flash-in-the-pan variety (Stuessy 1990, 112).

By late 1962, enormous crowds of screaming teenagers converged on their every performance. Five thousand caused a riot in Manchester. Four thousand lined up at three in the morning for a show seventeen hours later at eight in the evening. Dr. F. R. Casson, an English psychologist, likened the hysteria to voodoo worship, and said "beat music" had rhythmic stimulation on the brain, in a manner similar to a flickering light which can cause an epileptic fit (Szatmary 1987, 90).

In October 1963, the Beatles, now often called the Fab Four, performed at the London Palladium while fifteen million television viewers watched and thousands of fans struggle to get in. In November, at a command performance for the Queen, John Lennon issued his famous remark, "For our last number, I'd like to ask your help. Would the people in the cheaper seats clap your hands? And the rest of you, if you'll just rattle your jewelry."

Beatlemania

For the Beatles' first visit to America, Epstein orchestrated an advance-publicity campaign that rivaled the Normandy Invasion in its careful planning, timing, and execution. Epstein had articles in *Newsweek, Time, Life,* and all the major newspapers. Capitol Records (EMI's American subsidiary) sent out a million copies of a seven-inch Beatles interview record that gave radio listeners the impression that the Beatles had personally talked with every disc jockey in the country (Szatmary 1987, 92).

All the East Coast disc jockeys were on a Beatles countdown, "It's nine o'clock, kids, seventeen hours and twelve minutes until the Beatles touch American soil." January and February sales of "I Want to Hold Your Hand" and "She Loves You" were off the charts. When the Beatles finally arrived at Kennedy International Airport in New York on February 7, 1964, twenty-five thousand screaming teens were there. Fifty thousand fans competed for seven hundred twenty-eight tickets for the two appearances on *The Ed Sullivan Show*, and seventy million viewers tuned in. Sixty percent of all the single records sold in American during the first three months of 1964 were Beatles recordings (Belz 1972, 145).

During this first American trip, the Beatles played only two live concerts, one at the Coliseum in Washington, D. C., and the other at Carnegie Hall, New York. They returned to America later the same year for a month-long tour, from August 19 to September 21. Soon, America was just another stop on their nearly continuous world touring schedule. They returned in 1965 for another late summer tour, and, finally, again in 1966 for a seventeen-day tour, their last.

Beatlemania swept through America during each tour. In Kansas City, the pillow slips and bed sheets on which the Beatles slept were cut into 160,000 one-inch squares and sold for a dollar each. Girls hid in air-conditioning ducts, kids fell from balcony rails and elevated walkways. *The Wall Street Journal* estimated that the sale of Beatles' memorabilia – combs, sweaters, sunglasses, pillows, earrings, etc. – came to fifty million dollars, enough to change the balance of trade between Great Britain and America for 1964.

In their early days, they were a refreshing contrast to the growing San Francisco hippie culture. Innocent and charming, but sometimes cheeky, they seemed to be able to keep everything in good balance. They especially loved to joke with the reporters who wanted their opinion on everything. In Australia, one journalist asked, "How did you find America?" McCartney answered, "Went to Greenland, and turned left." In their first movie, *A Hard Day's Night*, George was asked what he called his haircut. The questioner expected him to say "A mop top," or something similar. Harrison replied, "Arthur."

As their fame grew, live performances became more and more difficult. By 1966 things were so out of hand that they couldn't hear each other singing or playing, even with their amplifiers and monitors wide open. To escape bodily harm, they had to leave each concert in an armored truck. Live shows had become mindless orgies of hysterical, screaming, fainting adolescents. Finally, they stopped all public appearances, and for the rest of their career just made records. Their last live concert was at Candlestick Park in San Francisco on August 29, 1966.

Had their career ended on that evening in San Francisco, the Beatles would have been remembered as just another very interesting rock and roll band. Instead, they went on to become the most important rock band of all time.

The Father of the Modern Pop Record

John, Paul, George, and Ringo were gifted, intuitive musicians, to be sure, but the creative things that happened on their albums from 1965 on were the work of George Martin, their musical adviser, spiritual big brother, and studio producer supreme. On "In My Life" from *Rubber Soul*, for instance, the instrumental break in the middle is not a harpsichord, but a piano (played by George Martin, incidentally) at half-speed an octave lower, then mixed in at double-speed for the proper pitch. The resultant sound was thus absolutely unique, although it approximates the sound of a harpsichord (Steussy 1990, 121).

Martin coaxed them into stretching every musical component – melody, harmony, rhythm, instrumentation, form, texture – the works. Every new album had something substantially different from any previous pop group in history, while at the same time reaffirming something from the group's past achievements. And among all the inventive gestures are some classic pop tunes that hold their own with the great songs of Irving Berlin, George Gershwin, and Jerome Kern – "Yesterday", for example, with over twenty-five hundred cover versions (Bronson 1985, 185).

On "I'm Only Sleeping", from the album *Yesterday and Today*, the guitar sounds are mixed in backward. On "I am the Walrus", from *Magical Mystery Tour*, vocal distortions and "stream of consciousness" nonsense lyrics would later be called psychedelic rock.

By this time, Martin had moved from two-track to four-track procedures. There were two versions made of "Strawberry Fields Forever", each recorded in a different key at different speeds. Lennon could not decide on the heavy guitar version or the lighter cellos-and-brass version. He liked the beginning of one and the ending of the other (Stuessy 1994, 124-125).

A simple splice would not work because of the different tempos and keys. With considerable technical skill and almost unbelievable good luck, George Martin managed to modify the tape speeds enough to bring the two versions together. The result is an eerie sounding piece that, with John's stream-of-consciousness lyrics, creates a purely psychedelic impression. Further coloration was added by mixing in (backwards and at varying speeds) pieces of tape with the sounds of piano runs and arpeggios. John, who was using LSD more and more frequently, had created (with George Martin's help) a real musical [psychedelic] drug trip (Stuessy 1994, 125).

A whole book could be written about *Sgt. Pepper's Lonely Hearts Club Band*, with its meter shifts, "songs within a song" for "A Day in the Life", falsetto voices, different speeds, strings and harp tone colors, calliope music recordings cut into pieces and randomly spliced together for "Being for the Benefit of Mr. Kite", rooster crows, saxophone bass lines, a wall of sound created by forty musicians near the end, and, at last, the final 45-second reverberation delay at the conclusion of the album.

Now, is this the work of lower-class Liverpool adolescents, two of whom never finished high school? Boys from the streets who spent their time drinking, taking drugs, and chasing girls? Hardly. The topics of the tunes, yes. The continuous stream of double meanings and tongue-in-cheek witticisms, yes. The anti-establishment feeling to the album, yes.

But all the other dazzling innovations, all those stunning musical surprises – many of them from *musique concrete*, a form of music that features electronic sounds derived from natural sounds, vocalizations, and electronic instruments – feel like the work of a man who knew about Edgard Varese, Milton Babbitt, Pierre Boulez, John Cage, Lucas Foss, and other modern classical composers. That man was George Martin, and he often said that the Beatles were quick to learn, and always asking questions.

> *We used a string quartet, for example, very early in their recording lives. I would suggest using a trumpet or a cor anglais. They would say, "What's a cor anglais? Then I'd demonstrate how it sounded, and they'd say, "Great. Let's try that!"*
>
> *I remember on one occasion using a saxophone section. I asked John what notes he wanted for the riff background. He played them on his guitar, and I transcribed the notes for the sax section. "But you're giving him the wrong note," John said. "I played A-flat, and you gave him an F.*
>
> *So I explained that John's A-flat was F for the alto saxophone. John just shook his head and said, "That's bloody stupid!" He was quite right of course* (Palmer 1976, 242, but modified because Palmer had the transposition reversed).

At every recording session from very earlier in their career, the Beatles' charming musical innocence and curiosity was given shape and substance by a very sophisticated musical intelligence – George Martin.

A Momentous Change in Pop Music History

The reason that the Beatles are given so much credit for the way they changed popular music really comes down to these two fundamental tenants: with the Beatles, 1) the act of recording became the act of composition, and 2) the primary aesthetic experience became the act of listening to a specific record, the sound of which would be almost impossible to recreate in a live setting.

Recording and composing became one. Even before they stopped performing in public, the Beatles would go into the recording studio (at ridiculously odd hours, incidentally, and often high on heaven knows what) with only a rough idea of what they might end up doing. The real inventive energies, the inspired moments of true creativity, came in the give-and-take of personalities and ideas during the dozens of play-backs, overdubs, mistakes, spontaneous experiments, and happy accidents. About that time John Lennon said, "We don't write songs anymore, we write recordings."

The Beatles and George Martin usually finished any given tune in a couple of intense studio sessions. Before long the industry modified and streamlined that general pattern. During the next thirty years, a predictable mode of operation took shape – a rhythm track laid down in Memphis, the voices added in Nashville, the horns dubbed in at Los Angeles, the strings put on by the London Symphony, the solo inserted in Chicago, and the final mix done in Arizona. Then, three different treatments of the final mix were released: one for radio stations, one for club disc jockeys, and one for high-powered auto stereo systems.

The record producer rose to power as he called the shots all along the way, even instructing the chief mixing engineer as to how the final product should sound.

(This still happens in many cases, of course, but the rap industry of the 1990s had its own method of creating a product: a rhythm track is sampled from an old James Brown release, and all other things are dubbed in or digitally created instantly new at the studio.)

In addition to the line between composing and recording being blurred beyond recognition in the 1960s, there developed another momentous change – the act of listening to that record became the primary aesthetic experience, the moment of artistic truth and pleasure. Concerts became less and less fulfilling because the band could not possibly create on stage what the kids had heard on the recordings and because the sound systems of the day weren't suitable for listening to music over the voices of thousands of screaming fans.

All of this was a change of great magnitude. The entire field of pop music was altered forever. In the old days, Glenn Miller's band played a tune to the delight of thousands of fans all across America. At the end of the tour, by which time the band had honed its performance to razor-sharp precision, they went into the studio and made a record. The record was purchased by the fans who would then re-visit that memorable moment when they heard the band live. The concert was the primary aesthetic experience. Listening to the record was a secondary experience. Owning the record gave them the chance to repeat the pleasure at will. But with the Beatles, and all pop music after them, the act of listening to the record was and is the moment of highest artistic satisfaction.

THE ROLLING STONES

From a street-level bar band, the Beatles seem to have stumbled into fame, wealth, and historical significance by the fortuitous mix of George Martin's musical insights and Brian Epstein's managerial gifts. The Rolling Stones, however, were a completely different story.

Their thirst for fame and wealth seems to have come from middle-class design. Mick Jagger's father, Joe, a physical education teacher, provided a comfortable home in Dartford and sent his son, Mick (b. 1943), to the prestigious London School of Economics. Keith Richards (b. 1943) was the son of an electrical engineer. Brian Jones' mother was a piano teacher, his father an aeronautical engineer, and Brian (1942-1969) worked as an architect's assistant for a while. Charlie Watts (b. 1941) was employed in an advertising agency before joining the Stones. Bill Wyman (b. 1936) was the only genuine working class kid. As Mick Jagger pointed out, "We weren't from poverty families. Our fans were people like us... more like a college crowd" (Szatmary 187, 101).

The Stones started out as nice guys. But it just didn't work for them as it did for the Beatles. Their manager, Andrew Loog Oldham, was getting worried. Finally, during a dismal American tour in June of 1964 when they drew only 600 people in an auditorium with 15,000 seats in Omaha, Nebraska, Oldham decided to change their image – immediately – to the exact opposite of the clean cut Beatles. He succeeded.

In their very next press conference, the Stones came on with strong, vulgar, and insulting language. The newspapers reacted as Oldham hoped they would. They complained about the dirty language, and the long hair, and the sexist remarks. The journalists were shocked that the Stones' behavior contrasted so unfavorably with the lovable Beatles who were such decent chaps.

"It's working! It's working!" Oldham screamed out. "They're plastering your pictures and your terrible statements all over the papers. Those Rolling Stones!" A short time later, one publication called them "five indolent morons, who seem to really enjoy wallowing in the swill-tub of their own repulsiveness." Another called them "the ugliest pop group in Britain... a caveman-like quintet" (Szatmary 1987, 102-103).

With "I Can't Get No Satisfaction", the Stones had their first genuine hit. It was No. 1 on the pop charts for four weeks in July 1965. They had arrived. By

1967, they were nearly always in trouble with drugs, alcohol, and sex scandals. "Ruby Tuesday" and "Let's Spend the Night Together" still sold very well, though. In fact, the more scandalous their off-stage activities were, the more records they sold, and the more violent and destructive their fans became.

Although Brian Jones left the band in 1969 (about a month prior to his "death by misadventure"), Ronnie Woods (b. 1947) joined as a guitarist after Jones' replacement, Mick Taylor (b. 1949), left the band in 1975, and American Darryl Jones (b. 1961) took over for Bill Wyman when he retired in 1993, the Rolling Stones are still going strong, fifty years after their rise to fame.

THE OTHER BRITISH GROUPS

The Yardbirds, the Kinks, the Who, the Dave Clark Five, the Animals, the Moody Blues, and dozens more British rock bands blazed across the musical horizon in the 1960s and '70s. Nearly all toured America at one time or another, and a number of them began their careers as outright imitators of Muddy Waters, John Lee Hooker, B. B. King, Bo Diddley, and the other American R&B patriarchs.

These British groups copied and covered hundreds of American blues songs as best they could until they developed their own repertoire and style. Then, when the American bands began to imitate the British groups, the over-and-back cultural transfer was complete. It was a rare period in American pop music.

Chapter 28
Psychedelic Rock

THE BEATNIKS

In 1951, disenchanted former Columbia University football star Jack Kerouac traveled around the country with Neal Cassady on a tour of self-indulgence and self-discovery. *On the Road*, the literary retelling of that trip, established Kerouac's place in underground literature. Two years later, beatnik poet Lawrence Ferlinghetti opened City Lights Bookstore in San Francisco, and the late Allen Ginsberg took up residence in the same city. William S. Burroughs, heir to the Burroughs Adding Machine Company's wealth, turned against his parents' social register in a scathing denouncement called *Naked Lunch*. This 1950s Beat Generation set the stage for the 1960s Psychedelic Scene.

Szatmary suggests that the term "beat" came from three sources: (1) a quest for beatitude (bliss) that could be found in Zen Buddhism, (2) an admiration for the drifters on the city streets who appeared to be "beat down", but who were in reality wonderfully free from material want, and (3) a respect for the beat of modern jazz (be-bop) and its sensuous effect at their poetry readings (1996, 140).

The "nik" comes from a Yiddish suffix, which, roughly translated, means "a person who..." The suffix gained popularity in the 1930s as part of the word "no-goodnik", and later in the 1950s as part of "Sputnik", the first manmade satellite to orbit the Earth.

By the early 1960s, the beatnik approach to music included whatever would expand the mind and magnify the sensory load. To achieve this they took all the old mind altering drugs – marijuana (and its relatives bhang, cannabis, and hashish), morphine/heroin, amphetamines, and various other traditional uppers and downers – but they also took a new one, lysergic acid diethylamide, the famous and deadly LSD, often called "acid".

First formulated in 1938 by Alfred Hoffman in Switzerland, LSD lay neglected until the early 1960s when the CIA asked Stanford University to run some experiments to see if LSD might be useful in the destabilization of foreign governments. College students and other free-spirited types were paid $20 for taking part in weekly clinical tests. Among them were poet Allen Ginsburg and novelist Ken Kesey.

The CIA discontinued the project when LSD proved to be ineffective as an agent for covert or psychological effects, since the drug's effects were too unpredictable. Ginsberg, Kesey, and several others had become fond of those unpredictable experiences, however, and, making their own formula, they decided to throw LSD parties in San Francisco's bohemian North Beach (Palmer 1995, 156).

Beatnik musicians on drug trips began using newly available electronic gadgets and techniques – early synthesizers, high decibel amplification, feedback, fuzztone, ring modulators, and anything else – to manipulate musical sensations in an attempt to achieve an intense hallucinogenic experience.

HEPCATS, HIPSTERS, AND HIPPIES

Back in the 1920s and 1930s a "hepcat" was a person who was street smart in matters of nightlife, drugs, jazz, and such. Bandleader Cab Calloway had a big recording of a tune called "Are You Hep?" Through the 1940s and 1950s, "hep" became "hip", but kept the same meaning. "Hipster" replaced "hepcat" as the term of choice. In the early 1960s, to be "hip" meant to be "savvy", generally an OK thing to be.

By the end of the 1960s, however, the word "hip" began to pick up a strong negative meaning as journalists wrote in anger not of "hipsters" but of "hippies", who were demonstrating in the streets of the nation. By this time, the term "hippies" had replaced the term "beatniks", referring to highly intelligent, but unstable, social activists, artists, musicians, addicts, and the like.

LOS ANGELES

Psychedelic rock, also known as acid rock, began in Los Angeles when Capitol Records released a documentary recording on which the studio musicians were said to be under the influence of LSD. Behind the narrator, a weird blend of fluttering flutes and verbal moaning can be heard. Soon there were several L.A.

groups with odd names like the Mushrooms and Ever Pretending Fullness (Shaw 1982, 4).

The Byrds

The Byrds arrived on the scene in March of 1965 with a strong album, *Mr. Tambourine Man*, containing a nicely harmonized version of the title song, written by Bob Dylan. Their 12-string guitar sound was called folk-rock, and it was well received. Jim McGuinn (also known later as Roger McGuinn, b. 1942) was on vocals and guitar, Chris Hillman (b. 1944) on vocals and bass, Gene Clark (1944-1991) on vocals and tambourine, David Crosby (b. 1941) on vocals and guitar, and Michael Clarke (1946-1993) on drums. They released a second album, *Turn! Turn! Turn!,* in November of the same year, and they seemed to be on their way.

Another album, *Fifth Dimension*, in the summer of 1966, contained the controversial "Eight Miles High", supposedly referring to a trip on LSD. Musically the tune was quite innovative – with unusual chord progressions, use of the Dorian mode (which, on a piano, uses only the white keys from D to D), and a repetitive bass line, along with the unique sound of McGuinn's 12-string guitar.

Looking back, it seems clear that the Byrds might have challenged the Beatles and the Beach Boys for originality and creativity. Constant personnel changes, however, destroyed any kind of sustained growth and development. By 1968, the group had lost its focus. There were many stylistic changes as well, with a foray into the country music realm, led by Gram Parsons, who was only with the band for a short time in 1968. In 1973, the original band members, along with Clarence White (1944-1973), who had joined the band in 1968, and Skip Battin (1934-2003), who had joined the band in 1969, reunited briefly in 1972 and put out an album in 1973, but things fizzled out quickly. Since then, various members have gotten together for occasional reunions, and *Rolling Stone* listed the Byrds at No. 45 on their list of *100 Greatest Artists of All Time* in 2004.

The Doors

Singer Jim Morrison (1943-1971) started the Doors while enrolled in the film department at UCLA. He got together with keyboard player Ray Manzarek (1939-2013) who recruited jazz drummer John Densmore (b. 1944) and guitarist Robbie Krieger (b. 1946).

The name of the group came from a line in a poem by William Blake: "There are things that are known and things that are unknown, in between the doors." Aldous Huxley later referenced the line in the title of his book on mescaline experimentation, *The Doors of Perception* (Dolgins 1993, 71).

The music of the Doors was dark, blues-based, mainstream rock, usually set in a minor key and heavily loaded with lyrics on death, violence, drugs, and sex. The picture was anything by upbeat (Stuessy 1994, 248).

One of their big hits, "Light My Fire", ran nearly seven minutes, but it caught on when a shorter version was released in July of 1967. Another hit, "People Are Strange", went to No. 12 in 1967.

By 1969, Morrison's alcohol and drug addiction was catching up with him. Quite often, he was nearly incoherent on stage, and his behavior was getting more bizarre all the time. In March 1969, he was arrested for exposing himself on stage. Still, the band turned out several more albums, one of which, *The Soft Parade*, had strings, brass, and a backup vocal group.

By the early 1970s, however, Morrison's health was so bad that he went to Paris for rest and rehabilitation. He allegedly died of a heroin overdose in 1971 at age twenty-seven. By that time, San Francisco had already become the center of acid rock.

SAN FRANCISCO

One of the high moments of early acid rock was orchestrated by Ken Kesey, author of *One Flew Over the Cuckoo's Nest*, when he and his Merry Pranksters hosted the Trips Festival in January of 1966. Music was provided by the Grateful Dead and Big Brother and the Holding Company, who set up five movie screens, onto which were projected continuous combinations of mind boggling colors and shapes. The punch was spiked with LSD, a concoction called "the Kool-aid acid test" (Szatmary 1987, 111).

Almost immediately, the intersection of Haight and Ashbury streets in San Francisco turned into a gathering center for a crowd of alienated youth. Thousands of adolescents from middle-class families somehow felt compelled follow Timothy Leary's advice to "turn on, tune in, drop out" in defiance of all that their parents had worked to achieve.

They rejected the nine-to-five work ethic and the conventional American dream of a steady job and a home in the suburbs. Searching for a greater depth and range of human experience, they plunged into mind-blowing drugs, Eastern mysticism, meditation, and the exotic cultures of various Native American tribes.

Musically, they ignored the world of jazz, Broadway musicals, and mainstream pop, and they went back to the simple, and, for them, more sincere musical styles of folk, country, and blues. An army of rock bands settled in San Francisco, with possibly five hundred groups rehearsing and working in the acid drenched scene (Shaw 1982, 156).

Jefferson Airplane

In 1965, singer Marty Balin (b. 1942) left his San Francisco folk group called the Town Criers, and took over a small club on upper Fillmore Street. He renamed the club The Matrix and recruited guitarists Paul Kantner (b. 1941) and Jorma Kaukonen (b. 1940) and female vocalist Signe Toly Anderson (b. 1941) to be the house band (Stuessy 1994, 239).

As they searched for a name, Kaukonen told of a white blues musician who had a dog he called Blind Thomas Jefferson Airplane – sort of like Blind Lemon Jefferson (the famous pioneer bluesman) with a twist (Doglins 1993, 112). Kaukonen had no explanation for the "Airplane" part of the dog's name. Still it had an off-the-wall feeling to it, so they named their new group Jefferson Airplane.

As the group became famous, fans gave the name Jefferson Airplane to roach [marijuana] clips made by splitting a paper match at one end. Balin insisted that the dog inspired name came first, acknowledging, "It was kind of nice that people named their roach clips after us" (Doglins 1993, 112).

Balin went through several drummers and bassists, then settled on Skip Spence (1946-1999) and Jack Casady (b. 1944). In 1965 RCA released *Jefferson Airplane Takes Off*. The album didn't sell much. Signe Toly Anderson left and was replaced by Grace Slick (b. 1939). Drummer Skip Spence was replaced by Spencer Dryden (1938-2005). With the new personnel, *Surrealistic Pillow* came out in 1967 and went to No. 3 on the rock album charts with two hit singles, "Somebody to Love" (No. 5) and "White Rabbit" (No. 8) (Stuessy 1994, 240).

In the 1970s, the group went through more painful and nearly continuous personnel changes. By 1974, the remaining members took the name Jefferson Starship, which eventually (with more personnel changes) spun off another group,

Starship, in 1984, which is best known for the hits "We Built This City" (1985), "Sara" (1985), and "Nothing's Gonna Stop Us Now" (1987).

For all their complex shifting around in musical styles and professional identities, Jefferson Airplane/Jefferson Starship/Starship had its moment in the sun, from acoustic folk-like charm to overpowering psychedelic hard rock. Their performance of "Volunteers" at the Woodstock festival was a highlight.

The Grateful Dead

Bassist Phil Lesh (b. 1940) called the band to his apartment one afternoon to explain that they should no longer call themselves the Warlocks, because there was another band with the same name. After many silly suggestions and increasing frustration, they chose the "Grateful Dead." Official publicist, Dennis McNally, told the story often.

...there was a dictionary lying there, and Jerry Garcia opened it, stabbed a finger in, and landed, honest to God, on 'grateful dead.' The entry was a reference to a motif in folklore.

In English folk literature, there was a grateful dead ballad... a traveler is going along the road, finds a man who hasn't been given a proper burial because he owed money – he was an indebted man. The traveler pays off the man's debts, and puts the body to rest, as it were. The body is then given a proper burial, and the traveler goes on his way.

Later in his journey, the traveler encounters a representation of the dead man's spirit, usually in the form of an animal that helps him in his own quest.

The whole meaning of course, is the notion of the resolved spirit of the dead and the idea of good karma and a cycle – death and life and rebirth and such (paraphrased from Dolgins 1993, 92).

With guitarist Jerry Garcia's (1942-1995) bluegrass roots, organist Ron "Pigpen" McKernan's (1945-1973) passion for the blues, guitarist Bob Weir's (b. 1947) love of the Beatles, and bassist Phil Lesh's interest in classical music, the Grateful Dead came up with an eclectic mix that didn't fit into any convenient style category. Drummers Bill Kreutzmann (b. 1946) and Mickey Hart (b. 1943) rounded out the group, which remained together until Garcia's death in 1995.

Into drugs from the very beginning, they became the world's most famous acid band, and that anti-establishment reputation kept them in demand even though their records didn't match their on-stage excitement.

When they signed with Warner Records in 1967, they refused to be molded into any kind of career path. Indeed, their loyal fans, the Deadheads, are proud that the band never caved in to the commercial facts of life.

Most fans and rock critics consider their 1969 live double album, *Live/Dead*, to be their best album of the 1960s. It contains a twenty-one minute version of "Dark Star", and "Turn On Your Lovelight". In the 1970s, the Grateful Dead moved toward country-rock when Garcia began to play pedal steel guitar. In 1975, the Grateful Dead released *Blues for Allah,* with strong jazz influences at work throughout. They added horns, strings, and a vocal chorus in 1977 on *Terrapin Station.*

The Dead went blissfully on their way for twenty years without ever racking up big hit singles or chart positions until 1987s "Touch of Grey", their first of only three singles to chart in Billboard's Top 10.

Big Brother and the Holding Company

Though known as Janis Joplin's backup band, Big Brother and the Holding Company predated her and continued on after she left. San Francisco music promoter Chet Helms (1943-2005), organized the group in 1965, and the guys called him "big brother", a conscious reference to Big Brother in George Orwell's *1984.*

"Holding" was a well-known euphemism for possessing drugs. "Are you holding anything?" meant "Do you have any stash?" Also, big corporations are often holding companies, and the members of the band (all cynical anti-establishment types) believed that megacorporations would someday rule the world (Dolgins 1993, 24).

Joplin joined the band in 1966. The August 1968 album, *Cheap Thrills*, made them instant celebrities.

> *...[the album] is a masterpiece of utterly raw psychedelic blues-based rock from the peak of the '60s San Francisco rock scene. Anyone who thinks Guns N' Roses mastered hard electric blues*

grunge hasn't heard Big Brother's James Gurley and Sam Houston Andrews duke it out on tracks like "Ball and Chain", "Summertime", and "Combination of the Two" (Rick Clark, reviewer, in Erlewine 1992, 45).

Janis Joplin

When she first appeared with Big Brother and the Holding Company at the Monterey International Pop Festival, Texas born Janis Joplin (1943-1970) got as close as a white girl could get to a genuine blues emotion. Albert Grossman, Bob Dylan's manager, was impressed by her passionate singing, and persuaded her to go solo.

She left Big Brother and the Holding Company in November of 1968 and formed a band called Full Tilt Boogie. They recorded the album *Pearl*, but before it came out, Janis Joplin was dead from a heroin overdose. When the album was finally released, it went to No. 1 for nine weeks. Over her brief but brilliant career, there were several memorable singles "Me and Bobby McGee", "Down On Me", "Summertime", "Get It While You Can", "Ball and Chain", and "My Baby" among them.

Her voice was rough, raspy, and raw, and her life was the same. She destroyed herself at age twenty-seven, but had made her indelible mark in the world of psychedelic rock and roll.

ELSEWHERE

The mixture of drugs and decibels known as psychedelic rock began to change as the music assumed more and more importance over communal political posturing. Two groups led the way from acid rock to hard rock and heavy metal.

The Jimi Hendrix Experience

James "Jimi" Marshall Hendrix (1942-1970) was born in Seattle, Washington, to an African-American father and a Cherokee mother. His parents gave him a guitar at age 12. As he was left-handed, he turned the guitar upside down and taught himself how to play by listening to recordings of Muddy Waters, B. B. King, Elmore James, Chuck Berry, and others.

At age nineteen he joined the Army but was honorably discharged in 1962. He was hired immediately as a guitarist for Sam Cooke, Little Richard, Ike and Tina Turner, Wilson Picket, Jackie Wilson, and several similar blues based groups.

In 1964, at age twenty-two, Jimi Hendrix relocated to New York where he played the club circuit with the Isley Brothers, King Curtis, and John Paul Hammond. Chas Chandler, who left the Animals to go into the field of artist management, heard Hendrix in 1966, and persuaded him to go to London to form a new group. They arrived in England, and soon recruited jazz drummer Mitch Mitchell (1947-2008) and bassist Noel Redding (1945-2003). The new trio was called the Jimi Hendrix Experience.

In no time at all, Jeff Beck, Jimmy Page, Eric Clapton, and other top level European guitarists became Jimi Hendrix fans and followers. He inspired them with his raw talent, enormous imagination, deep blues roots, technical skill, and creative stage innovations. A Jimi Hendrix concert was outrageous theater, to be sure, but the central focus was always a huge musical experience.

And shocking as they were, Jimi Hendrix's performances grew out of his early career.

In late 1966, Hendricks formed the Experience and amazed European audiences with an act modeled on such former employers as Little Richard and James Brown.

At the Paris Olympia he twisted, rolled, shook, and writhed in perfect time to every half-note of his thunderous electric blues. During the next few months, he staged similar shows for spectators at Stockholm's Tivoli, the Sports Arena in Copenhagen, and the Saville Theater in London (Szatmary 1996, 178).

At Woodstock in 1969, Hendrix turned "The Star Spangled Banner" into an exploration of pure sound as a musical artistic component. The tune was filled with "evocations of bombs falling and exploding, with screaming sirens, and with the howls of victims as Hendrix whipped up an entirely sonic conflagration" (Palmer 1995, 228).

Earlier, Hendrix had begun to close some of his shows by smashing his guitar, pouring lighter fluid on it, and setting it afire – all the time, however, keeping his amplifiers at full volume.

The sound of guitar strings vibrating and uncoiling as the instrument crumpled and went up in flames wasn't just showmanship, as in the Who's instrument smashing rampages, it was MUSIC (Palmer 1995, 228).

Jimi Hendrix lived a short, fast life and died of drug complications in London on September 18, 1970. His important recordings live on, however "Hey, Joe", "Purple Haze", "The Wind Cries Mary", "Wild Thing", "Like a Rolling Stone", "All Along the Watchtower", "Third Stone from the Sun", and many more.

The Jimi Hendrix Experience also provided "the principal model for the 'power trios' in particular and for the development of heavy metal in general" (Palmer 1995, 229).

Cream

Among those power trios was Cream, consisting of emerging superstars Eric Clapton (b. 1945) on guitar, Jack Bruce (b. 1943) on bass, and Peter "Ginger" Baker (b. 1939) on drums. Each had much experience going into the group, and each had an illustrious career when Cream dissolved.

During its brief existence, from June 1966 to November 1968, Cream captured the attention of the purists. With Clapton's passion for the blues and his jazz tinged improvisation skills, Bruce's inventive ostinato patterns (repeated riffs) on bass, and Baker's long and brilliant drum solos, Cream served as a bridge, a transition, between the fields of acid rock and heavy metal.

"I Feel Free", "Sunshine of Your Love", "Toad" (with a ten-minute drum solo), Robert Johnson's "Crossroads", Willie Dixon's "Spoonful", and many more great singles can be found on Cream's four ATCO albums *Fresh Cream, Disraeli Gears, Wheels of Fire,* and *Goodbye*.

***

Time now to turn our attention to another development in the story of American popular music, the fusion of jazz and rock into a style that is different from either. It was, and is, called by that very name, fusion.

Chapter 29
The Fusion of Jazz and Rock

Not all musicians in the 1960s were driven to the frightening boundaries of self-destruction so common in psychedelic and rock. And not all gifted musicians dropped out of college to protest against the establishment. There were many fine young musicians who found a way to balance their musical desires and goals with the realities of society and the market place.

What happened was a little surprising. A small number of jazz hopefuls who knew they would starve in the world of jazz turned to rock to make a living. And a small crowd of rock musicians who hungered for greater improvisatory freedom turned to jazz as a musical compromise.

The result was a new style that sounded sometimes like rock and sometimes like jazz. It was, in fact, a synthesis of each. Industry executives and journalists spoke openly about "jazz-rock" and everyone seemed comfortable. For discussion purposes, two terms can be used: (1) "rock-oriented fusion" which, for all the jazz elements, still has the even eighth-note feeling of rock, and (2) "jazz-oriented fusion" which, for all its rock elements, often has the uneven eighth-note feeling of jazz.

ROCK-ORIENTED FUSION

Blood, Sweat & Tears

As a band called Blues Project was dissolving in the late 1960s, two of its members, Al Kooper and Steve Katz, recruited drummer Bobby Colomby and bassist Jim Fielder, and formed a new band. They added four horn players and called their new band Blood, Sweat & Tears – a term taken from a famous speech by Winston Churchill during World War II.

Al Kooper explained the name to rock scholar Adam Dolgins for his book called *Rock Names*.

I was playing in an all-night jam session, and I had cut my finger but didn't know it. When they turned the lights on at the end of the evening, the organ keyboard was covered with blood. So I called everybody over, and I said, "Wouldn't this make a great album cover for a band called Blood, Sweat & Tears? And so we called it that, except we didn't use that picture because no one had a camera (page 28).

The horn players were Fred Lipsius on alto saxophone and clarinet (also keyboards and arranger); Dick Halligan on trombone (also flute, keyboards, and arranger); and Randy Brecker and Jerry Weiss on trumpets, who rounded out the original eight-man line up (Stuessy 1990, 260). Shortly after their first album, *The Child Is Father to the Man* (1968), Kooper, Brecker, and Weiss left, being replaced by Lew Soloff, Chuck Winfield, and David Clayton-Thomas. More personnel changes came in the 1970s.

Some of their best tracks includes "Spinning Wheel", "You've Made Me So Very Happy", "When I Die", "Hi-De-Ho", "Lucretia MacEvil", and their masterpiece "Symphony for the Devil/Sympathy for the Devil", a stunning rearrangement of the Rolling Stones' work (Stuessy 1990, 263).

With several bachelors and masters of music degrees among the members, Blood, Sweat & Tears served up exciting music that, for all its intellectual input and jazz-tinged sounds, still felt like it belonged in the broad tradition of mainstream rock.

In the late 1980s, David Clayton-Thomas re-formed Blood, Sweat & Tears with many new faces. Although Clayton-Thomas retired in 2004, Blood, Sweat & Tears still tours globally.

Chicago

Another horn-dominated rock-oriented fusion band started out as the Missing Links, then changed to The Big Thing, but then was renamed the Chicago Transit Authority by James William Guercio when he took over the band's management in 1967. Guercio had worked for Blood, Sweat & Tears, and he seems to have put the same kind of band together when he got control of Chicago Transit Authority.

Guercio recalls, "I came up with the name because I grew up on the northwest side of Chicago and I had a hell of a time getting to school. I used to have to take the bus. It was called the Chicago Transit Authority" (Dolgins 1993, 41-42). Guercio shortened the name of the band to avoid an expensive battle with Chicago mayor Richard Daley, who had filed a lawsuit.

From 1972 to 1975 the band had five consecutive number one albums, starting with *Chicago V* and going through *Chicago IX*, a greatest hits album. Their success and staying power is undoubtedly related to the continuity of personnel. By rock standards, they are most unusual, indeed – Robert Lamm (b. 1944) on keyboards, Peter Cetera (b. 1944) on bass, Terry Kath (1946-1978) on guitar, Danny Seraphine (b. 1948) on drums, Lee Loughnane (b. 1946) on trumpet, James Pankow (b. 1947) on trombone, and Walter Parazaider (b. 1945) on flute and saxophones. Cetera, Kath, and Lamm alternated as lead singers until Kath's death in 1978 and Cetera's departure for a solo career in 1986 (Stuessy 1994, 264-265). These days, lead vocal duties are shared among almost all of the current nine band members.

Some of their early hits, "Make Me Smile", "25 or 6 to 4", "Colour My World", "Saturday in the Park", and "Does Anybody Really Know What Time it Is?" have become rock classics. The band also had at least one Top 40 hit every year in the 1970s, and a total of ten gold albums and five platinum albums (Stuessy 1994, 264).

They change musical scenery every now and then (tours with the Beach Boys, an album with guest artist Maynard Ferguson), and they mix up their musical product with different styles. They are especially good with mixed meters: 2/4-time, 6/8-time, 3/4-time and so on, one after another. And they do it with assuredness.

By all standards, Chicago is one of the premier rock-oriented fusion bands in history of rock. Most successful fusion groups on the rock side followed Chicago's model with an even eighth-note rhythmic behavior, non-jazz voicing of the horns, and a fondness for stretching the pop traditions in form, texture, meter, phrase lengths, and such.

JAZZ-ORIENTED FUSION

Approaching the concept of fusion from the other side were a number of jazz-rooted musicians, a surprising number of whom had worked with, or were strongly influenced by, the veteran jazz giant Miles Davis.

Weather Report

Far and away the most popular and influential was Weather Report, formed by pianist Joe Zawinul (1932-2007) and saxophonist Wayne Shorter (b. 1933) in 1971. Using standard jazz instruments, but in most unusual ways, Weather Report captured the fancy of jazz and rock fans alike. When Jaco Pastorius (1951-1987) replaced Miroslav Vitouš (b. 1947) on bass, another dimension was felt – stunning virtuosity of bass lines, moods, and tone colors.

Zawinul was the musical mind most dominant in the group, and he composed many of the hits ("Mercy, Mercy, Mercy" and "Birdland", for example). Zawinul was a walking laboratory of new devices – ring modulators, exotic percussion instruments, ocarinas, thumb pianos, Fender Rhodes electric pianos, ARP and Oberheim Polyphonic synthesizers , Echoplex tape delay effects, and every other conceivable device to create a new and interesting sound.

The Mahavishnu Orchestra

John McLaughlin (b. 1942) organized the band in 1971, recruiting pianist Jan Hammer (b. 1948), drummer Billy Cobham (b. 1944), bassist Rick Laird (b. 1941), and violinist Jerry Goodman (b. 1943). McLaughlin, guitarist supreme, came out of British rock traditions, and came to America in the late 1960s where he began to work with Tony Williams' group, Lifetime. McLaughlin also recorded often with Miles Davis.

Birds of Fire (1972) is the Mahavishnu Orchestra's best work, and it shows off McLaughlin's high-intensity rapid-fire playing to great advantage. And he is just as competent on hollow-body standard guitars as he is on his custom-made double-neck, eighteen-string invention.

Other Jazz-Oriented Fusion Personalities

Chick Corea's band called Return to Forever produced the popular hit "Spain" from the *Light As a Feather* album. With bassist Stanley Clarke, guitarist Al

Dimeola, and drummer Lenny White, pianist Corea delivered a high level of jazz-rock offerings.

Herbie Hancock's album *Head Hunters* came out in 1973 and sold well, eventually going to No. 13 on the album charts. He followed with *Thrust* in 1974, and then the soundtrack album for the movie *Death Wish*, which starred Charles Bronson, in October 1974. All three albums were in the jazz-tinged fusion style, and Hancock revealed a keen understanding of the new thing called fusion.

Chuck Mangione, Jeff Beck, Steely Dan (pianist Donald Fagen and bassist Walter Becker), Carlos Santana, and several others fused jazz and rock into artistic statements on many albums through the 1970s.

THE FATHER OF FUSION

Jazz and rock historians invent a "father" for nearly everything. It's a bit contrived, of course, but it does serve to draw attention to the early giants who changed the history of the art form under discussion.

Miles Davis (1926-1991) is everyone's candidate for the Father of Fusion. A lot of things had already been done, but when Miles came out with *Bitches Brew* in 1969, the whole pop music world suddenly took notice. Here was a jazz giant, already a legend, steeped in acoustic be-bop sounds, and he had surrounded himself with electronic everything. The jazz world was stunned, and many jazz purists were greatly distressed by the thought that Davis had stepped off in the direction of rock.

What he did confused many scholars and critics, too, but it was a natural result of his burning curiosity about music and his relentless search for inventive and expressive ways to say what was on his mind.

Absorbing techniques from all around him like a giant sponge, Davis put it all together in his own intuitive manner – funky ostinato to patterns, mixed meters and odd meters, expanded percussion sounds and an enlarged percussion role in the overall musical fabric, electronic phase shifters and other sound distortion devices, Fender bass rather than acoustic bass, the works.

Fusion it was. Jazz and rock came together in subtle mixtures that produced a new age in each field. There was another new age developing, strangely enough, that sounds and feels considerably different from Weather Report or Blood, Sweat & Tears. That musical style, coincidentally, is commonly called New Age.

NEW AGE

In reaction against the decibel levels of acid rock and hard rock, in reaction against the staggering rhythmic complexities of two drummers and three guitars in the same fusion band, and in reaction against the philosophy such powerhouse musical experiences seem to symbolize, a whole new crowd of musicians gradually appeared on the American pop music scene.

They all seemed to have a common approach to music, best summed up, perhaps, by the phrase, "More is not necessarily better." It was almost as if they had said to themselves, "Enough is enough."

Back in 1964, Verve Records released *Music for Zen Meditation* with a Japanese koto, a shakuhachi flute, and a jazz clarinetist, Tony Scott (1921-2007). In 1967, Scott came out with another odd combination of instruments on *Music for Yoga Meditation*. Tony Scott was among the first to experiment with completely new sounds, but it took a while before the movement would attract a market.

Certain general characteristics of New Age appear over and over again in the various styles of the field. A lot of it is instrumental. It tries to evoke an image. It seems to be especially focused, almost a dialogue between the music and the listener. It has a meditative and reflective attitude, being for the heart and mind, not for the glands. It avoids negative feelings, and album notes use words like peaceful, gentle, special, lyric, tranquil, sensuous, lush. It often comes in compositions twenty minutes long, or more.

Critics called it Muzak for the Yuppies. Religious critics feared it was music for the cult crowd. Serious classical, rock, and jazz fans just yawned. Several schools of New Age are found.

Folk-Traditional-Acoustic

Guitarist William Ackerman (b. 1949) dropped out of college to become a carpenter. With natural business instincts, he soon formed a construction company called Windham Hill Builders. In his spare time, he composed guitar music for

Stanford University theater productions. His friends encouraged him to record an album of his own tunes.

Again his business instincts took over, and he formed Windham Hill Records in 1978, producing for George Winston, Alex de Grassi, Liz Story, and others. Ackerman was a most unusual businessman. He really listened to his composer-performers, and tried to capture their intent and content with the most sophisticated technology. He paid careful attention to the physical aspects of the record itself – with loving care given to an artistic cover, the highest quality paper used throughout, and intelligent liner notes. The total package was a work of art. It was refreshing.

The folk-traditional-acoustic school of New Age will occasionally have modest jazz nuances, but it is more likely to sound a bit like gentle mood music with a semi-classical folk feeling to the whole experience.

Ambient-Synthesizer

Sometimes called "space music", this school of New Age sounds like a film score in the making. Steve Roach, Michael Stearns, and others work in this area of "mood creating" music. Vangelis Parathanassiou popularized the style in 1982 with his background film score for *Chariots of Fire*.

Brian Eno (b. 1948) is the undisputed master of this kind of music, and his albums (over fifty at last count) have influenced the entire field of modern music, especially his 1979 masterpiece *Ambient 1: Music for Airports* which is now considered a sort of minimalist classic.

Jazz-Based New Age

Trained as a classical flutist, Paul Horn (1930-2014) had a strong jazz and studio recording career in progress when he began to yearn for more than financial security. He left Los Angeles, went to India, and studied Transcendental Meditation with Maharishi Mahesh Yogi at the same time as the Beatles. Horn's *Inside the Taj Mahal* (1991), made with just a solo flute inside the famous edifice, took full advantage of the 28-second reverberation factor to create a haunting, jazz-tinged blanket of free improvisation.

Alex DeGrassi's (b. 1952) nine albums have subtle jazz colors, too. A self-taught guitarist, DeGrassi had all the right genes and connections for success. His grandfather played violin in the San Francisco Symphony, his father was a classical pianist, and his cousin, William Ackerman, owned Windham Hill Records.

Environmental New Age

Paul Winter (b. 1939) has been concerned about the environment since his college days at Northwestern University in the 1960s. His jazz sextet won the Notre Dame Intercollegiate Jazz Festival in 1961, and went on a Latin American tour shortly thereafter for the U.S. State Department. Winter drifted away from pure jazz and left the group. The band regrouped and called themselves Oregon.

One of his most famous recordings is 1977's *Common Ground* which incorporates the sounds of birds, wolves, and humpback whales into the musical fabric. The retrospective *Wolf Eyes* (1988) features cuts from previous albums - with the sounds of birds, forest animals, and as many as fifteen different varieties of sea mammals. Winter often donates all his royalties to the World Wildlife Fund.

Most of the New Age musicians are sensitive to environmental causes, and many frequently put animal sounds into the sonic mix of their free-form poetic mood music.

***

Back in the day, New Age recordings were often found in health food stores, and several New Age magazines had music columnists who reviewed the current recordings in the field. As an industry, New Age music grew slowly right along with the various branches of alternative medicine – herbs, vitamins, macrobiotics, massage homeopathy, chiropractic manipulation, and other approaches to good health aimed at those Americans who are suspicious of the global drug corporations' chemical solutions to all of life's aches and pains. Nowadays, New Age has become a little more mainstream, with tracks played on jukebox-type machines in stores such as Target and Hallmark, encouraging passers-by to purchase a CD of instrumental "background music".

Chapter 30
Funk and Free-form Jazz

The be-bop revolution brought a new style of jazz into full bloom, but the seeds of its strength became the seeds of its decline. It was just too complex, too cerebral, too demanding in its pure form for any but the most dedicated aficionados. Two groups of jazz fans appeared: the free-form jazz crowd, who were quite happy to continue on the intellectual path before them, and the funky school, who yearned for a return to the black roots that seemed to have been lost in the shuffle.

FREE-FORM JAZZ

Under the leadership of Ornette Coleman (b. 1930), a small band of strong musicians plunged further into artistic exploration, and began to improvise without a pre-conceived basic scheme whatsoever. For example, Coleman and his colleagues jumped right over the problem of specific chord progressions ("changes") by rejecting them completely.

He also worked hard to avoid obvious melodic patterns and specific meters. He often refused to set down anything at all as a base of operations. His musicians were expected to listen to what he seemed to be suggesting, and then contribute whatever seemed appropriate to what he had first offered. Coleman would then pick up that thread and try to weave something new into the musical-emotional cloth.

In his early days, Coleman used two different groups, without a piano in either one – the first with Don Cherry on trumpet, Charlie Haden on bass, and Eddie Blackwell on drums; the second with Freddie Hubbard on trumpet, Eric Dolphy on multiple reeds, Scott Lafaro on bass, and Billy Higgins on drums. With no predetermined chords, bass lines, or rhythmic pulse, the musical results depended on the keen ears, quick reflexes, and fertile imaginations of its participants.

Sometimes it was very exciting, indeed, and sometimes it was not so exciting. Cecil Taylor tried many of the same procedures with remarkable results because as a pianist he was in complete control of the entire aesthetic intent and design. The Chicago-based Association for the Advancement of Creative Musicians has spent a good deal of their time exploring the precarious trails of free-form jazz.

THE FUNKY SCHOOL

The opposite reaction to an over-intellectualized be-bop style was to return to the original roots of jazz, to retrieve the blues and gospel feeling that had been pushed into the background by the hardline, mainstream musicians.

Several musicians set out to do just that. Pianist Horace Silver (1928-2014) was especially influential. His earthy, blues-drenched solos inspired a crowd of imitators – pianists Gene Harris, Ramsey Lewis, Les McCann, and organists Jimmie Smith, Richard "Groove" Holmes, and Jack McDuff. Silver's tunes became jazz standards – "The Preacher" and "Song for My Father" come to mind.

Julian "Cannonball" Adderly (1928-1975) also returned to gospel feelings and blues nuances to tell his story. A huge man with a huge sound, he played alto saxophone with wit, humor, astonishing velocity, and large doses of passion. He was among the most successful disciples of the great Charlie Parker.

Although the term "funk" came in during the late 1960s, it is now used more often to describe that special kind of black feeling associated with Earl "Bootsy" Collins (b. 1951), George Clinton (b. 1941) and Parliament Funkadelic, and a number of the Motown groups. The distinction between funk and soul is not clear in any of the literature on jazz and rock during the 1960s.

A THIRD OPTION

There was a third option, too, when be-bop got too complex. That was to move toward rock for fresh creative juices. And during the 1960s and 1970s, a large number of imaginative musicians who might have gone into jazz went into rock instead, because it seemed to offer more financial gain for the time and labor involved. That whole field came to be called fusion, which was covered in the previous chapter.

Chapter 31
Hard Rock

In the late 1960s, when the Jimi Hendrix Experience, Cream, and several other bands turned up the decibel level, the industry found itself on the edge of a new genre, an extension and synthesis of psychedelic/acid rock and hard blues-rock.

Before long, a variety of loud – *very loud* – bands paraded around both sides of the Atlantic Ocean. Physicians wondered if the human ear could take it all; electronics companies invented stronger amplifiers, speakers, and a host of tone modifiers; and audiologists designed special earplugs for the performers and their audiences.

Just being loud was not the *only* special characteristic of hard rock. It was also blue-collar, anti-establishment, blues-based, image-driven, concert-stage music – not music for dancing or listening, but music for ritual participation.

Being loud, however, *was* significant and fundamental to that communal-ritual experience. The physiological effects on the body of acoustic disturbances approaching the level of pain (130 decibels) were very real, indeed. Melody, harmony, and other traditional musical components soon lost out to reproducible details that could be manipulated to deliver a raw "sound".

Jazz and pop musicians had long ago manipulated the sound of their instruments with mutes, broken beer bottles, bathroom plungers, champagne buckets, hats, etc. – before that sound entered the amplifier. What was new about hard rock musicians was that they manipulated the sound during and after amplification.

As early as 1958, Link Wray (1929-2005) and his Ray Men distorted the sound for their instrumental hit, "Rumble", by poking a pencil through the speaker. In 1964, the Kinks cut a speaker cone with a razor blade for extra "buzz" on "You Really Got Me". Then, rock musicians discovered, probably accidentally, that a strange thing happened when the guitar was right in front of its own speaker – there was a ghastly squeal of reciprocal resonance, with the amplified sound feeding itself back into the guitar pickup. The Beatles tried this new "feedback" on "I Feel Fine" (1964), the Who on "My Generation" (1965), and the Yardbirds on "Shapes Of Things" (1966) (Charlton 1990, 175).

The "primal scream" quality of that feedback appealed to the hard rock musicians' hostility toward the establishment, and – ironically, it always happens – the very establishment rushed to profit with dozens of foot-pedal electronic sound distortion gadgets. A new industry appeared with a new name (Peavey, Boss, Roland, et al.).

WHY THE LATE 1960s?

The hard rock musicians were reacting intuitively to deep changes in the collective Euro-American mentality of the late 1960s. "Any pop phenomenon is a kind of cultural seismograph, revealing the large, subterranean forces that are at work beneath the surface of society, and that sometimes break through with convulsive effect" (Schechter 1988, 124).

Hard rock was a musical metaphor for the heinous aggressions of the time, shocking music at frightening levels of sound in a symbolic reflection and demonstration of the terrifying disequilibrium and hostilities of the day – race riots, the assassinations of Martin Luther King, Jr., and Robert Kennedy, protests and riots at the 1968 Democratic National Convention in Chicago, Vietnam protests at 400 colleges, the Kent State tragedy, and finally, the Watergate scandal.

The lyrics of songs, some of them surprisingly strong and meaningful, now had to be printed on the album jacket, since they were buried in the overall sonic package of the group's delivery. In concert, the audiences often sang along with the tunes, for they had learned the words from the record jacket.

NOTABLE HARD ROCK GROUPS

Grand Funk Railroad

For a while, the most popular American hard rock band was Grand Funk Railroad, formed in Michigan in 1968. Former rock singer Terry Knight managed Grand Funk, and got them into the 1969 Atlanta Pop Festival. They were an instant success, and immediately took America by storm, selling out big stadiums all over the country, including New York's Shea Stadium. Their hit singles "We're An American Band" and "Locomotion" put them at the top of the charts in the early and middle 1970s. The band continues to tour, playing 40 dates a year. They kicked off their "40 Years of Grand Funk" tour in January 2014.

Aerosmith

Formed in 1970 in New Hampshire and signed by Clive Davis for CBS in 1972, Aerosmith hit the top with a self-titled album in 1973 and *Toys in the Attic* in 1975. Mick Jagger look-alike Steven Tyler (b. 1948) carried the group along with guitarist Joe Perry (b. 1950). Interlacing their rock with occasional folk and country classics, Aerosmith had a special identity.

In July of 1978, they appeared as villains in the film *Sergeant Pepper's Lonely Hearts Club Band,* starring the Bee Gees and Peter Frampton. Their musical contribution was a revival of the McCartney-Lennon classic "Come Together" (Lazell 1989, 10). Major personality conflicts arose in the early 1980s, but by 1985 the band had regrouped, signed with Geffen Records, and entered a new chapter in their career.

In November 2012, Columbia released *Music from Another Dimension!,* making a total of fifteen studio albums, five live albums, and twelve compilation albums since they first entered the world of music in 1973.

Van Halen

The long line of virtuoso guitarists in rock continues with Eddie Van Halen's inventive pulling and hammering the strings with both hands on the fingerboard. Combine these skills with short solos on the upper partials (harmonics) of the strings, above and beyond the normal guitar technique, and the result is a unique and clearly marketable musical personality. Gene Simmons, from KISS, realized this when he financed Van Halen's first demo tape in 1976.

In the Netherlands, brothers Eddie (b. 1955) and Alex (b. 1953) Van Halen trained rigorously in classical piano, but upon their move to California in 1968, the boys fell in with the rock culture to form a band called Mammoth. When they regrouped later as Van Halen, they hired bassist Michael Anthony (b. 1954) from Snake and David Lee Roth (b. 1954) from the Redball Jets.

Van Halen risked criticism for not being true hard rock when Eddie Van Halen played keyboards on "Jump" and "I'll Wait" on their album titled *1984*. Their critics also predicted trouble and decline for Van Halen when their lead vocalist, the photogenic David Lee Roth, left in 1985. Sammy Hagar (b. 1947) joined the band within months after Roth's departure, however, and stayed until 1995, filling the role to everyone's satisfaction.

Hagar was replaced by former Extreme lead singer Gary Cherone (b. 1961), and Van Halen released *III* in 1998 (*III*, as in the third incarnation of the band). The album was not well-received by critics or fans, and this version of the band was defunct by the following year. Hagar returned to front the band from 2003 to 2005. Then, in 2006, two extraordinary line-up changes occurred: David Lee Roth returned to the band and original bassist Michael Anthony was replaced by Eddie's son Wolfgang Van Halen (b. 1991). This line-up released *A Different Kind of Truth* in 2012, containing a mixture of songs originally penned decades before (but never released) and new tracks.

Deep Purple

Formed in Germany from the remnants of the United Kingdom band Roundabout, Deep Purple moved in 1966 into hard rock from a pop-rock background. Classically trained pianist Jon Lord (1941-2012) balanced things nicely with Ritchie Blackmore's (b. 1945) street-level blues inclination. The band even made an appearance with the Royal Philharmonic Orchestra at London's Royal Albert Hall in 1969, but critics were reserved in their opinion of the main work for the evening, a concerto for rock band and symphony orchestra.

By the early 1970s, they were being compared favorably with Led Zeppelin. Deep Purple's big American hit singles, "Hush" and "Smoke on the Water", kept them in the public eye until they broke up in 1976. They regrouped in 1984, and went on a world tour in 1987. Although there have been some changes in the lineup (most notably, of the departures of Blackmore in 1993 and Lord in 2002), their latest studio album, *Now What?!*, was released in 2013 and the band toured the world to promote it.

Mötley Crüe

In 1981, bassist Frank Carlton Serafino Ferrana, Jr., (b. 1958) left his group called London, changed his name to Nikki Sixx, and formed a new band called Christmas. He then recruited guitarist Mick Mars (Bob Deal, b. 1951), vocalist Vince Neil (Vincent Wharton, b. 1961), and drummer Tommy Lee (b. 1962) to form Mötley Crüe. They played "increasingly outrageous gigs in the Los Angeles area, including dates at the Starwood Club, where they chain-sawed mannequins and set their own trousers on fire'" (Lazell 1989, 342).

Opening on tours for KISS in 1983 and for Ozzy Osbourne in 1984, Mötley Crüe began to attract an audience of their own, but suffered some career damage when Vince Neil wrecked his Pantera sports cars in an accident which killed Nick Dingley (from the group Hanoi Rocks). Neil was jailed for twenty days, paid $2.6 million in compensation to others injured in the crash, and served two thousand hours of community service by lecturing in high schools and colleges on the dangers of drugs and alcohol. At about the same time, December 1984, Mötley Crüe was named the No. 1 Rock Act by *Hit Parader* magazine.

Shout at the Devil and a single release of Brownsville Station's "Smokin' in the Boy's Room" put Mötley Crüe in a firm position near the top of hard rock in 1985. Kicking a heroin habit in 1986, Sixx regained his control of the band. Shortly thereafter, Mötley Crüe embarked in their Lear Jet on a worldwide "Girls" tour (Lazell 1989, 342). In 2014, the band went on a farewell tour, with plans to retire in 2015.

***

As with all genres of music, there are different subcategories for the different kinds of music being played. Hard rock is no different. Some of the more distinct subcategories of hard rock include progressive rock, heavy metal (which, in itself, has subcategories), grunge, and alternative rock.

PROGRESSIVE ROCK

What this really means is anyone's guess, but the word "progressive" has long history of suggesting something a bit more intellectual and sophisticated than the ordinary thing. It is favored by those who wish to separate themselves from the pedestrian crowd.

Stan Kenton (1940s) and Dave Brubeck (1950s) were called progressive jazzmen. In the 1960s and 1970s, "progressive rock" was very close to "art rock" – a term often used for Jethro Tull, Rick Wakeman and Yes, Procol Harum, Genesis (still with Peter Gabriel and only at the very beginning of Phil Collins' involvement), Frank Zappa, and Emerson, Lake, and Palmer, among others.

In the 1990s, the term "progressive metal" was occasionally found in reference to groups like Dream Theater, who had one foot in each of the subcategories of progressive rock and heavy metal.

Rush

For sustained musical rewards in the progressive rock genre, a Canadian power trio called Rush stands very high with knowledgeable critics and fans. Classical guitarist Alex Lifeson (b. 1953) changed to rock and joined bassist Geddy Lee (b. 1953) and stunning virtuoso drummer Neil Peart (b. 1952) to expand the potential of heavy metal in all directions. Their multi-movement song cycle *By-Tor & The Snow Dog* earned a Juno award, the Canadian equivalent of an American Grammy (Charlton 1990, 190-191).

Rush's lineup has remained constant since 1974. Concentrating on expert musicianship and avoiding the drama of most of their peers, Rush has relentlessly toured and released albums regularly for decades. While radio has not recognized the band in the way that critics and the record and concert-ticket buying public has, Rush was nonetheless finally inducted into the Rock and Roll Hall of Fame in 2013.

Pink Floyd

Although they are now considered to be more of a progressive rock group, because of their past forays into other areas of the hard rock realm, Pink Floyd is really in a category by itself as the premier political-intellectual-progressive spaced-out hard rock. They began in 1965 as a psychedelic-blues-rock synthesis of several previous groups. Their 1967 debut album, released in America under the title *Pink Floyd,* sold only moderately well, but established them as a special kind of band that would never sacrifice artistic principles for fame and wealth.

The tour that promoted *The Wall* album (1970) involved such elaborate logistics that only two American performances ever occurred – New York and Los Angeles, although twenty-nine performances took place worldwide. A complete brick wall 160 feet long and 30 feet high was built to symbolize the barrier that inevitably arises between a band and its fans. Roger Waters (b. 1943) came up with the original idea.

In 1970 Roger "Syd" Barrett (1946-2006) was coaxed out of the band. A sad victim of LSD abuse, he retired to a life of seclusion. Roger Waters (vocals and bass), Rick Wright (keyboards, 1948-2008), David Gilmour (vocals and guitars, b. 1946), and Nick Mason (drums, b. 1944) became a hard-core team. Their 1973 album, *The Dark Side of the Moon,* a sonic description of the hopelessness, despair, and madness of modern society, was on the charts for fifteen years (741 weeks), with over 50 million copies sold.

The band went through an acrimonious breakup in 1983, but the members reunited periodically (between and among dozens of lawsuits over who can legally still use the name Pink Floyd) to negotiate over financial matters and to turn out something to sell.

In 1995, for example, *P.U.L.S.E.* was released, a double-length album containing a 1994 live performance of *The Dark Side of the Moon.* The slipcover that held the two CDs contained a blinking red light, meant to symbolize the heartbeat, or pulse, of each listener. To draw attention to the event, the Empire State Building was splashed with pulsating red lights while excerpts from the album were simulcast over WNEW-FM (102.7) in New York.

Although their last studio album was 1994's *The Division Bell*, Pink Floyd reunited in 2004 for the Live 8 concert, both to commemorate the 20th anniversary of the Live Aid concerts and to influence the outcome of a G8 summit occurring over the same weekend. The organizers hoped the concert would shine a light on Make Poverty History campaigns, so that the G8 summit attendees would pass resolutions to combat global poverty.

Although Syd Barrett died in 2006, a new album of sorts is set for release in October 2014. *The Endless River* will consist mostly of ambient music, recorded during sessions for *The Division Bell*, that were later expanded upon after the death of keyboardist Rick Wright in 2008.

HEAVY METAL

This subcategory of hard rock took its original name from the Steppenwolf biker anthem "Born To Be Wild", which contains the phrase "heavy metal thunder" [referring to motorcycle sounds] taken from William Burroughs' famous novel, *Naked Lunch* (Clarke 1988, 532).

Struessy says that heavy metal is "an exaggeration of the hard-rock side of mainstream", with insistent eighth-note divisions of the beat and low range guitar riff [short, repeated melodic motives] (1990, 306-307). Clarke adds that it is "a genre developed from the late 1960s blues progressions: guitar-based rock with amplified guitar and bass reinforcing each other to create a thick, brutal wall of sound" (1988, 532).

From its early days, heavy metal came in two schools: (1) the hardcore purists for whom the music was the primary experience, Led Zeppelin, for example and (2) the drama-driven crowd for whom the theatrical event was of equal importance, Alice Cooper and KISS, for example. The distinctions blur easily, and the separation is an arbitrary scholar's device, of course.

A word of qualification – what was heavy metal in 1970 may sound a little tame compared to the much heavier metal of the late 1980s through the present. Led Zeppelin, AC/DC, and Blue Oyster Cult would be considered just "hard rock" today. And what one fan considers genuine metal another fan dismisses as pop schlock, too pedestrian to be considered metal at all.

So, with every effort to be objective, here follows a summary of the controversial genre from its beginnings in the '60s to its pinnacle in the early 1990s.

MUSIC-DRIVEN HEAVY METAL

Led Zeppelin

When the Yardbirds disbanded in 1968, highly respected session guitarist Jimmy Page (b. 1944) recruited bassist John Paul Jones (b. 1946), drummer John Bonham (1948-1980), and vocalist Robert Plant (b. 1948) to fulfill a few remaining concert dates. They finished out a Scandinavian tour as the Yardbirds, then changed their name to a phrase Keith Moon (the drummer for the Who) often used for a bad concert (gig) – "going down like a lead zeppelin." Page suggested that the spelling be modified to "led" so American kids wouldn't say "leed" (Edelstein and McDonough 1990, 153).

Manager Peter Grant got them a contract with Atlantic records. Self-titled albums *I*, *II*, *III*, and *IV* from 1968 to 1971 made them the most popular rock band in the world. They earned thirty million dollars in 1973, and set record attendance numbers everywhere on their American tour. (The previous records were set by the Beatles.) Two years later, fifteen thousand fans waited for twenty-four hours outside Madison Square Garden for tickets, and in Boston, Led Zeppelin fanatics rioted at the box office causing $75,000 in damage (Szatmary 1987, 153).

Their bone crushing, blues-drenched, riff-dominated style of rock became the artistic standard against which all other groups were measured. Big hits were Chicago bluesman Willie Dixon's "You Shook Me" and "I Can't Quit You Baby", Howlin' Wolf's "How Many More Years" (redone as "How Many More Times"), and the original "Whole Lotta Love". Their masterpiece, "Stairway to Heaven", was never released as a single.

In 1975, Robert Plant and his wife suffered serious injuries in an auto accident; two years later their son, Karac, died of a viral infection. Meanwhile Page dabbled in occult matters, and the group went into exile in Switzerland. In 1980, when John Bonham died after drinking forty shots of vodka, the group disbanded (Edelstein and McDonough 1990, 153).

Even after they disbanded, their albums influenced other music – several Led Zeppelin riffs were sampled in the rhythm tracks of the late 1980s, and Led Zeppelin albums still sell well as successive generations discover them. In 1994, Plant and Page released the album *No Quarter*, with live acoustic tracks recorded during MTV's *UnLedded* program, and a related tour. Robert Plant also made waves for doing things in other genres, such as his *Raising Sand* album (2007) with bluegrass-country star Alison Krauss (b. 1971), and as a founder of the Honeydrippers, a rock band with an R&B bent, most famous for their remake of "Sea of Love" (1985).

AC/DC

Moving from Glasgow, Scotland, to Australia in 1963, brothers Malcolm (b. 1953) and Angus (b. 1955) Young wanted to surpass older brother George's pop hit "Friday on My Mind" (1967), made with a group known as the Easybeats. Claiming to take their name from an inscription on a vacuum cleaner, the younger brothers plunged into the world of heavy metal with musical assuredness and strong business skills. Their first release, *High Voltage* (1975), put them on the international stage with their own special brand of "rumbling, deafening, chord-crashing, electric blues" (Szatmary 1987, 154).

There were many personnel changes in the band over the years, but when their lead singer, Bon Scott (1946-1980), died only months after recording their album *Highway to Hell*, many fans thought the band would never recover. With support from Scott's parents, the band continued on, releasing *Back in Black* (1980), which many rock fans consider to be the quintessential album of the hard rock/heavy metal genre.

Blue Oyster Cult

Using the names Soft White Underbelly, Oaxaca, and the Stalk-Forrest Group before settling on the name Blue Oyster Cult, the Long Island, New York band (rejected twice by Elektra Records) finally signed with Columbia in 1971, largely through the influence of *Crawdaddy* magazine writer Sandy Pearlman, their producer-manager (Lazell 1989, 49).

"(Don't Fear) The Reaper" (1976) showed a musical sophistication not common to heavy metal. In fact, their whole career, notwithstanding their early days travelling with Alice Cooper, shows a good mix of musical intelligence and marketing know-how. Their harmonized vocals and interesting melodies put them a cut above some of the other heavy metal bands. Patti Smith's two songs and a guest appearance on *Agents of Fortune* (1976) pushed the album to platinum million-plus sales.

Between major tours, Blue Oyster Cult played small clubs under their first name, Soft White Underbelly. For years, only a few select fans, who aware of the name camouflage, were rewarded by hearing Blue Oyster Cult in close quarters (Charlton 1990, 190-191).

Guns N' Roses

When genuine heavy metal was getting crowded off the charts by dance music and pop, Guns N' Roses brought the real, raw, ugly thing. Lead guitarist Slash (b. 1965) and rhythm guitarist Izzy Stradlin (b. 1962) traded vicious musical riffs while Axl Rose (b. 1962) screamed about sex, drugs and all that's wrong with the world.

They shot up to the top of the market in the late 1980s because they offered a quick fix for the teenagers so hungry for old-fashioned violence and raw energy once again. Under the shrewd marketing skills of David Geffen's publicity staff, Guns N' Roses became the hottest band in America with *Appetite for Destruction* in 1987. "Welcome to the Jungle", "Mr. Brownstone", "Rocket Queen", and "Paradise City" are among their best.

To everyone's surprise, they revealed a gentle streak with "Sweet Child o' Mine", which was picked up by MTV and played often. When Stradlin, their best songwriter, left the group, the energy level of Guns N' Roses seemed to decline.

After a 15-year break since their last album, Guns N' Roses released *Chinese Democracy* in 2008, widely regarded as the most expensive album ever produced (at a cost of approximately $14 million). The band continues to tour and has had multiple residencies in Las Vegas.

DRAMA-DRIVEN HEAVY METAL

All the heavy metal groups are dramatic, to say the least. Some, however, have put stage dress, bizarre mannerisms, and theatrical effects at the center of their act.

Black Sabbath

Shortly before Led Zeppelin arrived on the scene, a band first called Polka Tulk, then Earth, toured the United Kingdom and parts of Europe, breaking the Beatles' long held attendance figures at the Star Club in Hamburg, Germany (Lazell 1987, 46). Guitarist Tony Iommi (b. 1948) did what he had set out to do, create a pop blues-based success. In full agreement were bassist Terry "Geezer" Butler (b. 1949), drummer Bill Ward (b. 1948), and vocalist John "Ozzy" Osbourne (b. 1948).

In 1969, manager Jim Simpson changed their name top Black Sabbath, from Butler's tune based on the writings of black magic novelist Dennis Wheatley. At the same time, Simpson changed the band's image and music from pop-flavored blues to evil-gloom-doom heavy metal.

It was a very effective change, and Black Sabbath soon became popular. The music world was stunned, however, and then general public was outraged, when mass-murderer David Berkowitz said he was inspired to kill by some of those early Black Sabbath recordings (Edelstein and McDonough 1990, 151).

The hit single "Paranoid" from the 1970 album of the same name shows a big money formula at work. Iommi wanted to avoid the formula rut, and demanded horns and keyboards for creative growth. After many emotional battles and managerial squabbles, Osbourne left in 1978.

Ozzy Osbourne's anti-hero personality carried him into solo fame, alcohol addiction, an extended legal battle over the suicide of a teenage fan, and several painful rabies shots after biting the head off of a dead bat that had been thrown up on the stage. In his condition at the time, Osbourne wasn't sure what it was – one story even says it was a rubber imitation – but he got rabies shots, just in case. More recently, Osbourne and his family were the subjects of a reality show on MTV, *The Osbournes*.

Iommi, Butler, and Osbourne reunited in 1997 for a tour and the band released their nineteenth studio album, *13*, in 2013. For all its problems, rock historians put Black Sabbath right up next to Led Zeppelin as one of the most important and influential of the pioneer British heavy metal bands.

Alice Cooper

Originally the name of his band before adopting the name on his own in the 1970s, Vincent Furnier (b. 1948), a minister's son, took the name Alice Cooper from a sixteenth century witch who was burned at the stake. His theatrical routines caused enormous controversy. Strangling a chicken onstage, beating-stabbing-decapitating a female toy doll, and putting a huge boa constrictor around his neck kept Alice Cooper in the news every few weeks. Frank Zappa signed the band for a debut album, *Pretties for You,* when he heard that they could clear out a club quicker than any act on the West Coast.

Furnier was soon known as the Father of Shock Rock, but Alice Cooper began to deteriorate as Furnier slipped into a severe and dangerous alcohol problem. The albums of the late 1970s and 1980s did not sell well at all.

Alice Cooper came out of the slump in 1987 with *Raise Your Fist and Yell* followed with two commercial albums, *Trash* in 1989 and *Hey Stupid* in 1991. His album, *The Last Temptation* (1995), was accompanied by a comic book, illustrating the lyrical content of the album. It dealt with the dangers, insecurities, and struggles of youth, and the hardships and pressures of growing up. These days, compared to other definitively heavy metal artists, Alice Cooper might fit more into the broader "hard rock" category. His most recent album, *Welcome 2 My Nightmare*, was released in 2011.

KISS

Musically more hard rock than metal, but with an entirely metal attitude, is the band KISS. Inspired by the New York Dolls, Gene Simmons (b. 1949) formed a part-time rock band in late 1972 with guitarists Paul Stanley (b. 1952) and Ace Frehley (b. 1951). They recruited drummer Peter Criss (b. 1945), quit their day jobs, and launched one of the most eye-popping heavy metal bands in the business.

From their first professional job in January of 1973, KISS went for the bizarre and preposterous – fire breathing, imitation blood vomiting, dry-ice fog, fireworks, explosions, police lights, black leather shirts, spandex pants, and floating drum risers. With full-paint circus makeup and outrageous gestures, KISS emphasized all the gothic, bigger-than-life aspects of the glitter-glamour branch of heavy metal.

Dressed to Kill and *Alive* in 1975 put the band at the top of the industry, with a special following among the early teenage heavy metal fans. Marvel Comics issued a series of KISS comic books, and a movie called *KISS Meets the Phantom of the Park* was televised on NBC. For the first twelve years of their existence, KISS would not be photographed without their makeup.

As KISS and their audience have matured, their style has become decidedly "pop metal". In the 1980s, they went through the big personality fights that all rock groups seem to go through. Criss was replaced by Eric Carr (who died of cancer, 1950-1991), and Frehley was replaced by Vinnie Vincent (b. 1952) who was replaced by Mark St. John (1956-2007) who was replaced by Bruce Kulick (b. 1953).

Their latest album, *KISS 40* (2014), was released as a celebration of the 40th anniversary of the band. It contains forty songs – one from every album the band released, including live albums and some solo albums. Their current line-up still includes Simmons and Stanley, but they're now joined by Eric Singer (b. 1958) and Tommy Thayer (b. 1960), both of whom joined the band in the early 2000s.

Ted Nugent

A self-styled "wild man of rock," Ted Nugent (b. 1948) mastered many of Jimi Hendrix's theatrical gimmicks, including the art of plucking the guitar strings (or pretending to) with his teeth. In the late 1960s, Nugent toured relentlessly with his "heavy garage band, the Amboy Dukes," from Detroit, Michigan (Lazell 1989, 354).

A genuine virtuoso, Nugent often invited rock guitarists on stage for a musical battle, similar in spirit to the "cutting sessions" in the jazz clubs of old. He actively supports the National Rifle Association, is an expert shot, and often hunts wild game with a bow and arrow on his Michigan farm. He appears now and then on stage in a cave-man loincloth, performing what some rock journalists call "Neanderthal Rock." In 1978 he signed his autograph on fan's arm with the tip of a Bowie knife.

In contrast to most rock musicians, Ted Nugent is politically a staunch conservative; he's a fierce critic of drugs who has been known to dismiss a band member suspected of drug use, a board member of the National Rifle Association, and a strong supporter of the Republican Party. "Journey to the Center of the Mind" (1968) from an album of the same name is considered his best contribution to heavy metal. These days, his music fits more correctly into the broader hard rock category than the narrower heavy metal subgenre.

Judas Priest

Leading a new wave of heavy metal in the late 1970s, Judas Priest crashed the scene. Vocalist Rob Halford (b. 1951) adopted a biker image, and often roared out on stage with his Harley Davidson belching and barking full throttle. Black leather jackets with the full complement of metal studs and chains, punk-style haircuts, and Marlon Brando tough-guy snarls gave Judas Priest a following of Hell's Angels types who were similar in behavior to big-time wrestling fans.

After their first album, *Rocka Rolla,* in 1974, Judas Priest began to penetrate the market, and, by the early 1980s, the band was an invited guest at the first Castle Donington Monsters of Rock Festival in the United Kingdom. Lead singer Halford left the band in 1992, came out as gay in 1998, and then returned to the line-up in 2003, continuing with them today. Their latest offering, *Redeemer of Souls,* was released in 2014.

They share with Ozzy Osbourne the negative fame of a serious lawsuit. They had a long and involved legal battle with the families of James Vance and Raymond Belknap who committed double suicide after listening to six hours of Judas Priest recordings. Both court cases were eventually dismissed, both in favor of the musicians.

***

There are many other heavy metal bands of course – Skid Row, Stone Temple Pilots, Ugly Kid Joe, and Megadeath, just to name a few. Each band has a certain identity discernible to knowledgeable fans. Some of the bands have moved toward mainstream pop, becoming in essence pop music businessmen not all that different than Billy Joel, Mariah Carey, or Katy Perry. Some have maintained their antisocial beginnings with reasonable financial success. Some have fulfilled their early promise of self-destruction.

SUBSCHOOLS OF HEAVY METAL

By the 1990s, the distinction between "music-driven" heavy metal and "drama-driven" heavy metal was pointless as a scholarly device – all metal was spectacular in sight and sound beyond belief. Even the distinction between heavy metal and hard rock was a bit confusing. Rock journalists constantly struggled to define the concerts they were reviewing.

The industry needs categories to function, however, so record companies began to publicize their groups with specific new adjectives, music critics coined new descriptive terms for the parade of groups, and serious traditional heavy metal fans began to look down in contempt on all the variations on the old classic theme. Certain subschools have taken shape.

Christian Metal

Stryper and Petra are old-fashioned by now, but Christian metal is alive and well with groups like Fireflight, Skillet, and several others declaring their convictions, much to the delight of the faithful. Stylistically, Christian bands tend toward more melodic lines, fewer bass-line riffs, and a greater attention to the texts – all for reasons of their basic religious purpose.

Thrash Metal

Thrash metal seems to appear in two sub-categories: the up-tempo "speed" groups like Metallica, Anthrax, and Megadeth (Charlton 1990, 191), and the slow-tempo, gloom-doom-death groups who are the direct descendants of Black

336

Sabbath. The technical proficiency in thrash groups is surprisingly high, yet still consistent with the heavy metal instincts of not wanting to appear schooled or trained.

Industrial Metal

The term "industrial metal" is used occasionally in reference to groups making a supreme effort to recapture the savage purity of Led Zeppelin – groups like Iron Maiden, Ministry, Nine Inch Nails, and some others.

Pop Metal

Any band that loses its underground, anti-social, hostile stance, usually accompanied by actually being ranked on album or singles charts, is likely to be given the derogatory "pop" label indicating, of course, that all integrity has been sacrificed for fame and wealth. Guns N' Roses could fit into this category, especially when "Sweet Child o' Mine" was released in 1988.

Country Metal

Although the examples are much fewer in this genre, some do exist, most notably the group Jackyl.

SEATTLE GRUNGE

Coming out of Seattle, Washington, and very big in the early 1990s was a new thing called "grunge". The leader of the pack was Nirvana.

Nirvana combined strands of rock from all eras into one explosive burst of rage. Combining the melodic pop of the Beatles, the '70s sludge of Black Sabbath, the spiky song structure of the Pixies, and the fierce indie ethics of the indie underground of the '80s, the band came up with a signature pop-punk that was distinctly their own (Erlewine 1994, 233).

Among Nirvana's important recordings were "Smells like Teen Spirit" from *Nevermind* in 1991, "Negative Creep" from *Bleach* in 1989, and "Heart Shaped Box" from *In Utero* in 1993.

Jack Endino, who produced the recordings of most of the grunge rock bands in the early 1990s, said that the whole thing was an inside joke, at first. A garage band, Nirvana, went into the Sub Pop studios to make some party music for their friends, and they decided to have a few laughs by poking fun at punk. To everyone's surprise their parody on punk caught on, first with the Seattle underground, then with the nation – and the rest is history.

Nirvana was unprepared for stardom, and not very good at handling it, especially Kurt Cobain (1967-1994). And certain members of the several other Seattle bands got into fearsome drug and alcohol problems trying to learn how to live with fame and wealth. Kurt Cobain's suicide in April of 1994 was a painful reality check for everyone in the world of grunge.

Several other groups followed in the direction of Nirvana's post-punk musical language, each band with its own special kind of pop-grunge-punk – Pearl Jam, Soundgarden, and Alice in Chains come to mind.

ALTERNATIVE ROCK

The term "alternative" seems to mean "as intellectually stimulating and emotionally sophisticated as 'progressive rock', but more authentic and rewarding." Alternative rock has a more subtle lyric-musical agenda than other categories of hard rock, and it appeals to a large crowd of very knowledgeable fans with college-age underground tastes. R.E.M. is usually one of the first names to come up in conversations on alternative rock, as is Green Day.

Alternative bands have the musical integrity and professional self-confidence to challenge the conventional wisdom and to resist the commercial pressures of the recording industry. It is not easy, of course, and who is really "alternative" is a matter of personal opinion. Some of the acts that fall into this category are Blind Melon, Shawn Colvin, Sonic Youth, New Order, and the Sundays.

CONCLUSION

The world of hard rock music is a very specific field. It is not traditional mainstream pop, adult contemporary, golden oldies, or any other establishment thing. It is clearly the adolescent rebel of the music world, bashing the establishment at every opportunity with fierce political rhetoric and savage power.

THREE FINAL OBSERVATIONS

First, there is a startling similarity between modern hard rock concerts and the hedonistic orgies of the ancient Aztecs, Romans, and others. The blood, violence, and screaming spectators in the coliseums of Central America, Rome, and elsewhere would suggest that modern "arena" (how fitting) rock concerts are not all that unusual in the traditions of human behavior.

The substance and style of such ritualistic entertainment seems to be fairly constant throughout history – the result of a fundamental human craving for manufactured fear, for noise and its raw energy, for public sexual innuendoes, and for the electrifying emotional abandon of mob-crowd anonymity.

Second, the preponderance of shows that focus on sex, violence, and death is perfectly understandable. The rock stars may get old, but the market audience stays young, between fourteen and twenty-four, perhaps, in the midst of sexual awakening, ethical awareness, and a passionate search for personal identity – all of which translate into a temporary but powerful state of disequilibrium and a fascination with the forbidden, a suspicion of the conventional, and a fear of the unknown.

Third, the appropriation by white musicians of historically black music and its magical-mystical link to religious ecstasy explains much of the behavior on and off stage at a typical hard rock concert. The other-worldliness of all that angst thrills American teenage males whose pre-teen years seem to lack a really exciting commitment of any kind.

Chapter 32
Disco

In the middle and late 1970s, a special kind of dance music flashed across the horizon of big-city life in Europe and North America. It was just the kind of music the world seemed to want at the time – glitzy, sexy, and glamorous. Everyone said it would fade, like platform shoes and pet rocks. It eventually did, but it held on for about fifteen years, beginning to end.

The new dancing craze started in Paris in the mid-1950s in the after-hours and out-of-the-way nightclubs serving homosexuals as a place where they could meet, dine, and dance without being harassed by the police. The nightclub owners replaced their live bands with disc jockeys who offered a wide variety of musical styles from their extensive personal record collections. The clubs came to be called discothèques – from the 1950s' French word for "record library".

While on vacation in Europe in the early 1960s, Elmer Valentine, owner of a nightclub in Los Angeles, visited the Whiskey a-Go-Go, a very popular discothèque in Paris. In 1965, he opened his own Whiskey a-Go-Go in Los Angeles. It was a huge success as hundreds of young dancers gyrated (follow-the-leader style) with the go-go girls in the cages suspended above the dance floor.

Discos, as they came to be known, soon appeared all over America, losing their original function as homosexual hangouts. The Jet Set took over the disco fever, and it became the "in" thing for famous movie stars, wealthy heiresses, and young political wheeler-dealers to sniff cocaine and "shake their booty" all night long at the newest disco club.

An early disco hit, George McRae's "Rock Your Baby", was written and produced by two engineers at TK Studios in Hialeah, Florida, Harry Wayne Casey and Richard Finch. The song sold more than three million recordings, becoming a No. 1 hit in fifty-three countries of the world. The engineers formed their own nine-piece band called K.C. and the Sunshine Band, and had a string of giant hits – "Shake Your Booty", "Get Down Tonight", "Please Don't Go", "Give It Up", "Boogie Shoes", and several others.

In 1975, "The Hustle" by Van McCoy caught on and fired the imagination of American dancers. Soon there were a dozen Hustles – the California Hustle (often called the Bus Stop), the New York Hustle, the Latin Hustle, the Tango Hustle, as well as the Detroit Shuffle, the Bump, and the Time Warp. The Hustle and its variants became the basic disco dance style.

Also in 1975, Donna Summer co-wrote and recorded "Love to Love You, Baby". Its original three-minute version was extended to sixteen minutes and fifty seconds for record distributors catering to disco houses. Much of the recording consists of Summer's sensuous moaning and panting over and over again, "Love To Love You, Baby". It became a run-away hit, a smash, and it set the stage for a huge industry. Before long, entire twelve-inch records had only two songs, one on each side. The frequency range was greatly enhanced to offer the disc jockeys many sonic options for working the crowd.

John Travolta's appearance in *Saturday Night Fever* ignited the explosion and turned disco into a worldwide passion from 1977 well into 1979. The Bee Gees' soundtrack for the movie sold twelve million records. Disco records were suddenly hot – Gloria Gaynor's "I Will Survive", the Village People's "YMCA" and "Macho Man", and Taste of Honey's "Boogie-Oogie Oogie", along with the Boston Pops Orchestra's *Saturday Night Fiedler* and Barbra Streisand's "Enough Is Enough" (Shaw 1982, 106).

Twenty thousand disco clubs appeared out of nowhere. In Fennimore, Wisconsin (population 1,900), a $100,000 club was built in a matter of months. There were disco proms, disco wedding services, disco roller skating rinks, and non-alcoholic disco pre-teen clubs featuring disco dogs, disco burgers, and disco pizza. Two hundred radio stations soon changed to a 24-hour disco format.

Very quickly disco records gravitated toward one predominant tempo – 125 beats per minutes – to which any style or tune could be adapted. There were disco versions of Glenn Miller's "In the Mood", and "Chattanooga Choo Choo", and a Salsoul Orchestra disco version of Stravinsky's "Rite of Spring", and a special treatment of Beethoven's "*Symphony No. 5*" by Walter Murphy.

The record producer became a dictator. His word was law. Giorgio Moroder produced the sound track to the movie called *Midnight Express* in his $700,000 Musicland Studio in Munich, Germany, all by himself, playing all the instruments and programming all the other sounds. Producers usually started by laying down the rhythm track, then stacking up as many as forty-eight layers of sound from every conceivable synthesizer, ring modulator, and artificial tone generator possible, then, finally, the voices. "It's like sonic watercolors," said producer Patrick Adams.

Richard A. Peterson, Vanderbilt University sociologist, said that the four billion dollar disco industry was the music of a generation of young folks who wanted nothing more than to be left alone. No more Vietnam, no more Gulf Oil scandals, no more Watergate, no more government greed and corruption, no more commitments. "Just leave me alone."

> *I am good. I like my body, and I like what I am. I am a survivor, able to thrive in an anomic urban world of strangers. I can overcome alienating work and the stigma of race, sex, ethnicity. The day may belong to Them, but the night is Mine. Here I am, in control, and my fantasy is real* (Peterson 1978, 27).

Research studios found that disco dancers developed an alkaline condition in their bodies after long hours on the dance floor. They got a natural high, a sense of euphoria, almost like a long distance runner gets after "crashing the wall".

Disco came to an abrupt end, however. In November of 1979, Iranian militants captured ninety Americans and held fifty-two of them hostage for 444 days. Gasoline went from forty cents a gallon to a dollar forty cents a gallon. Suddenly it was no longer fashionable to say, "Leave me alone, don't bother me with political matters." The whole nation took a conservative turn, politically and economically. In this new atmosphere, disco somehow seemed childish and almost irresponsible.

In no time at all it was fashionable to *have* a commitment, to be patriotic, to believe in American values. And disco – the music of a "don't bother me" crowd – began to die out rapidly. It was replaced by strong music with traditional roots: country rock, with Willie Nelson, Waylon Jennings, and the Eagles singing about values, commitment, and relationships, imperfect perhaps, by there just the same.

Disco houses folded, ten every week for a year or more. Studio 54, the most glitzy of all went bankrupt, and its owners ended up in jail for income tax evasion.

As always, the popular music of the nation reflected quickly the shifting dreams and desires, values and attitudes, hopes and frustrations of the tribe. For a short time, though, disco reigned supreme as the music of the 1970s. It was indeed a colorful chapter in American pop music history.

Chapter 33
The Influence of MTV

THE HISTORY OF MUSIC VIDEOS

Although music videos looked like a new pop culture mini-art form when MTV appeared in 1981, the idea of adding a visual component to a musical offering was not new, of course. It had been around since the earliest days of sound movies. In 1920s film clips of Al Jolson and Rudy Vallee, there are hints of things to come. Then there were the 1930s big band "soundies", featuring Tommy Dorsey, Artie Shaw, and others playing their hits while the camera men created angle shots, fade in/fade out sequences, rearranged horn sections, superimposed images, overhead shots of the drummer, and many similar ingenious tricks.

The best example of the early use of these film devices is *The King of Jazz* (1930) with Paul Whiteman, Bing Crosby, and their friends, including the famous composer pianist George Gershwin performing his popular "Rhapsody in Blue". Another historic moment was Lena Horne's extended treatment of the title song in a 1943 all-black film *Stormy Weather*. By this time there were musical short subjects, ten minutes or so, before the feature films in all the movie theaters of America.

In the 1950s, video jukeboxes could be found in the better restaurants and drug store soda fountains of the land. A video jukebox was just that – a circular loop of film in a coin operated music machine. Many of the early rock and roll stars appeared there in action.

In the 1960s, music videos sometimes came in movie form, such as the Beatles' *Help!*, *Magical Mystery Tour*, and *Yellow Submarine,* and sometimes appeared as part of a television show, on programs like *The Monkees*, *The Partridge Family*, and on variety shows.

In 1977, with the creation of VHS and Beta, the music industry began to market videotapes of pop concerts, so fans could enjoy the music of their favorite artists in the comfort of their own homes.

THE ADVENT OF MTV

On August 1, 1981, the music industry changed as millions of young people gathered around their TVs to hear and see the band the Buggles predict the future with the first-ever video on MTV, "Video Killed the Radio Star". MTV (Music Television) was the first place that music videos could be watched, 24 hours a day, 7 days a week, all year long. (These days, with the advent of reality TV shows like *The Jersey Shore*, it no longer lives up to its original concept of "all music, all the time".) The music cable outlet broadcast all over America, Canada, Western Europe and Scandinavia, and selected big cities in South America, Africa, Australia, and the Orient. At the beginning of MTV, videos were seen as a new art form, a new way for fans to experience the music, but it didn't take long for the recording industry to realize the potential of videos as promotional tools for tours, albums, and even artists themselves, creating a whole new field of global art-vs.-commerce considerations.

Very simply, pop videos are a form of continuous sales promotion, and they grow out of the vocabulary, grammar, and syntax of the language of advertising. Born in this visual language of the advertising industry, pop videos follow their own aesthetic principles, which may or may not penetrate or derive from the music. The British journalist Don Watson said, "Never has the world of pop culture been so close to the world of advertising, the world of lifestyle sales" (quoted in Wicke 1987, 162).

Many major stars' careers began on MTV, including those of Michael Jackson, Madonna, the Beastie Boys, Duran Duran, and George Michael in the '80s; Nirvana, Nine Inch Nails, and TLC in the '90s; and, more recently, Beyoncé and Lady Gaga.

EARLY VIDEOS

During the 1980s, there were several different styles of pop videos, some with a social message, like "Beds Are Burning" by the Australian band, Midnight Oil. Some were mini dramas, like George Michael's "Father Figure". Some were wonderfully surrealistic and politically loaded, like Peter Gabriel's "Shock the Monkey". Regardless of any other motives that may have prompted the writing of the song in the first place, a video really only had one goal: to sell as many albums (later CDs, and later, downloads) as possible.

In his book *Rock Music: Culture, Aesthetics, and Sociology*, Professor Peter Wicke devoted several pages to a scholarly analysis of one of early videos, a prototype as it were, Russel Mulcahy's 1985 production of Duran Duran's "Wild Boys":

> The video of this song shows a surrealistic and apocalyptic world full of confusing symbolism. Nightmarish, dark, unconnected images rush by frantically in no particular order, bathed in bluish light or in the flickering glow of flames. The images change every few seconds, often merely leaving behind the fleeting trace of an impression, only to freeze again into painfully captivating detailed scenes.
>
> The camera perspective continually moves between all the imaginable angles, making any spacial orientation, any relation of up and down, right and left, practically impossible. The scenery is dominated by battle, attack, aggression, and stylized force. The members of Duran are included in these ghostly events, but at the same time stand outside them – they appear on video on a screen that is continually brought into the action.
>
> The collection of symbols is devoid of any logic: men knock tables over, bathed in flickering shadows, tongues of flame blaze from their mouths. A figure enveloped in a floating cape approaches dangerously slowly. A robot like man/machine head turns, spewing flames, to a video screen which shows Duran Duran playing "Wild Boys;" half naked savages, dressed in leather shorts, with painted upper bodies and punk hair styles perform archaic dances. On the screen a time bomb begins to tick. Flames leap up, and laboratory equipment becomes visible.
>
> A lift platform sinks into a metal structure. Bodies whirl through the air like bullets. A windmill appears with Duran Duran's lead singer tied to one of the sails, rotating through the air. Another of the group, locked in a cage, is working hard at the most modern

computers, while a third is undergoing a form of brain washing using photographs of himself.

The savages and their barbaric dance games dominate the scene again. Out of nowhere appears a mediaeval flying machine with a man in it. One of the savages tries to catch it with a lasso, but it races straight into the windmill, releasing the lead singer from his rotation torture. He then immediately finds himself in shimmering green water, threatened by a monster (Wicke 1987, 163-164)

Wicke continues on with several more paragraphs of descriptive details, then makes his point: what appears to be random and senseless is really very specific.

But for all this, the images are by no means meaningless. Looked at more closely, each scene is a carefully constructed quotation from the repertoire of action sequences from adventure and science fiction films, and thus refers to the viewer's previous media experiences, since he has probably seen the relevant scenes in hundreds of different versions in the cinema or on television. The viewer therefore has the visual stereotypes to hand. What is at work here is the aesthetic law of advertising (Wicke 1987, 165).

Advertising is based on juxtaposing two image packages so that the viewer subliminally attaches the characteristic virtues of one with the other. The huge Clydesdale horses are powerful, virile, even beautiful – so I'll drink Budweiser and be the same. The voluptuous beauty in the slinky dress slides into her Lexus with a smile – I'll bet driving a Lexus has the same sexy excitement that she could certainly provide. The nuances are much deeper, broader, and more layered with various levels of meaning, of course. Many of them are nonverbal and not even available for conscious consideration.

The pop video uses advertising principles, but the product to be sold, the record, is nearly absent from the scenario. It's so subtle that the video producer merely prints the relevant information before and after, and lets the viewer enjoy the playful nonsense of the indiscriminate and meaningless barrage of audio and visual sensations – all of which resonate, however, and make the viewer feel alive, knowledgeable, and "with it". It's the ultimate soft sales pitch, and it has special appeal for early adolescents who want desperately to feel alive, knowledgeable, and "with it".

Because of the nature of pop videos, musicians, singers, and even the songs are nearly interchangeable – like toothpaste, or shampoo, or beer, or headache remedies. The producers of the pop videos, like the producers of the advertisements, have become multi-talented magicians who can indeed sell anything to anyone on a really good day.

MICHAEL JACKSON

MTV provided the opportunity for the creation of a truly worldwide superstar for the first time. Technology was now in place to bring the sound and look of a performer, not just to the local movie theaters as the Beatles and Elvis Presley had done in earlier decades, but to every television, every home, in the civilized world. All that was needed was an artist who was a master at both the music and the new visual world of videos. That person was Michael Jackson.

Originally a member of the Jackson Five, Michael, the youngest of the five brothers, began his career as a solo artist with the release of the album *Got to Be There* (1972). Three other solo albums soon followed: *Ben* (1972), *Music and Me* (1973), and *Forever Michael* (1975).

After the Jackson Five left Motown in 1975, they signed with Epic Records, and continued to record and tour as the Jacksons. Michael remained a member of the group and became their lead songwriter, with hits such as "Shake Your Body (Down to the Ground)" (1979).

In 1978, Michael appeared as the Scarecrow in *The Wiz*, a Motown version of L. Frank Baum's *The Wizard of Oz*. Although the film did not do well at the box office, it gave Michael the opportunity to meet producer Quincy Jones, who would produce Michael's next solo album, *Off the Wall* (1979). It was this album that helped transition Michael's career away from his membership in the Jacksons and more into a solo performer in his own right. The album reached No. 3 on the Billboard charts and it has sold over 20 million copies worldwide, propelled by many strong singles, including "Rock with You" and "Don't Stop 'til You Get Enough".

Then, in 1981, along came MTV. Trained in Berry Gordy's Motown Machine from the age of 11, Jackson was the perfect artist for that moment in music history. He could sing passionately, dance like James Brown, interact effectively with the camera, and look attractive to the audience while doing it. He didn't drink, smoke, swear, or take drugs (that anyone was aware of), which fit in nicely with the conservative Reagan era of the early 1980s. He spoke politely, and seemed to show kindness to others at every turn. He was authentically "black enough" in his musical style to attract a large following in that community, while attracting a huge new white audience as well. Women liked him and so did most men. The old remembered him from his Motown Days, and the young just wanted to "dance like Michael".

The ultimate cross-over artist then ascended to the throne of pop king with the release of *Thriller*, one of the first albums to successfully use music videos as part of the promotional package. Although the first single, "The Girl is Mine", a duet between Jackson and Paul McCartney, failed to make waves on the pop charts, the second single, "Billie Jean", changed all of that with the release of the album's first video. With a fantastic bass line and catchy chorus, the song became an instant hit.

However, despite the radio success of the song, MTV initially thought that the video for "Billie Jean" was not for them, since it wasn't "rock" music. MTV only relented and began playing the video after CBS Records' chief Walter Yetnikoff threatened to pull all of their other videos. Directed by Steve Barron (who would also direct a-ha's groundbreaking video for "Take on Me"), "Billie Jean" became the first video by a black artist to receive heavy rotation on MTV. It would also be the video that propelled MTV from "that music video cable channel" into a mainstream media outlet.

The success of the third single off of the album, "Beat It", which featured guitarist Eddie Van Halen, sent sales of *Thriller* through the roof, at one point selling a million copies every 4 days. The album topped the charts in both 1983 and 1984 and it has sold an estimated 65 million copies to date, easily the best-selling album of all time.

The last video for the album – the one for the song "Thriller" – reached previously unimaginable heights when it was released in December 1983. Directed by John Landis (who, at the time, was best known for directing the films *National Lampoon's Animal House*, *The Blues Brothers*, and a segment in the *Twilight Zone* movie), and with a budget of $500,000, the video was the first "world premiere" on MTV. The almost 14-minute video featured zombies and other creatures created by Academy Award winning special effects makeup artist Rick Baker, and it is widely considered the most influential music video of all time.

Although "Thriller" and its accompanying video will always be considered his "crowning achievement", Jackson had many other successful videos, too, including "Bad", "Black or White", "Man in the Mirror", and "Scream" (with his sister, Janet Jackson).

When he was dubbed the "King of Pop" in 1989, few could argue. The most awarded artist in pop music history, Jackson dominated an entire decade of American pop. The fame was not without drawbacks, though. Tabloid reporters hounded him, following his every move, eventually forcing him into near seclusion on his private, custom-built, fantasyland estate, "Neverland", named for the place where Peter Pan never had to grow up.

Like James Brown before him, Jackson used his stardom to support various social causes, including efforts to fight world hunger (as co-writer of USA for Africa's "We Are the World" single, on which he also sang), drunk driving ("Beat It" was used in a prevention campaign sponsored by the Ad Council and the National Highway Transportation Safety Administration), HIV/AIDS research (which came to his attention after he befriended Ryan White, an Indiana teenager who contracted HIV after a blood transfusion), the United Negro College Fund (all profits from the single "Man in the Mirror" were donated to the charity), and as part of his Heal the World Foundation, which brought underprivileged children to the theme park at Neverland, as well as working with other children-focused charities to fight disease, hunger, and war.

Jackson's career was not without controversy, however. His short-lived marriage to Elvis Presley's daughter, Lisa Marie, created a firestorm of controversy in 1994, some of it certainly caused by the inter-racial nature of the marriage. A black man marrying the white daughter of "the King of Rock and Roll" was a bit hard for some to accept, even decades after the end of segregation.

And Jackson's fondness for children was endearing to some of his fans, but troubling to many others. Having been thrust into the spotlight as the lead singer of the Jackson Five at the tender age of six years old (before they signed with Motown), Jackson never experienced a traditional childhood himself. As a grown man, Jackson sought to find his lost childhood experience by inviting children, many of them poor or handicapped, to his Neverland ranch, a wonderland complete with trains, rides, Ferris wheels, and a large petting zoo. Allegations of sexual abuse of children surfaced in 1993 and continued for the rest of his career, but he was never convicted.

Other strange behaviors were rumored, as well, including that Jackson slept in a hyperbaric oxygen chamber, and that he bleached his skin and repeatedly had plastic surgeries in an attempt to look "whiter". There was also an incident where he dangled his baby son from a high balcony while fans looked on, horrified, from below.

Jackson died in 2009 at the age of 50, under questionable circumstances. Conrad Murray, a doctor hired by Jackson to treat a variety of conditions including stress and insomnia, medicated him with a lethal dose of anti-anxiety medications and anesthetics in order to "help him sleep". Michael never woke up. Murray was convicted of involuntary manslaughter and sent to jail.

Despite the oddities and allegations in his personal life, Michael Jackson remains the single greatest entertainer of the 1980s. Jackson is the only artist to have a song in the Billboard Hot 100 list in five different decades, and sales of all his recordings combined top 400 million copies. He perfected the art of pop video performance, and dance videos like "Beat It", "Billie Jean", and "Black or White" still stand as the standard against which all other pop dance videos are judged. The "King of Pop"? Undoubtedly.

YO! MTV RAPS

With the exception of Michael Jackson and a few other artists, MTV played very few videos by black artists in its earliest days, and very little rap at all. This changed dramatically in 1988 with the unveiling of an all-rap show on MTV entitled *Yo! MTV Raps.*

With the exception of some people who lived in New York or Los Angeles, few Americans had ever been exposed to hip-hop music and its accompanying style of dress, graffiti art, and break dancing specific to inner-city black America. *Yo! MTV Raps* brought hip-hop into the mainstream for the first time, so all of America could see and hear the new music as well and its artists.

The hosts of the show, Dr. Dre' (not the same Dr. Dre from N.W.A, to be discussed on page 367), Fab 5 Freddie, and Ed Lover were funny, irreverent and interesting. They were the perfect people to sell rap to a nation of white teenagers who knew nothing of hip-hop culture or rap mentality.

Yo! MTV Raps made rap accessible to everybody in the 1980s, just as Fats Domino had presented R&B as "safe" for whites in the 1950s. By the early 1990s, the show was airing three or more times a week, and the biggest names in rap were not only appearing on the show, but referencing it in their lyric, to garner more MTV airplay. *Yo! MTV Raps* went off the air in 1995, its job having been completed. Rap was now mainstream popular music for all of America's younger generations.

VIDEOS OF THE LATE 1990S THROUGH TODAY

Gone are the days when our minds had to create the pictures to accompany the songs we were enjoying with ears alone. Today every detail of the experience is provided for us by the genius producers and directors with clear visions of what it all should mean. Nearly every pop tune of any consequence now comes with video-clip availability on the artist's website and YouTube. It means, of course, that popular music is now in a new era, where the music is only one piece of the industry, and, in most cases, it will not stand on its own without a "look" to go with it. Unfortunately, this means that some bands are prefabricated for their looks and not necessarily their talent, which can lead to music that is formulaic and, frankly, just a rehashing of something that worked well before. However, in the age of MP3s, homemade websites, and file sharing, truly talented artists can have their music discovered and shared more quickly than artists of the past could have ever imagined.

Chapter 34
Reggae

In the middle of the 1960s, Jamaican reggae surfaced as a new music to catch the interest of record buyers, especially in the big cities of England and the United States.

Jamaica is a wondrous mix of many cultures. For four hundred years, though, Jamaica – a tiny corner of the Third World – has been a boiling caldron of human misery, greed, corruption, and deep multicultural hostilities. The aboriginal inhabitants, members of the Arawakan linguistic stock of native North Americans, called their homeland Xaymaca, "Isle of Springs". Visited by Christopher Columbus in 1494, Jamaica became an official Spanish colony in 1509. In an effort to make slaves of the Arawakan Indians, the Spanish killed them off almost completely. African natives were then imported to overcome the resultant labor shortage (Morse 1960, 5154).

England took over Jamaica in 1670, and it soon became a major producer of sugar cane and cacao, labor-intensive industries in the extreme. Kingston thus became one of the world's principal slave-trading centers, both for North America and Jamaica itself. Insurrections and armed warfare by maroons (bands of slaves who had escaped to interior hideouts) continued until the abolition of slavery in 1831, at which time 300,000 slaves were set free. However, even though they had gained their freedom, they were still mistreated by oppressive taxation, discriminatory legal rules and procedures, and land-exclusion measures, which caused widespread unrest among the blacks.

In 1940, the United States obtained a lease on various prime Jamaican land areas and important dockyard installations. These leases, turned over to huge American corporations, were renegotiated with local Jamaican officials when Britain gave Jamaica its independence in 1962.

MENTO

Of the several folk music styles in Jamaica, the one called mento leads directly to reggae. Mento, a slow version of a Cuban-styled rumba combined with African rhythms, comes from the Spanish verb *mentar,* meaning "to mention", referring to the subtle ways their song lyrics, sometimes accompanied by symbolic dance steps, express personal complaints and intense sociopolitical criticism of the ruling classes. Subtlety is necessary to avoid offending the audience, while still getting the point across (Charlton 1990, 221).

Mento is performed by street corner bands of guitar, banjo, drum, occasionally trumpet, and any other instruments available. Mento street music is, of course, looked down upon as insufferably low-class by all upper levels of society – native, black, white, and all mixtures thereof.

And in Jamaica, as everywhere in the world, adolescents from the upper levels of society find this low-class music wonderfully appealing when they arrive at the age of social consciousness in their late teens. It's a form of mildly acceptable temporary rebellion against the establishment – the very establishment they will most assuredly join in a few short years.

SKA

When mento street musicians heard 1950s' American R&B beamed down from the powerful radio stations in Florida, they began to work some of those musical ingredients into their music. The result was called ska coming, perhaps, from "skat", a simulation of the scratching sound made by strumming a guitar, probably much like Bo Diddley's strumming technique.

Thus ska emerged in the middle 1950s, with horns, R&B riffs, and a shuffle rhythm much like that made famous by Louis Jordan. The Jamaican ska musicians called that rhythm "chug-a-lug", and they accented the last part of each beat with such emphasis that it was often perceived as the main beat. Ska rhythm was thus said to have a "hesitation beat".

Recording studios arose in Jamaica to make money on this new and exciting music, the first and most famous being Clement "Coxone" Dodd's Studio One. Dodd's main studio musicians, a nineteen-piece resident house band, were the Skatalites – consisting of four trumpet-fluegelhorn players, two trombonists, two alto and two tenor saxophonists, two guitarists, three keyboard players, a bass guitarist, and three percussionists (Charlton 1990, 223). Not all musicians were used on every recording, of course.

The Skatalites backed up the Maytals, the Wailers, and the Heptones. "Guns of Navarone" by the Skatalites made the British charts in 1967. Earlier, in 1964, a Jamaican singer, Millie Small (b. 1946), came out with "My Boy, Lollipop" which placed in the American *Billboard* listings. That recordings was made in London (Rod Stewart played harmonica, incidentally) (Shaw 1982, 307), and the session was produced by a Jamaican of British ancestry, Chris Blackwell. Blackwell used the profits to set up his own Island Record Company in London.

Ska is not dead, at all. It comes and goes, picking up bits and pieces from other rock styles, but hangs on to a small crowd of fans, especially in college towns, it seems. In the 1990s, the Mighty, Mighty Bosstones were Lollapalooza's first mainstage ska band and one of ska's biggest American underground-to-minor-mainstream success stories with their hit "The Impression That I Get" (Mike Breen in [Cincinnati, Ohio], May 8-14, 1997, p. 17).

ROCKSTEADY

By 1966, the original pure ska style in Jamaica had begun to undergo changes. Wilson Pickett and Booker T. and the MGs injected gospel vocalisms and a heavy bass line into some of the ska they performed. Tempos were slowed, and the new style was called rocksteady. "Oh Ba-a-by" by the Techniques and "Rock Steady" by Alton Ellis made the English charts in the late 1960s (Charlton 1990, 223).

When Jamaican disc jockeys heard American radio personalities talk in and around the recordings, they (the Jamaican DJs) took the idea even further by talking in rhythmic patter while ska and rocksteady records were played. The practice was called "toasting" when it was just rhythmic chatter, but when it grew into actually changing the sound of the recording it was called "dubbing" (Charlton 1990, 223). They were, in a sense, dubbing in their contribution to the recording.

Dubbing was soon performed in the recording studios as an essential element of spoken patter over a rocksteady beat. When New York funk disc jockeys like Joseph Saddler, known as Grandmaster Flash, heard what the Jamaican disc jockeys were doing, they (the New Yorkers) began some techniques that lead very quickly to rap (Charlton 1990, 101).

REGGAE

In 1968, the Maytals released "Do the Reggay". Deriving from the Latin *regis*, meaning "king", reggae (the more common spelling) came to mean "king's music". The king referred to was the King of Ethiopia, Tafari Makonnen Woldemikael (1892-1975), who was considered to have fulfilled the prophecy of Marcus Garvey (1887-1940).

Garvey, a black Jamaican printer and editor, formed the Universal Negro Improvement Association, which aimed to lift the socioeconomic circumstances for all blacks worldwide. His most imaginative plan was the Black Star Line Steamship Company organized with the idea that the blacks would return from the United States and the West Indies to Africa to establish their own modern highly industrialized nations. After $500,000 in stock was sold, the project failed, and Garvey was imprisoned for mail fraud. Even with these issues, Garvey's dream caught the fancy of blacks throughout the West Indies, especially his "Back to Africa" theme which urged his followers to "Look to Africa for the crowning of a black king, and he shall be the redeemer" (Hebdige 1977, 52).

When Tafari Makonnen came of age and was crowned Emperor of Ethiopia, he took the name Haile Selassie I (Amharic for "Power of the Trinity"). His compassionate and humanitarian governing style, particularly his abolition of slavery, brought him hundreds of thousands of admirers all over the world, and the blacks in the West Indies began to believe he was their redeemer, the black Messiah that Marcus Garvey had spoken of.

Rastafarians (from the title "Ras", meaning "king", and his birth name "Tafari") in the West Indies have developed a set of guiding principles, beliefs, and rituals. Some grow dreadlocks and cite Biblical passages to explain why they don't cut their hair. Many smoke ganja (marijuana), believing it to be a holy herb. Many live as artists, fishermen, and craftsmen, and refuse to pay taxes or to work for the competitive commercial world which they call Babylon. Instead, they look toward Zion – black Africa. Many Rastafarians are vegetarians. Some wear the red, green, and gold colors of the Ethiopian flag. Others wear the red, green, and black of Marcus Garvey's UNIA jackets (Hebdige 1977, 53).

Borrowing from Burru folk drumming traditions, European harmonies, mento melodies, ska, and, rocksteady, the style known as reggae began to make its presence felt. Using modern amplified lead and rhythm guitars, piano, organ, bass guitar, drums, and assorted Jamaica percussion instruments, reggae's infectious beat moved into more commercial success than the earlier styles mentioned above.

Reggae bassists, with the lead guitarist sometimes doubling at the octave, typically set up syncopated ostinato patterns which often avoid the first beat. The percussionists offer a heavy back beat revealing their debt to American R&B. There is no single specific reggae style, however. It absorbs many subtleties from other styles.

Johnny Nash's "I Can See Clearly" (1972) and "Stir It Up" (1973) were early evidence of reggae's influence in American pop music. Reggae also influenced many British groups – especially the punk groups, who shared reggae's stance against police brutality, racism, corrupt business practices, and other establishment conditions. The Clash covered Junior Murvin's "Police and Thieves" (1977), and came out with their own "White Man in Hammersmith Palais" (1978). Madness came out with "The Prince" (1979). The Specials released "Gangsters" (1979) under their own label, 2 Tone Records.

The Body Snatchers, Bad Manners, the English Beat, and several other British punk-inclined bands took to ska-reggae easily, particularly the group called UB40 out of Birmingham, who cried out against English, rather than Jamaican, poverty. Their name, UB40, came from a code on the cards issued by the British government to apply for unemployment benefits (Charlton 1990, 228).

Perhaps the best-known British bank to use ska and reggae regularly in their music was the Police. Led by Gordon Sumner (b. 1951) on bass – nicknamed "Sting" by jazzman Gordon Soloman, because of the yellow and black striped t-shirt Sumner wore that made him look like a bee – with Andy Summers on guitar and Stewart Copeland on drums, the Police recorded *Reggatta de Blanc* ("white Reggae") in 1979. That album containing "Message in a Bottle", a No. 1 single in the UK. The ska and reggae influence is also heard in "Walking on the Moon", "De Do Do Do, De Da Da Da", "Spirits in the Material World", and many other songs by the Police.

Bob Marley

The real thing, however, had been around since 1964 with the formation of the Wailin' Rude Boys, a vocal group comprised of adolescents from the Trenchtown ghetto of West Kingston. They were Robert Nesta "Bob" Marley (1945-1981), Winston Hubert McIntosh (Peter Tosh) (1944-1987), Neville O'Riley Livingston (Bunny Wailer) (b. 1947), Junior Braithwaite (1949-1999), Cherry Smith (1943-2008) and Beverley Kelso (b. 1948). "Rude boys" were gangs of hostile Jamaican punk-style male teenagers who roamed around creating serious trouble, much like the British skinheads a few years later.

Gradually softening their rude boy image, the Wailers came out with several strong sociopolitical songs, "Small Ax" (1970) and "Get Up, Stand Up" (1973), all backed by the Upsetters, Lee "Scratch" Perry's resident studio band (Hebdige 1987, 78).

Catch a Fire Burnin' on Chris Blackwell's Island label brought them to international attention when Eric Clapton made a big hit out of a cover of "I Shot the Sheriff". By 1974, Tosh and Wailer left the group because they didn't want to tour. The group reorganized as Bob Marley and the Wailers with Marley, brothers Carlton "Carly" (1950-1987) and Aston "Family Man" Barrett (b. 1943) on drums and bass, Alvin "Seeco" Patterson (b. 1930) on percussion, Junior Marvin (b. 1949) and Al Anderson (b. 1950) on lead guitar, Tyrone Downie (b. 1956) and Earl "Wire" Lindo (b. 1953) on keyboards, and a backup female vocal trio called the I Three's, consisting of Judy Mowatt (b. 1953), Marcia Griffiths (b. 1949), and Marley's wife, Rita (b. 1946). Soon they played to huge crowds Europe and the United States.

Their last big show together was as the opening act for the Commodores in New York's Madison Square Garden in September, 1980. On May 11, 1981, Bob Marley died of cancer at age 36. Eventually, Marley's children entered show business, too, as Ziggy Marley and the Melody Makers, who disbanded in 2002.

Jimmy Cliff

James Chambers (b. 1948), calling himself Jimmy Cliff, dropped out of school to pursue a career in music. At age 14, his first effort at songwriting, "Hurricane Hattie", named for a storm that had swept the Caribbean in the early 1960s, went to No. 1 in Jamaica. He then went on tour in America as a new reggae "find". He appeared in 1972, at age 22, in a semi-autobiographical movie called *The Harder*

They Come, a story about the greed, corruption, and brutality in the Jamaican music industry.

In 1974, Cliff went to Nigeria for the first time to study Islam, which he eventually converted to. On a subsequent trip to South Africa in 1980, with the condition that the audience be racially diverse, he played to a crowd of 75,000 in Soweto, fourteen years before the end of apartheid (Lazell 1989, 101). He and his new backup band, called Oneness, began to draw notice in late 1982.

Jimmy Cliff co-headlined the World Music Festival at the Bob Marley Center in Montego Bay, Jamaica, in October, 1982. In 1984, on the first occasion of a reggae category in the awards, Cliff was nominated for a Grammy for "Reggae Night", written by LaToya Jackson and Amir Bayyan (of Kool and the Gang). "Trapped", Cliff's contribution to the USA for Africa recording on *We Are the World*, was performed by Bruce Springsteen.

He continues to tour and to record, with his last album, *Rebirth*, released in 2012.

CONCLUSION

The growth of reggae illustrates a common occurrence in the history of popular music in Western civilization: what starts out as the social protest music of an oppressed and poverty-stricken ethnic or racial community eventually becomes the fashionable pop "in thing" with middle-class Caucasian adolescents, a few of whom share the social concerns, but most of whom are the children of the fathers and grandfathers whose corporations are the very cause of that oppression and poverty in the first place. Strange are the ways of human behavior. Generation after generation, however, the same patterns seem to be at work.

Chapter 35
The Roots of Rap

One of the more controversial developments in American pop music – rap – is the latest in the series of deep-seated black socioeconomic protest movements that always precipitate a new musical style. The sequence of events is a matter of historical record. It starts out with field hollers, spirituals, and chain-gang blues, then proceeds to and through the urban blues, swing, be-bop, rhythm and blues, gospel, soul, funk, disco, and now rap.

The new musical styles are a way for the black community to, on one hand, protest against four hundred years of oppression, and on the other hand, bath its wounds in musical therapy.

Each time, the white community ignores the protest, cleans up what is too uncomfortable in the lyrics, "whitens" what is too "black" in the music, and turns the new musical style into a huge, new, profitable business. This is a blazing over-simplification of a frightfully complex chain of events, of course, but the generalization holds firm.

MUSICAL ROOTS OF RAP

The specific musical style that triggered the rap explosion in America seems to have been the 1970s' Jamaican street-pop music industry led, by and large, by the disc jockeys with their provocative "toasting" and "dubbing" performances (see the previous chapter). Jamaican disc jockeys like Duke Reid (1915-1975) and Prince Buster (b. 1938) would shout their favorite catch phrases over the microphone as they played their records. These talk overs ("toasts") became the way of the future.

Ewart Bedford (b. 1942), better known as U-Roy, began to deliver weird rambling monologues, yelps, screeches, and assorted blistering asides on "Wear You To the Ball", "Flashing My Whip", and "Tom Drunk". Roy Samuel Reid (1944-1999), known as I-Roy, followed with fatherly advice to "cool out the youth" in his talk-over patter on certain cuts on *Crisus Time* (1976). U-Roy and I-Roy challenged each other in the style of the old African boast songs, mocking each other with insults and putdowns – "playing the dozens" as it's called in American black culture (Hebdige 1987, 84).

All of this was done over the radio, and also on portable sound systems on the back of flatbed trucks, in open fields, on ghetto streets, in vacant lots, in a rental hall, wherever a crowd might gather to mingle and dance. Mixed in with the chatter were bits and pieces of local news – updates on the latest political indignities, corruption, murders, cover-ups, and other grassroots events the people would want to know about. In continuous three-way networking of artists, record producers, and the audience, the DJ served much like the "griots" in West Africa – resident story-telling historians for the exchange of information, tribal myths, and community attitudes and values.

SOCIAL AND POLITICAL ROOTS OF RAP

By the early 1980s, rap was a national craze. In no time at all it was all the rage in the pop music industry. A small crowd of artists pushed rap into the newspapers and the courts with their tough lyrics. The famous obscenity trial of 2 Live Crew in Florida caused quite a stir.

One of the nation's leading scholars in the field of black literature and culture, Henry Louis Gates, Jr., Chairman of the Black Studies Program at Harvard University, testified at the trial of 2 Live Crew. He explained that rap was a contemporary form of a four-hundred year tradition of "signifying" – rhythmic teasing, insulting, ridiculing indirectly to send a message to those listening in, punning often in lewd and off-color rhyme patterns, and teaching a lesson by circumlocution. Male adolescents have been signifying in the black community for a long time, he explained, and they do it partly in earnest, partly tongue-in-cheek. For them it was, and is, a release of pent-up anguish at the helplessness of their social circumstances. It's a survival strategy.

PIONEERS OF RAP

DJ Kool Herc

The Father of Rap is most certainly DJ Kool Herc (Clive Campbell (b. 1955)). In the 1970s when Herc moved from Jamaica to the West Bronx in New York, he brought with him an intimate understanding of the DJ's powerful leadership role in street-level affairs, and he also brought with him the best sound system anyone had ever heard up to that time – clean and crisp, with brilliant highs and deep, rich lows. Before long he was being copied by several neighboring disc jockeys.

In the clubs where he used to DJ, Herc switched between two turntables, both with the same song on them, so that he could extend percussion breaks for dancers. Eventually, a type of "one-upmanship" evolved, with each dancer creating more and more elaborate moves, leading to the type of dance now called breakdancing.

Herc also hired an MC (master of ceremonies), Coke La Rock (b. 1955) to do some of the talk-overs for him while he concentrated on the turntables. After Grand Wizzard Theodore (Theodore Livingston) (b. 1963) developed the technique of "scratching", that is, moving the record backward and forward in time with the beat of a tune on another turntable to produce a unique percussion accompaniment, Herc added that to his list of techniques as well.

Although he has since become a legend, DJ Kool Herc never switched from live performances to commercial recording.

These American modifications of Jamaican DJ techniques came to be known as "rap" and the funk-driven street music as "hip hop". Soon there were boast raps, party raps, insult raps, news raps, message raps, nonsense raps, and motherly-fatherly-sisterly-brotherly raps (Erlewine 1994).

Afrika Bambaataa

Afrika Bambaataa (b. 1957) was another major figure in the early days. He tried to turn black street culture into a positive force through his music. Born Kevin Donovan in the Bronx, Afrika Bambaataa Aasim took his name from a 19th-century Zulu chief. In his late teens, Bambaataa was one of the most skillful disc jockeys in the Bronx, and he began to organize block parties and breakdancing competitions to get the kids off the ghetto streets and into less violent and dangerous behavior.

Bambaataa entered the record business as a producer of a single by Soulsonic Force, "Zulu Nation Throwdown" (1980). Two years later he made his debut as a performer with "Jazzy Session" and "Planet Rock". "Planet Rock" introduced a new, technologically-driven style of black popular music, which Bambaataa referred to as "ElectroFunk". Inspired by German electronic band Kraftwerk, Bambaataa created his own uniquely African-American version of European electronic dance music. "Planet Rock" reached No. 4 on the R&B charts and joined the Sugarhill Gang's "Rapper's Delight" (1979) as one of the early classics of hip-hop.

Afrika Bambaataa went on to a big career, often collaborating with other artists: James Brown, John Lydon, George Clinton, UB40, Bootsy Collins, and Boy George. Afrika Bambaataa justly deserves his reputation as one of the founding fathers of rap (Erlewine 1994).

Grandmaster Flash

Another founding father of rap enjoys the same kind of respect. Calling himself Grandmaster Flash because of his speed and precision at the turntables, Joseph Saddler (b. 1958) put together a group called the Furious Five, consisting of Cowboy (Robert Keith Wiggins), Melle Mel (Melvin Glover), Kidd Creole (Danny Glover), Mr. Ness/Scorpio (Eddie Morris), and Rahiem (Guy Williams).

The trio of Cowboy, Melle Mel, and Kidd Creole called themselves the Three MCs, who are considered to be the first emcees in the history of rap, with Mel being the first to call himself an MC during a performance. Cowboy is also credited with creating the term "hip hop".

Grandmaster Flash made art forms out of manipulating records on his turntables – scratching them and repeating particular instrumental sections – and "punch phrasing" – hitting a particular break on one deck while the record on the other deck is still playing. The effect is like an acoustical exclamation point. He thus created new music out of collages of existing recordings. The most important recording of such a technique was the single "The Adventures of Grandmaster Flash on the Wheels of Steel" released in 1981 (Erlewine 1994).

Nearly all of the Grandmaster's recordings, however, consist of interlocking raps by the Furious Five. Their most important recording, "The Message" (1982), turned away from the party subjects of the time to focus on urban social issues – creating a new genre of rap.

In addition to the three pioneers mentioned above, several artists were especially influential in the growth and development of rap in America.

Run-D.M.C.

In the early 1980s, entrepreneur Russell Simmons (b. 1957), founder of Def Jam Records, coaxed his little brother, Joe "DJ Run" (b. 1964), and a friend, Darryl "D.M.C." McDaniel (b. 1964), to form a rap duo. Upon graduation from high school they did just that, and enlisted their friend Jason "Jam Master Jay" Mizell (1965-2002) to scratch turntables. All three members of Run-D.M.C. were from middle-class New York families in Hollis, Queens.

Their first single "It's Like That"/"Sucker MCs" (1983) sounded like no other rap at the time – it was spare, blunt, and skillful, with hard beats and with powerful, literate, daring vocals. Several other singles and a self-titled album appeared soon thereafter.

By 1985 and their second album, *King of Rock,* Run-D.M.C. had become the most popular and influential rappers in America, with dozens of imitators. They were breaking down the barriers between rock and rap, and single cuts from the album were lodged high up in the R&B charts: "King of Rock", "You Talk Too Much", and "Can You Rock It Like This?" Also in 1985, they appeared in the rap movie *Krush Groove.*

In 1986, Run-D.M.C. had a Top 5 hit (the first hip hop song to hit that high on the pop charts) with a cover of Aerosmith's "Walk this Way", featuring Steven Tyler and Joe Perry on vocals and guitars. The video featured the two bands on either side of a wall, until Tyler breaks through the wall and both bands join forces for a collaborative concert. It's considered a pivotal moment for the rap/hip hop genre, as it was the first hip hop video to be played in heavy rotation on MTV.

Although they continued to record together through 1993, personal issues and other business enterprises took precedence for the members of the group throughout much of the 1990s. Run-D.M.C. officially disbanded in 2002, after Jam-Master Jay was shot and killed outside of a recording studio in New York.

The Beastie Boys

White rappers had dabbled in the genre since its inception, but it was the Beastie Boys – three upper-middle-class white kids – who made rap a serious option for white musicians and popular with large numbers of white listeners. The Beasties attracted a large black fan base, too, a testament to their abilities to rap "authentically". Comprised of Michael "Mike D" Diamond (b. 1965), Adam "MCA" Yauch (1964-2012), and Adam "Ad-rock" Horovitz (b. 1966), the trio signed with Def Jam Recordings, which, due in part to the Beasties' success, would eventually become rap's biggest and most successful independent record label. Although they had released singles on the Def Jam label in 1985, it was their first full-length album, *License to Ill* (1986), which brought them worldwide fame.

Met with critical acclaim when it was first released, *License to Ill* became the biggest selling album of the year, and it went on to be the best selling rap album of the 1980s. Because of it, millions of kids all over America raised their voices with a new battle cry: "You've got to fight / for your right / to PAAARRR-TTTTYYYY."

The Beasties, former punk rockers, played up their obnoxious image at every turn. They were rude, crude, obscene, and well beyond what most audiences had seen before. Women in cages, simulated sexual acts, and mechanical and inflatable penises were all a regular part of the live show experience. The Beasties were teenage sexuality gone wild. But beneath all the theater and obnoxious behavior were solid rap lyrics, delivered over complex, sample-heavy music.

Largely because of, and in response to, the Beasties' music, the Parents Music Resource Center (PMRC) was formed in 1985 as a way of protecting children from harmful lyrics. PMRC introduced a content warning label to advise parents of lyrics about sex, drug use, violence or the occult.

After nearly thirty years of performing, the group finally disbanded in 2012, after member Adam Yauch died of cancer.

2 Pac Shakur

The late rapper Tupac Amaru Shakur had a controversial career, but there was no doubt about his raw talent, ambition, and skill in his chosen field of entertainment. The former member of Digital Underground became a solo performer with *2Pacalypse Now* (1992), and was highly praised for originality.

In 1996, he released the first double-disc set of all new material in hip-hop history, *All Eyez on Me*. It entered the charts at No. 1. In September, 1996, 2 Pac was shot in the chest as he was riding in a car in Las Vegas. He struggled for a week, but died on September 13, 1996 (Ron Wynn, AMG scholar).

Despite the fact that he's supposedly been dead for over 15 years now, 2 Pac (or his estate) have put out seven studio albums, two live albums, and ten compilation albums after his death, leading some to believe that he survived the shooting, but is living incognito under an alias for security reasons.

The Notorious B.I.G.

Chris Wallace (1972-1997), called The Notorious B.I.G., also known as "Biggie" and "Biggie Smalls" came out with his first album, *Ready To Die*, in 1994, and it was one of the most popular hip-hop releases of the year. In June of 1995, his single, "One More Chance", debuted at No. 5 in the pop singles chart, topping Michael Jackson's "Scream/Childhood" as the highest debut single of all time. The single later won the Grammy for Rap Single of the Year, and Biggie won the Grammy for Rap Artist of the Year.

As the Notorious B.I.G. was preparing his second album, Tupac Shakur was killed in Las Vegas. Many in the media speculated that Biggie's camp was responsible for the shooting, which Biggie and his producer, Sean "Puff Daddy/Puffy/Diddy/P. Diddy" Combs, denied emphatically.

Early on the morning of March 9, 1997, the Notorious B.I.G. was returning to his hotel in Los Angeles after a Soul Train Award party when a car pulled up aside his car and opened fire, killing him instantly.

The Notorious B.I.G.'s second album, the double-disc *After Death*, was released three weeks later, and entered the charts at No. 1 (Erlewine1994). As of this writing (2014), his murder still has not been solved.

Public Enemy

Born on the streets of New York, Public Enemy ushered in a new era of attitude-driven rap, combining biting lyrics with the hard edge of rock and roll. With videos produced by filmmaker Spike Lee, Public Enemy added a new topic to the world of rap that only folk rock had dealt with before: social criticism. While the Sugarhill Gang was rapping about dancing, drinking, and sexual exploits, Public

Enemy, who called themselves "the prophets of rage" were rapping about poverty, politics, and racism over complex beats, samples, and music provided by an expert team of DJ-producers referred to as "the Bomb Squad".

Rappers Chuck D (Carlton Douglas Ridenhour, b. 1960), Flavor Flav (William Jonathan Drayton, Jr., b. 1959) and the rest of Public Enemy called for social action with hits like "Fight the Power" and "Bring the Noise". The group caused controversy from its earliest days, openly aligning themselves with Muslim leader Louis Farrakhan, whom they frequently referred to as a prophet, who had made anti-Semitic remarks against Jews.

Flavor Flav got into legal trouble in the 1990s with an assault conviction and a charge of attempted murder. While the band stopped recording in the late 1990s, Chuck D continues a successful career as a college speaker, and Flavor Flav has hosted reality TV shows and opened a string of restaurants.

NWA (Niggaz With Attitude)

Perhaps the most notorious group in the history of rap, NWA were unapologetically violent in their raps. Blunt, harsh, and aggressive, this five-man rap crew seemed not only to discuss but also to celebrate the criminal life on the tough streets of Los Angeles. The fathers of gangsta rap sang of gang violence, police brutality, and drug use. Their 1988 album, *Straight Outta Compton,* received virtually no radio play at all, but cemented their image as hardcore rap outlaws with songs like "F*** tha Police" which resulted in a letter from the Federal Bureau of Investigations, warning the record company to "watch their step." Three years later, the group was disbanded, but members Dr. Dre and Ice Cube went on to successful solo careers of their own. Just as English punk band the Sex Pistols had done ten years earlier, NWA came onto the scene, created a violent hardcore version of their respective genre, and then disbanded.

RAP ARTISTS WHO MOVED INTO OTHER AREAS OF ENTERTAINMENT

LL Cool J

James Smith, known as LL Cool J (for "Ladies Love Cool James") (b. 1968), fused the beat box minimalism of Run-D.M.C. with a b-boy's snarl of defiant lyrics, and pushed rap into new terrain, opening the door for numerous hip-hop contenders. He was the first hip-hop act to appear on *American Bandstand*. His biggest hit was *Mama Said Knock You Out* (1990) (Erlewine 1994). These days, he appears on TV, on *NCIS: Los Angeles*.

Queen Latifah

Beginning as a beat boxer with the hip-hop group Ladies Fresh, Queen Latifah (b. 1970) made her first solo statement – "Ladies First" – count on her 1989 album *All Hail the Queen*, a nice mixture of soul, dub reggae, and straight hip-hop. Her persona was intelligent and no-nonsense.

Born Dana Owens in Newark, New Jersey, Latifah (an Arabic word translating as "delicate" and "very kind") landed an acting role as a cast member of the Fox sitcom *Living Single*, and then released *Black Reign* (1993), dedicated to her brother who had been killed in a motorcycle accident a year earlier. "U.N.I.T.Y.", a hit single on *Black Reign* won a Grammy for Best Rap Solo Performance in 1993.

Although she started out in the realm of hip-hop, these days she casts a wider net, including soul, jazz, and traditional pop (she sang "Who Can I Turn To" with Tony Bennett on his album, *Duets*) in her repertoire.

Latifah was later nominated for an Academy Award in the Best Supporting Actress category for her portrayal of Mama Morton in the film *Chicago* (2002). Latifah lost to one of her co-stars, Catherine Zeta-Jones. She also had a major role in the film version of *Hairspray* (2007), based on the Broadway show of the same name, which itself was based on an earlier movie, also called *Hairspray*, directed by John Waters.

Latifah continues to appear in films, and her last album, *Persona*, was released in 2009.

Chapter 36
Salsa

Since the middle 1800s, American music has been flavored with Latin spices – particularly from Cuba, Brazil, Argentina, and Mexico. What may be the earliest Texan *corrido*, "The Corrido de Leandro Rivera", dates from 1841, and begins a long line of such "story songs", [ballads] in the Great Southwest (Roberts 1979, 24). Sheet music of Cuban tunes was available in New York in the 1850s. The celebrated piano virtuoso, Louis Moreau Gottschalk (1829-1869) wrote and played dozens of Latin pieces to the delight of his fans. Various Latin groups toured America in the late 1800s, and soon the intoxicating rhythms found their way into the operettas of Victor Herbert, John Philip Sousa, and Sigmund Romberg.

Several of the early New Orleans jazzmen casually labeled "Creole" were, in fact, of Mexican ethnic origin – Lorenzo Tio, Sr., his brother Luis Tio, Frank Otera, Alcide "Yellow" Nuñez, Jimmy Palau, and Chink Martin, for example. Jelly Roll Morton spoke often of the Spanish tinge being a desirable thing in certain pieces of music.

But the explosion came in 1913, when an Argentine dance called the tango was danced by Vernon Castle and Julia Sanderson in a musical called *The Sunshine Girl*, by Paul Reuben. Suddenly all of the America went crazy over the tango. Restaurants and nightclubs catered to couples who were encouraged to tango between courses of their meals.

The wealthy Mrs. Ethel Fitch Conger of New York broke her leg dancing the tango. A high school student died in a trolley car after dancing the tango for seven hours. The headlines read "Death Attributed to Tango". In 1914, Yale made the front pages by banning the tango at its Junior Prom.

The New York Mail complained that "the tango – which appalls lovers of sound manner and morals – is an immodest and basely suggestive exercise tending to lewdness and immorality," and Bishop Schrembs, of Toledo, Ohio, denounced it as one of the "nauseating revels and dances of the brothel" (Roberts 1979, 46).

Very much the same thing happened when the several other Latin dances came to America – rumba, samba, bolero, beguine, mambo, merengue, cha cha, bossa nova, and others. Each time, the delightful rhythm patterns lifted American mainstream pop and jazz to a new level of interest and vitality. And each time, a number of people were duly offended and insulted by the evil they saw at work in the land.

The current term favored among the insiders in the Latin music industry for this whole body of musical dance rhythms is *salsa.* The term means "sauce", and is often used by dancers to urge the musicians to add more spice to their music. The older term "Latin music" has not entirely disappeared, but is used more and more to refer to the earlier times and earlier Latin bands – Xavier Cugat, Perez Prado, Tito Puente, Desi Arnaz, and the like.

But salsa is more precisely the music of a special crowd of people in a special location, after the 1960s.

> *Salsa is best distinguished from earlier styles of Latin music by defining it as the New York Sound, developed primarily by Puerto Rican New Yorkers, known as Nuyoricans (or Neoyoricans).*
>
> *The genesis of the music reflects several sometimes contradictory attitudes: a desire to forge roots in Cuban music, an interest in adopting the musical lexicons of jazz and rock, and an often politically motivated wish to create an all-inclusive Latin America music* (Gerard 1989, 3).

There are three styles within the broad field of salsa, and all of them come from New York: a traditional style called "tipica", that is, typical of the music of preceding generations; a jazz-flavored style, called salsa jazz; and a rock-flavored style, called salsa rock, or Latin-rock.

TIPICA

The Fort Apache Band, led by Jerry Gonzalez (b. 1949), who plays trumpet and conga drum with dazzling skill, reaches back to African-Cuban folk music like the rumba, the comparsa (African-Cuban carnival music), and the chants used in the

Santería religion. A large number of the salsa musicians in New York and Miami are practicing Santeros, and they subscribe to the beliefs of the Yorùbá people of West Africa, who talk to the Orishas (who are similar to Roman Catholic saints) with bata drum bands.

The large Cuban community in the Bronx called their local police station "Fort Apache", hence, the name of Gonzalez' group. They play music from before the Cuban Revolution (mambo, cha cha, pachanga, etc.), and after the Cuban Revolution (Mozambique and songo).

When Fidel Castro isolated Cuba from the rest of the Western Hemisphere, New York became the center of Cuban music. The queen of this tipica salsa was Celia Cruz (1925-2003), contralto, and she recorded with the important Cuban musicians – percussionists Julio Collazo, Carlos "Patato" Valdez, and Orestes Vilato; pianists Javier Vasquez and Lino Frias; and many others. (She also appeared a few times on the PBS kids program, *Sesame Street*.)

SALSA JAZZ

Argentine saxophonist Leandro "Gato" Barbieri (b. 1932), Cuban conga player Ray Barretto (1929-2006), and many others have added American jazz into the salsa mix with great success. John Coltrane (1926-1967) was very fond of Barbieri's explosive improvisation soaring over a battery of ethnic percussion instruments. Coltrane's album called *Chapter One*, recorded in Buenos Aires, has become a favorite. Barbieri's *The Third World* is his most successful album.

Latin tinged jazz is not new at all. Cuban conga player Chano Pozo (1915-1948) worked with Dizzy Gillespie in the 1940s. Brazilian guitarist Laurindo Almeida (1917-1995) recorded with jazz saxophonist Bud Shank (1926-2009) in the 1950s. Stan Getz (1927-1991) recorded with composer-guitarist Antônio Carlos Jobim (1927-1994), guitarist João Gilberto (b. 1931), and singer Astrud Gilberto (b. 1940) (João's wife) in the 1960s. Astrud was the singer on the giant hit "Girl from Ipanema" which came out in 1963.

Brazilian percussionist Airto Moreira (b. 1941) and his wife, vocalist Flora Purim (b. 1942), have been on the jazz scene for over forty years now, and they are well known in the industry. Airto was invited by Joe Zawinul to join Miles Davis for two cuts on *Bitches Brew*, and they (Airto and Purim) were quite influential in Chick Corea's group called Return to Forever.

Two Brazilian keyboard players contributed to a mixture of jazz, pop, and salsa in the 1970s. Eumir Deodato (b. 1943) had a big hit with his modified disco treatment of Richard Strauss' brilliant symphonic poem, *Also Sprach Zarathustra* — (well-known as the theme for the film *2001: A Space Odyssey).* Sérgio Mendes (b. 1941) recorded with Cannonball Adderly before moving on to a successful career in Latin-jazz with female voices used as instrumental colors, as in "Mas Que Nada", for example.

Salsa Rock

Among the many salsa influences in the world of rock, the most well-known is the career of guitarist Carlos Santana (b. 1947). He mixed rock and Brazilian rhythms for strong commercial sales in *Amigos* (1976) and *Festival* (1977). "Carnaval", which opens *Festival,* is pure Rio carnival music with a Cuban accent.

Earth, Wind and Fire's "Evil" and "Serpentine Fire" made good use of salsa rhythms, as did the group called War on their "Bailero" from *War Live* (1974). On Patty LaBelle's album *Tasty* (1978), "Teach Me Tonight/Me Gusta Tu Baile" is pure salsa (Roberts 1979, 208-209).

THE SALSA INDUSTRY

As often happens, financial matters greatly determine the growth and development of a give component in American pop culture. Salsa, for example, is almost the single-handed creation of Fania Records, started in the 1960s by Jerry Masucci, business manager, and Johnny Pacheco, music director.

Fania Records' underground promotion and marketing skills were so effective that salsa bands appeared in nearly every major American city and in many foreign countries, most notably Japan and Denmark. Fania wanted to control the genre so their product would be considered the real thing.

Masucci and Pacheco gave the impression that an entirely new music had been created in their studios. Many Cubans in America and in Cuba were greatly offended. It was, after all, the music of their people and their composers that had been recorded by Fania Records.

The Cubans were, and still are, very angry that the names of the Cuban composers were not, and are not, listed on most of the Fania record labels. Instead, the letters D.R. appear, meaning "Derechos Reservados", meaning "reserved rights". This means, of course, that no royalties were being paid to the composers (Gerard 1989, II).

For example, on Ray Barretto's *Indestructible* (1973), half of the eight tunes were listed as "D.R.", even though most Cubans knew quite well that the tunes were written by Ignacio Piñeiro and other Cuban songwriters now living in Cuba. Masucci and Pacheco were obviously taking advantage of the void between Cuba and the United States which obviates all normal international agreements on royalties, performance rights, and mechanical rights.

To add insult to injury, Fania Records released a movie on the Fania All-Stars and the salsa movement in America. It was called *Our Latin Thing*. It was the first movie made about Latinos and their music. There are scenes from a Santería religious ceremony and a brief cockfighting episode. Diaz Ayala, an authority on Cuban pop music, said that the movie created a completely false impression that salsa came directly from Africa to New York, by-passing Cuba entirely (Gerard 1989, 11).

Salsa has moved into the big time now. Gloria Estefan, along with her band, The Miami Sound Machine, had seven Top 10 hits, beginning with the horn-infused *Conga* in 1985. In 1989, Estefan went out on her own as a solo singer, and continues to tour and record today. Actress Jennifer Lopez (b. 1969) also dabbled in the realm of salsa, perhaps most notably when she portrayed slain Tejano singer-songwriter Selena Quintanilla-Pérez in the biopic, *Selena* (1997). Puerto Rican born pop star Ricky Martin (b. 1971) began his career with the boy band, Menudo. His single, "Livin' la Vida Loca", is often credited with starting the Latin music trend that began in the late 1990s and continues today in the music of artists such as Shakira.

CONCLUSION

Although salsa and other Latin music may never reach the same widespread popularity as some of the other genres in this book, the fact that people of Hispanic origin are now the largest ethnic and/or racial minority in the United States (as of 2012) will probably make it more mainstream as time goes on. If America's

Hispanic minority increases as projected – the US Census Bureau predicts that Hispanics will account for over 30% of the population of the United States by 2060 – the influence of salsa in mainstream American pop music may increase greatly.

What is certain, however, is that Latin spices will continue to flavor American pop music as they have for nearly two hundred years.

EPILOGUE

What does it all mean? As one of my students said recently, "I took your course last year, and got straight A's. It was a great course, and I learned a lot. But I still don't like country music, and New Age leaves me cold. Where did we fail?

My response surprised her. "We didn't fail, at all. The idea was not to get you to *like* any specific genre of music, but simply to *appreciate* that music as a part of the American story."

The purpose of this book is instruction. And the purpose of instruction should not be persuasion, but insight. I don't want to persuade anyone to "like" any kind of music. I do, however, very much want everyone who has read this book to understand how popular music came into being, who its major composer-performers were and are, and how it fits into the overall picture of American popular music in the last half of the 20th century and in the early 21st century.

If I have been successful, my students will now see what a potent force popular music is in the life of the nation, and how diverse are its forms and styles – and how deep are its dreams and desires for a given crowd of people at a given moment in history in a given geographical area of America.

Dr. Simon V. Anderson, Professor Emeritus
The University of Cincinnati's College Conservatory of Music
From the first edition of *Pop Music, U.S.A.*, June 1997

BIBLIOGRAPHY

Althouse, Jay. *Copyright: The Complete Guide for Music Educators*. East Stroudsburg, Pennsylvania: Music in Action, 1984.

Arlacchi, Pino. *Mafia Business: The Mafia Ethic and the Spirit of Capitalism*. Translated by Martin Ryle. London: Verso (the Imprint of New Left Books), 1986.

Baron, Stanley. *Benny: King of Swing*. New York: William Morrow and Company, Inc., 1979.

Breen, Mike. "The Ska Is the Limit," in *City Beat*: Weekly Issues, Arts and Events, Vol. 3, Issue 25. Cincinnati, Ohio.

Broven, John. South to Louisiana: The Music of the Cajun Bayous. Gretna, Louisiana: Pelican Publishing Company, 1983.

Brown, Charles T. *The Art of Rock and Roll*. Englewood Cliffs, New Jersey: Prentice-Hall Inc., 1983.

Case, Brian, ed. *The Illustrated Encyclopedia of Jazz*. London: Salamander Books, Ltd., 1978.

Chapple, Steve and Reebee Garafalo. *Rock'n'Roll Is Here To Pay*. Chicago: Nelson-Hall, 1977.

Charlton, Katherine. *Rock Music Styles: A History*. Dubuque, Iowa: Wm. C. Brown Publishers, 1990.

Chilton, John. *Who's Who of Jazz: Storyville to Swing Street*. Philadelphia: Chilton Book Company, 1979.

Clarke, Donald, ed. *The Penguin Encyclopedia of Popular Music*. Harmondsworth, Middlesex, England: Penguin Books, 1990.

Clifford, Mike, ed. *The Harmony Illustrated Encyclopedia of Rock*. London: Salamander Books, Ltd., 1988.

Costello, Mark and David Foster Wallace. *Signifying Rappers: Rap and Race In the Urban Present*. New York: The Ecco Press, 1990.

Dexter, Dave Jr. *The Jazz Story*. Englewood Cliffs, New Jersey: Prentice-Hall Inc., 1964.

Dolgins, Adam. *Rock Names: From ABBA To ZZ Top*. New York: Citadel Press, Inc., 1993.

Dixon, Keith. "Pat Boone, Minus Those White Bucks," *New York Times,* May 4, 1997, Section 2, page H-20.

Dubro, James. *Mob Mistress*. Toronto, Canada: Beacon Hill Productions, Inc., 1988.

Erlewine, Michael, editor. *All Music Guide*. San Francisco: Miller Freeman Books, 1994.

_____. Same as above, but on the Internet.

Ewen, David. *All the Years of American Popular Music*. Englewood Cliffs, New Jersey: Prentice-Hall Inc., 1977.

_____. *The Complete Book of the American Musical Theater*. New York: Henry Holt and Company, 1959.

Farley, Christopher John. "The New Video Wizards," *Time* (Vol. 150, No. 9) September 1, 1997, pp. 68-70.

Futrell, Jon, ed. *The Illustrated Encyclopedia of Black Music*. London: Salamander Books, Ltd., 1977.

Gates, Henry Louis, Jr. *The Signifying Monkey: A Theory of African-American Literary Criticism*. New York: Oxford University Press, 1988.

Geist, Christopher D. and Jack Nachbar, eds. *The Popular Culture Reader*. Third Edition. Bowling Green, Ohio: Bowling Green University Popular Press, 1983.

Gerard, Charley and Marty Sheller. *Salsa! The Rhythm of Latin Music*. Crown Point, Indiana: White Cliffs Media Company, 1988.

Girardin, G. Russell with William J. Helmer. *Dillinger: The Untold Story*. Bloomington, Indiana: Indiana University Press, 1994.

Giancana, Antoinette and Thomas C. Renner. *Mafia Princess: Growing Up In Sam Giancana's Family*. New York: William Morrow and Company, Inc., 1984.

Gleason, Harold. *American Music From 1620 to 1920*. Music Literature Outline Series. Rochester, New York: Lewis Store, 1955.

Green, Stanley. *Broadway Musicals: Show By Show*. Milwaukee, Wisconsin: Hal Leonard Books, 1985.

Gridley, Mark C. *Jazz Styles: History & Analysis*. Englewood Cliffs, New Jersey: Prentice-Hall Inc., 1988.

Hebridge, Dick. *Cut 'N' Mix: Culture, Identity, and Caribbean Music*. London: Methuen & Co., 1987.

Helander, Brock. *The Rock Who's Who*. New York: Schirmer Books, 1982.

Hemming, Roy and David Hajdu. *Discovering Great Singers of Classic Pop*. New York: Newmarket Press, 1991.

Ianni, Francis A. J. *A Family Business: Kinship and Social Control in Organized Crime*. New York: Russell Sage Foundation, 1972.

Jablonski, Edward, ed. *The Encyclopedia of America Music*. New York: Doubleday & Co., 1981.

Jacobs, Dick. *Who Wrote That Song?* White Hall, Virginia: Betterway Publications, Inc., 1988.

Jacoby, Neil H. and Peter Nehemkis and Richard Eells. *Bribery and Exhortation in World Business: A Study of Corporate Political Payments Abroad*. New York: Macmillan Publishing Co., 1977.

Lacey Robert. *Little Man: Meyer Lansky and the Gangster Life*. Boston: Little, Brown and Company, 1991.

Lazell, Barry ed. *Rock Movers & Shakers*. New York: Billboard Publications, Inc., 1989.

Logan, Nick and Bob Woffinden, eds. *The Illustrated Encyclopedia of Rock*. London: Salamander Books Ltd., 1977.

Lomax, John III. *Nashville: Music City U.S.A*. New York: Harry N. Abrams, Inc., 1985.

Malone, Bill C. *Country Music, U.S.A.* Austin: The University of Texas Press, 1968.

Maltby, Richard. *Passing Parade: A History of Popular Culture in the Twentieth Century*. Oxford: Oxford University Press, 1989.

Marre, Jeremy and Hannah Charlton. *Beats of the Heart: Popular Music of the World*. New York: Pantheon Books, 1985.

Martin, Henry. *Enjoying Jazz*. New York: Schirmer Books, 1986.

Megill, Donald D. and Richard S. Demory. *Introduction to Jazz History*. Englewood Cliffs, New Jersey: Prentice-Hall, 1989.

Nite, Norm N. *Rock On Almanac: The First Four Decades of Rock'n'Roll*. New York: Harper and Row, Publishers, 1989.

Noonan, John T., Jr. *Bribes*. New York: Macmillan Publishing Company, 1984.

Oliver, Paul. *The Story of the Blues*. Radnor, Pennsylvania: Chilton Book Company, 1982.

Palmer, Tony. *All You Need Is Love: The Story of Popular Music*. New York: Grossman Publishers, 1976.

_____. *Rock & Roll: An Unruly History*. New York: Harmony Books, 1995.

Palmer, Trisha, ed. *The Illustrated Encyclopedia of Country Music*. London: Salamander books, 1977.

Pleasants, Henry. *The Great American Popular Singers: Their Lives, Careers, & Art*. New York: Simon & Schuster, Inc., 1974.

Roberts, John Storm. *The Latin Tinge: The Impact of Latin American Music on the United States*. New York: Oxford University Press, 1979.

Shannon, Bob and John Javna. *Behind the Hits*. New York: Warner Books, Inc., 1986.

Shaw, Arnold. *Black Popular Music in America*. New York: Schirmer Books, 1986.

_____. *Dictionary of American Pop/Rock*. New York: Schirmer Books, 1982.

_____. *Honkers and Shouters: The Golden Years of Rhythm and Blues*. New York: Macmillan Publishing Company, 1978.

Shelton, Robert. *The Country Music Story*. Secaucus, New Jersey: Castle Books, 1966.

Shestack, Melvin. *The Country Music Encyclopedia*. New York: Thomas Y. Crowell Company, 1974.

Simon, George T. *The Big Bands*. New York: The Macmillan Company, 1967.

Smith, Wes. *The Pied Pipers of Rock'n'Roll: Radio Deejays of the 50s and 60s*. Marietta, Georgia: Longstreet Press, Inc., 1989.

Southern, Eileen. *The Music of Black Americans*. New York: W. W. Norton, Inc., 1971.

Strait, Raymond and Terry Robinson. *Lanza: His Tragic Life*. Englewood Cliffs, New Jersey: Prentice-Hall, Inc., 1980.

Stuessy, Joe. *Rock and Roll: Its History and Stylistic Development*. Englewood Cliffs, New Jersey: Prentice-Hall, Inc., 1990 and 2nd Edition 1994.

Szatmary, David P. *Rockin' in Time: A Social history of Rock and Roll*. Englewood Cliffs, New Jersey: Prentice-Hall Inc., 1987, and 2nd Edition 1991, and 3rd Edition 1996.

Taraborrelli, J. Randy. *Motown: Hot Wax, City Cool, and Solid Gold*. Graden City, New York: Doubleday & Co., 1986.

Thomas, Tony and Jim Terry. *The Busby Berkeley Book*. New York: New York Graphic Society Ltd., 1973.

Tobler, John, ed. *The Rock'n'Roll Years: The Chronicle of the Lives and Times of the Rock'n'Roll Generation from 1955 to the Present Day*. New York: Crescent Books, 1990.

Tosches, Nick. *Dino: Living High in the Dirty Business of Dreams*. New York: Doubleday, 1992.

Tracy, Steven C. *Going to Cincinnati: A History of the Blues in the Queen City*. Urbana, Illinois: University of Illinois Press, 1993.

Wicke, Peter. Translated by Rachel Fogg. *Rock Music: Culture, Aesthetics, and Sociology*. New York: Cambridge University Press, 1987, reprinted 1991.